DETERMINED TO SUCCEED?

DETERMINED TO SUCCEED?

*Performance versus Choice in
Educational Attainment*

Edited by Michelle Jackson

STANFORD UNIVERSITY PRESS
STANFORD, CALIFORNIA

Stanford University Press
Stanford, California

Printed in the United States of America on acid-free,
archival-quality paper

Library of Congress Cataloging-in-Publication Data

Determined to succeed? : performance versus choice in
educational attainment / edited by Michelle Jackson.
    pages cm
  Includes bibliographical references and index.
  ISBN 978-0-8047-8302-6 (cloth : alk. paper)
    1. Educational equalization—Cross-cultural studies.
2. Educational attainment—Cross-cultural studies.
3. Academic achievement—Cross-cultural studies.
I. Jackson, Michelle Victoria, editor of compilation.
LC213.D48 2013
379.2′6—dc23   2012016179

Typeset by Newgen in 10.5/14 Bembo

CONTENTS

In many countries, concern about social-background inequalities in educational attainment has focused on inequalities in test scores and grades, with interventions including early-childhood education and low-cost child care being proposed as necessary to reduce such inequalities. The presumption behind these increasingly widespread interventions is that the best way to reduce inequalities in educational *outcomes* is to reduce inequalities in *performance*. But is this presumption correct? Is it possible that children from disadvantaged backgrounds are less likely not just to perform well but also to proceed to higher levels of education even when they do perform well? Is part of the problem, in other words, the choices that these children are making? If it is, might it be more appropriate to focus on interventions that address such choices rather than those that focus solely on performance? The purpose of this book is to take on just such questions and to offer the first comprehensive cross-national examination of the roles of performance and choice in generating social-background inequalities in educational attainment.

This volume combines detailed analysis of educational transitions in different countries with general commentary on the roles of performance and choice in creating educational inequality. At the heart of the volume is a methodological approach that allows us to quantitatively assess the contributions of performance and choice. This approach is explained and developed early on in the volume and then applied throughout the balance of the book. The analyses based on this method are not of purely academic interest. By considering educational inequalities as the overall consequence of two separate processes (performance and choice), we do of course gain greater theoretical and empirical precision. But the policy implications are also clear and dramatic. The results presented here and in a web appendix (http://www. primaryandsecondaryeffects.com) allow us to begin developing an empirical foundation for choosing between interventions oriented toward performance and those oriented toward choice.

As do several other volumes in this field (e.g., Shavit and Blossfeld 1993; Shavit, Arum, and Gamoran 2007), this volume represents a collaborative approach to cross-national comparative research, with authors from European societies and the United States cooperating to produce comparable analyses across a range of institutional contexts. This cross-national cooperation came about through support from the European Union's Framework 6 Network of Excellence, EQUALSOC (Economic Change, Quality of Life, and Social Cohesion), a collaboration among research centers across Europe. The network is distinctive for its unwavering support of junior scholars and its willingness to fund projects over the long period necessary for cross-national collaborations to come to fruition. EQUALSOC provided funding for project meetings, research assistance, and conferences and meetings across Europe. This volume (alongside numerous other research papers) is the outcome of the collaborations fostered by the network. It is seemingly fashionable in the current political climate for British citizens to hold negative views of the EU, but it is hard to imagine a more effective and productive European-wide social science collaboration than that funded under EQUALSOC.

I suspect that few would recommend book editing as a way to make friends, given the cajoling and the issuing of (occasionally unreasonable) demands that accompany the role. But I am fortunate indeed that the authors in this volume were so committed to the project that they submitted to such cajoling with enthusiasm and good humor. In addition to the detailed comments and suggestions issued at project meetings, each draft chapter was subjected to careful, sustained, and insightful review by the other contributors. This is collegiality at its best. I am very grateful to have been part of such an exceptional group, and I thank all of the authors for their contributions to the project.

The wider scholarly community also contributed to this volume. Papers from the project were presented at many workshops and conferences, and particularly those of the EDUC (Education, Social Mobility and Social

Cohesion) group within the EQUALSOC network. Within EQUALSOC, I should like to particularly acknowledge Robert Erikson, John Goldthorpe, Jan O. Jonsson, Walter Müller, and Yossi Shavit, who offered perceptive comments, constructive suggestions, and calm counsel. Valuable contributions to the project also came from the twice-yearly meetings of the Research Committee on Social Stratification (RC28) of the International Sociological Association. The committee offers a welcoming and stimulating intellectual environment for those concerned with issues of social stratification and inequality, and many of the chapters in this volume have benefited greatly from the contributions of RC28 participants. The editors and reviewers of the Studies in Social Inequality series of Stanford University Press offered extremely helpful and constructive advice on revisions to the volume, and I particularly thank Kate Wahl for her thoughtful contributions to the project.

While preparing this volume, I was fortunate to be a part of academic communities on both sides of the ocean. I started the volume at Nuffield College and at the Centre for Research Methods in the Social Sciences at Oxford University, and I finished it at the Center on Poverty and Inequality and the Institute for Research in the Social Sciences at Stanford University. I am extremely grateful to the Center on Poverty and Inequality for its support of the project in recent years. I thank colleagues and friends associated with these institutions, many of whom offered constructive criticism and helpful suggestions on the project. While a great many individual scholars offered valuable comments and suggestions, I would particularly like to thank Richard Breen, David Cox, Geoffrey Evans, and Colin Mills. Their unwavering enthusiasm for the project and reassuring words are much appreciated.

Those who work on social stratification and the intergenerational transmission of inequality will perhaps be unsurprised to learn that the editor of a volume on educational inequality was borne of a family of schoolteachers. I thank my parents for their support and for illuminating discussions about educational inequalities as experienced by those attempting to tackle them head-on. I also appreciate the support of my two dear sisters, Catherine Rose and Alexandra Wall; my grandmother, Eva Jackson; and other family and friends. And finally, I wish to thank David Grusky. He is very special.

REFERENCES

Shavit, Yossi, and Hans-Peter Blossfeld, eds. 1993. *Persistent Inequality: A Comparative Study of Educational Attainment in Thirteen Countries*. Boulder, CO: Westview.

Shavit, Yossi, Richard Arum, and Adam Gamoran, eds. 2007. *Stratification in Higher Education: A Comparative Study*. Stanford, CA: Stanford University Press.

Charlotte Büchner is a research associate and doctoral student at the Research Centre for Education and the Labour Market (ROA), at Maastricht University. Her research interests include social stratification, educational inequality, and labor market transitions. Recent work focuses on the role of cognitive skills and education in explaining labor market outcomes of males and females and inter-generational earnings persistence.

Dalit Contini is a professor of social statistics in the Department of Economics, Cognetti de Martiis, at the University of Turin. Her research interests include statistical methods for the study of social mobility, inequalities in educational attainment and achievement, peer effects, and impact evaluation of social policies.

David R. Cox read mathematics at the University of Cambridge and worked for 5 years in industrial research before holding academic positions at the University of Cambridge; University of North Carolina at Chapel Hill; Birkbeck College, London; and for over 20 years at the Department of Mathematics, Imperial College, London. In 1988 he became the Warden of Nuffield College, Oxford, from which post he retired in 1994. He has published papers and books on a range of topics in theoretical and applied statistics and in applied probability. In 2000 he was awarded the Copley Medal of the Royal Society of London, thought to be the oldest medal given for scientific research.

Anders Holm is a professor in the Department of Education, Aarhus University. His research interests include quantitative methods, social mobility, and educational achievement. His work has appeared in peer-reviewed journals including *Sociological Methodology*, *Sociological Methods and Research*, and *Social Science Research*.

Mathieu Ichou is a doctoral student at Sciences Po (Paris). His thesis, cosupervised by Agnès van Zanten (Sciences Po) and Anthony Heath (Oxford and

Manchester Universities), focuses on second-generation immigrants and educational inequalities in France and the United Kingdom. His research interests also include class inequality in education and methodological triangulation. He recently published a paper in the *Oxford Review of Education* (vol. 37, no. 2, 2011) on the evolution of class inequality in French upper secondary school since the 1960s.

Michelle Jackson is a visiting scholar at the Institute for Research in the Social Sciences (IRiSS), Stanford University, and an associate member of Nuffield College, Oxford. Her main research interests lie in social inequality and the sociology of education. She examines the role of social background in conditioning educational and occupational opportunities, considering both the decisions that individuals make when developing their educational strategies and the decisions that employers make when they evaluate job applicants with different social backgrounds and educational levels.

Mads Meier Jæger is a professor in the Department of Education, Aarhus University. His research interests include social mobility, public opinion research, and applied econometrics. His work has appeared in peer-reviewed journals such as *Social Forces*, *Sociology of Education*, and *Social Science Research*.

Jan O. Jonsson is an Official Fellow of Nuffield College, Oxford, and a professor of sociology at the Swedish Institute for Social Research (SOFI), Stockholm University, where he directs the Swedish Level of Living Surveys. His research interests are social stratification, especially educational inequality and social mobility; ethnic stratification; and studies of young people's well-being.

Christiana Kartsonaki is a doctoral student in statistics at Nuffield College, Oxford. She previously worked as a research associate in the Cancer Research UK Genetic Epidemiology Unit at the University of Cambridge.

Stephen L. Morgan is the Jan Rock Zubrow '77 Professor in the Social Sciences at Cornell University. His current areas of research include education, labor market inequality, and methodology. In addition to journal articles on these topics, he has published two books: *On the Edge of Commitment: Educational Attainment and Race in the United States* (Stanford University Press, 2005) and, cowritten with Christopher Winship, *Counterfactuals and Causal Inference: Methods and Principles for Social Research* (Cambridge University Press, 2007).

Martin Neugebauer is a doctoral student at the University of Mannheim and a researcher at the Mannheim Centre for European Social Research (MZES). His research interests are educational inequality, social stratification, and teacher education and quality. Recent publications focus on primary and secondary origin effects and on the question of whether the increasing feminization of the teaching profession can explain the boy crisis in educational attainment.

David Reimer is an assistant professor of educational sociology in the Department of Education, Aarhus University. His research interests include social inequality in educational attainment and transitions from school to work. Recently he has also become interested in issues of teacher recruitment.

Frida Rudolphi is an assistant professor of sociology at the Swedish Institute for Social Research (SOFI), Stockholm University. She has published on educational stratification, especially on the processes behind class and ethnic inequality.

Andrea Scagni is a professor of statistics in the Department of Economics, Cognetti de Martiis, at the University of Turin. He currently teaches statistics and data management. His main current research interests concern the use of applied statistics in the evaluation of educational institutions and in the comparative analysis of national educational systems.

Steffen Schindler is a researcher and lecturer at the University of Hannover. His research interests include social stratification and inequality, sociology of education, and labor market transitions. Recent publications focus on long-term trends in social inequality in educational attainment and the mechanisms behind socially selective educational choices.

Michael W. Spiller is a doctoral candidate in sociology at Cornell University. His research interests include education, inequality, and methodology. His recent work includes studies of the role of family and demography in educational stratification, a large study of labor law violations in the United States, and research on sampling hidden populations.

Volker Stocké is a professor of Methods of Empirical Social Research at the University of Kassel and a cofounder of the National Educational Panel Study in Germany. His main research interests include educational inequality over the life course, effects of social capital and networks on educational achievement and labor market success as well as the role of education in processes of stratification and reproduction in society. Recent publications also focus on social science research methodology and empirical tests of sociological theories.

Jennifer J. Todd received her PhD in sociology from Cornell University and is currently working for the Kentucky Department of Education as a data fellow for the Strategic Data Project, Center for Education Policy Research, Harvard Graduate

School of Education. Her current research interests include education, inequality, race and ethnicity, and methodology.

Louis-André Vallet is a research professor in the French National Centre for Scientific Research (CNRS) and works within the Quantitative Sociology Unit in the Centre for Research in Economics and Statistics (CREST), the research center affiliated with the French Statistical Office. He belongs to the boards of *European Sociological Review*, *Revue Française de Sociologie*, and *Social Forces*. His main research interests and publications are in the areas of social stratification and mobility, sociology of education, and statistical modeling of categorical variables.

Rolf van der Velden is a professor at Maastricht University and the program director of the Education and Occupational Career program at the Research Centre for Education and the Labour Market (ROA). He is a fellow of the Interuniversity Center for Educational Research (ICO). He recently coordinated the international REFLEX project (http://www.reflexproject.org) and is currently one of the coordinators in the PIAAC project (http://www.oecd.org/els/employment/piaac). His current research interests include international comparisons in the transition from school to work, competence development during education, the long-term effects of education on occupational careers, overeducation, and skills mismatches and the effect of generic and specific competences on labor market outcomes.

DETERMINED TO SUCCEED?

CHAPTER ONE

Introduction

How Is Inequality of Educational
Opportunity Generated? The Case
for Primary and Secondary Effects

Michelle Jackson

When sociologists write about inequalities in educational attainment, they frequently get under way by emphasizing the extraordinary transformations of educational institutions over the course of the 20th century. And indeed, it is hard to imagine how to open a volume on inequalities in educational attainment without acknowledging the significant educational expansion and reform in all Western societies over the last century. The basic features of expansion and reform are well known and may be summarized as comprising three fundamental steps: the establishment of near-universal primary education at the beginning of the 20th century, the rise of near-universal secondary education toward the middle of the century, and the (as yet unfinished) development of a system of mass higher education toward the end of the century. An important consequence of this expansion has been an increase in the average level of educational attainment, such that most of the students who enter secondary education today can expect to obtain a tertiary-level qualification by the end of their educational career. Alongside increasing average levels of attainment, we also observe increasing differentiation in educational systems, so that students may choose from a range of academic and vocational courses in many diverse specialist fields.

The development of educational systems can be understood principally as a response to the demands of changing economic and occupational structures but also as an attempt to create a greater equality of educational opportunity. Yet a great deal of research has demonstrated that significant inequalities in educational attainment between members of different social groups remain. One important area of research focuses on social-class inequalities in educational attainment; children of professional or managerial background generally achieve higher levels of educational performance and make more ambitious educational choices than do children from working-class backgrounds (e.g., Shavit and Blossfeld 1993; Breen et al. 2009).

Arguably of more interest than the current state of class inequalities in educational attainment is the question of how far these inequalities have changed over time. *Persistent Inequality* (Shavit and Blossfeld 1993) argues that there has been a relatively high degree of temporal stability in the association between class origin and educational attainment. More recent work suggests that a trend toward a weakening association between class origin and educational attainment is present in many European countries, particularly if changes over a relatively long period are considered (Jonsson, Mills, and Müller 1996; Vallet 2004; Breen and Jonsson 2005; Breen et al. 2009, 2010). But this observation should not lead us to lose sight of the following: even if weaker now than in the past, class inequalities in educational attainment remain as a feature of modern societies and this feature is likely to linger for some time. The durability of these inequalities is particularly striking when compared to the far more substantial changes in gender, ethnic, and racial inequalities observed in many countries.

In this volume we aim to understand why social-background inequalities in educational attainment, or inequality in educational opportunity (IEO),[1] should exist and persist in eight Western countries. Should IEO be understood as a consequence of differences in academic ability and performance between members of different social classes? Or should it be understood as a consequence of differences in the educational decisions made by members of different social classes, such that students from advantaged backgrounds choose higher levels of education more frequently than students from disadvantaged backgrounds, regardless of their academic performance? These basic questions outline extreme positions on how IEO is created. In this volume we consider social-background inequalities in educational attainment to be a consequence of *both* social-background differences in academic performance and social-background differences in the choices that students make, holding performance constant. Our main aim is to determine the relative importance of these two features in creating IEO. Insofar as changes in IEO are observed, we ask whether they can be attributed to changes in the relationship between class and performance or to changes in the class-biased choices that are made, conditional on performance. If we observe declines in one or both effects, leading to a decline in IEO, this provides us with important evidence about which policies and institutional innovations hold most promise for further reducing class effects.

IEO is a term that carries some ambiguity in that it can refer either to a summary measure of *all* inequalities related to social background generated by an educational system or to only the social-background inequalities generated *at a given transition*. For example, Boudon defines IEO as meaning "differences in level of educational attainment according to social background" (1974, xi) but also states that "IEO rates are subject to variations as a function of national context, point in time, and school level. . . . [A] certain amount of IEO is present . . . at each school level" (1974, 41). In this volume we are concerned with IEO at given educational transitions, and we therefore take the latter understanding of IEO to be our own. In each chapter IEO is discussed in relation to the transition under consideration and to the risk set of students eligible for that transition. On the whole, we do not address the question of how far IEO assessed for different transitions and risk sets accumulates to a summary measure of all IEO generated by an educational system.[2]

DEFINING PRIMARY AND SECONDARY EFFECTS

Our understanding of IEO has at its heart an individual-level model, in which a student achieves a certain level of academic performance and then makes a decision about how to proceed in the educational system. The decision that students make when faced with an educational transition is shaped by their previous academic performance, which provides information about the likelihood of successful completion of higher levels of education. But the decision is also influenced by factors other than previous academic performance, because a student takes into account the costs and benefits of the different choices that might be made in relation to the transition.

The decomposition of IEO into a part determined by differences in previous performance across social groups and a part determined by the choices made by members of those groups is well established in the literature, in which performance effects are labeled primary effects and choice effects are labeled secondary effects[3] (Girard and Bastide 1963; Boudon 1974). As Breen and Goldthorpe write,

> Primary effects are all those that are expressed in the association that exists between children's class origins and their average levels of demonstrated academic ability. Children of more advantaged backgrounds . . . perform better, on average, than children of less advantaged backgrounds in standard tests, examinations, and so on. . . . [S]econdary effects . . . are effects that are expressed in the actual choices that children, together perhaps with their parents, make in the course of their careers within the educational system—including the choice of exit. (1997, 277)

The history of the conceptual distinction between primary and secondary effects is discussed in more detail below.

Before proceeding any further, an apology on the matter of terminology is in order. While the concepts of primary and secondary effects can be defined with precision, the labels attached to the concepts are unfortunately rather ambiguous. Although one can understand the rationale behind the labels once the concepts have been defined, in that social background *primarily* affects performance and then *secondarily* affects choices (conditional on performance), there are few clues to the meanings of these labels for the uninitiated. It is also curious that these terms should be used in a field concerned with education systems, in which "primary" and "secondary" are understood first and foremost to refer to different phases of the school career or school system, not to the decomposition of IEO presented here. Despite the problems with the terminology of primary and secondary effects, the terms are now fully established in the literature on IEO, and in this volume we continue to use these labels. We also refer to primary and secondary effects as "performance" and "choice" effects, so as to further emphasize their meanings. To avoid confusion, we largely avoid using "primary" and "secondary" in isolation to refer to the school career.

THE UTILITY OF PRIMARY AND SECONDARY EFFECTS

There are clear advantages to treating IEO as the overall consequence of the operation of primary and secondary effects: the concepts allow sociologists to gain greater precision in identifying the determinants of IEO, and they also have obvious implications for social policy.

As discussed below, primary and secondary effects are likely to be generated by different processes, and as a consequence, the explanatory tools needed to explain the primary effects of differences in performance between social groups differ from the tools needed to explain the secondary effects of the differences in choices, conditional on performance (e.g., Erikson and Jonsson 1996a). Therefore, by determining to what extent IEO should be understood as resulting from primary or secondary effects, sociologists obtain valuable information about where explanatory effort should be directed. If the distinction between primary and secondary effects is ignored, sociologists are in danger of attempting to explain IEO as an unwieldy whole, thus mistaking a dual phenomenon requiring distinct and separate explanations for a single composite requiring a single explanation.

Aside from the utility of primary and secondary effects for explaining IEO, the concepts are highly relevant to policy. Just as the explanatory tools differ depending on whether the focus is on primary or on secondary effects, the appropriate policy interventions will also differ depending on which type of effect is to be addressed. If differences in *performance* are the main drivers of educational inequality, policies aimed at reducing those differences will have a very large impact in reducing overall inequality. Early interventions, such as intensive preschool education or economic support for families with young children, seem to have great potential for reducing primary effects (see Cameron and Heckman 1999; Carneiro and Heckman 2003; Heckman 2006). On the other hand, if differences in the *choices* made by students at the same level of performance have a significant impact, policies aimed at changing constraints and incentives hold more promise (Jackson et al. 2007).

PRIMARY AND SECONDARY EFFECTS

History of the Concepts

The distinction between primary and secondary effects has a long and colorful history. It is a history marked principally by unrealized promise, a state of affairs that can perhaps be attributed to the lack of a rigorous operationalization of the concepts of primary and secondary effects but also to other idiosyncratic features that had a further suppressive effect.

Where to begin with this history? The distinction between primary and secondary effects is most commonly associated with Boudon's 1974 book *Education, Opportunity, and Social Inequality*. However, while Boudon's work is clearly the most extensive treatment of the roles of primary and secondary effects in creating educational inequality, the roots of these concepts are elsewhere. In the 1940s Boalt carried out an empirical analysis of social-class inequalities in educational attainment in Sweden, in which he considered the roles of previous performance and class background in the transition to secondary school (Boalt 1947; summarized in English in Boalt and Janson 1953). Calculating partial correlations between class, school performance, and school selection, on data describing all 5,000 students in primary school in Stockholm in 1936, Boalt concludes that

> "social class" measured by father's occupation gave a significant correlation with marks in primary schools (0.32) but a high correlation with selection to secondary schools (0.56). This latter correlation remained high even when partial correlations for marks, income, and the factor "known to social welfare authorities," were worked out. (Boalt and Janson 1953, 323)

Boalt clearly distinguishes between the effects of social-class background on performance and its effects on the transition to secondary school, conditional on performance. Here we find, therefore, a distinction between primary and secondary effects in all but name.

It is not apparent that Boalt's distinction was widely applied in the educational research of the time, and indeed the 1947 book and 1953 paper have been cited only 59 times.[4] However, Boalt's work has much in common with that of his contemporaries, in particular, with research in the 1950s and 1960s on the "reserve of talent." The talent reserve referred to "how many young people . . . with sufficient ability did for various reasons *not* proceed to upper secondary and university education" (Husén 1974, ix). In this literature, a concern about class inequalities in educational participation rates was expressed as concern about wastage of talent, in that there must be working-class children who were not realizing their full potential. Several studies aimed to assess the size of the talent reserve in relation to class origin, and these studies considered the gap between more advantaged and less advantaged students to be a consequence of differences in ability (or performance) between classes and differences in transition propensities conditional on ability (or performance) (see, e.g., Anderberg 1948; Ekman 1951; Wolfe 1954; Härnqvist 1958; Härnqvist 2003 provides an excellent summary of some of this research). Again, in all but name, these studies distinguished between primary and secondary effects in determining class inequalities in educational attainment. Indeed, the expectancy method, applied by Gösta Ekman (1951), in which the proportion of students from one class making a transition is compared with the proportion of students from another class making a transition for given ability levels, is a precursor of the methods applied in this volume.

In the 1960s the distinction that Boalt had recognized was once again applied in sociological research, although this application was seemingly independent of Boalt's work. In France, Girard and Bastide published two papers in the journal *Population* that discussed the effect of social background on performance and its effect on transitions conditional on performance (Girard and Bastide 1963; Girard, Bastide, and Pourcher 1963). In an analysis of a nationally representative sample of French schoolchildren facing the transition to secondary education, Girard and his colleagues demonstrated that students' grades were associated with their social origins, such that around 55 percent of students originating in the most advantaged social class achieved "good" or "excellent" grades while only 29 percent of students originating in the least advantaged class achieved equivalent grades. Social-class origins were also found to affect the chances of making the transition to secondary education, even after taking into account these differences in performance. So among the students with good or excellent grades, almost all of those from the most advantaged class made the transition to secondary education, while only 80 percent of those from the least advantaged class made the transition.

The work of Girard and his colleagues offered evidence that social-class inequalities in educational attainment were driven by both class differences in performance and class differences in transition propensities, given performance. But this research is probably more important for a theoretical than an empirical contribution: although not generally acknowledged, Girard and Bastide (1963) were the first to introduce the language of primary and secondary effects to the analysis of educational inequality.[5] They write, "C'est là la première cause de la non-démocratisation: l'influence du milieu familial sur le développement de l'enfant et, par suite, sa réussite scolaire" (437), and "C'est là la seconde cause de la non-démocratisation: même à égalité de notes, la chance pour l'enfant d'entrer en sixième est en relation avec sa condition sociale" (439).[6] In these two passages, Girard and Bastide describe a decomposition of overall educational inequality into a part determined by performance differences and a part determined by differences in choices, conditional on performance, and also identify these features as primary and secondary causes of the inequality.

Despite the relatively long history of primary and secondary effects in sociology, it was not until Boudon's 1974 book, *Education, Opportunity, and Social Inequality*, that these concepts received an extensive sociological treatment. Boudon's book put forward a general theory designed to explain why IEO and inequality of social opportunity (ISO, or social-class immobility) should exist and persist in modern, industrialized societies. The distinction between primary and secondary effects is part of the general theory of IEO.

Boudon argues that a puzzling feature of modern societies with well-developed educational systems is that children of less advantaged social background choose to acquire less education, on average, than children of more advantaged social background, even though these children must know that their chances in the labor market would be substantially improved if they obtained more education rather than less. He argues that this is a consequence of two different processes, which he labels as primary and secondary effects. His treatment of these effects is very similar to Girard and Bastide's, in that primary effects are seen to be the effects of social background on performance and secondary effects are seen to be the effects of social background on educational choices, conditional on performance. The existence of secondary effects, for Boudon, results from the differential costs and benefits attached to educational decisions for students from different social classes. In sum, he writes that

> IEO is generated by a two-component process. One component is related mainly to the cultural effects of the stratification system. The other introduces the assumption that even with other factors being equal, people will make different choices according to their position in the stratification system. In other words, it is assumed (1) that people behave rationally in the economic sense of this concept . . . but that (2) they also behave within decisional fields whose parameters are a function of their position in the stratification system. (1974, 36)

After the publication of Boudon's book, the distinction between primary and secondary effects was firmly established in the literature on IEO, although as Jackson and colleagues note, these concepts were "surprisingly neglected" by sociologists of education (2007, 212; see also Nash 2006). While many researchers discussed the primary-versus-secondary-effects distinction, no rigorous method was available for operationalizing the concepts and few shaped their empirical analyses around the distinction. But there are also two historically idiosyncratic reasons why the concepts were not more influential.

First, as Stephen Morgan, Michael Spiller, and Jennifer Todd note in this volume (Chapter 10), a crushing review of Boudon's book by Hauser (1976) in the *American Journal of Sociology* is unlikely to have encouraged scholars to take the distinction to heart.[7] Hauser's criticisms focused on Boudon's overarching theories of IEO and ISO and the tests of these theories (although because Hauser's review dealt with the whole of Boudon's book, many criticisms do not in fact relate to the conceptual distinction between primary and secondary effects).

Second, to some extent the primary-versus-secondary-effects distinction has been subsumed in the wider literature of rational choice theories in education. Many of the influential rational choice models of education, in which educational decisions are related to the costs, benefits, and expected probabilities of success of different courses of action, make the distinction between primary and secondary effects, either implicitly or explicitly. In the Breen-Goldthorpe model (1997), the distinction is acknowledged explicitly:

> We assume, to begin with, that class differentials in educational attainment come about through the operation of two different kinds of effect which, following Boudon (1974), we label as "primary" and "secondary." . . . Some educational choices may of course be precluded to some children through the operation of primary effects. . . . But, typically, a set of other choices remains, and it is further known that the overall patterns of choice that are made are in themselves—over and above primary effects—an important source of class differentials in attainment. (277)

Other rational choice models of educational decisions might not be linked to the primary-versus-secondary-effects distinction as explicitly as the Breen-Goldthorpe model is, but performance and choice effects are understood to have separate roles in determining the main components of many of these models (e.g., Erikson and Jonsson 1996a).

Aside from these two relatively particularistic explanations for why the distinction between primary and secondary effects has been underapplied in the sociology of education, another, more straightforward reason explains why the distinction did not achieve instant or wholesale adoption. The distinction between primary and secondary effects is most useful when applied to educational transitions: given a transition point, we wish to understand the separate roles of performance and choice in determining whether a student makes the transition. While western European systems are transition-based systems, in other school systems transitions are less easily identified, which limits the applicability of the distinction. For example, in the United States, the first major educational branching point is not a transition but instead relates to whether students complete the high school degree. In such a system, where years of schooling or completion of educational levels are treated as the appropriate components of educational systems, a transition-based analysis might not be seen as the most natural analytic approach.

RECENT DEVELOPMENTS

For all the foregoing reasons, the distinction between primary and secondary effects was to a certain extent neglected in the literature on IEO, yet recent years have seen a resurgence of interest in these concepts. In part this resurgence has been driven by methodological developments that allow researchers to assess the relative importance of primary and secondary effects in creating inequalities in educational attainment.

In the empirical literature on the talent reserve in the 1950s, researchers were concerned with estimating the size of the reserve of talent by comparing ability distributions across classes and comparing the transition rates for those same classes. In Ekman's expectancy method, as described in Härnqvist (1958, 2003), class differences in transition probabilities were calculated for different levels of performance, enabling the researchers to show that students from the highest class were more likely to make the transition to upper secondary school than students from the lower classes at all levels of academic performance (Härnqvist 2003, 487–89; see Duru-Bellat, Jarousse, and Mingat 1993 for a similar approach using French data). In a somewhat similar fashion, Erikson and Jonsson (1996b) observed that the primary and secondary effects of class origin could be represented graphically; Figure 1.1 shows how grade point average (GPA) distributions and transition propensities for two different social classes would be presented under this approach. First, to represent primary effects, they presented class-specific GPA distributions, to demonstrate that students from the highest class (EGP I) had higher average GPAs than students from the lowest class (EGP VII). Second, to represent secondary effects, they plotted

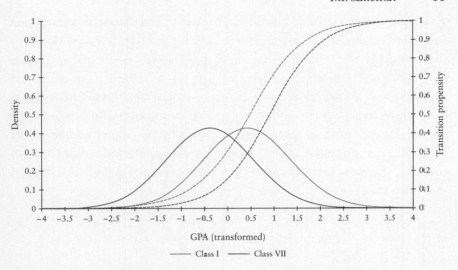

Figure 1.1. Grade point average (GPA) and transition propensities for two social classes

NOTE: Adapted from Erikson and Jonsson (1996b). The curves shown here are for illustrative purposes only and do not exactly correspond to the results reported in Erikson and Jonsson (1996b).

separate curves for each class showing the probability of making the transition (to upper secondary school) at every level of GPA (1996b, 76–77). Through integration, the two sets of curves could be used to estimate the total proportion of students making the transition for each class, how these proportions would be affected if arbitrary grade limits were defined, and the subsequent effect on IEO.

The Erikson-Jonsson approach was further developed in work by Erikson et al. (2005) and Jackson et al. (2007), in which class-specific performance distributions and transition probabilities were manipulated to obtain a quantitative estimate of the contributions of primary and secondary effects to IEO. This method will be applied throughout the volume, and it is described in detail and extended in Chapter 2. In essence, the method decomposes the odds ratios describing inequalities between social groups into a part due to primary effects and a part due to secondary effects; a percentage estimate of the relative importance of the two effects in creating IEO can thus be derived.

These recent methodological advances in measuring primary and secondary effects have been taken up in several papers (e.g., Erikson 2007; Erikson and Rudolphi 2010; Kloosterman et al. 2009; Relikowski, Schneider, and Blossfeld 2009). In all of these studies, results show that primary and secondary effects are important features of educational inequality and that inequalities in educational attainment would be substantially reduced if the secondary effects of choices were eliminated.[8] In this book we build on the research so far produced, by providing a systematic comparison of IEO and the roles of primary and secondary effects in creating IEO across countries and over time.

MECHANISMS IMPLICATED IN THE GENERATION OF PRIMARY AND SECONDARY EFFECTS

In this volume our main concern is to assess the extent to which IEO can be attributed to performance differences between students of different social groups or to differences in the choices that are made by those students, net of performance. We do not attempt the far more ambitious endeavor of attempting to explain IEO by reference to the genesis of primary and secondary effects, although we see the decomposition of IEO into the two effects as an important step toward a full explanation of how inequalities are created. Here I summarize the main mechanisms through which primary and secondary effects are likely to be generated. While the mechanisms will be familiar to those well acquainted with research on educational inequality, it is important to highlight that the mechanisms required to explain the generation of primary effects may differ from those required to explain the generation of secondary effects. Furthermore, in rehearsing these mechanisms, it will become clear that while some causes of educational inequality are deeply rooted and difficult to tackle, others are more amenable to policy intervention. It will also become clear that, for the most part, it is the mechanisms underlying the generation of secondary effects that are more malleable by social policy.

In general, primary effects are understood to be the consequence of a complex interaction between educational institutions and the cultural, economic, and social resources of individuals and their families. Six classes of mechanisms might be relevant to the generation of performance differences between groups: (a) genetic, (b) the home environment and its implications for economic, cultural, and social resources, (c) health and nutrition, (d) sibship size, (e) the cultural biases exhibited by schools, and (f) psychological mechanisms, particularly those that come into play in the interaction with schools (see Erikson and Jonsson 1996a [10–12], who discuss the first five classes). Genetic explanations aside, a wealth of research exists to demonstrate the power of these mechanisms in shaping social-background inequalities in performance.[9]

The class of mechanisms associated with the role of the home environment in generating performance inequalities is the subject of a great deal of research activity. Economic, cultural, and social resources have been found to be profoundly consequential for performance inequalities. Socioeconomically advantaged households are able to employ their superior economic resources in ways that boost their children's academic performance: investments in private tuition, summer schools, books, and school materials will all improve the performance of students from socioeconomically advantaged households. For example, Kaushal, Magnuson, and Waldfogel (2011) show that investment in learning-related activities and goods increases as family income increases, with children from economically advantaged households having substantially greater access to books, newspapers, and computers and more opportunities for educational trips and private tuition than those from economically disadvantaged households (see also Kornrich and Furstenberg 2010; Duncan and Brooks-Gunn 1997; Danziger and Waldfogel 2000). Cultural and social mechanisms also operate to the advantage of socioeconomically advantaged students; substantial inequalities in language skills are already observed in very young children (Feinstein 2003; Farkas and Beron 2004; Kloosterman et al. 2011), alongside inequalities in cultural capital (Bourdieu and Passeron 1977; Bourdieu 1984; De Graaf, De Graaf, and Kraaykamp 2001; Lareau 1987, 2003) and inequalities in access to educationally beneficial social networks (Coleman 1988). Differences in levels of health and nutrition between social groups have been shown to influence socioeconomic inequalities in performance (for a useful summary see Jukes et al. 2002; Behrman 1996), as have differences in fertility and subsequent differences in sibship size between groups (Blake 1989; Downey 1995). Recent work in neuroscience also points to the consequences of deprivation for brain development; although there is much work to be done in this relatively new field, it is known that environmental factors influence brain development and cognitive function both pre- and postbirth (Nelson and Sheridan 2011; Farah et al. 2006; Blair and Razza 2007; also see Duncan and Magnuson 2011), and differences in cognitive and other functions resulting from environmental factors are likely to have significant consequences for socioeconomic inequalities in performance.

The cultural, economic, and social inequalities present in the home environment are likely to be exacerbated by the practices of educational institutions, where the language styles and cultural practices of the socio-economically advantaged are rewarded (e.g., Bernstein 1971; Bowles and Gintis 1976). Psychological mechanisms may also come into play. One such mechanism likely to contribute to socioeconomic inequalities in performance is stereotype threat (Steele and Aronson 1995; Steele 1997): students of disadvantaged social origin, aware that they are from a group that performs poorly in school assessments, will underachieve when faced with similar exercises (Croizet and Claire 1998). Therefore, whether through individual psychology or through cultural mismatch between individuals and schools, the interaction between the school and individual family circumstances is expected to generate differences in performance between those of different socioeconomic backgrounds.

The mechanisms underlying the generation of primary effects relate to features of individuals, families, and societies that are difficult to change. Educational and social policies may reduce performance inequalities, but on the whole, the most successful of these policies are extremely expensive and time intensive. Perhaps the most well known and successful of the policies designed to tackle performance inequalities is early childhood education as practiced in initiatives such as Head Start, which has been shown to substantially improve the performance of those from disadvantaged social groups (e.g., Currie and Thomas 1995; Garces, Thomas, and Currie 2002). But the difficulty of breaking the association between socioeconomic background and performance by addressing the underlying mechanisms should not be underestimated.

In understanding how secondary effects are generated, the explanatory focus must be on how the costs, benefits, and expected probabilities of success associated with different educational outcomes differ according to socioeconomic background. Costs, benefits, and expected probabilities of success are rather standard components of rational choice models of educational decision making (e.g., Breen and Goldthorpe 1997; Erikson and

Jonsson 1996a), although it is of course not obligatory to look to rational choice models for explanations of how secondary effects are generated.

Most central to explanations of secondary effects are mechanisms linked to the home environment; one feature highlighted by both sociologists and economists as having the potential to generate secondary effects is the availability of economic resources, which may influence the perceived costs and benefits associated with different educational alternatives. Economic resources may be employed to cover the direct and indirect costs of education (e.g., tuition fees and living costs) and to assuage the opportunity costs associated with further study (Erikson and Jonsson 1996a). While inequalities in economic resources generate secondary effects and thus IEO, the policy implication is clear: a reduction in the magnitude of secondary effects would be expected if moves were made to equalize the resources available to students.

In addition to the straightforward transfer of economic resources from advantaged parents to their children, the home environment alters the decision calculus surrounding educational transitions because children's educational and career aspirations will be influenced by their parents' socioeconomic position. At the heart of the Breen-Goldthorpe model, for example, is the proposition that students will make educational choices that are most likely to allow them to obtain a class position that is "at least as advantageous as that from which they originate. . . . [T]hey seek to avoid downward social mobility" (Breen and Goldthorpe 1997, 283). Other models of educational decision making highlight the effect of the home environment on norms and values surrounding education. Akerlof (1997), for example, argues that educational decisions are social decisions, in that they are influenced by the norms and values held by significant others in the student's social network (see Goldthorpe 2007, chap. 4, for a detailed discussion of Akerlof's contribution to explanations of secondary effects and IEO). And although Bourdieu's explanation of educational inequality is clearly at odds with a decomposition of inequality into primary and secondary effects, one can perhaps understand secondary effects from the Bourdieuian perspective as originating in the different norms and values held by those from different social backgrounds; students from advantaged backgrounds hold educational norms and values in keeping with the dominant educational culture and thus are more likely to make ambitious educational decisions than students from disadvantaged backgrounds who do not share those norms and values (e.g., Bourdieu and Passeron 1977).

It is important to highlight the role of macrosocioeconomic factors in generating secondary effects, because these factors strongly influence the perceived costs and benefits of different educational trajectories and therefore provide the context in which the above-identified mechanisms will operate. Changes in the occupational structure have long been predicted to increase the demand for a highly educated labor force (e.g., Blau and Duncan 1967; Bell 1973), and if entering high-level occupational positions were possible only with high-level qualifications, the perceived benefits of continuing in the educational system would increase. Other features of the labor market, such as the level of unemployment or the availability of entry-level jobs, would be expected to change the decision calculus by changing the costs and benefits associated with particular educational transitions. While these macrosocioeconomic factors may at first glance appear difficult to change, there is much room for educational and social policies to respond to societal changes and to influence the perceived costs and benefits associated with educational transitions, thereby influencing the size of secondary effects. For example, we would expect secondary effects to be increased in a system in which certain educational tracks are associated with significant up-front tuition fees for all students. Conversely, policies that attempted to mitigate the costs of higher levels of education, by providing scholarships for students from disadvantaged households, would be expected to reduce the size of secondary effects.

POTENTIAL PROBLEMS WITH THE CONCEPTUAL MODEL

It is important to consider the criticisms that have been leveled at the attempt to understand IEO as a consequence of the operation of primary and secondary effects. Although these criticisms take various forms, all of them amount to a dissatisfaction with the implied causal model underlying the concepts of primary and secondary effects. As defined above, the model of behavior within this theory assumes that students receive information about their academic ability and subsequently make a decision about whether to proceed with an educational transition. Social-background inequalities in educational attainment therefore result from students from different social backgrounds achieving different levels of academic performance and then making different decisions about the transitions that they face.

One form of criticism of the concepts of primary and secondary effects is that the behavioral model does not take account of anticipatory decisions (see Erikson et al. 2005; Jackson et al. 2007). These are decisions made in relation to the transition, which would be classified as secondary effects, that influence the level of performance achieved and thus the primary effects. The decomposition of IEO into primary and secondary effects rests on the principle that these effects act independently to produce overall inequalities. If students anticipate that they will not make an educational transition, they may then decide to work less hard and subsequently achieve a lower level of performance; this behavior violates the principle of independence of primary and secondary effects. If students do routinely make anticipatory decisions of this kind, the size of secondary effects estimated under the principle of independence would be an underestimate of the true role of choice in creating IEO.

One way of testing how anticipatory decisions influence the relative importance of primary and secondary effects is to compare estimates derived using different measures of primary effects. While measures of performance taken close to the decision might be contaminated by anticipatory decisions, measures of academic ability taken long before any educational decision is made should be less prone to contamination. Jackson and colleagues (2007) compare estimates of the relative importance of primary and secondary effects for two different measures of performance: first, performance in public examinations at age 16, just before transition decisions are made, and second, a general-ability test taken at age 11. Secondary effects are estimated to be much smaller relative to primary effects when the measure of performance at 16 is used than when the measure of ability at age 11 is used. Erikson and Rudolphi (2010) show similar analyses for Sweden, with similar results. The results of these studies therefore suggest that ignoring the influence of anticipatory decisions might indeed lead us to underestimate the relative importance of secondary effects in creating IEO.[10]

As indicated above, the concern about anticipatory decisions is in fact a specific example of a more general criticism of the implied causal model underlying the theory. If we adjust estimates of the relative importance of primary and secondary effects to take account of anticipatory decisions, it is still not clear that we have the *correct* estimates, because the causal model is yet more complicated than we have supposed so far. A behavioral model

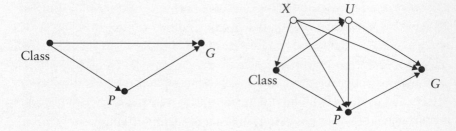

Figure 1.2. Proposed causal models describing primary and secondary effects on IEO (see text for description)

SOURCE: Figures 10.4a and 10.4d of this volume.

that took account of all possible causal paths in creating IEO would include any number of additional factors that influenced academic performance, choice, and even social background. Morgan, Spiller, and Todd consider alternative causal models in their chapter on the United States in this volume (Chapter 10), and in an important extension to this work, Morgan discusses in detail the issues of causality in the primary and secondary effects approach (2012). Morgan, Spiller, and Todd present diagrams to illustrate the factors that are omitted in the classic formulation of the role of primary and secondary effects in creating IEO, and I reproduce two of these diagrams in Figure 1.2.

The figure on the left presents the causal model implied by the primary and secondary effects approach: class has an indirect effect on transition (*G*) through performance (*P*) and also a direct effect on transition. The figure on the right presents what Morgan, Spiller, and Todd argue is a more realistic characterization of the causal model underlying behavior: *U* represents anticipatory decisions, which influence both performance and transition, and *X* represents variables that will exert their own influence on components of the model. Morgan, Spiller, and Todd argue that the misspecification of the causal model within the standard theory of primary and secondary effects, and the omission of potentially important variables, will lead researchers to draw erroneous conclusions about the role of choice in generating IEO.

At this point we may well ask, what is to be done? The criticism of the implied causal model arises because of the labeling of primary and secondary effects as performance and choice effects respectively; the decomposition of IEO into primary and secondary effects in itself raises no difficulties, as it is a simple matter of definition that IEO is the sum of primary and secondary effects. But the appeal to performance and choice effects does involve assumptions about the causal relationships between primary and secondary effects and overall IEO, and it is important to ask whether the approach is undermined if the causal relationships are indeed more complex.

Arguably, an approach that combines the simplicity of the primary-secondary effects decomposition with the complexity of a full causal analysis offers great potential. One significant advantage of the primary-secondary-effects approach is that it maps extremely well onto the structure of educational systems. In transition-based educational systems, students receive an assessment of their academic performance and subsequently make a decision about an educational transition. It would seem that there is value in maintaining a correspondence between the institutional structure of educational systems and the model of student behavior, even if this is at the cost of simplifying the complex causal relationships described above. Decomposing IEO into primary and secondary effects is an important first step in explaining inequalities. However, we should certainly acknowledge that primary and secondary effects have complex causes, and having estimated the magnitude of primary and secondary effects, we should subsequently try to *explain* these effects with additional variables; some variables will be shown to reduce the magnitude of primary effects, others will reduce the magnitude of secondary effects, and yet others will determine both primary and secondary effects. In this way we preserve the distinction between the formal and consequential decisions that are institutionally required, and the implicit and hidden decisions that lie behind these formal choices.

One might also argue that, given limited governmental resources for reducing IEO, policy interests are well-served by a simple model of primary and secondary effects. Regardless of the range of factors that may operate throughout children's lives to determine their educational performance and condition their choices, the institutional veracity of the simple model allows a good correspondence with the points at which interventions might be made. For example, secondary effects are supposed to operate after performance is known and when a decision is to be made. This decision is a real one: until the decision is recorded and acted on, students may still be moved from one decision to another through a policy intervention. In contrast, if we are wedded to a model that has full behavioral veracity, the moment of decision is downplayed and the potential to reduce inequalities through intervention at the decision point is diminished. It is this logic, coupled with the significant challenges of estimating a full and complete behavioral model, that lies behind the decision here to opt for a model with institutional veracity.

INSTITUTIONS AND PRIMARY AND SECONDARY EFFECTS

In this volume we consider the influence of primary and secondary effects on social-background inequalities in educational attainment in eight countries: Denmark, England, France, Germany, Italy, the Netherlands, Sweden and the United States. The authors describe the institutional contexts in which educational transitions are made and the constraints on students as they negotiate the examinations and choices that comprise the educational systems of the countries under investigation. For each country, the authors identify the important educational transitions and use the best available data to estimate the magnitude of social-background inequalities in the chances of making these transitions. These inequalities are then decomposed to determine the extent to which they are generated by primary effects or by secondary effects. Data selection, variable construction, and methodological approach are carried out according to a common metric (described below), to allow for comparison across countries. The detailed study of individual country cases allows for a careful assessment of the importance of performance and choice in determining educational outcomes in light of country-specific economic, social, and institutional circumstances. But by conforming to a common metric for analysis, the results from the individual country chapters can also be used for comparison *across* countries, an approach that has proved fruitful in previous studies of educational inequality (e.g., Shavit and Blossfeld 1993; Shavit, Arum, and Gamoran 2007). This comparative approach allows us to ask whether institutional features of educational systems and countries generate particularly large (or small) primary and secondary effects and overall IEO. These institutional features could provide us with important clues about the conditions that generate primary and secondary effects and how IEO might be reduced.

A priori, one would expect the influence of performance and choice to vary with the structure of educational systems, and in Chapter 11 Michelle

Jackson and Jan O. Jonsson ask whether institutional features do indeed have consequences for the size of primary and secondary effects. They examine the importance of two institutional features—stratification and selectivity—that are likely to interact with inequality of condition to generate primary and secondary effects.

Stratification describes the vertical differentiation of an educational system: in highly stratified systems students are filtered into distinct tracks early in their educational career, with few opportunities for switching tracks at later points, and in weakly stratified systems students follow a common curriculum. Selectivity describes whether educational systems are selective with regard to academic ability or choice driven. In purely selective systems, students are channeled into different educational tracks according to their performance in examinations or cognitive tests. In choice-driven systems, by contrast, students have much more freedom to decide which educational track they will pursue. Examination and test results may provide information to students about their academic potential and chances of success in different educational tracks, but the choice of track is open and any student may pursue any educational track. Thus while stratification structures the range of educational options available to students, selectivity structures the extent to which students (and their parents) are able to exercise free choice in deciding between those educational options. In practice, stratification and selectivity are associated, so that highly stratified systems are also highly selective and weakly stratified systems also exhibit weak selectivity. In anticipation of the final chapter, where we compare countries with different levels of stratification and selectivity, in this volume the country chapters are ordered by the stratification and selectivity of the education system under study, opening with the chapter on Germany and closing with the chapter on the United States.

A natural assumption would be that increasing stratification should lead to increasing secondary effects; as tracks become more highly differentiated and thus track choice becomes more consequential, students of advantaged background come to recognize that the importance of making the right choice increases, and thus secondary effects should increase. Similarly, one would also expect selectivity to influence the size of secondary effects; as educational systems become more selective, and therefore more reliant on examinations and test scores to assign students to tracks, the role of choice should be diminished (and in a purely selective system, eliminated), and thus secondary effects should decrease. But without giving too much away, neither stratification nor selectivity appears to provide the smoking gun of cross-national variability in primary and secondary effects.

A COMMON METRIC

We consider the influence of primary and secondary effects on social-background inequalities in educational attainment in seven European countries and the United States. In each country chapter we take a common approach to data selection, variable construction, and methodology, although inevitably compromises on one or more of these fronts are sometimes necessary to manage the idiosyncrasies of individual countries or datasets.

We analyze nationally representative data that capture the window of time in which major educational transitions are made. In many countries these data come from cohort surveys, but population register data and cross-sectional surveys are also analyzed in places. For some countries we are able to analyze data relating to several different cohorts, and we are therefore able to make over-time comparisons of the magnitude of primary and secondary effects and IEO.

We employ both parental class and parental education as measures of socioeconomic background. In part, this is to allow for cross-national comparison, because in some countries reliable data on either parental class or parental education are not readily available. But in addition, it is important to ask whether parental class and parental education have effects of similar magnitude on students' educational attainment and to consider changes in these effects over time. Both class and educational structures have changed substantially over the past half century, and although these structural changes need not have produced changes in IEO by necessity, we investigate whether changes in IEO did occur. We also consider whether the relative importance of primary and secondary effects differs depending on whether parental class or education is used as a measure of social background. Up to this point few comparative studies consider the influence of different measures of socioeconomic background on estimates of IEO and of primary and secondary effects. In countries in which measures of both parental class and parental education are available, it is additionally possible to consider inequalities in educational attainment with respect to a cross-classification of parental class and education, which allows us to compare the most socioeconomically advantaged group to the least socioeconomically advantaged group and thus provides an indication of the maximal inequalities related to class and educational background.

Our measure of parental class is based on the Erikson-Goldthorpe-Portocarero (EGP) classification schema that has been widely applied in comparative stratification research (Erikson, Goldthorpe, and Portocarero 1979). The schema classifies occupational positions in terms of their employment relations (see Erikson and Goldthorpe 1992; Goldthorpe 2007), and versions of the schema have been shown to demonstrate both construct and criterion-related validity (e.g., Evans 1992; Rose and Harrison 2009). We use a three-class version of the schema that distinguishes between the professional and managerial salariat (EGP classes I and II), the intermediate classes (classes IIIa, IV, and V), and the working classes (classes IIIb, VI, and VII). Parental education is measured as the highest-achieved educational qualification, and we distinguish between high (degree level and above), medium (upper secondary), and low (lower secondary and below) levels of qualifications. In contrast to many previous studies of IEO, we use information on both fathers and mothers to construct our measures of parental class and education. As women's education and labor market participation has increased, it has become more important to take the mother's influence on the household situation into account. In this volume, we use a dominance approach to determine the class and education of the household, whereby we compare the class positions and educational levels of the father and mother and take the higher class or higher level of education to represent the household position (see Erikson 1984).

We ask whether IEO is better understood as a consequence of differences in previous academic performance between social classes or educational groups or whether it should be understood as resulting from differences in educational decisions made by members of those groups, conditional on performance. Given the behavioral model that lies behind the concepts of primary and secondary effects, the students who are assumed to make educational decisions on the basis of their academic performance must have had access to information about that performance. In other words, primary effects must be measured through previous academic performance that is *known* to the students, such as examination results, rather than through performance that is known only to academic researchers, such as measures of IQ. In most countries, authors use public examination results that are known to students, teachers, and families, and where these are not available, the consequences of using other measures of performance are considered.

As discussed earlier, the theory of primary and secondary effects treats IEO as a consequence of sequential decisions about educational transitions. In this volume, we focus on the main educational transitions taken in each country; there is in fact a great deal of cross-national similarity in the important educational transitions. We identify three main educational transitions cross-nationally, two of which are generally present in any single country's educational system. The first transition identified is an early one, usually taken at around age 10, and is present in countries such as Germany and the Netherlands. This transition distinguishes between students who will pursue the higher-level academic tracks and those who will pursue lower-level academic tracks and vocational education. The second transition identified is that occurring at the end of compulsory schooling, usually at around age 16. This transition is present in a good many countries and usually distinguishes between students who continue to postcompulsory academic education, those who choose vocational education, and those who leave education. No country included in this volume has both first and second transitions. We expect the initial transition to be particularly important in determining overall IEO (see Breen et al. 2009). The third transition that we identify is that from school to university education, usually taken around age 18, and again present in most of the countries that we consider.

We use a common methodology in the country chapters, and in Chapter 2 Christiana Kartsonaki, Michelle Jackson, and David Cox present and outline the method that will be applied in all countries (see Erikson et al. 2005; Jackson et al. 2007). They first provide an outline of the method and subsequently extend the method by introducing standard errors and significance tests for estimates of primary and secondary effects.

The chapters on individual countries follow Chapter 2. I briefly summarize them here, leaving an in-depth analysis of the country findings to the final chapter.

In Chapter 3 Martin Neugebauer, David Reimer, Steffen Schindler, and Volker Stocké consider class inequalities in Germany for cohorts born in the 1980s and 1990s. They focus on the transitions from primary school to *Gymnasium* and from *Gymnasium* to university, and they relate the influence of primary and secondary effects in the transition to university to the decisions made at previous transition points. In Chapter 4, Charlotte Büchner and Rolf van der Velden assess IEO in relation to parental education in the Netherlands. They show the contribution of primary and secondary effects to IEO in the transitions to upper secondary and tertiary education for cohorts of students born in the 1970s and later. In Chapter 5, Mathieu Ichou and Louis-André Vallet present analyses of IEO in France for cohorts spanning 30 years. They assess inequalities related to both parental class and education and also comment on inequalities related to gender and ethnicity. In Chapter 6, Dalit Contini and Andrea Scagni use statistical techniques to deal with sample selection problems in order to determine the relative importance of primary and secondary effects in creating inequalities in Italy. They consider the influence of parental class and education in creating inequalities in the transitions to upper secondary and tertiary education. In Chapter 7, Frida Rudolphi analyzes register data for cohorts of Swedish students from the past 40 years, assessing IEO in relation to both parental class and education. She focuses on the transition that students make at age 16, from compulsory education to upper secondary education, and on the later transition to university. In Chapter 8 Anders Holm and Mads Meier Jæger assess IEO in Denmark, building on the basic analyses described in Chapter 2 to consider tripartite outcomes (academic tracks, vocational tracks, and exit). They compare parental class and parental education inequalities at the transition made at age 16 for two cohorts born around 30 years apart. In Chapter 9, Michelle Jackson examines IEO in England, focusing on the transitions from compulsory to postcompulsory academic education (A level), and from A level to university degree. She considers IEO in relation to both parental class and parental education and asks whether the association between social background and transitions has changed over the past half century. In Chapter 10, Stephen Morgan, Michael Spiller, and Jennifer Todd analyze data drawn from the National Education Longitudinal Study to assess the contribution of primary and secondary effects in creating class inequalities in the United States, considering both high school completion and the transition from high school to university degree. Additionally, they discuss the causal model underlying the primary-versus-secondary-effects distinction and consider alternative causal paths from social background to transition.

NOTES

I thank Dalit Contini, Robert Erikson, John Goldthorpe, David Grusky, Jan O. Jonsson, Pablo Mitnik, Walter Müller, Andrea Scagni, and Steffen Schindler for stimulating discussions on the material covered here and for helpful comments on an earlier version of this chapter.

1. *IEO*, or inequality in educational opportunity, is also used in the literature as shorthand for "inequality in educational attainment." This characterization sidesteps the thorny question of whether inequalities in *attainment* would remain if *opportunities* were equalized for members of different social classes; it is quite possible that class inequalities in educational attainment would persist even if educational opportunities were equalized.

2. Furthermore, a summary measure of inequalities in educational attainment will be influenced by both inequalities in transition rates *and* inequalities in completion rates. We do not systematically study completion as an outcome, largely because it is not simple to understand how completion might be influenced by primary and secondary effects. For example, which measure of performance do students use to glean information on their performance: their performance in the formal tests before the transition or their perceived performance on the higher-level courses?

3. The concepts of primary and secondary effects may of course also be understood as restatements of basic statistical concepts, in that they represent the indirect and direct effects of class origin on transition (e.g., Blau and Duncan 1967). The primary effects are the indirect effects of class origin on transition, operating through performance, and the secondary effects are the direct effects of class origin on transition (after taking into account all factors that operate through performance).

4. As of September 2012, searches for the term "Gunnar Boalt" in Google Scholar returned these results for the book and paper.

5. The lack of acknowledgment in the literature of Girard and Bastide's work on primary and secondary effects can perhaps be attributed to the relevant article being published only in French. During discussions of this book project, the authors in this volume learned of Girard and Bastide's work from Louis-André Vallet, to whom we are most grateful.

6. Mathieu Ichou and Louis-André Vallet's translation in Chapter 5, this volume, is the following: "the primary cause of nondemocratization: the influence of family background on the child's development and, in turn, on his or her school success," and "the secondary cause of nondemocratization: even at a given level of school performance, the likelihood of entering lower secondary school is linked to social background."

7. Of course, this is to some extent an unsatisfactory explanation given that, as we have seen, the concepts of primary and secondary effects were not proposed

by Boudon. However, as Boudon was the sociologist who gave these concepts the most systematic treatment, in a highly visible book, it is reasonable to ask why they were not more fully appreciated by sociologists of education.

8. It is important to acknowledge another strand of literature in the sociology of education in which the separate roles of academic performance and choice are recognized but not described as primary and secondary effects and in which there is no attempt to decompose total inequalities by assessing the relative importance of the two effects (e.g., Croxford 1994; Duru-Bellat 1996).

9. Genetic explanations for social-background inequalities in educational (and occupational) attainment are periodically mooted in the literature and are perhaps most famously associated with Herrnstein and Murray's *The Bell Curve* (1994). Such explanations generally focus on the role of intelligence in attainment processes, arguing first that intelligence determines educational and occupational outcomes and second that intelligence is largely transmitted through genes. There is in fact little evidence to support these claims. Research shows that social-background inequalities in educational attainment remain even after controlling for scores on intelligence tests (e.g., Erikson and Rudolphi 2010; and research on income and occupational attainment shows much the same, e.g., Fischer et al. 1996; Arrow, Bowles, and Durlauf 2000). Furthermore, social scientists favoring genetic interpretations of inequalities in attainment are accused of making simplistic and misleading assumptions regarding the heritability of intelligence and other social-psychological characteristics (see Block and Dworkin 1977 for reviews of research on intelligence and its heritability).

10. In further work, Rudolphi (2011) asks whether secondary effects are underestimated by ignoring anticipatory decisions as captured in children's early educational and occupational aspirations. She first estimates a model assessing the contribution of primary and secondary effects to IEO in Sweden and then estimates a second model assessing the contribution of these effects after controlling for early educational and occupational aspirations. Her findings suggest that estimates of the relative importance of primary and secondary effects are altered, but not substantially so, by taking account of early aspirations.

REFERENCES

Akerlof, George A. 1997. "Social Distance and Social Decisions." *Econometrica* 65:1005–27.
Anderberg, Rudolf. 1948. "Skolreform och intelligensnivå." *Folkskolan* 189–92.
Arrow, Kenneth, Samuel Bowles, and Steven N. Durlauf, eds. 2000. *Meritocracy and Economic Inequality.* Princeton, NJ: Princeton University Press.
Behrman, Jere R. 1996. "The Impact of Health and Nutrition on Education." *World Bank Research Observer* 11:23–37.

Bell, Daniel. 1973. *The Coming of Post-Industrial Society: A Venture in Social Forecasting*. London: Heinemann.

Bernstein, Basil B. 1971. *Class, Codes and Control: Theoretical Studies towards a Sociology of Language*. London: Routledge.

Blair, Clancy, and Rachel P. Razza. 2007. "Relating Effortful Control, Executive Function, and False Belief Understanding to Emerging Math and Literacy Ability in Kindergarten." *Child Development* 78:647–63.

Blake, Judith. 1989. *Family Size and Achievement*. Los Angeles: University of California Press.

Blau, Peter M., and Otis Dudley Duncan. 1971. *The American Occupational Structure*. New York: Wiley.

Block, Ned J., and Gerald Dworkin, eds. 1977. *The IQ Controversy*. London: Quartet Books.

Boalt, Gunnar, and Janson, Carl-Gunnar. 1953. "A Selected Bibliography of the Literature on Social Stratification and Social Mobility in Sweden." *Current Sociology* 2:306–27.

Boalt, Gunnar. 1947. *Skolutbildning och skolresultat för barn ur olika samhälls-grupper i Stockholm*. Stockholm: P. A. Norstedt.

Boudon, Raymond. 1974. *Education, Opportunity, and Social Inequality*. New York: Wiley.

Bourdieu, Pierre. 1984. *Distinction: A Social Critique of the Judgement of Taste*. Cambridge, MA: Harvard University Press.

Bourdieu, Pierre, and Jean Claude Passeron. 1977. *Reproduction in Education, Society and Culture*. London: Sage.

Bowles, Samuel, and Herbert Gintis. 1976. *Schooling in Capitalist America: Educational Reform and the Contradictions of Economic Life*. New York: Basic Books.

Breen, Richard, and Jan O. Jonsson. 2005. "Inequality of Opportunity in Comparative Perspective: Recent Research on Educational Attainment and Social Mobility." *Annual Review of Sociology* 31:223–43.

Breen, Richard, and John H. Goldthorpe. 1997. "Explaining Educational Differentials: Towards a Formal Rational Action Theory." *Rationality and Society* 9:275–305.

Breen, Richard, Ruud Luijkx, Walter Müller, and Reinhard Pollak. 2009. "Non-persistent Inequality in Educational Attainment: Evidence from Eight European Countries." *American Journal of Sociology* 114:1475–521.

———. 2010. "Long-Term Trends in Educational Inequality in Europe: Class Inequalities and Gender Differences." *European Sociological Review* 26:31–48.

Cameron, Stephen V., and James J. Heckman. 1999. "Can Tuition Combat Rising Wage Inequality?" In *Financing College Tuition: Government Policies and Educational Priorities*, edited by Marvin H. Kosters, 76–124. Washington DC: American Enterprise Institute Press.

Carneiro, Pedro, and James J. Heckman. 2003. "Human Capital Policy." In *Inequality in America*, edited by James J. Heckman and Alan B. Krueger, 77–239. Cambridge, MA: MIT Press.

Coleman, James S. 1988. "Social Capital in the Creation of Human Capital." In "Organizations and Institutions: Sociological and Economic Approaches to the Analysis of Social Structure." Supplement, *American Journal of Sociology* 94: S95–S120.

Croizet, Jean Claude, and Theresa Claire. 1998. "Extending the Concept of Stereotype Threat to Social Class: The Intellectual Underperformance of Students from Low Socioeconomic Backgrounds." *Personality and Social Psychology Bulletin* 24:588–94.

Croxford, Linda. 1994. "Equal Opportunities in the Secondary-School Curriculum in Scotland, 1977–1991." *British Educational Research Journal* 20:371–91.

Currie, Janet, and Duncan Thomas. 1995. "Does Head Start Make a Difference?" *American Economic Review* 85:341–64.

Danziger, Sheldon, and Jane Waldfogel, eds. 2000. *Securing the Future: Investing in Children from Birth to College.* New York: Russell Sage.

De Graaf, Nan Dirk, Paul M. De Graaf, and Gerbert Kraaykamp. 2001. "Parental Cultural Capital and Educational Attainment in the Netherlands: A Refinement of the Cultural Capital Perspective." *Sociology of Education* 73:92–111.

Downey, Douglas B. 1995. "When Bigger Is Not Better: Family Size, Parental Resources, and Children's Educational Performance." *American Sociological Review* 60:746–61.

Duncan, Greg J., and Katherine Magnuson. 2011. "The Nature and Impact of Early Achievement Skills, Attention Skills, and Behavior Problems." In *Whither Opportunity. Rising Inequality, Schools, and Children's Life Chances*, edited by Greg J. Duncan and Richard J. Murnane, 47–70. New York: Russell Sage.

Duncan, Greg J., and Jeanne Brooks-Gunn. 1997. *Consequences of Growing Up Poor.* New York: Russell Sage.

Duru-Bellat, Marie. 1996. "Social Inequalities in French Secondary Schools: From Figures to Theories." *British Journal of Sociology of Education* 17:341–50.

Duru-Bellat, Marie, Jean-Pierre Jarousse, and Alain Mingat. 1993. "Les scolarités de la maternelle au lycée. Étapes et processus dans la production des inégalités sociales." *Revue française de sociologie* 34:43–60.

Ekman, Gösta. 1951. "Skolformer och begåvningsfördelning." *Pedagogisk Tidskrift* 87:15–37.

Erikson, Robert. 1984. "Social Class of Men, Women and Families." *Sociology* 18:500–514.

———. 2007. "Social Selection in Stockholm Schools: Primary and Secondary Effects on the Transition to Upper Secondary Education." In *From Origin to Destination: Trends and Mechanisms in Social Stratification Research*, edited by Stefani Scherer, Reinhard Pollak, Gunnar Otte, and Markus Gangl. Frankfurt, Germany: Campus Verlag.

Erikson, Robert, and John H. Goldthorpe. 1992. *The Constant Flux: A Study of Class Mobility in Industrial Societies*. Oxford: Clarendon Press.

Erikson, Robert, John H. Goldthorpe, Michelle Jackson, Meir Yaish, and David R. Cox. 2005. "On Class Differentials in Educational Attainment." *Proceedings of the National Academy of Sciences* 102:9730–33.

Erikson, Robert, John H. Goldthorpe, and Lucienne Portocarero. 1979. "Intergenerational Class Mobility in Three Western European Societies: England, France and Sweden." *British Journal of Sociology* 33:1–34.

Erikson, Robert, and Jan O. Jonsson. 1996a. "Introduction: Explaining Class Inequality in Education: The Swedish Test Case." In *Can Education Be Equalized? The Swedish Case in Comparative Perspective*, edited by Robert Erikson and Jan O. Jonsson, 1–64. Boulder, CO: Westview.

———. 1996b. "The Swedish Context: Educational Reform and Long-Term Change in Educational Inequality." In *Can Education Be Equalized? The Swedish Case in Comparative Perspective*, edited by Robert Erikson and Jan O. Jonsson, 65–94. Boulder, CO: Westview.

Erikson, Robert, and Frida Rudolphi. 2010. "Change in Social Selection to Upper Secondary School—Primary and Secondary Effects in Sweden." *European Sociological Review* 26:291–305.

Evans, Geoffrey. 1992. "Testing the Validity of the Goldthorpe Class Schema." *European Sociological Review* 12:211–32.

Farah, Martha J., David M. Shera, Jessica H. Savage, Laura Betancourt, Joan M. Giannetta, Nancy L. Brodsky, Elsa K. Malmud, and Hallam Hurt. 2006. "Childhood Poverty: Specific Associations with Neurocognitive Development." *Brain Research* 1110:166–74.

Farkas, George, and Kurt Beron. 2004. "The Detailed Trajectory of Oral Vocabulary Knowledge: Differences by Class and Race." *Social Science Research* 33:464–97.

Feinstein, Leon. 2003. "Inequality in the Early Cognitive Development of British Children in the 1970 Cohort." *Economica* 70:73–97.

Fischer, Claude S., Michael Hout, Martín Sanchez Jankowski, Samuel R. Lucas, Ann Swidler, and Kim Voss. 1996. *Inequality by Design: Cracking the Bell Curve Myth*. Princeton, NJ: Princeton University Press.

Garces, Eliana, Duncan Thomas, and Janet Currie. 2002. "Longer-Term Effects of Head Start." *American Economic Review* 92:999–1012.

Girard, Alain, and Henri Bastide. 1963. "La stratification sociale et al démocratisation de l'enseignement." *Population* 18:435–72.

Girard, Alain, Henri Bastide, and Guy Pourcher. 1963. "Enquête nationale sur l'entrée en sixième et la démocratisation de l'enseignement." *Population* 18:7–48.

Goldthorpe, John H. 2007. *On Sociology.* 2nd ed. Vol. 2, *Illustration and Retrospect.* Stanford, CA: Stanford University Press.

Härnqvist, Kjell. 1958. *Reserverna för högre utbildning. Beräkningar och metoddiskussion. 1955 års universitetsutredning III.* Swedish Government Official Report (SOU) 1958:11. Stockholm: Idun.

———. 2003. "Educational Reserves Revisited." *Scandinavian Journal of Educational Research* 47:483–500.

Hauser, Robert M. 1976. "Review: On Boudon's Model of Social Mobility." *American Journal of Sociology* 81:911–28.

Heckman, James J. 2006. "Skill Formation and the Economics of Investing in Disadvantaged Children." *Science* 312:1900–1902.

Herrnstein, Richard J., and Charles Murray. 1994. *The Bell Curve: Intelligence and Class Structure in American Life.* New York: Free Press.

Husén, Torsten. 1974. *Talent, Equality and Meritocracy: Availability and Utilization of Talent.* The Hague: Martinus Nijhof.

Jackson, Michelle, Robert Erikson, John H. Goldthorpe, and Meir Yaish. 2007. "Primary and Secondary Effects in Class Differentials in Educational Attainment: The Transition to A-Level Courses in England and Wales." *Acta Sociologica* 50:211–29.

Jonsson, Jan O., Colin Mills, and Walter Müller. 1996. "A Half Century of Increasing Educational Openness? Social Class, Gender and Educational Attainment in Sweden, Germany and Britain." In *Can Education Be Equalized? The Swedish Case in Comparative Perspective*, edited by Robert Erikson and Jan O. Jonsson, 183–206. Boulder, CO: Westview.

Jukes, Matthew, Judith McGuire, Frank Method, and Robert Sternberg. 2002. "Nutrition and Education." In *Nutrition: A Foundation for Development.* Geneva: ACC/SCN.

Kaushal, Neeraj, Katherine Magnuson, and Jane Waldfogel. 2011. "How Is Family Income Related to Investments in Children's Learning?" In *Whither Opportunity. Rising Inequality, Schools, and Children's Life Chances*, edited by Greg J. Duncan and Richard J. Murnane, 187–206. New York: Russell Sage.

Kloosterman, Rianne, Natascha Notten, Jochem Tolsma, and Gerbert Kraaykamp. 2011. "The Effects of Parental Reading Socialization and Early School Involvement on Children's Academic Performance: A Panel Study of Primary School Pupils in the Netherlands." *European Sociological Review* 27:291–306.

Kloosterman, Rianne, Stijn Ruiter, Paul M. de Graaf, and Gerbert Kraaykamp. 2009. "Parental Education, Children's Performance and the Transition to Higher Secondary Education: Trends in Primary and Secondary Effects over Five Dutch School Cohorts (1965–1999)." *British Journal of Sociology* 60:377–98.

Kornrich, Sabino, and Frank Furstenberg. 2010. "Changes in Parental Spending on Children, 1972 to 2007." United States Studies Centre, University of Sydney. Working Paper, March.

Lareau, Annette. 1987. "Social Class Differences in Family-School Relationships: The Importance of Cultural Capital." *Sociology of Education* 60:73–85.

———. 2003. *Unequal Childhoods: Class, Race, and Family Life.* Berkeley: University of California Press.

Morgan, Stephen L. 2012. "Models of College Entry in the United States and the Challenges of Estimating Primary and Secondary Effects." *Sociological Methods and Research* 41:17–56.

Nash, Roy. 2006. "Controlling for 'Ability': A Conceptual and Empirical Study of Primary and Secondary Effects." *British Journal of Sociology of Education* 27:157–72.

Nelson, Charles A., III, and Margaret A. Sheridan. 2011. "Lessons from Neuroscience Research for Understanding Causal Links between Family and Neighborhood Characteristics and Educational Outcomes." In *Whither Opportunity. Rising Inequality, Schools, and Children's Life Chances*, edited by Greg J. Duncan and Richard J, Murnane, 27–46. New York: Russell Sage.

Relikowski, Ilona, Thorsten Schneider, Hans-Peter Blossfeld. 2009. "Primary and Secondary Effects of Social Origin in Migrant and Native Families at the Transition to the Tracked German School System." In *Raymond Boudon— A Life in Sociology: Essays in Honour of Raymond Boudon*, edited by Mohamed Cherkaoui and Peter Hamilton, 3:149–70. Oxford: Bardwell Press.

Rose, David, and Eric Harrison, eds. 2009. *Social Class in Europe: An Introduction to the European Socio-Economic Classification.* Abingdon, UK: Routledge.

Rudolphi, Frida. 2011. "Class Differences in Educational and Occupational Aspirations and Subsequent Educational Success among Swedish Youth." In *Inequality in Educational Outcomes: How Aspirations, Performance, and Choice Shape School Careers in Sweden*. PhD diss. 86. Stockholm: Stockholm University, Swedish Institute for Social Research.

Shavit, Yossi, and Hans-Peter Blossfeld, eds. 1993. *Persistent Inequality: A Comparative Study of Educational Attainment in Thirteen Countries.* Boulder, CO: Westview.

Shavit, Yossi, Richard Arum, and Adam Gamoran, eds. 2007. *Stratification in Higher Education: A Comparative Study.* Stanford, CA: Stanford University Press.

Steele, Claude M. 1997. "A Threat in the Air: How Stereotypes Shape Intellectual Identity and Performance." *American Psychologist* 52:613–29.

Steele, Claude M., and Joshua Aronson. 1995. "Stereotype Threat and the Intellectual Test Performance of African-Americans." *Journal of Personality and Social Psychology* 69:797–811.

Vallet, Louis-André. 2004. "Change in Intergenerational Class Mobility in France from the 1970s to the 1990s and Its Explanation: An Analysis Following the CASMIN Approach." In *Social Mobility in Europe*, edited by Richard Breen, 115–47. Oxford: Oxford University Press.

Wolfe, Dael. 1954. *America's Resources of Specialized Talent*. New York: Harpers.

CHAPTER TWO

Primary and Secondary Effects
Some Methodological Issues

Christiana Kartsonaki, Michelle Jackson,
and David R. Cox

In Chapter 1 the author argues that social-background inequalities in educational attainment may be seen as the consequence of social-background inequalities in both educational performance and the propensity to make educational transitions, conditional on educational performance. In other words, both primary and secondary effects operate to create inequalities in educational attainment.

In this chapter we discuss a method for providing quantitative estimates of the relative importance of primary and secondary effects in creating educational inequalities. The method was introduced by Erikson et al. (2005) and applied by Jackson et al. (2007) and is used in this volume in the individual country chapters. Here, we describe the method as laid out in the Erikson et al. and Jackson et al. papers and extend their approach by deriving standard errors for the estimates both of primary and secondary effects and of the relative importance of these effects. We illustrate the method with analyses of real data.

As discussed in Chapter 1, at the heart of the method is an idealized process that links social background, academic performance, and the transition. A student achieves a level of academic performance and then makes his or her choice about whether to continue to higher levels of education. Social background (from this point forward referred to as class) influences both the level of performance and the choice about whether to make the transition. The two paths from class to outcome are therefore primary effects (the indirect effect, from class to performance to transition) and secondary effects (the direct effect, from class to transition). The objective of this analysis is to assess the relative strength of the two paths from class to transition.

To investigate the relative importance of primary and secondary effects, the choice distribution of students of one class is combined with the performance distribution of students of another class to produce a synthesized,[1] or potential, outcome. That is, a hypothetical intervention is considered in which the choice characteristics change while the performance distribution remains the same and vice versa. The synthesized estimates can be compared to the actual estimates obtained when a class maintains its own performance and choice distributions. In this way, we can ask what proportion of, say, working-class students would make an educational transition if they maintained their own performance distribution but had the same choice distribution as students from the salariat, and we can compare this to the proportion of working-class students who actually made the transition. Such comparisons form the basis of the method to distinguish the relative importance of primary and secondary effects, as described below.

METHOD

Three components of the idealized process underlie the method: class, performance, and the transition. Class is treated as a nominal variable, here with three categories (salariat, intermediate, and working class). The performance scores of students are assumed to be normally distributed within each class.[2] We treat the choice at any given educational transition as simply binary, distinguishing, for example, students who stay in full-time education after the completion of compulsory education from those who do not.

The primary and secondary effects can be represented in graphical form, as shown in Figure 2.1. The performance scores for each class are represented by the normal distribution curves; the mean and variance of the performance scores are estimated for each class, and a normal distribution with these parameters is fitted within each of the classes. The distribution of performance differs across the classes, and primary effects will therefore influence the overall inequality between classes. The S-shaped curves represent the secondary effects. For each class, a binary logistic regression is fitted, with the response variable indicating whether a student continues in education, given his or her performance score. Hence, within each class,

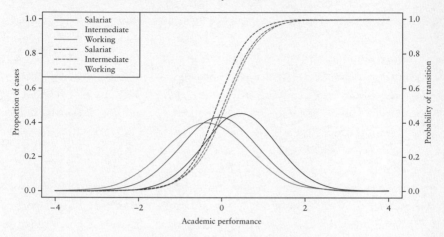

Figure 2.1. Performance distributions (solid lines) and transition probabilities (dashed lines) for each class

for a given performance score x, the probability of continuing in education can be written in the form

$$\Lambda(\alpha + \beta x) = \frac{e^{\alpha+\beta x}}{1+e^{\alpha+\beta x}},$$

where $\Lambda(\cdot)$ denotes the logistic function and α and β are the parameters of the logistic curve. Thus $-\alpha/\beta$ is the value of performance, x, at which there is a 50 percent probability of staying in full-time education.[3]

The probability that an individual makes the transition given performance x can be written as $\Lambda\{\gamma + \beta(x - \mu)\}$, where $\gamma = \alpha + \beta\mu$.

Thus, given the assumption that the performance x follows a normal distribution with mean μ and variance σ^2, that is, $x \sim \mathcal{N}(\mu, \sigma^2)$, the proportion of individuals making the educational transition within a given class is

$$\int \sigma^{-1} \phi\left(\frac{x-\mu}{\sigma}\right) \Lambda(\alpha + \beta x)\, dx, \qquad (2.1)$$

where $\phi(\cdot)$ is the standard normal density function.

The integral cannot be evaluated in closed form, but it can be calculated by numerical integration. However, $\Lambda(t)$ can be approximated by $\Phi(kt)$, where $\Phi(\cdot)$ is the standard normal cumulative distribution function and k is a tuning constant. With $k = 0.61$, the approximation has a small relative error except when the probability of success is either very close to 0 or very close to 1. In that case the normal curve approaches its limit more rapidly than the logistic (Cox and Snell 1989).

Thus, for a given class, the proportion making the transition can be written as

$$\int \sigma^{-1}\phi\left(\frac{x-\mu}{\sigma}\right)\Phi\{k\gamma + k\beta(x-\mu)\}dx = \Phi\left(\frac{k\gamma}{\sqrt{1+k^2\sigma^2\beta^2}}\right) = \Phi\left(\frac{k\gamma}{\omega}\right), \quad (2.2)$$

where $\omega = \sqrt{1+k^2\sigma^2\beta^2}$. The normal integral is then approximated by a logistic function, by applying the above approximation in reverse order.

Then the probability of transition is

$$\Lambda\left\{\frac{\gamma}{\omega}\right\} \qquad (2.3)$$

so that the log odds of transition are

$$\frac{\gamma}{\omega} = \frac{\alpha + \beta\mu}{\omega}. \qquad (2.4)$$

The transition probabilities for each class can be calculated using either (2.2) or (2.3); the difference in the values obtained by the two formulae is very small.

Inequalities between different classes are expressed by odds ratios, or equivalently by log odds ratios, comparing the transition propensities of a given class with those of a less advantaged class. Equation (2.4) is used for estimating the log odds of transition for each class and also synthesized combinations, in which the parameters of the performance distribution of one class and the parameters of the choice distribution of another class are used.

Decomposition of Primary and Secondary Effects

Let P_{jk} denote the probability that an individual with performance characteristics of class j and choice characteristics of class k continues in education. Then the odds ratio for the transition propensities of class j relative to class k is

$$Q_{jj \cdot kk} = \frac{P_{jj}/(1-P_{jj})}{P_{kk}/(1-P_{kk})}.$$

The actual odds for class j are compared with a synthesized case in which the performance distribution or the choice distribution, respectively, of class j is replaced by that of class k. The synthesized odds of transition, when using performance characteristics of class j and choice characteristics of class k, are

$$Q_{jk} = \frac{P_{jk}}{1 - P_{jk}}.$$

Then we have the synthesized odds ratios

$$Q_{jj \cdot kj} = \frac{P_{jj} / \left(1 - P_{jj}\right)}{P_{kj} / \left(1 - P_{kj}\right)}$$

and

$$Q_{jj \cdot jk} = \frac{P_{jj} / \left(1 - P_{jj}\right)}{P_{jk} / \left(1 - P_{jk}\right)}.$$

Thus

$$Q_{jj \cdot kk} = Q_{jk \cdot kk} Q_{jj \cdot jk}$$

and

$$Q_{jj \cdot kk} = Q_{jj \cdot kj} Q_{kj \cdot kk}.$$

If $L = \log Q$, then

$$L_{jj \cdot kk} = L_{jk \cdot kk} + L_{jj \cdot jk}$$

and

$$L_{jj \cdot kk} = L_{jj \cdot kj} + L_{kj \cdot kk}.$$

Thus primary and secondary effects can be isolated and can be expressed as a proportion of the total effect.

Here, $Q_{jj \cdot kj}$ is the odds ratio of students from class j making the transition compared to students with performance characteristics of class k (corresponding to primary effects) and choice characteristics of class j (corresponding to secondary effects). That is, the choice characteristics are the same, thus this quantity measures the effect due to performance (primary effects). Similarly, $Q_{jj\cdot jk}$ compares two sets of individuals who differ only in their choice characteristics and have the same performance characteristics; hence it measures secondary effects.

The relative importance of secondary effects can be expressed as

$$\frac{L_{jj\cdot jk}}{L_{jj\cdot kk}} \tag{2.5}$$

or

$$\frac{L_{kj\cdot kk}}{L_{jj\cdot kk}}. \tag{2.6}$$

Thus the relative importance of primary effects can be written as

$$1 - \frac{L_{jj\cdot jk}}{L_{jj\cdot kk}} \text{ or } 1 - \frac{L_{kj\cdot kk}}{L_{jj\cdot kk}}.$$

This method provides useful estimates only if the log odds are in the same direction, in other words, if they have the same sign. These ratios would not be informative if the performance of one class was higher than the performance of another and the transition probability for students of the former class was lower than that of the latter (or vice versa). If this were the case, the log odds ratio representing primary effects would be negative and the log odds ratio representing secondary effects positive, or vice versa.

Consider as an example the following situation, in which there are two groups, 1 and 2: subjects from group 1 are more likely to make the transition than those from group 2, but at the same time the performance of students in group 2 is higher, on average, than that of students in group 1. Thus the log odds for secondary effects are x and for primary effects $-y$ (where $x, y > 0$ and $x + y = 1$) for group 1 relative to group 2. So, for example, in comparing group 1 to group 2, if the relative importance of secondary effects was 1.4 and that of primary effects -0.4, this could be interpreted as 140 percent primary and -40 percent secondary effects, the differential operating in favor of group 1. Thus in this situation secondary effects would be in the opposite direction to the overall differential (and to the primary effect), and the absolute magnitude of the primary effect would be 3.5 times that of the secondary effect.

Moreover, as this method involves ratios of log odds ratios, it cannot be applied when the odds ratio expressing inequalities between two classes is (approximately) equal to 1, since in that case the denominator would be (approximately) 0. However, this situation would arise only if two classes had (approximately) equal probabilities of transition. In this case, there would be no class differences in educational attainment, and hence it would not be of interest to decompose into primary and secondary effects.

It can be shown that the two formulae for the relative importance of secondary effects, (2.5) and (2.6), give similar results. Because there are small differences between the results obtained by the two ways of calculating relative importance, the average of the two results can be reported instead.

The two expressions of relative importance of secondary effects differ only in the numerator, while the denominator is the actual log odds ratio for the two classes under comparison. For two classes i and j, i being more advantaged than j, the numerator of (2.5) is written algebraically as

$$\frac{\alpha_i}{\sqrt{1+k^2\sigma_i^2\beta_i^2}} + \frac{\beta_i\mu_i}{\sqrt{1+k^2\sigma_i^2\beta_i^2}} - \frac{\alpha_j}{\sqrt{1+k^2\sigma_i^2\beta_j^2}} - \frac{\beta_j\mu_i}{\sqrt{1+k^2\sigma_i^2\beta_j^2}}$$

and that of (2.6) is

$$\frac{\alpha_i}{\sqrt{1+k^2\sigma_j^2\beta_i^2}} + \frac{\beta_i\mu_j}{\sqrt{1+k^2\sigma_j^2\beta_i^2}} - \frac{\alpha_j}{\sqrt{1+k^2\sigma_j^2\beta_j^2}} - \frac{\beta_j\mu_j}{\sqrt{1+k^2\sigma_j^2\beta_j^2}}.$$

Thus the difference in the values obtained by the two expressions of relative importance arises from the differences between μ_i, μ_j and σ_i, σ_j. As there are no major differences between the variances of the classes, the differences in the estimates obtained are mainly due to the different values of μ involved in each expression. As i is the more advantaged class of the two classes involved, μ_i will be greater than μ_j and thus (2.5) will give a greater value than the one obtained by (2.6).

Illustration

To illustrate how the method works, we present analyses of a dataset from an unnamed country.[4] Our sample consists of 10,897 students who responded to a questionnaire about their social background, educational history, and current situation. Around 55 percent of the students in the

TABLE 2.1
*Means and standard deviations of performance scores, estimated
parameters of logistic curves, and 50 percent point of transition for
each class*

Class	$\hat{\mu}$	$\hat{\sigma}$	$\hat{\alpha}$	$\hat{\beta}$	$-\hat{\alpha}/\hat{\beta}$
Salariat	0.440	0.875	0.313	2.754	−0.114
Intermediate	−0.064	0.922	−0.081	2.510	0.032
Working	−0.371	0.995	−0.200	2.480	0.081

sample made the transition to postsecondary education after the completion of compulsory education. From information provided by the students
on their social background, we allocate the students to one of three classes:
salariat, intermediate class, and working class, of size 4,519, 3,905, and
2,473, respectively. The percentage of students of salariat background who
made the transition is 71 percent and the percentages of students from the
intermediate and working classes are 48 percent and 37 percent, respectively. The (standardized) performance scores for our sample of students
range from −3.59 to 1.44.

Table 2.1 shows the estimates of the parameters of the logistic regression and the distribution of performance scores for each class.

The estimated actual and synthesized probabilities and log odds of
transition for each class combination, as calculated using (2.3) and (2.4),
respectively, are presented in Table 2.2 (probabilities in the upper panel, log
odds in the lower panel). The diagonal elements of the table are the actual
probabilities and log odds, while the off-diagonal elements give the synthesized probabilities and log odds combinations, calculated using the performance distribution of the class of the corresponding row of the table and the
choice distribution of the class of the corresponding column. Comparing
the actual probabilities with a synthesized case with transition propensities
equal to those of a more advantaged class shows how much the probability
of transition increases if students of one class take on the choice characteristics of a more advantaged class.

The total class effects on transition are captured by log odds ratios, and
we use (2.5), (2.6), and their average to estimate the relative importance
of secondary effects for each combination of classes. The log odds ratios
and estimates of the relative importance of secondary effects are given in
Table 2.3.

TABLE 2.2
Probabilities and log odds of transition

	Choice		
Performance	S	I	W
Probabilities			
S	0.700	0.646	0.628
I	0.518	0.466	0.449
W	0.412	0.367	0.353
Log odds			
S	0.858	0.612	0.537
I	0.074	−0.140	−0.209
W	−0.363	−0.555	−0.619

NOTE: S = salariat; I = intermediate class; W = working class.

TABLE 2.3
Log odds ratios and estimates of relative importance of secondary effects

		RELATIVE IMPORTANCE OF SECONDARY EFFECTS		
Class	Log odds ratio	Using equation (2.5)	Using equation (2.6)	Average
Salariat-intermediate	0.998	0.246	0.215	0.231
Salariat-working	1.477	0.217	0.173	0.195
Intermediate-working	0.479	0.144	0.133	0.139

STANDARD ERRORS AND CONFIDENCE INTERVALS

The calculation of standard errors for the estimates of log odds of transition, log odds ratios, and relative importance of primary and secondary effects allows assessment of the precision of comparisons to be made between two datasets, for example, to find whether these quantities differ over time. Standard errors are also necessary for investigating whether the estimates significantly differ between classes or from some hypothesized value.

Approximate standard errors are derived using the delta method. The estimates of log odds, log odds ratios, and the relative importance of primary and secondary effects converge in distribution to the normal distribution; the asymptotic normality of the estimates is used for the derivation of confidence intervals and hypothesis tests.

In the following sections we outline the statistical derivation of standard errors and confidence intervals for our estimates. We then apply these calculations to the data described above.

Standard Error of Estimate of Log Odds of Transition

For a given class, let $\hat{\alpha}, \hat{\beta}$ be the maximum likelihood estimates of the parameters of the logistic regression and $\hat{\mu}, \hat{\sigma}$ the estimates of the parameters of the normal distribution, and let Σ denote the covariance matrix of $\hat{\alpha}, \hat{\beta}, \hat{\mu}$, and $\hat{\sigma}$.

Then the covariance matrix of the estimates of the parameters is

$$\Sigma = \begin{pmatrix} \text{var}(\hat{\alpha}) & \text{cov}(\hat{\alpha}, \hat{\beta}) & & \\ \text{cov}(\hat{\alpha}, \hat{\beta}) & \text{var}(\hat{\beta}) & & \mathbb{O} \\ & & \text{var}(\hat{\mu}) & 0 \\ \mathbb{O} & & 0 & \text{var}(\hat{\sigma}) \end{pmatrix},$$

since $\hat{\alpha}, \hat{\beta}$ are independent of $\hat{\mu}, \hat{\sigma}$ and $\hat{\mu}, \hat{\sigma}$ are mutually independent. Equivalently,

$$\Sigma = \text{diag}\{I_{\alpha,\beta}^{-1}, \Sigma_{\hat{\mu},\hat{\sigma}}\},$$

where $I_{\alpha,\beta}^{-1}$ is the inverse of the Fisher information matrix for $\hat{\alpha}, \hat{\beta}$ and $\Sigma_{\hat{\mu},\hat{\sigma}} = \text{diag}\{\sigma^2 / n, \sigma^2 / (2n)\}$.

For a function $f = f(\alpha, \beta, \mu, \sigma)$, let ∇f denote the vector of partial derivatives of f. By the delta method, as $n \to \infty$,

$$\frac{\hat{f} - f}{\sqrt{\text{var}(\hat{f})}} \xrightarrow{d} \mathcal{N}(0, 1),$$

where $\text{var}(\hat{f}) \approx (\nabla f)^T \Sigma (\nabla f)$ and $\xrightarrow{d}$ denotes convergence in distribution.

Using

$$f = \frac{\alpha + \beta\mu}{\sqrt{1 + k^2 \sigma^2 \beta^2}},$$

the asymptotic variance of the estimate of the log odds of transition is given by

$$\text{var}\left(\hat{f}\right) \approx \frac{I^{11}}{\omega^2} + \frac{2\left(\mu - 2\alpha k^2 \sigma^2 \beta\right) I^{12}}{\omega^4} + \frac{\left(\mu - 2\alpha k^2 \sigma^2 \beta\right)^2 I^{22}}{\omega^6}$$

$$+ \frac{\sigma^2 \beta^2}{n\omega^2} + \frac{2k^4 \beta^4 \sigma^4 \left(\alpha + \beta\mu\right)^2}{n\omega^6}, \tag{2.7}$$

where I^{ij} denotes the (i, j) element of the inverse of the Fisher information matrix for the logistic regression and $\omega = \sqrt{1 + k^2 \sigma^2 \beta^2}$.

Then the standard error of the estimate of the log odds of transition is $\text{SE}(\hat{f}) = \sqrt{\text{var}(\hat{f})}$.

Because normal distributions and logistic curves are fitted within each class separately, the estimates of the parameters of the normal distribution of one class are independent of the estimates of the parameters of the logistic distribution of another class. Therefore, (2.7) applies also for the calculation of the variance of the estimate of the synthesized log odds.

As a check on the proposed method for calculating standard errors, non-parametric bootstrap samples were used. For each class separately, pairs of performance scores and binary variables indicating whether a student made the transition were resampled with replacement from the original dataset. If f denotes the true value of the log odds of transition for a given class; $\hat{f}$ the estimated value of the log odds, by (2.4); and $\hat{f}^*$ the estimate obtained by the bootstrap, the bootstrap is used to assess the variability of $\hat{f}$ about the unknown true f by the variability of $\hat{f}^*$ about $\hat{f}$ (Davison and Hinkley 1997). The values of the standard errors of the log odds of transition obtained by the bootstrap were very close to those obtained by the delta method.

Separation of Variance into Components. If $\bar{I}_{\text{obs}}$ denotes the information per observation, the information of the sample is $I_{\text{sample}} = n\bar{I}_{\text{obs}}$. Thus $I^{-1} = n^{-1}\bar{I}^{-1}$.

When the parameters α, β are estimated using a different sample size from that used in estimating μ, σ, the covariance matrix of $\hat{\alpha}, \hat{\beta}, \hat{\mu}$, and $\hat{\sigma}$ is

$$\Sigma = \text{diag}\left\{ \frac{\bar{I}_{\alpha,\beta}^{-1}}{n_1}, \text{diag}\left\{ \sigma^2 / n_2, \sigma^2 / (2n_2) \right\} \right\}$$

$$= \text{diag}\left\{ \frac{\bar{I}_{\alpha,\beta}^{-1}}{np_1}, \text{diag}\left\{ \sigma^2 / (np_2), \sigma^2 / (2np_2) \right\} \right\},$$

where $n_1 = np_1$, $n_2 = np_2$, and $p_1 + p_2 = 1$. Therefore, the variance of the estimate of the log odds of transition can be written as

$$\operatorname{var}\left(\hat{f}\right) \approx \frac{1}{n_1}\left(\frac{\bar{I}^{11}}{\omega^2} + \frac{2\left(\mu - 2\alpha k^2\sigma^2\beta\right)\bar{I}^{12}}{\omega^4} + \frac{\left(\mu - 2\alpha k^2\sigma^2\beta\right)^2 \bar{I}^{22}}{\omega^6}\right)$$

$$+ \frac{1}{n_2}\left(\frac{\sigma^2\beta^2}{\omega^2} + \frac{2k^4\beta^4\sigma^4\left(\alpha + \beta\mu\right)^2}{\omega^6}\right). \tag{2.8}$$

The first component of this equation depends on the sample size used for estimating the choice distribution, while the second component depends on the sample size used in the estimation of the performance distributions. However, the same sample should preferably be used for estimating all parameters.

Covariance between Log Odds of Transition. Covariances between the log odds of transition need to be calculated to perform hypothesis tests that compare log odds estimates and also to obtain standard errors for the estimates of relative importance.

If $f_i = f(\alpha_i, \beta_i, \mu_i, \sigma_i)$ and $f_j = f(\alpha_j, \beta_j, \mu_j, \sigma_j)$, for two classes i, j ($i \neq j$), the covariance matrix of the estimates of the parameters for the two classes is

$$V_{ij} = \operatorname{diag}\left\{I_{\alpha_i,\beta_i}^{-1}, \Sigma_i, I_{\alpha_j,\beta_j}^{-1}, \Sigma_j\right\},$$

where Σ_i is the 2×2 covariance matrix of the estimated parameters of the normal distribution for class i, that is, $\Sigma_i = \operatorname{diag}\{\operatorname{var}(\hat{\mu}_i), \operatorname{var}(\hat{\sigma}_i)\}$. The covariance between two functions of the parameters is

$$\operatorname{cov}\left(\hat{f}_i, \hat{f}_j\right) \approx \left(\nabla f_i\right)^{\mathrm{T}} V_{ij}\left(\nabla f_j\right),$$

and thus for two classes i, j ($i \neq j$), $\operatorname{cov}(\hat{f}_i, \hat{f}_j) = 0$.

If $f_{ij} = f(\alpha_j, \beta_j, \mu_i, \sigma_i)$ denotes the synthesized log odds of transition, with performance parameters of class i and choice parameters of class j, then

$$\operatorname{cov}\left(\hat{f}_{ii}, \hat{f}_{ij}\right) \approx \left(\nabla f_{ii}\right)^{\mathrm{T}} \Sigma_{ij}\left(\nabla f_{ij}\right),$$

where Σ_{ij} is the covariance matrix of the parameters involved in f_{ii} and f_{ij}. Hence

$$\mathrm{cov}\left(\hat{f}_{ii}, \hat{f}_{ij}\right) \approx \frac{\sigma_i^2 \beta_i \beta_j}{n_i \omega_{ii} \omega_{ij}} + \frac{\sigma_i^4 k^4 \beta_i^2 \beta_j^2 \left(\alpha_i + \beta_i \mu_i\right)\left(\alpha_j + \beta_j \mu_i\right)}{2 n_i \omega_{ii}^3 \omega_{ij}^3}, \tag{2.9}$$

where $\omega_{ij} = \sqrt{1 + k^2 \sigma_i^2 \beta_j^2}$. Similarly,

$$\mathrm{cov}\left(\hat{f}_{ii}, \hat{f}_{ji}\right) \approx \left(\nabla f_{ii}\right)^{\mathrm{T}} \Sigma_{ji} \left(\nabla f_{ji}\right),$$

where Σ_{ji} is the covariance matrix of the parameters involved in f_{ii} and f_{ji}, and

$$\mathrm{cov}\left(\hat{f}_{ii}, \hat{f}_{ji}\right) \approx \frac{I_i^{11}}{\omega_{ji} \omega_{ii}} + \left(\frac{\mu_i - \alpha_i \beta_i k^2 \sigma_i^2}{\omega_{ji} \omega_{ii}^3} + \frac{\mu_j - \alpha_i \beta_i k^2 \sigma_j^2}{\omega_{ii} \omega_{ji}^3}\right) I_i^{12}$$
$$+ \frac{\left(\mu_i - \alpha_i \beta_i k^2 \sigma_i^2\right)\left(\mu_j - \alpha_i \beta_i k^2 \sigma_j^2\right)}{\omega_{ii}^3 \omega_{ji}^3} I_i^{22}, \tag{2.10}$$

where I_i is the information matrix for $\hat{\alpha}_i, \hat{\beta}_i$.

Standard Errors of Estimates of Relative Importance

The relative importance of secondary effects compared to the total effect for classes i, j, by (2.5), can be written as

$$F_{ij_{(1)}} = \frac{f_{ii} - f_{ij}}{f_{ii} - f_{jj}}.$$

Similar odds for classes i and j would lead to a denominator close to 0, and thus this method is not sensibly applied in this case. Then

$$\mathrm{var}\left(\hat{F}_{ij_{(1)}}\right) \approx \left(\nabla F_{ij_{(1)}}\right)^{\mathrm{T}} V_{(1)} \left(\nabla F_{ij_{(1)}}\right),$$

where $V_{(1)}$ is the covariance matrix of $\hat{f}_{ii}, \hat{f}_{ij}$, and $\hat{f}_{jj}$. Hence

$$\mathrm{var}\left(\hat{F}_{ij_{(1)}}\right) \approx \frac{\left(f_{ij} - f_{jj}\right)^2}{\left(f_{ii} - f_{jj}\right)^4} \mathrm{var}\left(\hat{f}_{ii}\right) + \frac{\left(f_{ii} - f_{jj}\right)^2}{\left(f_{ii} - f_{jj}\right)^4} \mathrm{var}\left(\hat{f}_{ii}\right) + \frac{1}{\left(f_{ii} - f_{jj}\right)^2} \mathrm{var}\left(\hat{f}_{ij}\right)$$

$$-\frac{2\left(f_{ij}-f_{jj}\right)}{\left(f_{ii}-f_{jj}\right)^{3}}\text{cov}\left(\hat{f}_{ii},\hat{f}_{ij}\right)-\frac{2\left(f_{ii}-f_{ij}\right)}{\left(f_{ii}-f_{jj}\right)^{3}}\text{cov}\left(\hat{f}_{ij},\hat{f}_{jj}\right). \qquad (2.11)$$

Similarly, for

$$F_{ij_{(2)}}=\frac{f_{ji}-f_{jj}}{f_{ii}-f_{jj}},$$

using (2.6),

$$\text{var}\left(\hat{F}_{ij_{(2)}}\right)\approx\left(\nabla F_{ij_{(2)}}\right)^{\text{T}}V_{(2)}\left(\nabla F_{ij_{(2)}}\right),$$

where $V_{(2)}$ is the covariance matrix of $\hat{f}_{ii}$, $\hat{f}_{ji}$, and $\hat{f}_{jj}$, thus

$$\text{var}\left(\hat{F}_{ij_{(2)}}\right)\approx\frac{\left(f_{ji}-f_{jj}\right)^{2}}{\left(f_{ii}-f_{jj}\right)^{4}}\text{var}\left(\hat{f}_{ii}\right)+\frac{\left(f_{ii}-f_{ji}\right)^{2}}{\left(f_{ii}-f_{jj}\right)^{4}}\text{var}\left(\hat{f}_{jj}\right)+\frac{1}{\left(f_{ii}-f_{jj}\right)^{2}}\text{var}\left(\hat{f}_{ji}\right)$$

$$-\frac{2\left(f_{ji}-f_{jj}\right)}{\left(f_{ii}-f_{jj}\right)^{3}}\text{cov}\left(\hat{f}_{ii},\hat{f}_{ji}\right)-\frac{2\left(f_{ii}-f_{ji}\right)}{\left(f_{ii}-f_{jj}\right)^{3}}\text{cov}\left(\hat{f}_{ji},\hat{f}_{jj}\right). \qquad (2.12)$$

Also

$$\frac{\hat{F}_{ij_{(m)}}-F_{ij_{(m)}}}{\sqrt{\text{var}\left(\hat{F}_{ij_{(m)}}\right)}}\xrightarrow{d}\mathcal{N}\left(0,1\right),\text{ as }n\rightarrow\infty,\ m=1,2.$$

Using the average of (2.5) and (2.6),

$$F_{ij_{(\text{avg})}}=\frac{1}{2}\left(1+\frac{f_{ji}-f_{ij}}{f_{ii}-f_{jj}}\right) \qquad (2.13)$$

and

$$\text{var}\left(\hat{F}_{ij_{(\text{avg})}}\right)\approx\left(\nabla F_{ij_{(\text{avg})}}\right)^{\text{T}}V_{(\text{avg})}\left(\nabla F_{ij_{(\text{avg})}}\right),$$

where $V_{(\text{avg})}$ is the covariance matrix of $\hat{f}_{ji}$, $\hat{f}_{ij}$, $\hat{f}_{ii}$, and $\hat{f}_{jj}$. Then

$$\text{var}\left(\hat{F}_{ij_{(\text{avg})}}\right) \approx \frac{1}{4\left(f_{ii}-f_{jj}\right)^2}\left(\text{var}\left(\hat{f}_{ji}\right)+\text{var}\left(\hat{f}_{ij}\right)\right)+\frac{\left(f_{ji}-f_{ij}\right)^2}{4\left(f_{ii}-f_{jj}\right)^4}\left(\text{var}\left(\hat{f}_{ii}\right)+\text{var}\left(\hat{f}_{jj}\right)\right)$$

$$+\frac{f_{ji}-f_{ij}}{2\left(f_{ii}-f_{jj}\right)^3}\left(\text{cov}\left(\hat{f}_{ji},\hat{f}_{ii}\right)+\text{cov}\left(\hat{f}_{ij},\hat{f}_{jj}\right)-\text{cov}\left(\hat{f}_{ji},\hat{f}_{jj}\right)-\text{cov}\left(\hat{f}_{ij},\hat{f}_{ii}\right)\right)$$

$$(2.14)$$

and

$$\frac{\hat{F}_{ij_{(\text{avg})}}-F_{ij_{(\text{avg})}}}{\sqrt{\text{var}\left(\hat{F}_{ij_{(\text{avg})}}\right)}}\xrightarrow{d}\mathcal{N}(0,1), \text{ as } n\to\infty.$$

Confidence Intervals for the Relative Importance of Primary or Secondary Effects

The convergence in distribution of the estimators of log odds and relative importance to the normal distribution can be used for the derivation of confidence intervals and significance tests.

Approximate confidence intervals can be calculated using the delta method approximations, with limits $\hat{f}\pm z_{1-\alpha/2}\sqrt{\text{var}(\hat{f})}$ for confidence level $1-\alpha$, where $z_{1-\alpha/2}$ is such that $P(|Z|\le z_{1-\alpha/2})=1-\alpha$, for any $Z\sim\mathcal{N}(0,1)$.

All estimates of the relative importance of primary or secondary effects involve ratios of log odds ratios or, equivalently, ratios of differences of log odds. This may result in nonrobust estimates and standard errors. As synthesized odds ratios approach 1, their logarithms will get close to 0, and in that case the estimates and their standard errors will be inflated. Then the delta method approximations and confidence intervals based on them may be inaccurate. An alternative method of obtaining confidence intervals for ratios of normally distributed random variables is Fieller's method (Cox 1967).

Confidence Intervals for the Relative Importance of Primary and Secondary Effects Using Fieller's Method. Because the synthesized log odds ratios approximately follow a normal distribution, Fieller's method can alternatively be used to obtain confidence intervals for the estimates of the relative importance of primary or secondary effects. Fieller's method is used for deriving confidence intervals for the ratio of two possibly correlated normal variables. Let X and Y be random variables that jointly follow a normal distribution with mean (μ_X, μ_Y) and covariance matrix V. Then $X - \rho Y \sim \mathcal{N}(0, \tau^2)$, where $\rho = \mu_X / \mu_Y$ and τ^2 is a function of ρ and the elements of the covariance matrix V, quadratic in ρ. Then

$$\frac{(X - \rho Y)^2}{\tau^2} \sim \chi_1^2$$

and therefore

$$P\left(\frac{(X - \rho Y)^2}{\tau^2} \leq \chi_{1,(1-\alpha)}^2 \right) = 1 - \alpha,$$

where $\chi_{1,(1-\alpha)}^2$ is the $(1 - \alpha)$ quantile of the chi-square distribution with 1 degree of freedom, such that $P(W \geq \chi_{1,(1-\alpha)}^2) = \alpha$ for any random variable $W \sim \chi_1^2$, and the limits of the corresponding $(1 - \alpha)$ confidence interval will be the two real roots of the quadratic equation, given that these exist. Fieller's method is in principle the most secure way to calculate confidence intervals for a ratio, but in the present context large-sample approximations are adequate.

Illustration. Using the same dataset as previously, the proposed method is applied to provide standard errors and confidence intervals for the measures of interest. We use the free R package DECIDE (Kartsonaki 2010; on R, see R Development Core Team 2011) to obtain our results.

In Table 2.4 we present standard errors and approximate 95 percent confidence intervals for the log odds of students' transition for each class. As shown in Table 2.4, students of salariat background are significantly more likely to continue in education than not to, while students of intermediate and working class background are more likely to leave education. We can derive standard errors for both the actual and the synthesized log odds of transition.

Standard errors and approximate 95 percent confidence intervals for the log odds ratios comparing differences in the log odds of transition between classes are shown in Table 2.5. The confidence intervals demonstrate that the log odds ratios are significantly greater than 0, confirming that inequalities do exist between all classes.

TABLE 2.4

Standard errors and approximate 95 percent confidence intervals for the log odds of transition

Class	Log odds	Standard error	95% CI
Salariat	0.858	0.0357	(0.788, 0.928)
Intermediate	−0.140	0.0331	(−0.205, −0.075)
Working	−0.619	0.0436	(−0.704, −0.533)

TABLE 2.5

Standard errors and approximate 95 percent confidence intervals for the log odds ratios

Class	Log odds ratio	Standard error	95% CI
Salariat-intermediate	0.998	0.0487	(0.902, 1.093)
Salariat-working	1.477	0.0563	(1.367, 1.587)
Intermediate-working	0.479	0.0548	(0.372, 0.587)

TABLE 2.6

Estimates and standard errors for the relative importance of secondary effects

Class	RELATIVE IMPORTANCE OF SECONDARY EFFECTS (STANDARD ERROR)		
	Using equation (2.5)	Using equation (2.6)	Average
Salariat-intermediate	0.246 (0.0333)	0.215 (0.0272)	0.231 (0.0302)
Salariat-working	0.217 (0.0288)	0.173 (0.0219)	0.195 (0.0249)
Intermediate-working	0.144 (0.0795)	0.133 (0.0642)	0.139 (0.0757)

The standard errors of the estimates of relative importance are shown in Table 2.6. The standard errors are calculated using (2.11), (2.12), and (2.14), for the estimates of relative importance from (2.5), (2.6), and their average, respectively.

In Table 2.7 we present 95 percent confidence intervals for the relative importance of secondary effects, based on the normal approximations. The contribution of secondary effects is significant for the differentials between the salariat and the intermediate class, as well as between the salariat and the working class. For those comparisons the contribution of secondary effects ranges from 13 percent to 31 percent of the total effect. The same cannot be said of the comparison of intermediate with working class, where the confidence intervals include 0. This could be due to a greater level of

TABLE 2.7
Approximate 95 percent confidence intervals for the relative importance
of secondary effects

Class	Using equation (2.5)	Using equation (2.6)	Using average
Salariat-intermediate	(0.181, 0.312)	(0.161, 0.268)	(0.171, 0.290)
Salariat-working	(0.161, 0.274)	(0.130, 0.216)	(0.146, 0.244)
Intermediate-working	(−0.012, 0.300)	(0.007, 0.259)	(−0.010, 0.287)

variability in the transition propensities of working-class students, which is shown by larger standard errors and hence wider confidence intervals.

HYPOTHESIS TESTING

Test for Overall Differences over Time

To examine whether there is a significant difference overall between the values obtained from two datasets, a χ^2 test of the overall difference may be used. This test can be used to examine whether the overall differences between log odds, log odds ratios, or estimates of relative importance of primary and secondary effects obtained from two datasets are significant.

Let $d^{\mathrm{T}} = (d_1, d_2, \ldots, d_p)$ denote the differences between the values of p functions at two time points. To investigate whether the overall difference is significant, the test statistic

$$d^{\mathrm{T}} \Sigma_d^{-1} d$$

is compared with a quantile of the χ_p^2 distribution.

Hence the null hypothesis of zero differences ($d_1 = d_2 = \cdots = d_p = 0$) is rejected at significance level α if $d^{\mathrm{T}} \Sigma_d^{-1} d \geq \chi_{p,(1-\alpha)}^2$, where $P(W \geq \chi_{p,(1-\alpha)}^2) = \alpha$ for any $W \sim \chi_p^2$.

The elements of the covariance matrix Σ_d are obtained by the delta method approximations described above. Covariances between estimates of relative importance of secondary effects are obtained similarly by the delta method.

Illustration

To illustrate the comparisons that may be made between two datasets, we use a second dataset from the same country that includes data for students who were at the same transition point at an earlier time point than those in the original dataset. All differences taken below are of the estimates obtained from the most recent dataset minus those of the older one.

The log odds ratios of transition, which quantify the overall differentials between classes, can be compared over time to examine whether the magnitude of the between-class differentials changes. Table 2.8 shows 95 percent confidence intervals for the differences in log odds ratios over time. The confidence intervals include 0, suggesting that the inequalities between classes have not changed substantially over time, even though the transition propensities for all classes have increased. This is confirmed by testing whether the overall difference in log odds ratios differs from 0; the test is not significant (value of test statistic is 0.412, $p = 0.94$).

Using similar reasoning, confidence intervals for the difference of the relative importance of secondary effects for the two time points are obtained, to assess whether the relative contribution of secondary effects significantly differs over time. These 95 percent confidence intervals are presented in Table 2.9, and they show that the relative importance of secondary effects has not changed significantly over time (as each confidence interval includes 0).

Sampling Issues. The standard errors calculated here are based on simple random sampling. Clustering of samples could affect the distribution of the observations and the variances. If more complicated sampling procedures are thought likely to have a major effect on the overall precision of the conclusions, the simplest procedure would be to multiply the component standard errors by inflation factors derived from the sampling procedures used.

TABLE 2.8
*Estimates and approximate 95 percent confidence intervals
for the differences of log odds ratios over time*

	LOG ODDS RATIO			
Class	*Recent dataset*	*Older dataset*	*Difference of log odds ratios*	*95% CI for difference*
Salariat-intermediate	0.998	1.029	−0.031	(−0.166, 0.103)
Salariat-working	1.477	1.512	−0.035	(−0.197, 0.128)
Intermediate-working	0.479	0.482	−0.003	(−0.165, 0.158)

TABLE 2.9
Estimates and approximate 95 percent confidence intervals
for the difference in relative importance of secondary effects over time

	DIFFERENCE IN RELATIVE IMPORTANCE OF SECONDARY EFFECTS (95% CI)		
Class	Using equation (2.5)	Using equation (2.6)	Using average
S-I	−0.049 (−0.144, 0.046)	−0.060 (−0.146, 0.026)	−0.054 (−0.137, 0.029)
S-W	−0.075 (−0.166, 0.017)	−0.054 (−0.131, 0.022)	−0.065 (−0.138, 0.009)
I-W	−0.042 (−0.292, 0.207)	−0.004 (−0.247, 0.239)	−0.023 (−0.253, 0.207)

N O T E : S = salariat; I = intermediate class; W = working class.

Weighting Issues. In many datasets analyzed by social scientists, weights are provided that are based on the sampling design. These are required whenever the main objective is estimation of descriptive features of the population under investigation, for example, the proportions of the population in various social classes. In our context, however, the object is the study of conditional relations; for example, given that an individual is in such and such a social class, what is the probability of a specific educational choice. If that relation is stable, there is in general no need for weighting (Snijders and Bosker 2011). If, however, the relation is appreciably different in different parts of the population and an average across the population is required, some simple form of weighting may be desirable.

If weighting is required, relatively standard methods are available in which least squares regression is involved, but for logistic regression the position is not so simple. We recommend the following procedure. Round the weights to simple integer multiples avoiding extremely high values, say, integers between 1 and 5. Produce a synthetic dataset with appropriate repetition of some data values. From the logistic regression of the synthetic data, find the standard maximum likelihood estimates. Compute the standard errors from the original data unweighted. These standard errors are likely to be slightly too small.

CONCLUSION

Because all results rely on approximations, which in principle need checking in each case, the conclusions should be interpreted with caution. The logistic approximation to the normal distribution is unsafe in some cases when the probabilities used for generating the binary variables of transition are very close either to 0 or 1. Thus the approximation to the log odds may give biased estimates when probabilities of transition critically depend on the tails of the distribution. In that case, standard errors calculated using the delta method are likely to be underestimated.

NOTES

1. Throughout this chapter we label the estimates obtained by this analysis as synthesized and not counterfactual, as they were called by Erikson et al. (2005) and Jackson et al. (2007). While the synthesized estimates represent counterfactual situations, which are contrasted with actual situations, the term *counterfactual* is not used here so as to avoid potential confusion with *counterfactual analysis*.

2. Buis (2010) provided an alternative approach for decomposing primary and secondary effects that does not assume normality of performance scores.

3. Although different parameters, α_i and β_i, are used in the logistic regressions for each class, where i indexes classes, in many applications the same β could be used for all classes subject to reasonable consistency with the data. If the same variance were used for the performance distributions of all classes and the same slope used in the logistic regressions for all classes, the estimates obtained would be close to those obtained using different parameter values for each class. The consequence of using common parameter values would be some apparent increase in precision accompanied by some risk of inducing bias.

4. We do not identify the country from which the data are drawn to avoid foreshadowing the results presented in the individual country chapters. Our aim is to provide an illustration of the method, rather than to present an analysis from which substantive conclusions should be drawn.

REFERENCES

Buis, Maarten L. 2010. "Direct and Indirect Effects in a Logit Model." *Stata Journal* 10:11–29.

Cox, David R. 1967. "Fieller's Theorem and a Generalization." *Biometrika* 54:567–72.

Cox, David R., and E. Joyce Snell. 1989. *The Analysis of Binary Data*. 2nd ed. London: Chapman and Hall.

Davison, Anthony C., and David V. Hinkley. 1997. *Bootstrap Methods and Their Application*. Cambridge: Cambridge University Press.

Erikson, Robert, John H. Goldthorpe, Michelle Jackson, Meir Yaish, and David R. Cox. 2005. "On Class Differentials in Educational Attainment." *Proceedings of the National Academy of Sciences* 102:9730–33.

Jackson, Michelle, Robert Erikson, John H. Goldthorpe, and Meir Yaish. 2007. "Primary and Secondary Effects in Class Differentials in Educational Attainment: The Transition to A-Level Courses in England and Wales." *Acta Sociologica* 50:211–29.

Kartsonaki, Christiana. 2010. "DECIDE: DEComposition of Indirect and Direct Effects." R package. http://CRAN.R-project.org/package=DECIDE.

R Development Core Team. 2011. *R: A Language and Environment for Statistical Computing*. Vienna, Austria: R Foundation for Statistical Computing. http://www.R-project.org.

Snijders, Tom A. B., and Roel J. Bosker. 2011. *Multilevel Analysis. An Introduction to Basic and Advanced Multilevel Modeling*. London: Sage.

CHAPTER THREE

Inequality in Transitions to Secondary School and Tertiary Education in Germany

Martin Neugebauer, David Reimer,
Steffen Schindler, and Volker Stocké

One of the most stable findings in educational research is that, on average, students of low socioeconomic origin choose less ambitious educational pathways than their peers from more privileged backgrounds (e.g., Breen et al. 2009; Shavit and Blossfeld 1993). In Germany the most consequential educational decision is the transition from elementary school to one of several secondary school tracks when students are 10 or 11 years old. Among the available options, only successful completion of the classical academic track (*Gymnasium*) directly qualifies students for entry into tertiary education. Students who qualify reach a second important decision point: whether to enter some type of tertiary education. At both transition points inequality of educational opportunity stems from two sources: the primary effects of social origin, which can be understood as the association between origin and academic performance, and the secondary effects, which are differences in transition probabilities for students with the same level of academic performance but different social origin.

The level of educational inequality in Germany is high compared with other industrialized nations (Jonsson, Mills, and Müller 1996). To locate and understand the mechanisms behind this inequality, it is useful to obtain estimates of the relative importance of primary and secondary effects at the transition to both secondary school and university. Furthermore, the nature of the selection process and the influence of primary and secondary effects at the transition from elementary school to secondary education affects the relative strength of both types of effects at subsequent transition points: If, for example, class inequality at the transition from elementary school to secondary education were entirely attributable to academic performance, the secondary effects of social origin might then play a larger role when students and their parents make the decision to enter or forgo university education. In any case, an understanding of the relative importance of primary and secondary effects in the stratified German education system allows us to make inferences about where to direct policy measures to reduce inequality of educational opportunity.

With this policy perspective in mind, the aim of our chapter is to provide comparable estimates of primary and secondary effects for the two key transitions in the German educational system. The remainder of this chapter is structured as follows: We provide a brief sketch of the German educational system. We emphasize two institutional characteristics that we believe are most relevant for understanding inequality in educational opportunity in Germany: first, the early and very consequential sorting of students into stratified secondary school tracks after primary school, where school performance serves as the prime allocation principle, and second, the existence of an attractive system of vocational training that constitutes a popular educational alternative even for those students who obtain the qualification to go on to university. We discuss relevant literature on educational inequality in the German context. We describe our datasets and variables before presenting our findings in two parts: In the first part we evaluate the relative importance of primary and secondary effects at both major transitions, employing the method outlined in Chapter 2 of this volume. In the second part we expand on this method and simulate how eliminating primary and secondary effects separately or simultaneously at both transitions would affect the inequality related to participation in tertiary education. Finally, we conclude by summarizing our results and providing some tentative policy recommendations.

EDUCATIONAL SYSTEM

In the German school system the institutional framework and regulations vary to a substantial degree among the 16 federal states (*Bundesländer*). We thus describe (and display in Figure 3.1) the institutional setup that is predominant in most of the federal states and note important deviations from the majority regulations. If not stated otherwise, the description refers to the situation in 2001 when the transitions analyzed in the empirical section took place.

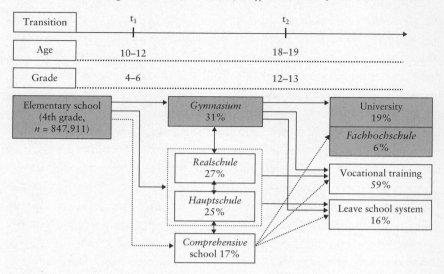

Figure 3.1.   Important educational pathways through the stylized German educational system

SOURCE: Kultusministerkonferenz (KMK) (nos. 171–12/03), KMK (nos. 184–11/07), Bundesministerium für Bildung und Forschung (BMBF) Grund- und Strukturdaten 94/95 (p. 64), and our calculations based on Mikrozensus (2005).

NOTE: In 1993, 847,911 students of the 1983 birth cohort attended the last grade in elementary school. The percentages indicate the distribution of this cohort over tracks at age 15 (during secondary school) and at age 22 (after transfer to a postcompulsory schooling activity). The distribution is taken as a national average, and percentages differ between federal states because of the different alternatives offered. The gray boxes depict the typical academic route into tertiary education. Not displayed for the sake of clarity are additional secondary and postsecondary school types, which vary between federal states.

The Transition from Elementary to Secondary School

Schooling is compulsory from age 6, when students typically enter primary school, up until students have completed 9 or in some states 10 years of schooling. Elementary school lasts for 4 years (until age 10) or 6 years (until age 12), depending on the state. At the end of elementary school students are selected into one of the secondary school types. The main types are *Hauptschule*, *Realschule*, and *Gymnasium*. The lowest secondary track (*Hauptschule*) is academically least demanding and provides very limited career opportunities. This track takes only 5 years to complete, in addition to the 4 years of elementary schooling. The intermediate secondary track (*Realschule*) lasts 6 years and leads to a degree that permits entry into white-collar, business, or skilled trade occupations. Completion of this track alone is not sufficient for admission to university, but it can provide access to the tertiary track through the completion of additional programs. Since this is a relatively rare educational pathway, it is not shown in Figure 3.1. In recent years, there has been a trend toward integrating *Hauptschule* and *Realschule* into one lower secondary school type, so that today the majority of the federal states do not distinguish between them.

Upper secondary school (*Gymnasium*) is the most demanding, prestigious, and academically oriented track. In 2001 students had to attend *Gymnasium* for 9 years before they received an upper secondary certificate (*Abitur*).[1] Although the upper secondary school track is the main pathway to obtain eligibility for tertiary education, several additional, but relatively rarely used pathways lead to eligibility for tertiary education.[2] Besides these tracked institutions, most states offer comprehensive schools, in which students are not separated by secondary school track. In these schools students are grouped into different courses according to their academic ability. In 2001 just under 20 percent of all students attended some kind of comprehensive school (Avenarius et al. 2003, 56). With respect to the construction of the dependent variable of our analyses, note that because of the heterogeneity of the German school system, *Gymnasium* is the only distinct track available in all federal states.

Because of the early first transition point and the rare instances of track mobility (Mühlenweg 2008; Schneider 2008), the German school system must be regarded as highly stratified. In this institutional context the educational decision made after elementary school is consequential for educational success. Despite the importance of this transition, the institutional practices that determine which school track students attend after primary school vary substantially across German states. In all states primary school teachers provide a formal recommendation for one or more school types that they regard as appropriate for the students' further school careers. Two types of practices determine the relative significance of these recommendations vis-à-vis families' own wishes. In one group of states parents are free to choose whichever school type they want. The recommendations serve only to provide relevant information for the families' school choice decisions. In other states the recommendation of the primary school is binding and parents must accept it or choose a less demanding secondary school track, although parents can also force a revision of the recommendation.[3]

In these cases, students must pass a special entrance examination for the school type they wish to enter.

Although the educational decision after elementary school is consequential for obtaining eligibility for tertiary education, the selected type of secondary school in the tracked system does not completely determine the highest degree obtained. First, a total of 14.4 percent of all students attending secondary school change school type at least once (Bellenberg, Hovestadt, and Klemm 2004, 81). About 11 percent change to a less demanding and 3 percent to a more demanding track. Second, after completing a lower or intermediate secondary school degree, students can continue their school career to earn an upper secondary degree. However, students from more privileged backgrounds are more likely to change to more ambitious tracks or continue schooling and are less likely to change downward (Jacob and Tieben 2010). Thus, the social inequality observed at the first transition point after elementary school is actually an underestimation of the differentiation of completed secondary school degrees (Hillmert and Jacob 2005).

The Transition from Upper Secondary to Tertiary Education

The tertiary-education system in Germany comprises two types of institutions: the traditional research universities and the more practically oriented universities of applied sciences (*Fachhochschulen*). Before the implementation of the Bologna reforms (see Reinalda and Kulesza 2005), completing a degree at traditional universities took on average 6.7 years, which is 1.4 years longer than it takes to graduate from universities of applied sciences (Mayer 2008, 620). Although students from universities of applied sciences have somewhat less favorable career prospects, since the 1980s and 1990s they have caught up with university degree holders in terms of access to favorable social class positions (Müller, Brauns, and Steinmann 2002). In some German states, universities of cooperative education (*Berufsakademien*) and universities of administrative education (*Verwaltungsfachhochschulen*) are also present; these institutions combine tertiary-level education with vocational training and constitute alternative postsecondary options. However, only a relatively small proportion of all students choose these semitertiary institutions.[4] In the German educational system, vocational training offers an attractive and frequently chosen postsecondary alternative to tertiary education. While completing an apprenticeship within the dual system, the apprentice receives a small salary. Completing an apprenticeship usually takes only two or three years. Thus, vocational training can be regarded as less costly. Furthermore, academic demands are lower in the vocational than in the tertiary track. Both arguments lead to the prediction that students from lower social origins, even when eligible for tertiary education, will be deterred from a university career (e.g., Becker and Hecken 2009a).

As a summary, Figure 3.1 illustrates the flow of students through the German school system for the 1983 birth cohort. Less than a third of all students enter *Gymnasium* after elementary school, whereas 27 percent pursue an intermediate secondary school degree at the *Realschule*, and 25 percent pursue a lower secondary school degree at the *Hauptschule*. Altogether, 17 percent attend some kind of integrated school type.[5] However, as already mentioned, some students change (upward or downward) the initially selected secondary school track and complete a degree different from the initial secondary school choice. Among those who obtain eligibility for higher education, almost two-thirds enter a tertiary track, while about one-third start vocational training (Reimer and Pollak 2010).

PREVIOUS RESEARCH

The level of educational inequality is relatively high in Germany. This applies to the attainment of educational credentials (Jonsson, Mills, and Müller 1996) as well as to the distribution of academic ability (Ehmke and Baumert 2007). Because attendance patterns across the different school tracks highly depend on students' social origin, the initial differentiation of academic abilities is reinforced during the school career. Recent research confirms that inequality in academic ability increases substantially between elementary and secondary school in Germany (Hanushek and Wößmann 2006; Schütz, Ursprung, and Wößmann 2008). Accordingly, inequality in educational attainment in Germany can be regarded as the cumulative result of origin-specific transition decisions at different branching points of the educational system and of different learning opportunities before and within the tracked system of secondary schooling.

Recent research within the German context demonstrates that inequality in cognitive competencies is already strong during elementary school. At the transition to secondary school, social origin explains between 5 and

11 percent of the variance in students' academic ability (Ditton and Krüsken 2009). Additionally, the selection of different secondary school tracks is highly differentiated according to parental social class and education (Schauenberg and Ditton 2004; Stocké 2007b), and even when controlling for students' school grades, significant effects of family background are observed (Stocké 2007a).

For Germany, four studies investigate the relative importance of primary and secondary effects at the transition to *Gymnasium* compared to lower secondary school types, and all studies have (different) limitations (Müller-Benedict 2007; Neugebauer 2010; Relikowski, Schneider, and Blossfeld 2009; Stocké 2007a).[6] Müller-Benedict (2007) finds that primary and secondary effects are equally strong, although the validity of this study might be questioned because it draws on cross-sectional Program for International Student Assessment (PISA) data, in which academic performance was assessed when students were in the ninth grade. The studies of Stocké (2007a) and Relikowksi, Schneider, and Blossfeld (2009) are longitudinal and thus better suited to distinguishing primary and secondary effects, but in both studies the samples are restricted to one or two federal states. The analyses of Stocké (2007a) show for Rhineland-Palatinate that secondary effects account for 53 percent of the class differentials and for 71 percent of the inequality attributable to parental education at the transition to *Gymnasium*. In contrast, Relikowski, Schneider, and Blossfeld (2009) find with data from Bavaria and Hesse that secondary effects account for only 40 percent of the inequalities related to class origin and for 43 percent of those related to the educational background of the students. Finally, Neugebauer (2010), employing a nationwide-panel dataset, finds that secondary effects account for 59 percent of the total inequality related to parental education. Furthermore, the study shows that the relative importance of secondary effects is higher when parents can freely choose a secondary school track and lower when a binding school recommendation restricts freedom to choose. However, Neugebauer provides estimates for only a crude two-category measure of parental education.

Less direct evidence for the relative strength of primary and secondary effects is available for the transition from secondary school to tertiary education. Many studies have analyzed social selectivity at the transition to tertiary education, conditional on having reached eligibility for this educational option (Becker and Hecken 2009a; Becker and Hecken 2009b;

Lörz and Schindler 2009; Maaz 2006; Mayer, Müller, and Pollak 2007; Reimer and Pollak 2010). Estimates for the relative strength of primary and secondary effects at the transition to tertiary education are provided in two studies. On the basis of a school-leaver survey in Saxonia, Becker (2009) finds that 63 percent of social-origin effects in the transition to higher education are due to secondary effects, although the study measures only the intention rather than the decision to study at a tertiary institution. The study by Schindler and Reimer (2010) uses data based on real transitions for a nationally representative sample of students who were eligible for tertiary education. Applying the method described in Chapter 2, the authors find that 86 percent of the inequality between the upper and lower classes at the transition to tertiary education can be attributed to secondary effects for the most recent cohort in their study. However, this conditional estimate ignores the influence of primary and secondary effects at previous transitions. Two studies have addressed this issue by employing a simulation approach across subsequent transitions to assess the importance of primary and secondary effects. Both the study by Becker (2009) and the study by Neugebauer and Schindler (2012) point to the pivotal role of the first transition in influencing social selectivity in access to tertiary education, and both studies show that taking account of this early selectivity results in larger estimates of the overall impact of secondary effects at the tertiary level.

DATA AND VARIABLES

Unfortunately, the data coverage and quality is not ideal in the German case. First of all, no longitudinal data exist that cover the two crucial educational transitions under consideration. As a result, we use two separate cross-sectional datasets, which each relate to one of the transitions, and make them as comparable as possible. In each case the data represent nationwide representative samples of the relevant population under consideration.

IGLU-E 2001 Data

For the first transition from elementary to secondary school, we use data from the German extension of the Progress in International Reading Literacy Study (PIRLS). This study was conducted by the International Association for the Evaluation of Educational Achievement (IEA) in 2001, to assess the reading literacy of 9- and 10-year-old students (Mullis et al. 2002, 2003). In Germany this study was extended; the IGLU-E (Erweiterungsstudie zur Internationalen Grundschul-Lese-Untersuchung) included not only reading literacy test scores but also performance tests in mathematics and science and school grades in all three subjects. Data were collected in a two-stage stratified sampling design toward the end of fourth grade, when the decision about secondary school choice had been made for most students.

Because the sample was drawn at the end of the fourth grade and because we are interested in secondary school choice, we exclude students from federal states in which no tracking into different secondary school tracks has taken place, because either primary school comprises six instead of four years or students transfer to an orientation school (*Orientierungsstufe*). In 2001 this was the case in Berlin, Brandenburg, Bremen, Mecklenburg-Vorpommern, and Niedersachsen. After weights are applied to compensate for unequal probabilities of inclusion in the sample and to ensure representativeness, we have complete information for 2,818 students. The participation rate of 84 percent can be regarded as sufficiently high.

Upper Secondary School-Leaver Survey

For the second transition we draw on a dataset from a large-scale upper secondary school-leaver mail survey, collected in 2002 by the German Higher Education Information System (HIS) Institute. The dataset comes from a stratified random sample of students with entrance qualifications for higher education in Germany. Students in the survey were interviewed twice: six months and then three and a half years after graduation. To observe real postsecondary schooling decisions rather than intentions, we construct our dependent variable using information from the second wave, even though there is considerable panel attrition in addition to the nonresponse in the first wave of the survey.[7] To correct for sample selection bias due to panel attrition, we weight the observations in each dataset inversely to their predicted dropout probabilities.

For our analyses we use the subsample of students in the second wave of the HIS data who obtained their degree in 2002 via the conventional academic route, which is an upper secondary degree at a *Gymnasium* without any detours through the vocational training system.[8] This sample is completely compatible with the student population in the IGLU-E data. To avoid problems with outliers we also exclude students who were older than 21 at the time of graduation (approximately 1 percent of the sample).

Dependent Variables

For the first transition the dependent variable is based on the answer to the following question in the parental questionnaire: "Which type of secondary school will your son/daughter most likely attend in the next school year?" Even though the question refers to intentions rather than final decisions, the interviews were conducted, depending on the federal state, either shortly before or after the students registered at the secondary school they were to attend the following school year. We assume that this variable in the vast majority of cases approximates the enrollment decision.

Because *Gymnasium* is the only distinct track available in all federal states, we construct a binary variable separating it from all lower school types. The lower category combines students who transferred to *Hauptschule*, *Realschule*, or school tracks that integrate the two.[9] Out of 2,818 families, 1,229 (44 percent) chose *Gymnasium*, while 1,239 (44 percent) did not. The remaining 350 families (12 percent) had not opted for or against *Gymnasium*, because either the pupil had to repeat the school year or a fully comprehensive track (*Gesamtschule*) was selected. These families are excluded, leaving a sample of 2,468 families for the following analyses.[10]

For the second transition, we consider whether students enroll at a tertiary institution within the first three and a half years after graduation. We do not distinguish between enrollment at traditional universities and universities of applied sciences (*Fachhochschulen*), although there are also social-class differences in the choice between these two tertiary options (Schindler and Reimer 2011; Trautwein et al. 2006).

Independent Variables

Social Origin. We consider inequalities with respect to parents' social class and education. We use the father's and the mother's social class and education as indicators of the occupational and educational background of each student. If information on both parents is available, we use the dominance model to arrive at a single indicator for the family. In the remainder of the chapter we refer to parents' class and education even if we used either the only available or in most cases the higher parental status position.

To measure class we employ the standard threefold collapse of the Goldthorpe (also known as the Erikson-Goldthorpe-Portocarero, or EGP) class schema: salariat (classes I and II), intermediate class (classes IIIa, IV, and V), and working class (classes IIIb, VI, and VII).[11] We categorize parental education into high (tertiary degree), medium (upper secondary degree, or *Abitur*), and low (lower and intermediate secondary degrees, or *Haupt-* and *Realschulabschluss*).[12]

Academic Performance. At both transitions, we measure primary effects through the average of teacher-assigned grades. In our view this is the best measure of primary effects in the German school system since, first, results of standardized achievement tests conducted by researchers are not known to families and, second, no standardized achievement tests are conducted in the school context. Consistent with this reasoning, grades explain educational decisions to a much higher degree than standardized test results (Stocké 2007a). At the transition from elementary to secondary school we calculate the average of the three most important grades in the midterm report of the fourth grade. These grades were reported by the teachers. At the transition to university, we use the self-reported grade point average (GPA) obtained in the graduation certificate (*Abitur*). GPAs have been standardized to a mean of 0 and a standard deviation of 1. Positive values denote above-average performance and negative values below-average.

Methodological Approach

To partition the total social-origin effect into its primary and secondary elements we apply the decomposition method outlined in Chapter 2 of this volume.[13] In the second part of our analysis, results regarding origin-specific continuation rates are used to simulate social inequalities in the entire educational career up to the transition to tertiary education. The simulation enables us to estimate how many students of a given social group would enter tertiary education if we assumed different hypothetical combinations of counterfactual transition rates at either of the two transition points.

RESULTS

Descriptive Overview

To begin with, we inspect the characteristics of the students at the different educational stages (Table 3.1). First, we evaluate the representativeness

TABLE 3.1
Distribution of students with different social backgrounds at different educational stages

	MZ PARENTS WITH CHILDREN AGE 13 OR 14 (1990–91 BIRTH COHORT)	IGLU-E (APPROX. 1990–91 BIRTH COHORT)		HIS (APPROX. 1981–83 BIRTH COHORT)	
	% Total	% Total	IGLU-E % Gymnasium	% Gymnasium	% University
Parental education					
Low	69	57	37	37	33
Medium	11	12	16	9	9
High	20	31	47	54	58
Parental class					
Working	40	31	16	10	9
Intermediate	27	32	30	34	32
Salariat	32	37	54	56	59
N	28,186 (education) 26,897 (class)	2,515	1,247 (= 50%)	5,431	4,374 (= 81%)

NOTE: MZ = German Microcensus 2004; IGLU-E = Erweiterungsstudie zur Internationalen Grundschul-Lese-Untersuchung 2001; HIS = Higher Education Information System School Leaver Panel 2002.

of the IGLU-E data by comparing distributions with population estimates drawn from the German Microcensus 2004 (MZ 2004). Students from more advantaged families with respect to educational background are to some extent overrepresented in the IGLU-E data, so that 31 percent of those in the IGLU-E data come from families with high education compared with 20 percent in the German population (the difference between the two data sources for those with low education is 12 percentage points).

Whereas the sample composition according to educational origin deviates to a certain degree from the population, there are only small deviations with respect to social class. In the IGLU-E data the working class is underrepresented by 9 percentage points, while the salariat and families with intermediate class positions are overrepresented by 5 percentage points (see columns 1 and 2). The observed differences may be due to selective nonresponse or sampling procedures in the IGLU-E survey and to not all German federal states being included in the selected IGLU-E sample. Additionally, there are slight deviations between the class and educational background composition of families who selected *Gymnasium* for their children in the IGLU-E dataset (column 3) and the HIS sample at risk of selecting the tertiary option (column 4). Comparing the social origin of the students eligible (column 4) with those who actually enter university (column 5) shows only a modest increase in social selectivity at this transition.

In Table 3.2a we present the transition rates of students according to their parents' educational background at the two key transitions in the German educational system. We also report GPAs for populations at risk of selecting *Gymnasium* and tertiary education and for the subgroups actually selecting these options. In line with many previous studies, we observe substantial inequality at the entry to *Gymnasium* at the first transition (see column 1). About three-quarters of students with highly educated parents go on to *Gymnasium* compared to a mere 32 percent of the students with low educational background (the odds ratio for this comparison is 6.75). The difference in the transition rates to *Gymnasium* between families with medium and low education is much greater (odds ratio of 3.63) than between those with high and medium education (odds ratio of 1.86). We also observe large discrepancies in academic achievement according to parental educational status: whereas the GPA of students with low educational background is 0.27 standard deviations below the average, the medium educational group performs 0.18 and the high educational group even 0.42 standard deviations above the average (see column 2).

TABLE 3.2A

Transition rates and grade point averages (GPAs) at the transition to Gymnasium
(first transition) and to tertiary education (second transition) of students from
different educational backgrounds

	FIRST TRANSITION			SECOND TRANSITION		
Parental education	*Transi- tion rate (%)*	*GPA of entire group*	*GPA of subgroup continuing to Gymna- sium*	*Transi- tion rate (%)*	*GPA of entire group*	*GPA of sub- group con- tinuing to university*
Low (L)	32	−0.27	0.65	72	−0.24	−0.08
Medium (M)	63	0.18	0.66	76	−0.14	0.02
High (H)	76	0.42	0.71	87	0.18	0.28
			ODDS RATIOS			
	H/L	H/M	M/L	H/L	H/M	M/L
	6.75	1.86	3.63	2.69	2.19	1.23

N O T E : Grades were *z* standardized for each dataset with a mean of 0 and a standard deviation of 1.
Odds ratio calculations were based on nonrounded transition rates.

The disparity in continuation rates across educational background groups is less pronounced at the second transition: 72, 76, and 87 percent of students of low, medium, and high educational background, respectively, enroll for a tertiary option (see column 4). The odds ratios for the differences between the three educational groups vary between 1.23 (medium vs. low education) and 2.69 (high vs. low education). As a result of the previous selection processes there is weaker inequality of educational opportunity at the transition to tertiary education than at the transition to *Gymnasium*. Accordingly, the differences in academic achievement by social origin are less pronounced in the group of *Gymnasium* graduates than in the group of primary students at the transition to secondary school: in the group of *Gymnasium* graduates, students with the highest and lowest educational backgrounds differ by 0.42 standard deviations, whereas in the group of primary students, the gap is 0.69 standard deviations.

In Table 3.2b we present equivalent analyses for the transition rates of students according to their social-class origin. We find that 26 percent of students with working-class background but 73 percent with parents from the salariat enter *Gymnasium* at the first transition (see column 1). The odds ratio for this contrast is 7.78. The difference in the transition rates to *Gymnasium* between families from the salariat and the intermediate class is greater (odds ratio of 3.13) than between those from intermediate- and

TABLE 3.2B

*Transition rates and grade point averages (GPAs) at the transition to Gymnasium
(first transition) and to tertiary education (second transition) of students from
different class backgrounds*

	FIRST TRANSITION			SECOND TRANSITION		
Parental class	Transition rate (%)	GPA of entire group	GPA of subgroup continuing to Gymnasium	Transition rate (%)	GPA of entire group	GPA of subgroup continuing to university
Working (W)	26	−0.49	0.61	72	−0.32	−0.15
Intermediate (I)	46	0.04	0.66	75	−0.11	0.03
Salariat (S)	73	0.38	0.71	85	0.13	0.25
			ODDS RATIOS			
	S/W	S/I	I/W	S/W	S/I	I/W
	7.78	3.13	2.48	2.23	1.86	1.20

NOTE: Grades were *z* standardized for each dataset with a mean of 0 and a standard deviation of 1.
Odds ratio calculations were based on nonrounded transition rates.

working-class backgrounds (odds ratio of 2.48). Thus, the transition rates
to *Gymnasium* are on average more strongly differentiated according to
social class than parental education. The same is true for the differences in
academic achievement. We also see that class inequality at the transition to
tertiary education is much weaker than at the first transition: 72, 75, and
85 percent of students from the working class, the intermediate class, and
the salariat, respectively, make this transition (see column 4), and odds ratios for the differences between the three social classes range from 1.20 (intermediate vs. working class) to 2.23 (salariat vs. working class). As in the
case of educational background, the class differences in academic achievement are much weaker in the group of *Gymnasium* graduates than in the
group of elementary school students: whereas in the group of *Gymnasium*
graduates the differences in GPA between the most and least favorable class
background amounts to 0.45 standard deviations, the gap amounts to 0.87
standard deviations in the group of elementary school students.

Estimation of Primary and Secondary Effects

We start the analysis by displaying the factual and synthesized transition
rates into *Gymnasium* and tertiary education that are generated when we
combine different background-specific performance distributions and transition propensities. This is done first for the effect of parental education

TABLE 3.3
Estimated factual and synthesized transition rates (%)
into Gymnasium (first transition) with respect to parental
education and parental class

| | PARENTAL EDUCATION | | |
| | Choice | | |
Performance	*High*	*Medium*	*Low*
High	75	71	53
Medium	65	60	44
Low	49	44	30

| | PARENTAL CLASS | | |
| | Choice | | |
Performance	*Salariat*	*Intermediate*	*Working*
Salariat	71	56	49
Intermediate	58	43	37
Working	40	28	24

NOTE: In a given row, academic performance is held constant. In a given
column, transition propensity is held constant. The diagonal figures in
boldface represent factual combinations. Percentages can deviate from those
shown in Table 3.2 due to the estimation procedure (cf. Chapter 2).

and social-class background on the transition to *Gymnasium*. The rows
of Table 3.3 denote manipulations of the performance distribution and the
columns denote the transition rates after exchanging the conditional transition functions for different social-origin groups. Looking at students from
low educational backgrounds, their factual transition rate into *Gymnasium*
is 30 percent (see upper part of Table 3.3). If this group had the performance
distribution of students with highly educated parents, their estimated transition rate would increase substantially, by 23 percentage points to 53 percent. If the students with low educational background were assigned the
transition propensity of the high-education parent group, their transition
rate to *Gymnasium* would increase by 19 percentage points, to 49 percent.

In the lower part of Table 3.3 the same analyses are presented for
social-class background. Students of working-class origin have a factual
transition rate of 24 percent. If these students had instead had the academic
performance distribution of the salariat, 49 percent would have entered
Gymnasium. However, if working-class students had been assigned the
transition propensity of the salariat, their transition rate would have increased to only 40 percent.

Turning to the second transition (see Table 3.4) we see that students with low-educational-background would increase their transition rate to university only marginally, from 72 to 77 percent, if they were assigned the performance distribution of students with a high educational background (see upper part of Table 3.4). Exchanging their transition propensities with those from higher educational backgrounds leads to a larger increase, of 12 percentage points (from 72 to 84 percent entering tertiary education).

The lower part of Table 3.4 reports synthesized transition rates to tertiary education for the social classes. Here, 72 percent of students from the working class enter university. If these students had instead had the academic performance distribution of the salariat, they would have increased their transition rate to tertiary education by 6 percentage points (an increase from 72 to 78 percent). In common with the results based on parental education, equalizing transition propensities appears to have a comparatively larger effect on class inequalities than equalizing academic abilities. Working-class students' transition rates to tertiary education would increase by 9 percentage points if they were assigned the salariat's "choices" (from 72 to 81 percent).

TABLE 3.4

Estimated factual and synthesized transition rates (%) into tertiary education (second transition) with respect to parental education and social class

PARENTAL EDUCATION		
	Choice		
Performance	High	Medium	Low
High	88	80	77
Medium	85	**76**	73
Low	84	75	**72**

PARENTAL CLASS		
	Choice		
Performance	Salariat	Intermediate	Working
Salariat	86	78	78
Intermediate	84	**76**	75
Working	81	73	**72**

NOTE: In a given row, academic performance is held constant. In a given column, transition propensity is held constant. The diagonal figures in bold-face represent factual combinations. Percentages can deviate from those shown in Table 3.4 due to the estimation procedure (cf. Chapter 2).

To derive more precise estimates of the relative importance of primary and secondary effects, we follow the method outlined in Chapter 2. The resulting estimates are reported in Tables 3.5a and 3.5b. Standard errors for the log odds ratios for each contrast and approximated 95 percent confidence intervals for the relative importance of secondary effects are included in parentheses.

Results for the transition from elementary to secondary school indicate that secondary effects account for 33–51 percent (average of 44 percent) of the total inequality in relation to educational background (see upper part of Table 3.5a). Because the confidence intervals for all estimates include 50 percent, we cannot reject the hypothesis that primary and secondary effects are equally important in determining the overall inequality. At the transition to tertiary education, secondary effects consistently account for 72 percent across all educational-origin groups (see lower part of Table 3.5a). With one exception the lower-bound estimates for the confidence intervals at the second transition indicate that secondary effects are indeed the main source of educational inequality at the transition to tertiary education.

In Table 3.5b we present the relative importance of primary and secondary effects for inequality in educational opportunity according to social class. We see that at the first transition only 25–54 percent (average of

TABLE 3.5A

Log odds ratios for inequalities related to parental education and the relative importance of secondary effects[a]

	Log odds ratio	Standard error	Secondary effects (%)	95% CI
	FIRST TRANSITION			
High-medium	0.70	0.12	33	(0.08, 0.57)
High-low	1.98	0.03	47	(0.41, 0.52)
Medium-low	1.29	0.05	51	(0.41, 0.61)
	SECOND TRANSITION			
High-medium	0.77	0.12	72	(0.60, 0.83)
High-low	0.98	0.08	72	(0.65, 0.78)
Medium-low	0.21	0.12	72	(0.31, 1.13)[b]

[a]Estimates are calculated using the R package DECIDE and average of methods a and b (Kartsonaki 2010).

[b]The confidence intervals in this case include extreme values (below 0 or above 1). As noted in Chapter 2, when inequalities between groups are very small and log odds ratios approach 0 the confidence intervals may be inaccurate. We display the confidence intervals for this estimate for the purpose of completeness.

TABLE 3.5B
Log odds ratios for inequalities related to social class and relative importance of secondary effects[a]

	Log odds ratio	Standard error	Secondary effects (%)	95% CI
	FIRST TRANSITION			
Salariat-intermediate	1.19	0.11	54	(0.45, 0.63)
Salariat-working	2.07	0.12	41	(0.35, 0.47)
Intermediate-working	0.88	0.12	25	(0.10, 0.41)
	SECOND TRANSITION			
Salariat-intermediate	0.62	0.08	76	(0.67, 0.85)
Salariat-working	0.80	0.11	60	(0.48, 0.73)
Intermediate-working	0.17	0.11	21	(−0.75, 1.16)[b]

[a]Estimates are calculated using the R package DECIDE and average of methods a and b (Kartsonaki 2010).
[b]The confidence intervals in this case include extreme values (below 0 or above 1). As noted in Chapter 2, when inequalities between groups are very small and log odds ratios approach 0 the confidence intervals may be inaccurate. We display the confidence intervals for this estimate for the purpose of completeness.

40 percent) of the class differentials in selecting secondary school tracks can be attributed to secondary effects. An inspection of the confidence intervals confirms that with the exception of the contrast between the salariat and the intermediate class, primary effects are significantly more important for explaining class inequality at this transition. In the case of the transition to tertiary education, secondary effects account for 21–76 percent (average of 53 percent). In general, secondary effects appear to be more important at the transition to tertiary education than at the transition to secondary school.

Early versus Late Interventions and Tertiary Enrollment

In the following section we compare the relative effectiveness of possible policy interventions aimed at reducing either primary or secondary effects at the first transition to *Gymnasium* (t_1, age 10), or the second transition to tertiary education (t_2, ages 18–22). More concretely, we estimate the proportion of students from the working class who *would* successfully enter tertiary institutions *if* certain policy interventions were in place to eliminate primary or secondary effects at the first or the second transition. To evaluate the scope for policy leverage, we simulate the impact of ideal-typical interventions that would successfully neutralize primary or secondary effects. Of course, realistic interventions are unlikely to completely eliminate primary or secondary effects and hence would have less noticeable impact. However, we aim to produce upper-bound estimates of potential interventions to identify the available scope for policy leverage at different phases in the educational life course. We introduce a simple simulation procedure based on the decomposition method described in Chapter 2. The basic idea is to follow students from each class across both transitions and to estimate where working-class students get lost along the way to tertiary enrollment.[14] This procedure allows us to derive concrete numerical estimates for the relative effectiveness of policy measures aimed at reducing primary or secondary effects at the first or the second transition. Additionally, the simulation shows the consequences of early interventions (at t_1) for later transitions. A reduction of either primary or secondary effects at t_1 will affect the number of students from different backgrounds who reach the second transition (i.e., the number of the students at risk), the distribution of academic ability, and the distribution of other unobserved characteristics, such as academic motivation and educational aspirations of these students (see Mare 1980, 298–99).

To reduce complexity we focus our simulation on social-class differentiation and on the contrast only between the salariat and the working class. The results of our simulation are depicted in Table 3.6.[15] Reading the table from left to right, we see the number of students at each educational stage. We start in elementary school with a hypothetical number of 100 students from the salariat (row 1) and 100 students from the working class (row 2) (100 students represents the entire population in each class, allowing for a percentage interpretation at subsequent educational stages). As explained in Chapter 2, two pieces of information are needed to estimate transition rates for each class: the class-specific performance distribution and the class-specific transition function. Both pieces of information can be obtained from the IGLU-E data. We denote the group from which we draw the observed performance distribution in column 2 and the observed transition function in column 3. "S" stands for students from salariat backgrounds and "W" for students from working-class backgrounds.

As column 4 shows, 73 salariat students and only 26 working-class students make the transition to *Gymnasium*. This approximately corresponds to the factual transition rates reported in Table 3.3. Next, we turn to the time span between enrollment in *Gymnasium* and graduating from it. Two

TABLE 3.6

Factual and counterfactual movement through the German educational system

	Age 10	TRANSITION T₁, TO GYMNASIUM		Age 11	TIME SPAN DURING GYMNASIUM		Age 18–19	TRANSITION T₂, TO TERTIARY EDUCATION		Age 19–22	
	(1) N	(2) Performance distribution	(3) Transition function	(4) N	(5) Performance development	(6) Net survival	(7) N	(8) Performance distribution	(9) Transition function	(10) N	(11) OR S/W
					FACTUAL SITUATION						
(1)	100	S	S	73	S	S	68	S	S	58	1.00
(2)	100	W	W	26	W	W	21	W	W	15	7.83
					LATE INTERVENTIONS						
(3)	100	W	W	26	W	W	21	W	S	17	6.74
(4)	100	W	W	26	CF	W	21	S	W	16	7.25
					EARLY INTERVENTIONS						
(5)	100	W	S	42	W	W	35	CF	W	24	4.37
(6)	100	S	W	51	W	W	42	CF	W	34	2.68

SOURCE: IGLU-E 2001; Higher Education Information System (HIS) School Leaver Panel 2002; our calculations.

NOTE: OR = odds ratio; S = students of salariat background; W = students of working-class background; CF = counterfactual performance distribution. Manipulated variables are indicated by boldface characters.

related processes happen during this period, which we take into account. First, the performance distribution for each class observed at graduation is not identical to the one at the time of enrollment. Students from salariat backgrounds are more successful in improving their academic performance throughout secondary education relative to students from working-class families. To account for these differential performance developments, we apply a weighting procedure that we label "performance development" (column 5). Applying this procedure allows us to compute and manipulate class-specific performance developments during the time at *Gymnasium*.[16] Second, students of more advantaged social origin are more likely to change to more ambitious tracks and less likely to move downward during secondary school. Furthermore, they are more likely to continue schooling after having completed a first secondary degree. We account for these fluctuations and adjust the number of students in each class. The net survival rate at *Gymnasium* is 93 percent for the salariat and 82 percent for the working class (see Neugebauer and Schindler 2012). Thus, while 73 students from the salariat enter upper secondary school, only 68 (73 × 93 percent) graduate from it. Out of the 26 working class students entering upper secondary school, only 21 (26 × 82 percent) graduate from it.

We now turn to the transition to tertiary education. We observe (from the HIS data) class-specific performance distributions (column 8) as well as class-specific transition functions (column 9). If we apply these to our at-risk population, we can compute the number of students who successfully enter tertiary education. Out of the 68 salariat students reaching the second transition, 58 go on to university (column 10). Out of the 21 working-class students, only 15 enter university. As an indicator of social inequalities in tertiary-education participation, column 11 denotes the odds ratios of enrollment in tertiary education between the salariat reference group (row 1) and the working-class group. When the entire educational career up until tertiary enrollment is taken into account, salariat students are 7.83 times more likely than working-class students to reach tertiary education (row 2). This odds ratio can thus be interpreted as an unconditional measure of educational inequality in access to tertiary education.

In the next step we manipulate the progress through the educational system of working-class students by replacing their performance distributions or transition functions with the respective values of the other group. In Table 3.6, manipulated variables are indicated by boldface letters. We simulate four relevant scenarios that enable us to compare the effect of late versus early interventions on tertiary enrollment of working-class students: no secondary effects at t_2 (row 3), no primary effects at t_2 (row 4), no secondary effects at t_1 (row 5), and no primary effects at t_1 (row 6).

We start by neutralizing secondary effects at t_2. In this scenario, we replace the working-class transition function at t_2 with the salariat transition function, leaving everything else unaltered. As can be seen in row 3, we gain two additional students compared to the factual situation. Next, we neutralize primary effects at t_2 (row 4). Such an intervention increases the number of working-class students who enter universities by only one. Overall, interventions at t_2 result in a very small increase in the number of working-class students. Given that we are dealing with a highly selective subsample of students, this is not surprising. Observed performance distributions and transition rates (also affected by unobserved factors such as motivation) do not differ much between classes. Before turning to possible interventions at t_1, note that neutralizing primary effects at t_2 automatically implies a counterfactual performance development up to this point. Performance distributions cannot simply be changed by a timely intervention. If performance distributions at t_2 are to be identical for both groups, working-class students would have to catch up during their time at *Gymnasium* (or even before). We have indicated this in the table with "CF" (counterfactual) in row 4, column 5.

Next we simulate a situation in which secondary effects at t_1 are eliminated (row 5). In such a scenario the number of working-class students would increase across all educational stages. It would result in 42 instead of 26 *Gymnasium* entrants, 35 instead of 21 *Gymnasium* graduates, and 24 instead of 15 tertiary-education students. Note that these early interventions would automatically imply counterfactual performance distributions at subsequent stages (we have denoted this in column 8). Neutralizing primary effects (row 6) would increase the number of working-class students at all educational levels to an even greater extent. Out of all working-class students entering elementary school, 34 percent (compared to 15 percent in the factual situation) would enroll in tertiary education if primary effects at t_1 could be successfully eliminated. Hence, primary effects at the first transition seem to be the major source of social inequalities on the pathway to tertiary education.

CONCLUSION

In the first part of this chapter we analyzed the relative strength of primary and secondary effects at the two most important educational transitions in the German school system: (a) the transition to different types of secondary school tracks after elementary school at age 10 and (b) the transition to tertiary education after having obtained a university entrance qualification (ages 18–22). Our results show that at the first transition secondary effects account for, on average, 44 percent of the total effect of students' educational origin and for 40 percent of the effect of social-class background on the probability of entering *Gymnasium*. Keeping in mind the imprecision of the point estimates for the relative importance of primary versus secondary effects, the majority of the evidence points to, at this early point in the educational career, differences in students' academic abilities being slightly more relevant for inequality of educational opportunity than differences in decision behavior. Once students attend and graduate from *Gymnasium*, secondary effects seem to be the more important source of unequal transition rates to tertiary education: we estimated that across the board 72 percent of the effects of educational background and 53 percent of the inequality related to the families' social-class position are due to differential decision behavior when performance is held constant.

In the second part of the analysis we departed from the static analysis of isolated transitions and asked how the neutralization of secondary or primary effects influences inequality across the educational career. More specifically, we expanded the analysis by simulating how the number of students from the working class who enter tertiary education changes if we eliminate either primary or secondary effects at the first or the second transition. We uncovered two important results. First, neutralizing primary or secondary effects at the first transition in both cases leads to considerably more students from less advantaged backgrounds entering university (an increase from 15 percent to 34 and 24 percent, respectively), compared with eliminating primary or secondary effects at the second transition (an increase from 15 percent to 16 and 17 percent, respectively). This is the result of the considerably higher absolute degree of inequality at the first transition to *Gymnasium* and the presence of much stronger class differences in academic performance at the first transition. Second, neutralizing primary effects in the transition to *Gymnasium* seems more efficient than neutralizing secondary effects in bringing more working-class students into tertiary education.

Before drawing tentative policy conclusions, we acknowledge and discuss some limitations of our data and methodology. Unfortunately, the IGLU-E data contain only a proxy measure for secondary school choice. In most cases this is not problematic because the interviews took place after the families had reached a final decision. However, in federal states that have a binding recommendation for secondary school, the final decision about the secondary school track is likely to take place later—if parents challenge the recommendation. Here our data most likely capture the recommended school type and miss late upward corrections, typically obtained by families with higher social status. This may cause a slight underestimation of secondary effects. In fact, our finding of a greater importance of primary effects at the first transition contradicts the results of previous studies that find a greater relative impact of secondary effects (Becker 2009; Neugebauer and Schindler 2012; Neugebauer 2010). However, it is unlikely that this can be attributed only to our measure of secondary school choice. Moreover, all these studies have measures of performance that rely on self-reported grades. Our measures of grades, in contrast, were reported by teachers and are probably more reliable. Teacher-reported grades were also consulted in the study by Relikowski, Schneider, and Blossfeld (2009), who also find a greater impact of primary effects. Hence, it is likely that the deviating results can be at least partially attributed to the measurement of primary effects.

We should emphasize that our results are valid only for the average institutional setup in the heterogeneous German school system. As pointed out earlier, the status of the recommendation for secondary school may be particularly relevant in this respect. Five of the 11 states in our study have a binding school recommendation. In school systems without binding recommendations the aspirations of parents rather than the teachers' recommendations can be regarded as more important for educational decisions. As recent research suggests, secondary effects are stronger in school systems that leave parents free to decide the secondary school type (Dollmann 2011; Neugebauer 2010). We also had to exclude five federal states from our analyses, because the decision regarding secondary school types is made after the sixth rather than the fourth grade. In all of these states the families are free to select the type of secondary schools (no binding recommendation). Hence we may *underestimate* the total strength of secondary effects in Germany. Apart from the issue of the school recommendation, students in the excluded states completed grade six and are thus comparatively older. They might therefore be more independent from their parents and their educational motivations may be less associated with social origin. Excluding the federal states with a later transition may thus lead to an *overestimation* of secondary effects. Both directions of bias may cancel one other out. Evidence from two previous studies points in this direction. On the one hand, Stocké's (2007a) study, in which only Rhineland-Palatinate, a federal state with no binding recommendation, was included in the analyses, reported considerably higher estimates of secondary effects. On the other hand, the results of the study by Relikowski, Schneider, and Blossfeld (2009), who include one state with binding recommendation (Bavaria) and one state without (Hesse), are consistent with those of our study, in which the school recommendation is binding in 5 of the 11 included states.

A different potential problem is that the high nonresponse and the panel dropouts in the HIS data may lead to sample selection bias. In particular, it is likely that students with weaker academic abilities and motivation and those who are in general less academically inclined, are underrepresented in the sample. Since these characteristics relate to primary as well as to secondary effects, it is difficult to predict whether the sample selection causes biased estimates of the relative strength of primary and secondary effects.

Finally, another possible critique of this study relates to the analysis of the transition from *Gymnasium* to university. Educational transition research that uses the so-called Mare model (Mare 1980, 1981) has been criticized for not accounting for selection bias, that is, for unobserved variables that influence earlier transitions biasing social-origin estimates, even if they are not initially correlated with social origin (Cameron and Heckman 1998, 2001; also see Holm and Jæger 2011). As in the case of nonresponse, we cannot be sure to what extent important unobserved variables that affect the earlier transition bias the results and affect the estimates of the relative magnitude of primary versus secondary effects.

To conclude, we ask whether it is possible to derive policy implications from the analysis for reducing the level of inequality of educational opportunity in Germany. In light of primary effects at the first transition seeming to be quite pronounced, we discuss measures that could elevate average performance levels of students from disadvantaged backgrounds.

Early childhood intervention programs are an obvious choice to achieve such an endeavor (e.g., Heckman and Masterov 2006), and in fact, research in the German context has shown that more extensive preschool enrollment tends to reduce social inequality in reading achievement (Schütz, Ursprung, and Wößmann 2008). Another possible measure frequently discussed in the German context is the introduction of all-day schools (*Ganztagsschulen*) (Palentien 2007), which would allow teachers to work longer and more intensively with weaker students. These measures, as desirable as they may seem, require extensive and long-term interventions to have lasting effects and may not be the most cost-effective way to reduce disparities in educational achievement (see Jackson et al. 2007, 225).

Are there less costly measures to reduce the strong secondary effects at the first transition? An often-discussed option is shifting the selection point of the first transition to a later phase of the educational career (e.g., Bauer and Riphahn 2006). One of the rationales behind this measure is that particularly bright students with less favorable social backgrounds might be less inclined to abstain from the *Gymnasium* track when they are older. Lower-status parents may gain more faith in their children's academic abilities and their chances to successfully complete higher school tracks when they have the opportunity to observe positive performances over a longer period. Postponing the first transition would of course also influence primary effects, given the different learning environments in the different schooling tracks. Another way to reduce the impact of secondary effects at the first transition could be to allow for more flexibility in changing tracks and to institutionalize practices and pathways that allow students in the tracks below *Gymnasium* to enter a *Gymnasium*-level path (Jacob and Tieben 2010). Undoubtedly, this practice is desirable, but correcting initial placement after the event seems to be much more cumbersome and inefficient compared to sending students who have the academic potential to a more ambitious track straightaway. The same applies for all channels that allow students with lower-level secondary degrees to acquire the *Abitur* later in their educational career.

Finally, the considerable importance of secondary effects at the second transition is in our opinion by and large a consequence of an attractive low-risk alternative to tertiary education in Germany: vocational training (Becker and Hecken 2009a). While we do not suggest abandoning vocational training programs or making such programs less attractive, the relative risks and, particularly, the costs attached to a tertiary course of study should be reduced. Many eligible students from less privileged backgrounds choose vocational training over tertiary education because they want to gain financial independence (e.g., Schindler and Reimer 2011). Thus, the current system of financial support for students with lesser means should be reformed.

NOTES

1. In two states (Thüringen and Sachsen) the *Abitur* took only eight years to complete.

2. Over 89 percent of the general university entrance qualifications awarded in 2007 were obtained by those attending *Gymnasium* (Statistisches Bundesamt [Federal Statistical Office] 2008, our calculations).

3. In 2001 school recommendation had a binding character in 5 of the 16 German states (Baden-Württemberg, Bayern, Sachsen, Saarland, and Thüringen) (Cortina et al. 2005, 356).

4. We follow conventional procedures for Germany and categorize these options as nontertiary. Because relatively few students enroll in these institutions, social-origin effects do not substantially change whether these institutions are classified as tertiary or nontertiary (e.g., Schindler and Reimer 2011).

5. In principle all three secondary degrees can be obtained at the integrated institutions. Because of the heterogeneity of integrated secondary schools across states, no precise information about the share of different degrees awarded at these institutions is available.

6. Only two of these studies (Neugebauer 2010; Relikowski, Schneider, and Blossfeld 2009) employ the decomposition method described in Chapter 2.

7. The response rate in the first wave was 22.4 percent; the panel attrition rate between the first and second waves was 41.8 percent (numbers provided by HIS).

8. The full sample also includes individuals who acquired their degree via different pathways than *Gymnasium*, such as after vocational training periods or through alternative institutions of upper secondary education. We repeated all analyses with this more inclusive sample and found no substantial deviations from the results that we present below.

9. *Hauptschule* exists as an independent track in 10 of 16 states, while *Realschule* exists as an independent track in only 8 states.

10. Our estimates for *Gymnasium* and comprehensive schools deviate somewhat from the estimates reported in Figure 3.1 because we code students who chose distinct tracks for *Gymnasium* within (cooperative) comprehensive schools into the *Gymnasium* category.

11. Because the IGLU-E data lack a variable indicating whether the parent has supervisory status or is self-employed, we cannot identify supervisors of

manual workers (class V) and small proprietors (IV). This leads to an underrepresentation of the intermediate-class category.

12. In the IGLU-E data a single question asks for information on the highest general educational degree and professional vocational qualification. As a result, for all who indicated that a vocational (apprenticeship) degree was their highest level of education (about 44 percent of the sample), no information about their completed general educational degree is available. Since the majority of individuals with a vocational degree have completed not more than an intermediate secondary school degree, we code them into the low education category, even if some might also have achieved an upper secondary (*Abitur*) degree.

13. See Fairlie (2005) for a similar method.

14. Neugebauer and Schindler (2012) have a complete account of this method and its application.

15. Unfortunately, we do not have real cohort data. Thus, we have to assume that our estimates are not influenced by cohort and period effects. Plausibility checks with other data sources suggest that our estimates are robust.

16. More specifically, we apply weights for each point of the GPA scale to transform the grade distribution from t_1 to the grade distribution at t_2, separately for each class. The weights are obtained by dividing the graduates' performance curves specific to their social background (from the HIS data), by the respective *Gymnasium* entrants' curve (from the IGLU-E data) at each point of the GPA scale (see Schindler 2010 for details).

REFERENCES

Avenarius, Hermann, Hartmut Ditton, Hans Döbert, Klaus Klemm, Eckhard Klieme, Matthias Rürup, Heinz-Elmar Tenorth, Horst Weishaupt, and Manfred Weiß. 2003. *Bildungsbericht für Deutschland*. Opladen, Germany: Leske and Budrich.

Bauer, Philipp C., and Regina T. Riphahn. 2006. "Timing of School Tracking as a Determinant of Intergenerational Transmission of Education." *Economics Letters* 91:90–97.

Becker, Rolf. 2009. "Wie können bildungsferne Gruppen für ein Hochschulstudium gewonnen werden? Eine empirische Simulation mit Implikationen für die Steuerung des Bildungswesens." *Kölner Zeitschrift für Soziologie und Sozialpsychologie* 61:563–93.

Becker, Rolf, and Anna E. Hecken. 2009a. "Why Are Working-Class Children Diverted from Universities? An Empirical Assessment of the Diversion Thesis." *European Sociological Review* 25:233–50.

———. 2009b. "Higher Education or Vocational Training? An Empirical Test of the Rational Action Model of Educational Choices Suggested by Breen and Goldthorpe and Esser." *Acta Sociologica* 52:25–45.

Bellenberg, Gabriele, Gertrud Hovestadt, and Klaus Klemm. 2004. *Selektivität und Durchlässigkeit im allgemein bildenden Schulsystem: Rechtliche Regelungen und Daten unter besonderer Berücksichtigung der Gleichwertigkeit von Abschlüssen.* Essen, Germany: Universität Duisburg-Essen. http://www.gew.de/Binaries/Binary34032/Studie_Selektivitaet_und_ Durchlaes sigkeit.pdf.

Breen, Richard, Ruud Luijkx, Walter Müller, and Reinhard Pollak. 2009. "Nonpersistent Inequality in Educational Attainment: Evidence from Eight European Countries." *American Journal of Sociology* 114:1475–521.

BMBF (Bundesministerium für Bildung und Forschung). 1994. *Grund- und Strukturdaten 1994/95.* Bonn, Germany: Bock.

Cameron, Stephen V., and James J. Heckman. 1998. "Life Cycle Schooling and Dynamic Selection Bias: Models and Evidence for Five Cohorts of American Males." *Journal of Political Economy* 106:262–333.

———. 2001. "The Dynamics of Educational Attainment for Black, Hispanic, and White Males." *Journal of Political Economy* 109:455–99.

Cortina, Kai S., Jürgen Baumert, Achim Leschinsky, Karl Ulrich Mayer, and Luitgard Trommer. 2005. *Das Bildungswesen in der Bundesrepublik Deutschland: Strukturen und Entwicklungen im Überblick.* 2nd ed. Reinbek, Germany: Rowohlt.

Ditton, Hartmut, and Jan Krüsken. 2009. "Denn wer hat, dem wird gegeben werden? Eine Längsschnittsstudie zur Entwicklung schulischer Leistungen und den Effekten der sozialen Herkunft in der Grundschulzeit." *Journal for Educational Research Online* 1:33–61.

Dollmann, Jörg. 2011. "Verbindliche und unverbindliche Grundschulempfehlungen und soziale Ungleichheiten am ersten Bildungsübergang." *Kölner Zeitschrift für Soziologie und Sozialpsychologie* 63:595–621.

Ehmke, Timo, and Jürgen Baumert. 2007. "Soziale Herkunft und Kompetenzerwerb: Vergleiche zwischen PISA 2000, 2003 und 2006." In *PISA 2006: Die Ergebnisse der dritten internationalen Vergleichsstudie,* edited by Manfred Prenzel, Cordula Artelt, Jürgen Baumert, Werner Blum, Marcus Hammann, Eckhard Klieme, and Reinhard Pekrun, 309–36. Münster, Germany: Waxmann Verlag.

Fairlie, Robert W. 2005. "An Extension of the Blinder-Oaxaca Decomposition Technique to Logit and Probit Models." *Journal of Economic and Social Measurement* 30:305–16.

Hanushek, Eric A., and Ludger Wößmann. 2006. "Does Educational Tracking Affect Performance and Inequality? Differences-in-Differences Evidence across Countries." *Economic Journal* 116:C63–C76.

Heckman, James J., and Dimitriy Masterov. 2006. "The Productivity Argument for Investing in Young Children." *Early Childhood Research Collaborative Discussion Paper,* August 2006. http://jenni.uchicago.edu/human-inequality/papers/Heckman_final_all_wp_2007-03-22c_jsb.pdf.

Hillmert, Steffen, and Marita Jacob. 2005. "Zweite Chance im Schulsystem? Zur sozialen Selektivität bei 'späteren' Bildungsentscheidungen." In *Institutionalisierte Ungleichheit: Wie das Bildungswesen Chancen blockiert*, edited by Peter Berger and Heike Kahlert, 155–76. Weinheim, Germany: Juventa Verlag.

Holm, Anders, and Mads Meier Jæger. 2011. "Dealing with Selection Bias in Educational Transition Models: The Bivariate Probit Selection Model." *Research in Social Stratification and Mobility* 29:311–22.

Jackson, Michelle, Robert Erikson, John H. Goldthorpe, and Meir Yaish. 2007. "Primary and Secondary Effects in Class Differentials in Educational Attainment: The Transition to A-Level Courses in England and Wales." *Acta Sociologica* 50:211–29.

Jacob, Marita, and Nicole Tieben. 2010. "Wer nutzt die Durchlässigkeit zwischen verschiedenen Schulformen? Soziale Selektivität bei Schulformwechseln und nachgeholten Schulabschlüssen." In *Vom Kindergarten bis zur Hochschule— Die Generierung von ethnischen und sozialen Disparitäten in der Bildungsbiographie*, edited by Birgit Becker and David Reimer, 145–78. Wiesbaden, Germany: VS-Verlag.

Jonsson, Jan O., Colin Mills, and Walter Müller. 1996. "A Half Century of Increasing Educational Openness? Social Class, Gender and Educational Attainment in Sweden, Germany and Britain." In *Can Education Be Equalized? The Swedish Case in Comparative Perspective*, edited by Robert Erikson and Jan O. Jonsson, 183–206. Boulder, CO: Westview.

Kartsonaki, Christina. 2010. DECIDE: DEComposition of Indirect and Direct Effects. R package version 1.0. http://CRAN.R-project.org/package=DECIDE.

KMK (Statistische Veröffentlichungen der Kultusministerkonferenz). 2003. *Dokumentation Nr. 171: Schüler, Klassen, Lehrer und Absolventen der Schulen, 1993–2002.*

———. 2007. *Dokumentation Nr. 184: Schüler, Klassen, Lehrer und Absolventen der Schulen, 1997–2006.*

Lörz, Markus, and Steffen Schindler. 2009. "Educational Expansion and Effects on the Transition to Higher Education: Has the Effect of Social Background Characteristics Declined or Just Moved to the Next Stage?" In *Expected and Unexpected Consequences of the Educational Expansion in Europe and USA*, edited by Andreas Hadjar and Rolf Becker, 97–110. Bern, Germany: Haupt.

Maaz, Kai. 2006. *Soziale Herkunft und Hochschulzugang. Effekte institutioneller Öffnung im Bildungssystem*. Wiesbaden, Germany: VS Verlag für Sozialwissenschaften.

Mare, Robert D. 1980. "Social Background and School Continuation Decisions." *Journal of the American Statistical Association* 75:295–305.

———. 1981. "Change and Stability in Educational Stratification." *American Sociological Review* 46:72–87.

Mayer, Karl Ulrich. 2008. "Das Hochschulwesen." In *Das Bildungssystem der Bundesrepublik Deutschland—Strukturen und Entwicklungen im Überblick*, edited by Kai S. Cortina, Jürgen Baumert, Achim Leschinsky, Karl Ulrich Mayer, and Luitgard Trommer, 599–645. Hamburg, Germany: Rowohlt Taschenbuch Verlag.

Mayer, Karl Ulrich, Walter Müller, and Reinhard Pollak. 2007. "Germany: Institutional Change and Inequalities of Access in Higher Education." In *Stratification in Higher Education. A Comparative Study*, edited by Yossi Shavit, Richard Arum, Adam Gamoran, and Gila Menahem, 240–66. Stanford, CA: Stanford University Press.

Mühlenweg, Andrea M. 2008. "Educational Effects of Alternative Secondary School Tracking Regimes in Germany." *Schmollers Jahrbuch* 128:351–79.

Müller, Walter, Hildegard Brauns, and Susanne Steinmann. 2002. "Expansion und Erträge tertiärer Bildung in Deutschland, Frankreich und im Vereinigten Königreich." *Berliner Journal für Soziologie* 12:37–62.

Müller-Benedict, Volker 2007. "Wodurch kann die soziale Ungleichheit des Schulerfolgs am stärksten verringert werden?" *Kölner Zeitschrift für Soziologie und Sozialpsychologie* 59:615–39.

Mullis, Ina V. S., Michael O. Martin, Eugenio J. Gonzalez, and Ann M. Kennedy. 2003. *PIRLS 2001 International Report: IEA's Study of Reading Literacy Achievement in Primary Schools*. Chestnut Hill, MA: Boston College.

Mullis, I. V. S., Michael O. Martin, Ann M. Kennedy, and Cheryl L. Flaherty. 2002. *PIRLS 2001 Encyclopedia: A Reference Guide to Reading Education in the Countries Participating in IEA's Progress in International Reading Literacy Study (PIRLS)*. Chestnut Hill, MA: Boston College.

Neugebauer, Martin. 2010. "Bildungsungleichheit und Grundschulempfehlung beim Übergang auf das Gymnasium: Eine Dekomposition primärer und sekundärer Herkunftseffekte." *Zeitschrift für Soziologie* 39:202–14.

Neugebauer, Martin, and Steffen Schindler. 2012. "Early Transitions and Tertiary Enrolment: The Cumulative Impact of Primary and Secondary Effects on Entering University in Germany." *Acta Sociologica* 55:19–36.

Palentien, Christian. 2007. "Die Ganztagsschule—als Möglichkeit zur Überwindung ungleicher Bildungschancen." In *Perspektiven der Bildung. Kinder und Jugendliche in formellen, nicht-formellen und informellen Bildungsprozessen*, edited by Marius Harring, Carsten Rohlfs, and Christian Palentien, 279–90. Wiesbaden, Germany: VS Verlag für Sozialwissenschaften.

Reimer, David, and Reinhard Pollak. 2010. "Educational Expansion and Its Consequences for Vertical and Horizontal Inequalities in Access to Higher Education in West Germany." *European Sociological Review* 26:415–30.

Reinalda, Bob, and Ewa Kulesza. 2005. *The Bologna Process: Harmonizing Europe's Higher Education*. Opladen, Germany: Barbara Budrich Publishers.

Relikowski, Ilona, Thorsten Schneider, and Hans-Peter Blossfeld. 2009. "Primary and Secondary Effects of Social Origin in Migrant and Native Families at the

Transition to the Tracked German School System." In *Raymond Boudon— A Life in Sociology: Essays in Honour of Raymond Boudon*, edited by Mohamed Cherkaoui and Peter Hamilton, 3:149–70. Oxford: Bardwell Press.

Schauenberg, Magdalena, and Hartmut Ditton. 2004. "Zur Reproduktion von Bildungsungleichheit beim Übertritt auf weiterführende Schulen." In *Soziale Ungleichheit, Kulturelle Unterschiede. Verhandlungen des 32. Kongresses der Deutschen Gesellschaft für Soziologie in München 2004*, edited by Karl-Siegbert Rehberg, Dana Giesecke, Susanne Kappler, and Thomas Dumke. Frankfurt, Germany: Campus Verlag.

Schindler, Steffen. 2010. "Assessing the Cumulative Impact of Primary and Secondary Effects on the Way from Elementary to Tertiary Education. A Simulation Study for Germany." EQUALSOC working paper 2010/2.

Schindler, Steffen, and David Reimer. 2010. "Primäre und sekundäre Effekte der sozialen Herkunft beim Übergang in die Hochschulbildung." *Kölner Zeitschrift für Soziologie und Sozialpsychologie* 62:623–53.

———. 2011. "Differentiation and Social Selectivity in German Higher Education." *Higher Education* 61:261–75.

Schneider, Thorsten. 2008. "Social Inequality in Educational Participation in the German School System in a Longitudinal Perspective: Pathways into and out of the Most Prestigious School Track." *European Sociological Review* 24:511–26.

Schütz, Gabriela, Heinrich Ursprung, and Ludger Wößmann. 2008. "Education Policy and Equality of Opportunity." *Kyklos* 61:279–308.

Shavit, Yossi, and Hans-Peter Blossfeld, eds. 1993. *Persistent Inequality. Changing Educational Attainment in Thirteen Countries*. Boulder, CO: Westview.

Statistisches Bundesamt. 2008. *Fachserie 11. Reihe 1. Bildung und Kultur. Allgemeinbildende Schulen*. Wiesbaden, Germany: Statistisches Bundesamt.

Stocké, Volker. 2007a. "Strength, Sources, and Temporal Development of Primary Effects of Families' Social Status on Secondary School Choice." Working Paper 07-70, Sonderforschungsbereich 504. Mannheim, Germany: University of Mannheim.

———. 2007b. "Explaining Educational Decision and Effects of Families' Social Class Position: An Empirical Test of the Breen-Goldthorpe Model of Educational Attainment." *European Sociological Review* 23:505–19.

Trautwein, Ulrich, Kai Maaz, Oliver Lüdtke, Gabriel Nagy, Nicole Husemann, Rainer Watermann, and Olaf Köller. 2006. "Studieren an der Berufsakademie oder an der Universität, Fachhochschule oder Pädagogischen Hochschule? Ein Vergleich des Leistungsstands, familiären Hintergrunds, beruflicher Interessen und der Studienwahlmotive von (künftigen) Studierenden aus Baden-Württemberg." *Zeitschrift für Erziehungswissenschaft* 9:393–412.

CHAPTER FOUR

How Social Background Affects Educational Attainment over Time in the Netherlands

Charlotte Büchner and Rolf van der Velden

There has been much research in the Netherlands on inequality of educational opportunity (IEO) for pupils of different socioeconomic backgrounds. Beginning with the seminal work of Van Heek (1968), the focus of this research has mostly been on the transition that pupils face at age 12, the transition from primary to secondary education, with an overall conclusion that IEO in the Netherlands has decreased only slightly in recent decades (e.g., Bakker, Dronkers, and Schijf 1982, 1986; Bakker and Cremers 1994; Bakker and Schouten 1991; De Graaf and Ganzeboom 1993; De Jong, Dronkers, and Saris 1982; Dronkers 1983, 1993; Kloosterman et al. 2009; Peschar, Ten Vergert, and Popping 1986; Sieben, Huinink, and De Graaf 2001; Tieben, De Graaf, and De Graaf 2010; Vrooman and Dronkers 1986; Willemse 1987). However, over a longer period, the Netherlands underwent a "process of opening-up and equalization" (Blossfeld and Shavit 1993, 18). A recent study by Buis (2010) replicates the study of De Graaf and Ganzeboom (1993) but with improved data and modeling techniques. He shows that the trend toward decreasing IEO was most notable in the middle decades of the 20th century: for men, in the 1940s and 1950s, and for women, in the 1950s and 1960s. For more recent decades he found no significant trend. He also showed that at the beginning of the 20th century total IEO was mainly driven by inequalities in the transition from primary to secondary education, while toward the end of the century inequalities in the transition to postsecondary education become more relevant.

One problem with the above-mentioned studies that deal with long-term trends is that they lack data on children's academic performance. Few studies even ask whether changes in the distribution of academic performance across social groups or changes in the propensity to make particular educational choices across social groups might have influenced IEO. In other words, it is not possible to identify whether the observed changes in IEO were due to changes in the magnitude of primary or of secondary effects, and we do not at present have a good understanding of whether these underlying processes that drive IEO are stable or changing over time.

The studies that include data about school performance have used different modeling techniques. To our knowledge, only one study in the Dutch context assesses the relative importance of primary and secondary effects when analyzing IEO. Kloosterman et al. (2009) apply the methodological approach introduced by Erikson et al. (2005) and Jackson et al. (2007) to examine the educational transition faced by Dutch pupils at age 12 (the transition from primary to secondary education), analyzing changes in primary and secondary effects over five birth cohorts. Using performance scores and parents' education to measure primary and secondary effects, they find that the secondary effects of social background have been more or less stable, while the primary effects have fluctuated (or somewhat increased) over the cohorts. Regarding the development of IEO, the results suggest that inequalities in the transition from primary to secondary education remained more or less stable over time.

Those studies that have analyzed the relationship between social background and the transition to higher education in the Netherlands have found a positive correlation between higher social background and the propensity to make the transition to higher education (e.g., Bosma and Cremers 1996; De Graaf and Ganzeboom 1993; De Graaf and Wolbers 2003; Rijken, Maas, and Ganzeboom 2007; Tieben and Wolbers 2010). However, none of these studies considered possible changes in the relative importance of primary and secondary effects at this transition.[1]

In this chapter we look at the development of primary and secondary effects over time by analyzing the transitions at age 12 and at age 17 or 18, the transition to higher education, using the models described in Chapter 2 of this book. The next section provides an overview of the Dutch educational system and the distribution of students in educational tracks over time. We then introduce the data and the model specification before presenting our findings. Finally, we summarize our findings and draw conclusions.

THE DUTCH SCHOOL SYSTEM

The school system in the Netherlands is highly stratified from secondary education onward and can generally be divided into vocationally oriented tracks and academic tracks. The first transition, from primary education to secondary education, takes place at age 12. The transition to higher education (vocational colleges and universities) takes place at age 17 or 18, depending on which secondary education track the student followed (see Figure 4.1). The structure of the secondary education system in the Netherlands was largely shaped by the Mammoth Law of 1968, which moved the country toward an integrated system. Before this law came into effect, secondary education consisted of four educational tracks organized in different institutions. Pupils were admitted to one of these tracks at age 12 on the basis of entry examinations, and they had little or no possibility of moving to a higher track. The Mammoth Law maintained the different hierarchical school types of the old system but facilitated transitions to secondary education through orientation classes (*brugklas*) in the first and

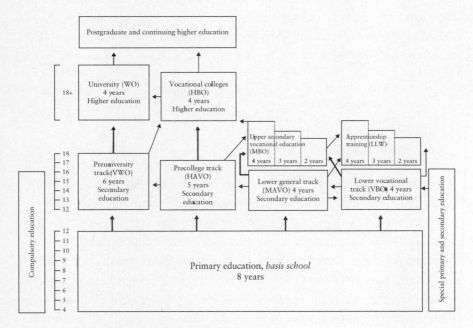

Figure 4.1. The Dutch educational system

sometimes second grade of secondary education. These orientation classes were meant to postpone track placement until the end of the first or second grade. In many cases the orientation classes combined two adjacent tracks, but schools were autonomous in the way that they implemented this: some maintained separate classes for each track, and others combined all four tracks of secondary education. The Mammoth Law also stimulated the formation of school communities in which different tracks of secondary education were combined within one building, which made it possible for more students to change tracks without changing schools. Furthermore, at the end of primary school, nationwide standardized skills tests (the so-called CITO[2] tests) and class teacher recommendations were introduced to structure the selection into different tracks in secondary education (see Dronkers 1993, 262–63). The CITO tests are used to measure school performance in the final grade of primary education in language, mathematics, and information processing. Although the CITO tests are not mandatory, most primary schools (about 92 percent) use them to assess their pupils (CITO 2010).

As shown in Figure 4.1, compulsory education starts with primary education at age 4 and ends at age 16.[3] Primary education, organized in the so-called *basisschool*, lasts for eight years, until age 12. Secondary education is distinguished in four tracks, three general and one vocational:

- preuniversity education (VWO): the preuniversity track
- higher general secondary education (HAVO): the precollege track
- intermediate general secondary education (MAVO): the lower general track
- prevocational education (VBO): the lower vocational track

Both primary education and secondary education also have a system of special education for pupils with learning problems or physical disabilities.[4]

The arrows in Figure 4.1 indicate the possible routes for proceeding from one track to another in the educational system, with bold arrows indicating the main routes. Vertical upward transitions to the higher school tracks are allowed when appropriate levels beneath them have been completed. Downward transitions to lower tracks are possible at any time. Only the two highest tracks in secondary education prepare students for higher education: the precollege track (HAVO) prepares for vocational colleges (HBO) and the preuniversity track (VWO) prepares for university

(WO). Both the lower general track (MAVO) and the lower vocational track (VBO) mainly prepare for upper secondary vocational education (MBO). In general, the lower general track (MAVO) aims to prepare students for the long (three- or four-year) tracks in upper secondary vocational education (MBO), while the lower vocational track (VBO) aims to prepare them for the short (one- or two-year) tracks and apprenticeship training. Each track after primary education follows a specified path to the next track. The system thereby also allows transitions within the secondary and postsecondary levels. The most relevant within-level transitions at the secondary level are from the lower general track (MAVO) to the precollege track (HAVO) and from the precollege track (HAVO) to the preuniversity track (VWO). At the postsecondary level, the most relevant transitions are from upper secondary vocational education (MBO) to vocational colleges (HBO) and from vocational colleges (HBO) to university (WO).

In 2000 the Dutch Ministry of Education, Culture, and Science introduced the concept of a starting qualification (*startkwalifikatie*) to establish a minimum credential for young people that confers eligibility for the labor market. Those who do not attain a starting qualification are considered to be early school leavers. Diplomas from the precollege track (HAVO), preuniversity track (VWO), and upper secondary vocational education of at least two years (MBO at level two, which is the level of a basic skilled worker [Traag and Van der Velden 2011]) all provide a starting qualification. Although compulsory education ends in the year that pupils turn 16 (*leerplicht*), they are obliged to stay in school until obtaining the starting qualification or turning 18 (*kwalificatieplicht*).

The two transition processes under study, the transition at age 12 from primary to secondary education and the transition at age 17 or 18 from secondary to higher education, are quite different in terms of the underlying process. At the transition at age 12, pupils are selected mainly on the basis of their performance on the CITO test and their schoolteacher's recommendation. Although this seems to leave little room for nonmeritocratic factors, the secondary effects of social stratification do play a role. First, the teacher's advice is not only based on a pupil's past performance but also on motivational aspects and expected success in secondary education. The children of higher social classes are expected to be more successful and are consequently steered toward higher courses (Dronkers 1993). Second, much of the advice is mixed (e.g., MAVO and HAVO, or HAVO and VWO),[5] which leaves room for the parents to negotiate placement in the higher of the two tracks, an option that parents from higher social classes are usually keen to embrace. Finally, the management of secondary schools has autonomy when it comes to decisions about whether to admit pupils and can therefore diverge from test results or advice. This again opens up room for negotiation by the parents.

The transition to higher education at age 17 or 18 depends very much on attainment at the secondary education level. Having gained a diploma from the preuniversity track (VWO), the student gains automatic access to university (WO), while a diploma from a precollege track (HAVO) gives automatic access to vocational college (HBO). Both types of diplomas are awarded on the basis of nationwide and schoolwide examinations. The examinations ensure that the quality of diplomas is more or less similar nationwide. Some programs in higher education, however, may impose additional requirements on students (for example, access to higher-education programs in medicine and the arts is restricted). Although a preuniversity track (VWO) diploma grants access to university (WO) and a precollege track (HAVO) diploma to vocational college (HBO), not every student will choose to take that path. Some preuniversity track (VWO) students choose the less prestigious vocational college (HBO) programs and some precollege track (HAVO) students choose an upper secondary vocational education (MBO) program that is not considered part of higher education. Alternatively, these students may decide not to study at all. As there are no entrance criteria other than having the required diploma from secondary education, we expect that the transition at age 17 or 18 to higher education is driven by secondary effects rather than by primary effects of social stratification.

In the web appendix (http://www.primaryandsecondaryeffects.com) we provide additional information on the development in enrollment for the different types of education over time (see Figures A4.1 and A4.2).

DATA AND MODEL SPECIFICATION

Our analysis is based on panel datasets of four education cohorts provided by Statistics Netherlands (Centraal Bureau voor de Statistiek; CBS 1992). Each dataset is a nationally representative sample, and pupils are observed, starting at age 12 when they enter secondary education, in 1977 (N = 37,280), 1982 (N = 16,813), 1989 (N = 19,524), and 1993 (N = 20,331). The pupils in each cohort are followed until the end of their full-time education or until age 28. We refer to the cohorts by the year the pupils were born, that is, 1965, 1970, 1977, and 1981. Each dataset provides comparable information on the socioeconomic background and standardized skills tests of pupils at the entry to secondary education. School track choices and whether a final examination was passed are documented by the schools participating in the four surveys and are provided each year for all students.[6]

Unlike for other countries in this book, our measure of social background is based solely on the highest educational level achieved by the parents. The occupational information in the data does not allow differentiation into social classes as conventionally defined. However, as demonstrated by several Dutch studies (e.g., Bakker and Cremers 1994; De Graaf and Ganzeboom 1993), the impact of father's occupational status on children's educational attainment appears to have decreased over time, while father's educational level is a much stronger and more stable predictor of children's educational attainment. This finding supports the assumption that the Netherlands, compared to other European countries (e.g., England), is a "knowledge-based" society rather than a "class" society (Kraaykamp, Van Eijck, and Ultee 2010). The lack of social-class measures in our data, however, means that we cannot compare the role of social class and parents' education in educational inequality, nor can we consider the role of social class in determining the relative importance of primary and secondary effects.

Dependent Variables

As discussed above, we aim to investigate the relative importance of primary and secondary effects over time at two stages of the educational career: the transition to secondary education, when pupils are 12 years old, and the transition to higher education, when pupils are aged 17 or 18. Figure 4.2 illustrates the transitions in the Dutch school system for the 1981 cohort and shows the transition and completion rates for the secondary and postsecondary levels. The proportions of students making the transitions to the different tracks in secondary education have hardly changed over time.[7] Around 30 percent of all pupils of each cohort go to one of the higher tracks (the precollege track HAVO or the preuniversity track VWO). The vast majority of them also complete their chosen track. The share of pupils completing a precollege track is even higher than the share of pupils

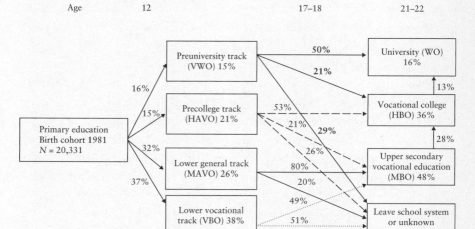

Figure 4.2.   Transition and completion rates in secondary and postsecondary education, 1981 birth cohort

SOURCE: 1981 CBS cohort; our calculations.

NOTE: The arrows represent the transition from one track to another track and add up to 100%. The figures in the boxes represent the highest completed level of secondary or post-secondary education. These can differ from the inflow as a result of upward or downward mobility. For the transition at age 12 we have information for all students. For the transition at age 17–18 we lack information for students who dropped out of the panel or who left school altogether; they are in the category "Leave school system or unknown."

entering the track, because of upward movements of pupils from the lower general track (MAVO) (for completion rates see percentages in Figure 4.2).

Clearer changes over time occur at the transition to postsecondary education (see Table 4.1). The share of pupils from the preuniversity track (VWO) entering university (WO) increased from 45 percent in the 1965 cohort to 50 percent in the 1981 cohort. The largest increase occurred with the transition to vocational colleges (HBO). The rates of transition from the precollege track (HAVO) to vocational college continuously increased from 31 percent (1965 cohort, see web appendix Figure A4.3) to 53 percent (1981 cohort, see Figure 4.2). The growing popularity of vocational college is also evident from completion rates and transfers to this track. In the 1965 cohort 26 percent of all pupils obtained a vocational college certificate. Included in this group are 11 percent of those who entered upper secondary vocational education (MBO), later transferring to vocational college. By the 1981 cohort the number of vocational college graduates had increased to

TABLE 4.1
Descriptive statistics (%)

	1965	1970	1977	1981
Parents' education				
Low	53	51	44	30
Medium	31	29	36	45
High	16	20	20	25
Transition at age 12 to precollege track (HAVO) or preuniversity track (VWO)	29	31	28	31
Transition at age 12 to preuniversity track (VWO)	17	17	15	16
Transition at age 17–18 from precollege track (HAVO) or preuniversity track (VWO) to vocational college (HBO)/university (WO)	49	57	60	60
Transition at 17–18 from preuniversity track (VWO) to university (WO)	45	54	48	50
Unconditional transition of all to vocational college (HBO) or university (WO)	20	21	20	22
Unconditional transition of all to university (WO)	8	10	7	8
N at age 12	37,050	7,864	19,287	19,994
N at age 17–18	18,123	4,242	12,193	11,965

SOURCE: CBS cohorts 1965, 1970, 1977, and 1981 and our calculations.

36 percent and transfers from upper secondary vocational education (MBO) to the vocational college certificate continuously increased over time to reach 28 percent (see Figure 4.2 and web appendix Figures A4.3, A4.4, and A4.5).

In constructing our measure of the transition at age 12, we consider two definitions that could be considered appropriate in the Dutch case. First, we look at only pupils entering the preuniversity track (VWO), and then—in line with Kloosterman et al. (2009)—we consider pupils entering precollege track (HAVO) *or* preuniversity track (VWO). We think that this is a crucial distinction in the Dutch school track system, since the preuniversity track is typically considered to be an elite track, while the precollege track is usually regarded as a track for talented students from the intermediate and lower social classes. Combining these two tracks is likely to lead to an underestimation of IEO. The same type of distinction applies at the transition to higher education: the vocational track in higher education (HBO) has absorbed much of the increase in enrollment rates, so that vocational college typically has the status of mass education, while the university (WO) maintained its status of elite education.

Summing up, in the analyses we use the following model specifications:[8]

    1. The probability of entering either precollege track (HAVO) or preuniversity track (VWO)

    2. The probability of entering preuniversity track (VWO)

    3. The conditional probability of making the transition to vocational college (HBO) or university (WO) given a diploma from a precollege track (HAVO) or a preuniversity track (VWO)

    4. The conditional probability of making the transition to university (WO) given a diploma from a preuniversity track (VWO)

    5. The unconditional probability of all students making the transition to vocational college (HBO) or university (WO)

    6. The unconditional probability of all students making the transition to university (WO)

Independent Variables

Social Background. As a measure of social background we use the highest educational level achieved by either the father or the mother. We distinguish between low educated (primary education, lower vocational track VBO or lower general track MAVO), medium educated (precollege track HAVO, preuniversity track VWO, or upper secondary vocational education MBO), and high educated (vocational college HBO or university WO).[9]

The upper part of Table 4.1 shows that the share of low educated parents decreased over time, while the shares of medium and high educated parents clearly increased over time. Cross-tabulating parents' educational attainment with the child's first transition at age 12 shows that the relationship between social background and educational choices is rather stable over time (see Table A4.1 in the web appendix). In every cohort, some 60 percent of children from high educated households continue to precollege track (HAVO) or preuniversity track (VWO), while the corresponding figures for children from households with low educated parents are 14–19 percent across the cohorts.

Academic Performance. As a measure of academic performance we use the average performance scores taken from arithmetic and language tests at age 12. The tests in the four surveys are based on a nationwide compulsory test that is developed by CITO. These compulsory tests are usually conducted at the end of primary education and estimate the pupil's level of school-based knowledge, in line with national curriculum requirements. The test scores in the surveys are derived from a shortened version of the national CITO tests,[10] which we have standardized to have a mean of 0 and a standard deviation of 1. These scores are used as indicators of the performance level of the students at the beginning of secondary education. The test results in the data are comparable with those of the real CITO tests at the end of primary education (Hustinx et al. 2005).[11]

Measuring performance before the transition at age 17 or 18 to higher education is more challenging. It is not possible to use grades as measures of performance, because grades are specific to the different tracks in secondary education and therefore cannot be compared across tracks. Furthermore, test scores at age 17 or 18 are also unavailable, because the CITO test is administered only once in the survey, at age 12. Given these constraints, we are therefore forced to use the age 12 CITO test results in our analyses of the transition at age 17 or 18. It is possible to check the effect of using early test scores rather than scores measured close to the transition. For two cohorts (the 1977 and the 1981 cohorts), an additional test in mathematics and language was constructed by CITO and carried out in the third year of the cohort study, at around age 15. We will therefore repeat some analyses of primary and secondary effects using the test scores at age 15.[12]

Table 4.2 displays the average performance scores of the pupils at age 12 across the four cohorts. Pupils with high educated parents perform best out of the three groups, with an average standardized score of 0.59. Pupils with low educated parents have the lowest performance scores of the three groups. Over time, the average level of performance of children with low and medium educated parents slightly decreased, while the average

TABLE 4.2

Means and standard deviations (in parentheses) of standardized performance scores at age 12, by birth cohort

Parents' education	1965	1970	1977	1981
Low	−0.22 (0.971)	−0.26 (0.937)	−0.31 (0.965)	−0.36 (0.942)
Medium	0.14 (0.947)	0.15 (0.961)	0.10 (0.931)	0.06 (0.931)
High	0.59 (0.890)	0.53 (0.955)	0.60 (0.872)	0.60 (0.857)

SOURCE: CBS cohorts 1965, 1970, 1977, and 1981 and our calculations.

scores for children with high educated parents remained more or less stable. The average performance scores in the second test at age 15, for the 1977 and 1981 cohorts, do not differ much from those at age 12. Some deviations can be found for pupils with high educated parents; in the 1977 cohort, 15-year-olds performed slightly better than at age 12, while they did worse at 15 than at 12 in the 1981 cohort (see Table A4.2 in the web appendix).

RESULTS

We analyze the relative importance of primary and secondary effects on the basis of the method described in Chapter 2 of this book, which provides us with the opportunity to disentangle performance and choice in the context of social-background differences. We use this method for educational transitions at both age 12 and age 17 or 18.

Before discussing the estimated relative importance of primary and secondary effects, we first discuss the factual and synthesized proportions of students making each transition.

Transition at Age 12

The diagonal numbers from the upper left corner to the lower right corner for each cohort in Table 4.3 show the actual probabilities of students from each social-background group making the transition to preuniversity track (VWO) and to precollege (HAVO) or preuniversity track (VWO). As a general observation we can note that the actual transition probabilities for all children have decreased by 3–4 percentage points over time. In our reference cohort (1981), 6 percent of students with low educated parents, 14 percent of students with medium educated parents, and 40 percent of students with high educated parents proceeded to the preuniversity track (VWO). All other numbers in the table show synthesized proportions. To give an example, if in the 1981 cohort students from low educated parents had the average performance of students with high educated parents but had kept their own choice behavior constant, their probability of entering the preuniversity track would have increased from 6 percent to 21 percent. In contrast, if students from low educated parents had the choice behavior of the students with high educated parents but had kept their own performance constant, their probability of entering the preuniversity track would have increased from 6 percent to 14 percent.

TABLE 4.3

Estimated factual and synthesized transition rates (%), from primary education to preuniversity track (VWO), age 12

	1965 Choice			1970 Choice			1977 Choice			1981 Choice		
Performance	Low	Medium	High	Low	Medium	High	Low	Medium	High	Low	Medium	High
Low	9	12	21	7	11	20	6	8	14	6	8	14
Medium	13	18	29	12	18	30	10	13	22	11	14	23
High	22	29	43	18	26	40	18	23	37	21	26	40

SOURCE: CBS cohorts 1965, 1970, 1977, and 1981 and our calculations.

If we look at the synthesized proportions in Table 4.3, we can make two observations. First, for students from low educated backgrounds in the 1965 cohort, whether they adopted the performance level or adopted the choice behavior of students from high educated parents made little difference: both cases would lead to an increase in the probability of making the transition to the preuniversity track from the (actual) rate of 9 percent to a (synthesized) transition probability of 22 percent or 21 percent, respectively. In the 1981 cohort, however, these same transition propensities changed from 6 percent to 21 percent and 14 percent, respectively. That is, the performance-related differences between children from low and high educated parents increased over time, while the choice-related differences (with the exception of the 1970 cohort) remained more or less constant.

Table A4.3 in the web appendix shows results for a similar analysis of entry to precollege track (HAVO) *or* preuniversity track (VWO). Students with high educated parents have a high and relatively stable probability over time to proceed to one of these tracks (61 percent on average). In turn, the probability of going to precollege track or preuniversity track is for students with low educated parents on average 17 percent and for students with medium educated parents 32 percent, and for both groups slightly decreasing over time. In the 1981 cohort, 15 percent of the students with low, 30 percent with medium, and 64 percent with high educated parents proceeded to either precollege track or preuniversity track. Note that, regardless of changes over time, the probability of going to precollege track or preuniversity track, rather than to preuniversity track only, is about twice as high for students with low and medium educated parents and about 1.5 times higher for students with high educated parents. It suggests that the precollege track provides a crucial opportunity for students with low and medium educated parents to proceed to higher education. Again we can note that the performance-related differences between those with low and high educated parents have increased over time (especially between the first two and the last two cohorts), while the choice-related differences have stayed more or less the same.

Primary and Secondary Effects at the Age-12 Transition

Table 4.4 confirms these findings and shows that secondary effects on average declined in importance over time at the transition at age 12 (see also Figures A4.6 and A4.7 in the web appendix). Between the first two cohorts and the last two cohorts, the relative importance of secondary effects at

TABLE 4.4

Relative importance (%) of secondary effects at age-12 transition from primary education to (1) preuniversity track (VWO) and (2) precollege track (HAVO) or preuniversity track (VWO)

	1965		1970		1977		1981	
	(1)	*(2)*	*(1)*	*(2)*	*(1)*	*(2)*	*(1)*	*(2)*
Medium-low	45	40	46	47	34	36	30	34
High-low	48	44	52	53	43	41	39	40
High-medium	50	47	57	58	48	45	44	44
Average	48	44	52	53	42	41	38	39

SOURCE: CBS cohorts 1965, 1970, 1977, and 1981 and our calculations.

the transition to the preuniversity track (VWO) decreased from around 50 percent to around 40 percent. For the transition to either precollege track (HAVO) or preuniversity track (VWO), the percentages fluctuated a little more (with a clear outlier in the 1970 cohort), but we also note a (smaller) decrease from 44 percent in the 1965 cohort to 39 percent in the 1981 cohort. The relative importance of secondary effects over all cohorts is thus on average 45 percent at the transition to preuniversity track and 44 percent at the transition to precollege track *or* preuniversity track. Primary effects are on average slightly more important at this transition. Interestingly, the relative importance of secondary effects is highest when explaining the difference between students with medium and high educated parents.

The results we have obtained are, with small deviations, in line with those of Kloosterman et al. (2009) for the same cohorts. When we consider the 1965, 1977, and 1981 cohorts, the relative importance of primary effects increased between students from medium and low, high and low, and high and medium educated parents over time. The 1970 cohort interrupts this linear trend, and we observe a decrease in the relative importance of primary effects from 1965 to 1970. Summarizing our findings, we can say that the primary effects outweigh the secondary effects at the transition at age 12, but that nonetheless secondary effects are still substantial, even if their relative share appears to decrease over time.

The Conditional Transition at Age 17 or 18

Compared to the first transition at age 12, the actual transition rates at age 17 or 18 from preuniversity track (VWO) to university (WO) and from precollege (HAVO) or preuniversity (VWO) tracks to vocational college (HBO) or to university (WO) of students with low, medium, and high educated parents very clearly increased over time. The selection process at the first transition already functions as an important selection mechanism for the future transition into higher education. As Table 4.5 shows, students with low educated parents who graduated in the preuniversity track increased their probability of making the transition to university from 34 percent in the 1965 cohort to 42 percent in the 1981 cohort. Students with medium and high educated parents had generally higher, but—with the exception of the 1970 cohort—rather constant transition rates over time (with medium educated parents, 43 percent in the 1965 cohort and 46 percent in the 1981 cohort; with high educated parents, 54 percent in the 1965 cohort and 55 percent in the 1981 cohort). The increase in actual transition rates for those from low educated households is even clearer when looking at the transition to vocational college or to university (see Table A4.4 in the web appendix). The expansion of Dutch higher education, which mostly occurred because of an increase in enrollment in vocational colleges, facilitated access to higher education over time for students with low and medium educated parents.

The synthesized proportions in the off-diagonal numbers in Table 4.5 reveal that secondary effects are much stronger than primary effects at the transition at age 17 or 18 (see also Table A4.4 in the web appendix). Table 4.5, for example, shows for the 1981 cohort that if students with low educated parents keep their own performance distribution but have the transition propensity of students from high educated parents, their transition rate to university would be 54 percent (actual transition rate is 42 percent). The opposite is reported for students from high educated parents: if their average performance distribution is combined with the transition propensity of students with low educated parents, their transition rate to university would be 42 percent (actual transition rate is 55 percent). Differences in performance (vertical differences) are practically nonexistent at this transition. All differences between students from different educational backgrounds are therefore driven by secondary effects (horizontal differences). This is also true for the transition to vocational college or university (see Table A4.4 in the web appendix), supporting the argument that there are few differences in performance between students from different social backgrounds at this transition (no primary effects), but there are different preferences in choosing higher education (secondary effects).

TABLE 4.5

Estimated factual and synthesized transition rates (%), from preuniversity track (VWO) to university (WO), conditional transition at age 17 or 18

Performance	1965 Choice			1970 Choice			1977 Choice			1981 Choice		
	Low	Medium	High	Low	Medium	High	Low	Medium	High	Low	Medium	High
Low	34	42	53	42	50	62	41	44	52	42	46	54
Medium	35	43	53	42	51	62	41	44	53	42	46	55
High	36	43	54	42	51	63	42	34	54	42	46	55

SOURCE: CBS cohorts 1965, 1970, 1977, and 1981 and our calculations.

To sum up, primary effects at the transition at age 17 or 18 are quite small and change very little over time. The secondary effects are larger (although not as large as at the first transition at age 12) and explain most of the differences in observed social-background effects, although these effects clearly decrease over time.

The Unconditional Transition at Age 17 or 18

An unconditional analysis, that is, of all pupils to university (WO) and all pupils to vocational college (HBO) or university (WO), allows us to take into account the possibility of upward movements through alternative tracking paths in the Dutch educational system and thus provides a picture of overall IEO at this transition stage. As Table 4.1 illustrates, students are less likely to enter vocational college (HBO) or university (WO) in the unconditional model than in the conditional model, which suggests that students move on rather straight career paths. In the 1981 cohort, for instance, 50 percent of the students who graduated in the preuniversity track (VWO) made the transition to university, while only 8 percent did so when alternative tracking paths are considered. However, if we consider the transition to *both* vocational college and university, the share of students proceeding to higher-education tracks at the transition at age 17 or 18 clearly increases compared to the option to enroll only in university. A relatively constant share over time, of about 21 percent of the students coming from different school tracks, proceeds to either vocational college or university, while the average share proceeding to university is about 8 percent over time.

As would be expected, Table 4.6 shows that the factual and synthesized proportions in the unconditional model are much lower than in the conditional model (see Table A4.5 in the web appendix for equivalent proportions for the unconditional transition to vocational college or university). The factual transition probabilities to university and to vocational college or university for students with low, medium, and high educated parents are low and even decreasing over time. Over time, the unconditional average transition probability of students with the average performance and transition propensity of those with low educated parents is 3 percent to university and 10 percent to vocational college or university. Students with medium educated parents have an average transition probability of 7 percent to university and 21 percent to vocational college or university. The corresponding figures for students with high educated parents are on

TABLE 4.6

Estimated factual and synthesized transition rates (%) of all students to university (WO), unconditional transition at age 17 or 18

	1965 Choice			1970 Choice			1977 Choice			1981 Choice		
Performance	Low	Medium	High	Low	Medium	High	Low	Medium	High	Low	Medium	High
Low	3	6	11	3	6	13	3	3	7	2	3	7
Medium	5	8	16	5	9	19	4	6	12	4	5	11
High	8	13	24	8	13	27	8	10	20	7	10	20

SOURCE: CBS cohorts 1965, 1970, 1977, and 1981 and our calculations.

average 23 percent to university and 45 percent to vocational college or university. Again, including vocational college as a higher-education track clearly increases the probability of all groups participating in higher education. The percentage of students with low and medium educated parents going to vocational college or to university is three times as large as the percentage going exclusively to university. For students with high educated parents, this percentage is two times as large. The synthesized proportions suggest some higher influence of secondary effects in the first two cohorts, while the relationship between primary and secondary effects becomes more balanced in the two younger cohorts.

Primary and Secondary Effects at the Age-17–18 Transition

The relative importance of secondary effects in the conditional models in Table 4.7 somewhat fluctuates, indicating neither a clear decrease nor increase over time. The proportion of total inequality explained by secondary effects is generally high at an overall average level of 94 percent at the transition from preuniversity track (VWO) to university (WO) and at an overall average level of 81 percent at the transition from precollege track (HAVO) or preuniversity track (VWO) to vocational college (HBO) or university (WO) (see also Figures A4.8 and A4.9 in the web appendix). The relatively high importance of secondary effects at the transition from preuniversity track to university consolidates the transition to university as an elite path. The conditional transition to vocational college or university generates lower proportions of secondary effects than the transition to only university, but it does not offer too much in terms of a distinctive decrease

TABLE 4.7
Relative importance (%) of secondary effects at conditional transition at age 17 or 18: (1) from preuniversity track (VWO) to university (WO) and (2) from precollege track (HAVO) or preuniversity track (VWO) to vocational college (HBO) or university (WO)

	1965		1970		1977		1981	
	(1)	*(2)*	*(1)*	*(2)*	*(1)*	*(2)*	*(1)*	*(2)*
Medium-low	90	79	93	87	91	71	94	84
High-low	93	79	96	88	91	78	95	80
High-medium	95	80	99	89	91	82	96	77
Average	93	79	96	88	91	77	95	80

SOURCE: CBS cohorts 1965, 1970, 1977, and 1981 and our calculations.

TABLE 4.8

Relative importance (%) of secondary effects at unconditional transition at age 17 or 18: all students to (1) university (WO) and (2) vocational college (HBO) or university (WO)

	1965		1970		1977		1981	
	(1)	*(2)*	*(1)*	*(2)*	*(1)*	*(2)*	*(1)*	*(2)*
Medium-low	56	54	54	57	39	42	39	49
High-low	58	55	61	60	50	48	48	48
High-medium	59	56	66	62	56	52	54	46
Average	58	55	60	60	48	47	47	48

SOURCE: CBS cohorts 1965, 1970, 1977, and 1981 and our calculations.

in IEO over time. The findings at this transition suggest that, to a large extent, the dominance of secondary effects results from the selection process at the first transition.[13]

Looking at the unconditional models in Table 4.8, we note that the relative importance of secondary effects is clearly lower than in Table 4.7 and on average also decreases somewhat over time. It suggests that, insofar as any change occurred, this change appears at the transition at age 12, rather than at the transition at age 17 or 18. A comparison of these results with the relative importance of secondary effects at the first transition (Table A4.5 in the web appendix) suggests that at the transition at age 17 or 18 there are no possibilities to repair previous decisions: later choices do not compensate for the choices made at the first transition. The proportions of secondary effects both at the transition to university and at the transition to vocational college or university are even higher than at the first transition at age 12, suggesting an ongoing selection in favor of pupils with high educated parents. Over time, the relationship between students with high and low, and high and medium educated parents shows that those of lower social background did catch up to some extent with those of higher social backgrounds but that secondary effects appear to remain more important than primary effects at these later transitions. The unconditional models suggest an average overall relative importance of secondary effects of 53 percent.

CONCLUSION

This chapter has assessed the relative importance of primary and secondary effects at the transitions at age 12 (entry to secondary education) and age 17 or 18 (entry to higher education) in the Dutch educational system over time. Using panel data from four birth cohorts, we made an explicit distinction between the most prestigious and less prestigious routes in the higher tracks of secondary and higher education. In particular, we differentiate between the preuniversity track (VWO) and the precollege track (HAVO) in secondary education and between university (WO) and vocational college (HBO) in higher education. Usually regarded as the less prestigious track in higher education, vocational college has gained in popularity among students over time. In particular, students from low and medium educated parents who complete a precollege track or a preuniversity track are choosing to enter higher education through vocational college. Students from high educated parents, in contrast, are more likely to choose straight career paths from preuniversity track to university.

Our results show that the relative importance of secondary effects at the first transition at age 12 has decreased over time and now amounts to an average of 38 percent of total IEO at this transition. While secondary effects lose some of their power at this transition, their importance clearly grows at later educational transitions. At the conditional transition to higher education at age 17 or 18, secondary effects gain a great deal in importance and almost exclusively explain the (conditional) transition to university (WO). While the proportions in the conditional model stay rather stable over time, the unconditional model at this transition shows a modest decrease in the relative importance of secondary effects, due to changes in the importance of secondary effects at the first transition. Although the Dutch educational system claims to be meritocratic in its selection into the different tracks of secondary education, we can observe that a large proportion of IEO is still related to differential preferences across social-background groups. At this point, almost 40 percent of the IEO differences are choice related.

The situation does not improve if we look at later transitions. At age 17 or 18 secondary effects have increased rather than decreased over the career, despite the Dutch educational system offering opportunities to repair mistakes by allowing moves between tracks. The decrease in secondary effects over time (from some 60 percent to some 48 percent) is mainly due to changes at the first transition at age 12.

These findings imply that policy measures by the Dutch government to reduce IEO have mainly been successful at the first transition to secondary education but have largely failed at later transition stages. To provide an example, a 1993 reform aimed to restructure secondary education. The so-called *Basisvorming* was supposed to provide pupils of all secondary education tracks with a standardized basic curriculum in the first three years of secondary education and an opportunity to prove their abilities and preferences over a longer period before deciding on a final track. However, as shown in the evaluation by the Dijsselbloem parliamentary committee (see Borghans et al. 2008), this reform did not lead to a considerable reduction in IEO. Pupils in our most recent birth cohort (the 1981 cohort) should have profited from this restructuring and subsequently experienced reduced inequality after entering secondary education. And yet the difference in IEO between this cohort and the previous cohort in our analysis is hardly detectable.

NOTES

1. Although Kloosterman (2010) includes an analysis of the transition to postsecondary education in her doctoral dissertation, she focuses on upward and downward movements *within* tertiary education.

2. CITO stands for Centraal Instituut voor Toets Ontwikkeling, which is the Dutch central institute for test development that provides the tests to primary schools nationwide.

3. At age 17 students are still obliged to follow formal education for at least two days per week.

4. These cases are included in the lower vocational track (VBO) in our analysis.

5. Teachers often give mixed recommendations for secondary school tracks if, for instance, the CITO test results are not clear-cut or they diverge from the overall impression that a teacher has of a pupil.

6. A student is understood to have successfully completed an educational track if he or she passed the final examination. If a student dropped out before finishing a grade, we consider the most recent available information about his or her educational transitions.

7. Corresponding figures for the other cohorts are available in Figures A4.3–A4.5 of the web appendix (http://www.primaryandsecondaryeffects.com). See also Table 4.1 for changes over time.

8. Each of the transition variables is binary, taking a value of 1 when making the transition and 0 otherwise. In the case of mixed tracks in the orientation years of secondary education, we look at the first clear track decision after the orientation phase (cf. Kloosterman et al. 2009, 383).

9. In the CBS survey of the 1970 cohort, information on parents' education was collected differently from the surveys of the other three cohorts. This may cause some distinct deviations from a trend when we compare results over time.

10. Pupils in the survey thus complete these tests twice; once, officially, at the end of primary education and once as a respondent in the survey. Choices for subsequent school tracks have already been made on the basis of the regular CITO test. In contrast to the 1965, 1977, and 1981 cohorts, the 1970 cohort took the survey-specific CITO test at the same time as the real CITO test, i.e., one year earlier. This leads to comparably lower performance scores in the survey for pupils of the 1970 cohort (CBS 1992).

11. According to Hustinx et al. (2005), the Cronbach's alpha of the CITO tests in the 1965 and 1970 birth cohorts is 0.80.

12. The use of the second test is unfortunately still problematic, due to three factors. First, as a result of the design of the data collection, pupils who had to repeat classes at any stage before the second test did not participate in this test. Second, the tests were not the same for each pupil. There was a relatively simple test for those who at age 15 were in the lower general track (MAVO) or the lower vocational track (VBO) and another, more difficult, test for pupils in the precollege track (HAVO) and the preuniversity track (VWO). Although some recalibration has taken place, the resulting test scores do not provide a perfect estimate of performance at age 15. Third, since the higher-education track is chosen at age 17 or 18, the second test at age 15 cannot provide a perfect proxy for pupils' performance at this later transition. Given these restrictions, the second test will not guarantee a completely unbiased comparison between performance and choice at the transition to higher education across different social backgrounds.

13. We performed an additional test using performance test scores at age 15 (see Table A4.6 in the web appendix). There are some differences between the results using performance tests at age 15 and those using performance tests at age 12. Table A4.6 shows that when employing performance scores at age 15 the average relative importance of secondary effects at the transition to vocational college (HBO) or university (WO) is lower in the 1977 cohort (38 percent) and almost the same in the 1981 cohort (47 percent), compared to the analyses employing performance scores at age 12. In comparing particular background groups, we see that, when employing performance scores at age 15, for both cohorts the relative importance of secondary effects is lowest between pupils of medium and low educated background, moderate between pupils of high and low educated background, and highest between pupils of high and medium educated background. While this trend is also found using test scores at age 12 in the 1977 cohort, it differs for the 1981 cohort.

REFERENCES

Bakker, Bart F. M., and Peter G. J. Cremers. 1994. "Gelijke kansen in het onderwijs? Een vergelijking van vier cohorten leerlingen in hun overgang naar het voortgezet onderwijs." *Tijdschrift voor Onderwijsresearch* 19:191–203.

Bakker, Bart F. M., Jaap Dronkers, and Huibert Schijf. 1982. "Veranderingen in individuele schoolloopbanen tussen 1959 en 1977 in de stad Groningen." *Mens en Maatschapij* 57:253–66.

Bakker, Bart F. M., and Siebe P. Schouten. 1991. "Trends in onderwijskansen: Een vergelijking van de overgang naar het voortgezet onderwijs van de generaties geboren rond 1953, 1965, en 1971." *Sociale Wetenschappen* 34:1–22.

Blossfeld, Hans-Peter, and Yossi Shavit. 1993. "Persisting Barriers: Changes in Educational Opportunities in Thirteen Countries." In *Persistent Inequality: Changing Educational Attainment in Thirteen Countries*, edited by Yossi Shavit and Hans-Peter Blossfeld, 1–24. Boulder, CO: Westview.

Borghans, Lex, Rolf van der Velden, Charlotte Büchner, Johan Coenen, and Christoph Meng. 2008. "Het meten van onderwijskwaliteit en de effecten van recente onderwijsvernieuwingen." In *Commissie Parlementair Onderzoek Onderwijsvernieuwingen. Tijd voor Onderwijs, Deelrapport IV*, 3–114. The Hague: SDU uitgevers.

Bosma, Hans, and Peter G. J. Cremers. 1996. "Sociaal-economische Verschillen bij de Doorstroom naar de Universiteit." *Mens en Maatschapij* 71:142–253.

Buis, Maarten L. 2010. "Inequality of Educational Outcome and Inequality of Educational Opportunity in the Netherlands during the 20th Century." PhD diss. Amsterdam: Free University.

CBS (Centraal Bureau voor de Statistiek). 1992. "Schoolloopbaan en herkomst van leerlingen bij het voortgezet onderwijs; vergelijking tussen de cohorten 1977 en 1982." Unpublished manuscript.

CITO. 2010. *Terugblik en resultaten 2010*. Eindtoets Basisonderwijs, Groep 8, versie April 20, 2010. Arnhem: Centraal Instituut voor Toetsontwikkeling.

De Graaf, Paul M., and Harry B. G. Ganzeboom. 1993. "Family Background and Educational Attainment in the Netherlands for the 1891–1960 Birth Cohorts." In *Persistent Inequality: Changing Educational Attainment in Thirteen Countries*, edited by Yossi Shavit and Hans-Peter Blossfeld, 75–100. Boulder, CO: Westview.

De Graaf, Paul M., and Maarten H. J. Wolbers. 2003. "The Effects of Social Background, Sex, and Ability on the Transition to Tertiary Education in the Netherlands." *The Netherlands Journal of Social Sciences* 39:172–201.

De Jong, Uulkje, Jaap Dronkers, and Willem E. Saris. 1982. "Veranderingen in de Schoolloopbanen tussen 1965 en 1977: Ontwikkelingen in de Nederlandse Samenleving en in haar Onderwijs." *Mens en Maatschapij* 57:26–54.

Dronkers, Jaap. 1983. "Have Inequalities in Educational Opportunities Changed in the Netherlands? A Review of Empirical Evidence." *The Netherlands Journal of Sociology* 19:133–50.

———. 1993. "Educational Reform in the Netherlands—Did It Change the Impact of Parental Occupation and Education?" *Sociology of Education* 66:262–77.

Erikson, Robert, John H. Goldthorpe, Michelle Jackson, Meir Yaish, and David R. Cox. 2005. "On Class Differentials in Educational Attainment." *Proceedings of the National Academy of Sciences* 102:9730–33.

Hustinx, Paul W. J., Hans Kuyper, Margaretha P. C. van der Werf, and Djurre Zijsling. 2005. *Beschrijving Leerlingsbestanden VOCL '89*. Groningen, Netherlands: Gronings Instituut voor onderzoek van onderwijs, opvoeding en ontwikkeling.

Jackson, Michelle, Robert Erikson, John H. Goldthorpe, and Meir Yaish. 2007. "Primary and Secondary Effects in Class Differentials in Educational Attainment: the Transition to A-Level Courses in England and Wales." *Acta Sociologica* 50:211–29.

Kloosterman, Rianne. 2010. "Social Background and Children's Educational Careers. Studies into the Primary and Secondary Effects of Social Background over Transitions and over Time in the Netherlands." PhD diss. Nijmegen, Netherlands: Radboud University Nijmegen.

Kloosterman, Rianne, Stijn Ruiter, Paul M. de Graaf, and Gerbert Kraaykamp. 2009. "Parental Education, Children's Performance and the Transition to Higher Secondary Education: Trends in Primary and Secondary Effects over Five Dutch School Cohorts (1965–1999)." *British Journal of Sociology* 60:377–98.

Kraaykamp, Gerbert, Koen Van Eijck, and Wout Ultee. 2010. "Status, Class and Culture in the Netherlands." In *Social Status and Cultural Consumption*, edited by Tak Wing Chan, 159–88. Cambridge: Cambridge University Press.

Peschar, Jules L., Els Ten Vergert, and Roel Popping. 1986. "From Father to Son and from Father to Daughter: Educational Mobility in Hungary and the Netherlands for the Birth Cohorts from 1925 to 1955." *Quality and Quantity* 20:377–403.

Rijken, Susanne, Ineke Maas, and Harry B. G. Ganzeboom. 2007. "The Netherlands: Access to Higher Education—Institutional Arrangements and Inequality of Opportunity." In *Stratification in Higher Education. A Comparative Study*, edited by Yossi Shavit, Richard Arum, and Adam Gamoran, 266–93. Stanford, CA: Stanford University Press.

Sieben, Inge, Johannes Huinink, and Paul M. De Graaf. 2001. "Family Background and Sibling Resemblance in Educational Attainment: Trends in the Former FRG, the Former GDR and the Netherlands." *European Sociological Review* 17:401–30.

Tieben, Nicole, Nan Dirk De Graaf, and Paul M. De Graaf. 2010. "Changing Effects of Family Background on Transitions to Secondary Education in the Netherlands. Consequences of Educational Expansion and Reform." *Research in Social Stratification and Mobility* 28:77–90.

Tieben, Nicole, and Maarten H.J. Wolbers. 2010. "Transitions to Post-Secondary Education in the Netherlands: A Trend Analysis of Unconditional and Conditional Socio-Economic Background Effects." *Higher Education* 60:85–100.

Traag, Tanja, and Rolf K. W. Van der Velden. 2011. "Early School-Leaving in the Netherlands. The Role of Family Resources, School Composition and Background Characteristics in Early School-leaving in Lower Secondary Education." *Irish Educational Studies* 30:45–62.

Van Heek, Frederik. 1968. *Het Verborgen Talent. Milieu, Schoolkeuze en Schoolgeschicktheid.* Meppel, Netherlands: J. A. Boom.

Vrooman, Cok, and Jaap Dronkers. 1986. "Changing Educational Attainment Processes: Some Evidence from the Netherlands." *Sociology of Education* 59:69–78.

Willemse, Paula. 1987. "Overleving in de Bovenstroom van het Voortgezet Onderwijs: Veranderde Milieu-Effekten voor Jongens en Meisjes." *Tijdschrift voor Onderwijsresearch* 12:329–43.

CHAPTER FIVE

Academic Achievement, Tracking Decisions, and Their Relative Contribution to Educational Inequalities

Change over Four Decades in France

Mathieu Ichou and Louis-André Vallet

The development of mass postcompulsory education is a key feature of all economically developed societies, a feature that is all the more important given the central role of educational attainment in allocating individuals to class positions (Ishida, Müller, and Ridge 1995). Unfortunately, this quantitative expansion of education has not resulted in a substantial equalization of educational opportunities, as many had expected. Indeed, inequalities in educational attainment based on class, gender, and ethnicity still represent an important and well-established phenomenon (Shavit and Blossfeld 1993; Jonsson, Mills, and Müller 1996; Breen and Jonsson 2005; Duru-Bellat, Kieffer, and Reimer 2008).

In France an early study emphasized that there was little change in the pattern of association between social origins and educational certification from the onset of the 20th century to 1970 (Garnier and Raffalovich 1984). To some extent, this conclusion has been subsequently challenged on the basis of more numerous data and more powerful statistical methods. Smith and Garnier (1986) and then Thélot and Vallet (2000) demonstrated a notable decline among cohorts born in the 1940s in the strong association between father's occupation and highest degree obtained but a much less marked decrease in inequality in more recent cohorts. Indeed, most of the change occurred before, and seems to be independent of, the major secondary school reforms that were introduced in France from the late 1950s to the mid-1970s to promote equality of educational opportunity (Vallet 2004). If rather than considering highest degree obtained, the focus is instead on successful completion of upper secondary school, there is no doubt that the gap between social classes has diminished somewhat (Selz and Vallet 2006; Vallet and Selz 2007). Even in the context of a slightly decreasing association between class origin and educational attainment, the distinction popularized by Boudon (1974) between two fundamental causes of educational inequality remains an important analytic tool, which we apply to France in this chapter.

PRIMARY AND SECONDARY EFFECTS IN FRANCE: FROM CONCEPTUALIZATION TO EMPIRICAL INVESTIGATION

In his book *Education, Opportunity, and Social Inequality*, Raymond Boudon introduced the distinction between the "primary effects of stratification" and the "secondary effects of stratification" in the creation of educational inequality (1974, especially chap. 2). Primary effects are those expressed in the statistical association between children's class or social origin and their average level of academic performance or ability. Secondary effects are those that, at a given level of performance, are expressed in the actual choices and decisions that children, their parents, and the school make in the course of an educational career, especially at branching points. When he proposed this distinction in 1974,[1] Boudon took much of his inspiration from empirical results established by Girard and Bastide (1963) from the French Institut National d'Études Démographiques (INED). Indeed, Girard and Bastide clearly distinguished between "la *première cause* de la non-démocratisation: l'influence du milieu familial sur le développement de l'enfant et, par suite, sa réussite scolaire" and "la *seconde cause* de non-démocratisation: même à égalité de notes, la chance pour l'enfant d'entrer en sixième est en relation avec sa condition sociale" (437, 439, emphasis added).[2] Of course, Boudon developed a more detailed and analytic version of this distinction, which was part of a systematic theoretical ambition. Nevertheless, it is useful to bear in mind that this distinction has its roots in empirical findings derived from the first French large-scale longitudinal study focused on education: the 1962–1972 INED survey, which happens to be one of the empirical bases of this chapter.

It is also worth noting that Boudon was not the only famous French sociologist to use INED empirical research to develop and consolidate a theory of educational inequality. Bourdieu, as early as 1966, explicitly cited INED researchers Girard and Bastide (1963) and Clerc (1964) to show that class inequality in education was not reducible to differences in academic performance. Bourdieu was well aware of the existence of what Boudon later called "secondary effects." Both authors differed only in their interpretation.[3] Therefore, 1960s INED researchers, perhaps more so than Boudon or Bourdieu, should be credited for shedding light on primary and secondary effects as key methodological notions in the study of educational inequality.

The distinction between primary and secondary effects, though influential in the field of social stratification and mobility (Goldthorpe 1996a; Breen and Goldthorpe 1997), has not been applied very often in empirical research on education, as Nash (2006) rightly noted. The absence is even more conspicuous in France, where although inspired by evidence on the French school system and created by a French sociologist, the distinction has almost been nonexistent. One notable exception is the work of Duru-Bellat and her colleagues, in which the authors employed logistic regression models to estimate the relative importance of primary and secondary effects of social stratification in creating educational inequality during compulsory schooling (Duru-Bellat, Jarousse, and Mingat 1993; Duru-Bellat 1996). Using a sample of 2,352 pupils from 17 Burgundian high schools in the early 1980s, they found that, in the transition from lower to upper secondary school, academic performance accounted for about 53.5 percent of the differential between children of manual workers and those from the upper service class, while secondary effects explained the remaining 46.5 percent (Duru-Bellat, Jarousse, and Mingat 1993, 52).[4]

Until recently, a major limitation of all scientific attempts to empirically assess the share of primary and secondary effects has been the lack of a convincing and effective statistical method. Decomposing primary (or indirect via academic performance) effects and secondary (or direct) effects of social background is feasible and relatively simple in linear regression models because, in this instance, the total effect is the exact sum of the primary and secondary effects (Alwin and Hauser 1975). This is, however, much more complicated in the context of models for categorical dependent variables, such as school tracks. This chapter aims to demonstrate the usefulness of Boudon's distinction by using the method described in Chapter 2 (see Erikson and Jonsson 1996; Erikson et al. 2005; Jackson et al. 2007), as well as recent alternative techniques, to analyze educational inequalities in France from a historical perspective. Two periods are studied, which correspond to five school transitions. We first describe the French school system during the two periods under study, namely, the 1960s and the late 1990s to early 2000s, and then describe the data and methods. Results are presented and finally discussed.

TWO STATES OF THE FRENCH EDUCATIONAL SYSTEM, FIVE SCHOOL TRANSITIONS

This chapter empirically investigates the primary and secondary effects of social stratification in creating educational differentials for two cohorts of pupils: the first is composed of students born around 1951; the second is composed of pupils who were born around 1984.[5] These two cohorts were differently affected by educational inequalities within two very different institutional configurations of the French school system. Comparing educational inequalities across two cohorts faced with these different institutional configurations is potentially problematic (Sartori 1991), and inequalities should not be directly compared between the cohorts without being put back into the context in which they occur (Maurice 1989). Specifically, inequality in educational opportunity cannot be studied without looking at the institutional constraints (supply-side) that influence the educational decisions of families (demand-side) (Prost 1992).

In the 1960s the French school system was still organized in a strongly tracked way and was characterized by rather elitist functioning. Since the 19th century, two distinct types of schooling had existed: on the one hand, the classical track leading its overwhelmingly upper-class pupils to the academic upper secondary *lycée*, to the *baccalauréat*, and in some cases, to higher education. On the other hand, postprimary classes confined working-class pupils to shorter vocational schools. Logically, these two closed schooling tracks channeled pupils toward unequal class positions. Thus, until the late 1950s, the school system was not organized to fight against social inequalities but rather to correspond to them (Prost 1997). The post-1950s period coincided with a dramatic expansion of secondary schooling, which stemmed from both a rise in the social demand for education and a political will to train more skilled workers. The age of compulsory schooling was raised from 14 to 16 in 1959 for pupils born from 1953 onward. The move toward a unified comprehensive school system was just beginning, and it reached its height with the *Collège unique* Act of 1975. The first cohort under study, which entered lower secondary school in 1962,

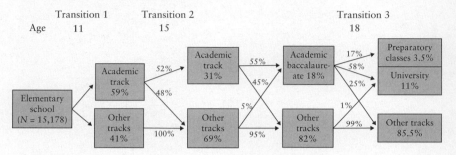

Figure 5.1. Important educational pathways through the stylized French educational system, 1962 to 1972 (1951 cohort)

SOURCE: 1962–1972 INED survey; our calculations.

NOTE: Percentages in boxes are of entire cohort; percentages in lines between boxes are transition rates of each group.

experienced the French educational system at the beginning of this era of reforms. In the 1960s the two-tier system was still formally in place, but differences between the classical upper-class type of schools (*lycée*) and the shorter working-class courses (*cours complémentaire* and *collège d'enseignement général*) had progressively diminished in administrative as well as pedagogical terms (Lelièvre 1990). Most importantly, access to the academic track of upper secondary school, leading to the *baccalauréat*, was no longer restricted to pupils coming from the first type of school.

For the 1951 cohort considered here, there were three main branching points through the educational system. As Figure 5.1 shows, only 59 percent of pupils attending the final year of elementary school gained access to the academic track of lower secondary school (transition 1, at age 11),[6] which enabled them to continue toward the second transition. At transition 2, at age 15, of pupils who had successfully made transition 1, 52 percent were admitted to the academic track of upper secondary school. They constituted 31 percent of the cohort. Of these, 55 percent passed their academic-oriented school-leaving certificate (*baccalauréat général*), which was a requirement to apply to higher education. At transition 3 (age 18), three-quarters of these *baccalauréat général* holders entered academic higher education, that is, university (58 percent) or preparatory classes to elite schools (*classes préparatoires aux grandes écoles*) (17 percent). On the whole, the system was very selective at each stage and only a tiny proportion of a generation attained higher education.

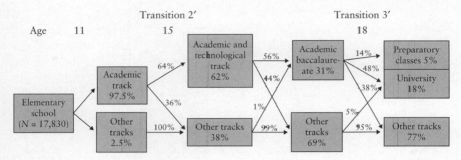

Figure 5.2. Important educational pathways through the stylized French educational system, 1995 to 2006 (1984 cohort)

SOURCE: 1995–2006 Ministry of Education Panel study; our calculations.

The situation is completely different for the 1984 cohort moving through the education system in the 1990s and 2000s, a system that is now far more unified and massified. The transition between elementary and lower secondary school turns out to be virtually automatic for all pupils (Brauns and Steinmann 1999), corresponding to a transition rate of 97.5 percent in our data (see Figure 5.2). After the 1975 act, lower secondary school (*collège*) progressively became an undifferentiated four-year middle school. At age 15, transition 2′ to upper secondary school is the first real branching point in the present-day French educational system. At the end of *collège*, institutional diversification between different tracks begins. On the basis of their family preferences and their level of academic achievement, pupils are allocated to the academic and technological *lycée*, on the one hand, or to other tracks, especially the vocational *lycée*, on the other. In fact, 62 percent of pupils are channeled into the former, while the rest go to other tracks. Three years—or more if they repeat a class—after entering upper secondary school, pupils take a final examination, the *baccalauréat*, that corresponds to the type of curriculum that they followed. Three types of *baccalauréat* exist: vocational, technological, and academic. Fifty-six percent of pupils who attended the academic and technological *lycée* passed the academic *baccalauréat*. Each type of *baccalauréat* formally grants access to higher education (transition 3′, at age 18). In reality, only 5 percent of pupils who do not hold an academic *baccalauréat* enter university, while 48 percent of academic *baccalauréat* holders do so; in addition, 14 percent of them are accepted in preparatory classes to elite schools.

DATA, VARIABLES, AND METHODS

We present evidence from two large-scale longitudinal datasets, the only datasets in France that are available for such an analysis. Fieldwork for the first survey was conducted between the 1961–1962 and 1971–1972 school years by the French Institut National d'Études Démographiques. A nationally representative sample of 17,461 pupils, born around 1951, who attended the last class of elementary school in June 1962 was selected through a complex sampling design and followed for 10 years. At the last point of observation, in September 1971, the attrition rate was as low as 10.6 percent and socially unbiased (Girard and Bastide 1973, 573, table A). Information on pupils, their school trajectories, their families, and their schools was collected annually through postal questionnaires sent to pupils' schools and parents. The data allow us to study the three main school transitions of that time: the transition from elementary to secondary school (transition 1, at age 11), the transition from lower to upper secondary school (transition 2, at age 15) and the transition from upper secondary to higher education (transition 3, at age 18).

The second dataset is a panel study carried out by the French Ministry of Education between 1995 and 2006. A representative sample of 17,830 individuals was randomly selected from all pupils, born around 1984, who entered lower secondary school for the first time in September 1995. They were followed up within and after secondary school. Attrition over the course of the 1995–2006 panel survey is low and without substantial social bias (INSEE 2006). Not only pupils but also heads of schools and parents participated in the survey through mail and telephone questionnaires. For the 1984 cohort, the two essential branching points to be analyzed are the transition from lower to upper secondary school (transition 2′, at age 15), and the transition from upper secondary school to higher education (transition 3′, at age 18). The core method and variables used here are similar to those employed in the other chapters of this book (see Chapter 2 for a discussion of the method). We build the variables as follows.

Parental Class and Education

For the 1951 cohort, the occupation of the head of the household, most usually the father, was precisely recorded. For sake of comparability, both between the two cohorts studied and with other chapters in this book, we recoded this variable into three categories following the Erikson-Goldthorpe-Portocarero (EGP) class schema. What is referred to as the "salariat" corresponds to EGP classes I and II; the "intermediate class" corresponds to EGP classes III, IV, and V; and the "working class" corresponds to classes VI and VII. Although widely recognized as a key independent variable in educational research, parental educational attainment was unfortunately not included in the 1962–1972 INED survey.

For the 1984 cohort, we have precise information on both mother's and father's occupation, but for comparative purposes we use data only on the occupation of the head of the household. This variable was recoded into three categories exactly as described above. Data on both parents' levels of education are also available in the 1995 panel study. We recode the parents' highest level of educational attainment into three categories, labeled as follows: "low" corresponds to parents who, at best, completed elementary school; "medium" corresponds to parents who left school between the end of lower and upper secondary education; and "high" corresponds to pupils whose parents obtained any university degree.

Ethnicity

In the 1962 INED survey, we were able to measure ethnicity only through a remote proxy: pupil's citizenship, contrasting French to foreign children. In the 1995 panel study, in addition to pupil's citizenship that we use when comparing with the former survey, we derived our information on ethnicity from a far more precise source, mother's and father's country of birth. We first cross-classified mother's and father's country of birth, but because of low frequencies, we recoded the ensuing variable into seven categories: both parents born in (1) France, (2) the rest of Europe, (3) North Africa, (4) the rest of Africa, (5) Turkey, (6) the rest of the world, and (7) parents from mixed origins.

Academic Performance Scores

For the 1951 cohort, no perfectly standardized test score is available. The academic level of pupils is individually assessed by the teacher on a five-point scale (excellent, good, average, below average, and bad) during each school year immediately preceding a transition. However, the last such assessment was made in the 1968–1969 school year. At that time, only half the pupils were present in the final class of upper secondary school to undergo the final transition. The remaining half had repeated one or two classes in their school career and, thus, approached this transition one or two years later. As a consequence, for these pupils the academic performance variable corresponding to transition 3 was recorded one or two years before they experienced the transition.

For the 1984 cohort, we have information on test scores, which are reliable quantitative indicators of demonstrated academic ability. For transition 2′, from lower to upper secondary school, the raw performance variable consists of the sum of the grades obtained during the school year in mathematics and French, both subjects having the same weight. As a consequence, some of the variation in grades may be due to not only variation in individual ability but also to the school and class contexts. In the absence of any other better proxy of demonstrated ability, we do, however, think that this variable is a solid indicator. For transition 3′, from upper secondary school to higher education, the performance variable is derived from the average grade obtained at a nationally homogeneous examination, the academic *baccalauréat*. At transition 2′ and before standardization, the grades range from 0.75 to 19.5 out of 20, with a mean of 10.95 and standard deviation of 2.77. For transition 3′, the grades range from 1.55 to 18.39, with a mean of 11.30 and standard deviation of 1.82. For both cohorts, all the performance variables were transformed into z scores with a mean of 0 and a standard deviation of 1 to allow comparability.

Track Variables

At transition 1, only pupils who attended the final year of elementary school (*Cours Moyen* 2, or equivalently *septième*) in 1961–1962 were included in the analysis. The academic track of lower secondary school contains all classes defined as *6e* (6th grade), whether they are part of a public or private school, purely academic or more technical, because all of them formally allow the possibility of continuing in education until the end of lower secondary school. Then, pupils did not reach the end of lower secondary school (*3e*, or 9th grade) at the same time: 47.8 percent reached it four years after 6th grade, that is, in 1965–1966; 42.4 percent repeated one year and attended *3e* in 1966–1967; and 9.8 percent repeated twice and thus spent six years in lower secondary school. All pupils who reach 9th grade face transition 2. The academic track of upper secondary school corresponds to *2nde* (10th grade), either in a private or public school. Finally, at transition 3, all pupils who reached the end of upper secondary school and who took and passed an academic baccalaureate (*baccalauréat général*) between school years 1968–1969 and 1970–1971 are taken into account. The academic track of higher education comprises all types of *classes préparatoires aux grandes écoles* (selective two- or three-year preparatory classes to elite graduate schools) and undergraduate studies in humanities, sciences, law, and medicine (*lettres*, *sciences*, *droit*, and *médecine*) in universities. As discussed below, we distinguished both types of tracks in most analyses. When studying the transition to university, we excluded pupils who were admitted to preparatory classes; symmetrically, when studying the transition to the latter track, we excluded pupils who entered university (see Table 5.2 note).

For the 1984 cohort, pupils who reached *3e* in 1998–1999 (71.4 percent), in 1999–2000 (26.3 percent), and in 2000–2001 (2.2 percent) are included in the analysis of transition 2'. The academic track of upper secondary school corresponds to what is called *2nde générale et technologique* (academic and technological 10th grade), as opposed to entering vocational tracks or leaving school. If pupils took and passed a *baccalauréat général* between 2002 and 2006, they are considered for the analyses related to transition 3'. The academic track of higher education includes the same two types of tracks as in transition 3.

The decomposition of the primary and secondary effects of class stratification in historical perspective is the aim of this chapter. We will now present results pertaining to this central issue before we expand on further results regarding the role of parental education, gender, and ethnicity.

FROM SECONDARY TO PRIMARY EFFECTS OF CLASS: THE HISTORY OF EDUCATIONAL INEQUALITIES IN FRANCE REVISITED

Total Class Inequality

The total level of class inequality needs to be precisely assessed before we move on to measure the relative importance of primary and secondary effects. Figures 5.3 and 5.4 display observed transition rates of pupils from each social class for the three historical and the two contemporary transitions.

In the 1951 cohort, sharp class differentials exist at each level of the school system. For pupils from the salariat, the transition rates are always

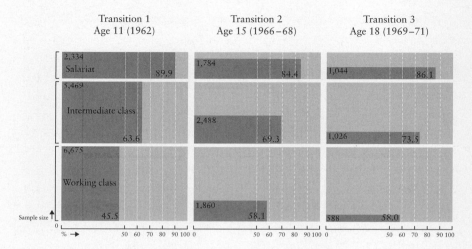

Figure 5.3. Transition rates showing class inequality at each transition (1951 cohort)

SOURCE: 1962–1972 INED survey; our calculations.

NOTE: The horizontal width of the rectangles is proportional to the transition rates. The vertical height of the rectangles corresponds to the numerical proportion of each class.

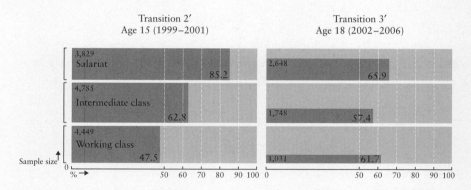

Figure 5.4. Transition rates showing class inequality at each transition (1984 cohort)

SOURCE: 1995–2006 Ministry of Education Panel study; our calculations.

NOTE: The horizontal width of the rectangles is proportional to the transition rates. The vertical height of the rectangles corresponds to the numerical proportion of each class.

around 85–90 percent, while they never exceed 60 percent for their working-class counterparts (see the horizontal axis of Figure 5.3). Both because of these lower transition rates and because of higher dropout rates between branching points, the total number of working-class pupils surviving in the educational system dramatically decreases from one transition to the next (see the vertical axis of Figure 5.3). By contrast, higher transition rates and lower dropout rates mean that the population of salariat pupils decreases much less in size from the first to the last transition. From the end of elementary school to higher education, each branching point reinforces previous class inequality to eliminate most working-class pupils from the educational system. Considerable inequalities are still at play in contemporary France, that is, for the 1984 cohort, but their magnitude has decreased (see Figure 5.4). At transition 3′ especially, the transition rates for the three classes move closer to one another. The transition rate of working-class pupils even exceeds the rate of their intermediate-class counterparts.

As does the remainder of the chapter, Figures 5.3 and 5.4 address transition-specific class inequality, that is, only for pupils at risk of making the transition. However, if we do not condition on whether pupils made the previous transition and we thus examine the whole sample of students, the odds of attaining the academic track of upper secondary school are 10.2 times higher for salariat than for working-class pupils in the 1951 cohort, compared with an odds ratio of 6.6 in the 1984 cohort. These odds ratios are respectively 12.0 and 4.3 when we consider the transition to the academic track of higher education.

In both periods, the academic track of higher education (transitions 3 and 3′) is characterized by a dual structure, distinguishing university from elite preparatory classes. These alternatives are not equally selective. Indeed, for those in the 1951 cohort who achieved an academic *baccalauréat*, the transition rate to university was as high as 62.9 percent and 46.6 percent for salariat and working-class children, respectively. These rates fall to only 23.2 percent and 11.3 percent if we consider *classes préparatoires*. In the present-day school system, that is, for the 1984 cohort, preparatory classes are still very socially selective and prized: the transition rates of salariat and working-class pupils are 20.3 percent and 6.7 percent, respectively. Most strikingly, beside these tracks of excellence, the social selectivity of university has reversed. Working-class pupils' transition rate (55.0 percent) stands *above* that of their salariat schoolmates (45.7 percent). This constitutes a key point in the understanding of the French contemporary field of higher education. Many upper-class parents would now advise their offspring *not* to enroll in traditional public universities, except to study law or medicine, while these universities still attract most working-class pupils who hold an academic *baccalauréat*. By contrast, the parallel preparatory-classes system is highly prized by upper-class families, because it prepares students for the very selective *grandes écoles*, which in turn likely grant them access to well-paid managerial and professional positions in the labor market. On the whole, there has been a clear, and likely growing, academic and social hierarchy between mass universities and elite *classes préparatoires aux grandes écoles*. This type of horizontal inequality within a given level of education is an essential feature of inequality in France (on inequality at the end of upper secondary school, see Ichou and Vallet 2011). To render this hierarchy, university and preparatory classes are distinguished in the analyses below.

On the whole, these descriptive statistics clearly show that overall class inequality, though decreasing, is still large enough for us to decompose the inequalities into primary and secondary effects.

Class Differentials in Academic Performance

Table 5.1 presents the average level of academic performance for each class and for each transition. In the three historical transitions, faced by the 1951 birth cohort, the ranking of test scores systematically corresponds to the social ladder. On average, salariat pupils have better school results than intermediate-class children, who in turn outperform pupils from the working class. The other conspicuous trend is the dramatic reduction in the performance gap over the course of pupils' educational careers. The difference between the mean score of salariat and working-class pupils is 10 times higher at the end of elementary school (0.614) than at the end of upper secondary school (0.062). At this stage, class differences in performance have almost disappeared. In terms of academic performance, and compared to the difference between classes at the end of elementary school, working-class pupils who have stayed in education until the end of upper secondary school are indeed far less different from their upper-class classmates.

Once again, in contemporary France (the 1984 cohort) the academic and social hierarchies closely parallel one another, as Table 5.1 also shows. But in contrast to the earlier cohort, the performance gap between classes is much wider now than it was 40 years ago at the end of both lower (0.675

TABLE 5.1

*Means of standardized test scores at each transition by class in the 1951
and 1984 cohorts*

Class	Mean	N	Mean	N	Mean	N
			1951 COHORT			
	TRANSITION 1: AGE 11 (1962)		TRANSITION 2: AGE 15 (1966–1968)		TRANSITION 3: AGE 18 (1969–1971)	
Salariat	0.426	2,334	0.075	1,784	0.028	1,044
Intermediate	0.047	5,469	−0.012	2,488	−0.009	1,026
Working	−0.188	6,675	−0.056	1,860	−0.034	588
Total	0	14,478	0	6,132	0	2,658
Salariat/ working gap	0.614		0.131		0.062	
			1984 COHORT			
			TRANSITION 2': AGE 15 (1999–2001)		TRANSITION 3': AGE 18 (2002–2006)	
Salariat			0.383	3,829	0.163	2,648
Intermediate			−0.034	4,785	−0.120	1,748
Working			−0.292	4,449	−0.214	1,031
Total			0	13,063	0	5,427
Salariat/ working gap			0.675		0.377	

SOURCE: 1962–1972 INED survey and 1995–2006 Ministry of Education Panel Study; our calculations.

versus 0.131) and upper (0.377 versus 0.062) secondary schools.[7] Finally, the performance gap between classes is strikingly similar when the whole population of pupils is considered, that is, at the *very first* transition each cohort experienced: 0.675 at age 15 in the 1984 cohort compared to 0.614 in the 1951 cohort at age 11.

Relative Importance of Primary and Secondary Effects

The panels of Table 5.2 are of key importance since they show, for each transition, the estimated transition rates for real and synthesized combinations of academic performance and transition propensities, which are at the heart of the method described in Chapter 2. Let us examine transition 1 undergone by the 1951 cohort at age 11, focusing on the two extreme classes (first panel of Table 5.2). Pupils from the salariat, with their actual level of performance and their specific transition propensity given performance, have an estimated transition rate of 91.1 percent, which is quite close to the

TABLE 5.2

Estimated factual and synthesized transition rates (%) for the 1951 cohort

	TRANSITION 1 AGE 11 (1962)			TRANSITION 2 AGE 15 (1966–1968)			TRANSITION 3[a] AGE 18 (1969–1971)			TRANSITION 3[b] AGE 18 (1969–1971)		
							Decision					
Perfor-mance	S	I	W	S	I	W	S	I	W	S	I	W
S	91.1	74.0	63.1	85.0	70.3	59.9	82.2	69.0	52.5	62.5	36.0	23.2
I	85.2	63.3	51.5	84.0	69.2	58.7	82.2	69.0	52.5	61.4	34.5	22.2
W	81.0	56.6	44.6	83.6	68.7	58.0	81.6	69.0	52.5	59.5	32.6	21.1

SOURCE: 1962–1972 INED survey; our calculations.

NOTE: Within each panel of the table, academic performance is fixed in a given row and transition propensity is fixed in a given column. The diagonal figures represent real combinations (i.e., performance and transition propensity measured for the same class), while off-diagonal cells contain synthesized combinations (performance and transition propensity of two different classes). S = salariat; I = intermediate class; W = working class.

[a]In this panel, we compare pupils who entered university to pupils who were channeled into all other tracks *excluding those who were accepted in preparatory classes.* We do this to reduce the heterogeneity of the other tracks category, which would have been extremely diverse had it brought together elite preparatory classes, short vocational studies, and dropouts. For this reason, the estimated real transition rates differ from the transition rates to university described in the previous section on total class inequality.

[b]In this panel, we compare pupils who entered preparatory classes to pupils who went into other tracks *excluding those who entered university.* See above for an explanation.

observed rate (89.9 percent). For working-class children, this real combination of their two actual attributes generates an estimated transition rate of 44.6 percent—close to the observed 45.5 percent. The real analytic value of these tables is related to their off-diagonal cells, which alone encompass the most distinctive feature of the method: counterfactual reasoning. In transition 1, if salariat pupils kept their real transition propensity but had the academic performance distribution of working-class pupils, their transition rate would be 81.0 percent, lower than the actual salariat rate. If the salariat level of academic performance is now combined with the transition propensity of working-class pupils, the estimated transition rate is even lower, reaching only 63.1 percent.

As can be inferred from the previous description, all vertical differences in transition rates arise from variations in academic performance, that is, primary effects. In comparison, horizontal contrasts stem only from differences in transition propensities controlling for performance, that is, secondary effects. This allows us to quickly interpret each one of the four panels. In creating class differentials in transition 1 (1951 cohort at age 11),

TABLE 5.3
Estimated factual and synthesized transition rates (%) for the 1984 cohort

	TRANSITION 2' AGE 15 (1999–2001)			TRANSITION 3'[a] AGE 18 (2002–2006)			TRANSITION 3'[b] AGE 18 (2002–2006)		
				Decision					
Performance	S	I	W	S	I	W	S	I	W
S	85.9	74.9	68.4	57.1	53.7	59.4	37.7	28.5	25.2
I	75.8	63.2	55.6	56.7	52.8	58.9	26.6	18.0	15.9
W	68.3	55.3	47.5	56.5	52.4	58.7	24.3	15.8	14.0

SOURCE: 1995–2006 Ministry of Education Panel Study; our calculations.

NOTE: Within each panel of the table, academic performance is fixed in a given row and transition propensity is fixed in a given column. The diagonal figures represent real combinations (i.e., performance and transition propensity measured for the same class), while off-diagonal cells contain synthesized combinations (performance and transition propensity of two different classes). S = salariat; I = intermediate class; W = working class.
[a]See Table 5.2 note a.
[b]See Table 5.2 note b.

secondary effects are more consequential than primary effects, because the horizontal differences are greater than the vertical ones. This is even truer for transition 2 (1951 cohort at age 15), where the horizontal differences, created by differences in transition propensities, are much wider than the vertical differences, created by differences in academic performance (see the second panel of Table 5.2). In transition 3 (1951 cohort at age 18), whether university or *classes préparatoires* are considered, primary effects virtually disappear and inequality is almost entirely created by secondary effects (see the final two panels).

Four decades later, the situation has changed. At transition 2' (1984 cohort at age 15, see the first panel of Table 5.3), primary and secondary effects appear to have the same magnitude. In the two extreme off-diagonal cells, the estimated transition rates of both counterfactual combinations are indeed similar (68.3 percent and 68.4 percent). At transition 3' (1984 cohort at age 18), figures related to university (second panel) and those linked to preparatory classes (third panel) tell a different story. In the first case, the overall differential between salariat and working-class pupils appears to be too small to be decomposed into primary and secondary effects. However, comparing the rates of intermediate-class children to those of the two other classes points to the influence of secondary effects. In the case of *classes préparatoires*, both types of effects seem to have a roughly similar weight in accounting for the higher transition rate of salariat pupils. On the whole, the share of primary effects in determining overall inequalities appears to be much larger in contemporary France than for the 1951 cohort.

By transforming the previous estimated rates into odds and following the method described in Chapter 2, we are now able to precisely assess the relative importance of primary and secondary effects at each of the five transitions (Table 5.4). To improve the robustness of the overall picture, we also display the results obtained using three alternative decomposition methods. The first alternative technique is in every respect similar to the one presented in Chapter 2, except that it releases the rather strong assumption of normality in the academic performance distribution (Buis 2010). The second alternative method was conceived by Fairlie (2005) and is an extension to binary outcome models of the classical Blinder (1973) and Oaxaca (1973) decomposition, which applied only to continuous dependent variables. The third alternative method was designed by Karlson, Holm, and Breen (2012) to solve the scaling problems of logistic regression.[8]

Though not perfectly equal, the figures delivered by the four decomposition methods are reassuringly close, and they all tell the same story. In the 1960s and early 1970s, for the 1951 cohort, secondary effects were crucial. Their share even increased as pupils progressed through the educational system. Secondary effects rose, from accounting for about three-quarters of the total inequality in transition 1 at age 11 to accounting for almost 95 percent in transition 2 at age 15. For the transition to university, all the inequality between salariat and working-class pupils is accounted for by secondary effects. In the transition to preparatory classes, the relative importance of secondary effects lies between 92.7 percent and 93.3 percent, depending on the method considered.

In the contemporary school system, for the 1984 cohort, primary effects play a far more important role. Secondary effects account for "only" half the overall inequality between salariat and working-class pupils in the transition from lower to upper secondary school. Because no significant differential exists between salariat and working-class children in the transition to university, no decomposition can sensibly be carried out. In the transition to preparatory classes, the share of secondary effects corresponds to around 50 percent of the salariat class advantage.

The core of this chapter lies here. A key—but never clearly demonstrated before—feature of the post–World War II French school system is the sharp historical rise of the share of primary effects in creating class

TABLE 5.4

Relative importance of secondary effects of class in the 1954 and 1981 cohorts (as a percentage of salariat vs. working-class inequality—four methods of decomposition; standard errors in parentheses)

1951 COHORT

	TRANSITION 1 AGE 11				TRANSITION 2 AGE 15				TRANSITION 3—UNIVERSITY AGE 18				TRANSITION 3—PREPARATORY CLASSES AGE 18			
	E.	B.	F.	K.	E.	B.	F.	K.	E.	B.	F.	K.	E.	B.	F.	K.
	68.4 (1.9)	67.4 (1.3)	77.7	68.6	93.7 (2.3)	93.7 (1.7)	95.0	94.1	100.0 (0.5)	100.0 (0.5)	100.0	100.0	93.3 (3.4)	93.3 (2.9)	93.1	92.7

1984 COHORT

	TRANSITION 2' AGE 15				TRANSITION 3'—UNIVERSITY AGE 18				TRANSITION 3'—PREPARATORY CLASSES AGE 18			
	E.	B.	F.	K.	E.	B.	F.	K.	E.	B.	F.	K.
	49.8 (1.9)	50.3 (1.5)	54.7	52.0	No significant total effect				48.2 (7.6)	46.9 (6.1)	51.1	51.6

SOURCE: 1962–1972 INED survey and 1995–2006 Ministry of Education Panel Study; own calculations.

NOTE: E. = Erikson et al. (2005) decomposition method described in Chapter 2; B. = Buis (2010) decomposition method; F. = Fairlie (2005) decomposition method; K. = Karlson, Holm, and Breen (2012) decomposition method. Standard errors have been computed with the R DECIDE package for the Erikson et al. method (as described in Chapter 2) and with the Stata ldecomp add-on program for the Buis method (using bootstrap). Software related to the other two methods does not provide standard errors for relative importance statistics.

inequality in educational attainment. To emphasize this result, we have represented it in graphical form. The following graphs describe total class inequality and its decomposition in primary and secondary effects as expressed on a log odds scale. The reference category is always the working class. Within each graph, the same transition is compared for the 1951 and 1984 cohorts.

If as we mentioned above, the 1960s school system was more socially unequal than the contemporary one, it is chiefly because of the existence of a first branching point operating as early as age 11. This transition no longer exists (Figure 5.5, left); the reader should bear this in mind when looking at later transitions (Figure 5.5, right, and Figure 5.6). In the 1951 cohort, pupils had already been through a selection process, which is not the case for children belonging to the 1984 cohort.

Figures 5.5 and 5.6 highlight and summarize our key results. The main difference between the two cohorts now becomes self-evident: primary effects were almost nonexistent; they are now highly consequential. While secondary effects were the almost sole mechanism creating class inequality for the 1951 cohort, they are much less decisive now.

Controlling for Differences in the Measurement of Performance

One methodological remark could undermine our conclusion: what if the trend identified here was due to differences in measurement between the two surveys? All variables have been constructed to be exactly comparable, with the exception of the performance variables (see above). In the 1962–1972 INED survey, the academic level of pupils is assessed by the teacher on a five-point scale before each transition, while in the 1995–2006 panel study, continuous test scores are available. In analyses not shown here, we assessed the claim that the upward trend in primary effects could stem from a better measurement of performance in the latter dataset. To do this, we deliberately impaired the two continuous performance variables for the 1984 cohort by splitting them into five categories. Three different categorizations for both variables were implemented: first, a normalization in five categories;[9] second, a reproduction of the distribution of the categorical performance variable observed at the same transition in the first survey; and third, a transformation into quintiles. We ran all the calculations again, following the method described in Chapter 2, for the transitions undergone by the 1984 cohort at age 15 and age 18, using these new

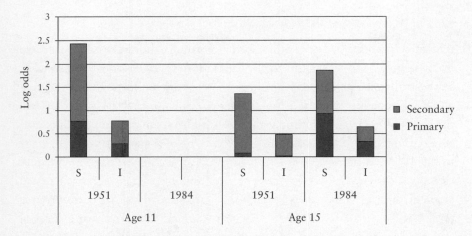

Figure 5.5. Total class inequality and its decomposition into primary and secondary effects, transitions at age 11 (1951 cohort) and age 15 (1951 and 1984 cohorts)

SOURCE: 1962–1972 INED survey and 1995–2006 Ministry of Education Panel study; our calculations.

NOTE: All bars represent log odds ratios (for total inequality, primary and secondary effects) expressed relative to working-class pupils. S = salariat; I = intermediate.

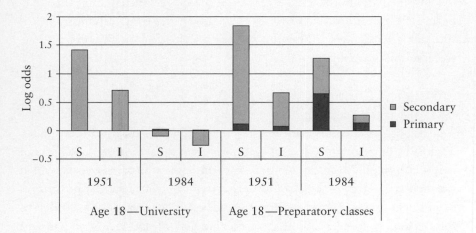

Figure 5.6. Total class inequality and its decomposition into primary and secondary effects, transitions at age 18 (1951 and 1984 cohorts)

SOURCE: 1962–1972 INED survey and 1995–2006 Ministry of Education Panel study; our calculations.

NOTE: All bars represent log odds ratios (for total inequality, primary and secondary effects) expressed relative to working class pupils. At the transition to university, we compare pupils who entered university to pupils who were channeled into all other tracks excluding those who were accepted in preparatory classes. Symmetrically, in the transition to preparatory classes, we compare pupils who entered preparatory classes to pupils who went into other tracks excluding those who entered university. S = salariat; I = intermediate class.

five-category performance variables. In no instance did the results generated by these new analyses lead us to question our first conclusion. For example, at the transition at age 15, the share of secondary effects is 57.8 percent and 58.4 percent for the first two categorizations, respectively. Even when the original variable is split into quintiles and thus undergoes the most severe damage, secondary effects still account for 66.1 percent of total effects in the 1984 cohort, which is still a substantial decline on the 93.7 percent estimated for the 1951 cohort.[10] A second possible source of measurement error in the first survey lies in pupils being assessed not by standardized tests but by their own teachers. It could well be that, at a given level of true performance, teachers are socially biased in favor of upper-class pupils at the expense of working-class pupils (Bourdieu and Saint-Martin 1975; Merle 2007). However, if this were the case,[11] the average performance gap between these two social classes would be artificially enlarged, which, all things being equal, would result in an overestimation of the share of primary effects for the 1951 cohort and an underestimation of the historical rise of primary effects.

On the basis of these checks, we can therefore conclude that there has been a clear and decisive historical increase in the relative importance of primary effects. Before drawing further conclusions on this main story, some subplots are now depicted.

PARENTAL CLASS OR PARENTAL EDUCATION?

Educational researchers widely agree that parental education often has a greater influence than parental class on many aspects of a child's school career. This could be particularly true in the case of primary effects, which are closely related to socialization processes influenced by the possession of cultural capital (e.g., De Graaf, De Graaf, and Kraaykamp 2000; see Lareau and Weininger 2003 for a critical review). Information on parental education was unfortunately not recorded in the 1962 INED survey. We are therefore able to measure the share of primary and secondary effects of parental education for only the 1984 cohort. As expected, the relative importance of primary effects is somewhat larger when we look at parental education instead of class in transition 2' at age 15. Compared to the figures in Table 5.4, secondary effects are indeed slightly lower: 44.6, 44.8,

46.4, and 46.6 percent, respectively, obtained with the Erikson et al. (2005) (see Chapter 2), Buis (2010), Fairlie (2005), and Karlson, Holm, and Breen (2012) methods of decomposition. For parental education, just as for class, no significant total inequality is observed in the transition to university (vs. short vocational tracks or leaving school). Contrary to what we observe at age 15, the share of secondary effects is generally higher at age 18 for parental education than for class in the transition to *classes préparatoires* (vs. short vocational tracks or leaving school): respectively 54.4, 52.9, 49.9, and 53.1 percent with the four methods of decomposition. All in all, and despite slight alterations in one direction or the other, the overall picture thus remains essentially unaltered.

EXPLAINING SECONDARY EFFECTS

The importance of primary effects has been rising over time. However, secondary effects have by no means disappeared and indeed tend to increase throughout the educational career. We here use further attitudinal and institutional variables to investigate factors responsible for secondary effects.

Because secondary effects are those effects of class origin that appear at a given level of academic performance, we anticipate that they will be explained especially by variables linked to parents' and children's educational and occupational aspirations and to the choices of field of study related to these aspirations. The 1995–2006 panel study contains detailed information on many aspects of pupils' educational trajectories, which can help us understand the origin of secondary effects.[12] Using the Fairlie (2005) decomposition method, we can assess the contribution of specific variables in explaining the difference between two groups of individuals as regards a binary outcome, for example, the difference between salariat and working-class pupils in the probability of making a given school transition. Now, to explain secondary effects specifically, we examine this difference in the probability of transition after controlling for academic performance, on top of other explanatory variables of interest, as in a regression model.[13]

For the transition at age 15, after taking academic performance into account, we tried to explain secondary effects by including the family's official first choice of track at the end of lower secondary school (academic track or otherwise), a parental subjective assessment of the child's academic level (from "very bad" to "excellent" in four categories), and the type of degree that was considered the most useful for finding a job (academic, vocational, or other degrees). The result is perfectly clear: family choice explains almost all (93.5 percent) of the difference between salariat and working-class pupils that is not linked to performance. How parents assess the level of their child explains another 3.1 percent of secondary effects. The third variable has no significant influence.

For the transition at age 18, after controlling for academic performance, we included the type of academic *baccalauréat* passed (major in literature, sociology and economics, or sciences) and the planned characteristics of the pupil's future occupation (yes or no answers to the following items: financially profitable, allowing free time, captivating, secure, enabling meeting people, and entailing travel or staying close to home).[14] Again, the transition to university was not considered, since no significant differential exists between salariat and working-class pupils here. We therefore implemented this model to explain secondary effects in the access to preparatory classes. Beyond academic performance, the type of *baccalauréat* passed is the only variable that helps explain the class gap in the access to *classes préparatoires*. It accounts for 22.2 percent of secondary effects: majoring in the sciences section of the academic *baccalauréat* increases the likelihood of accessing preparatory classes. We see this result as reflecting the fact that, even after controlling for performance, the institutional opportunities for entering different types of *classes préparatoires* are the largest for pupils holding a sciences-oriented academic *baccalauréat*, which is considered in France to be the most prestigious one (Ichou and Vallet 2011, graph 3).

In a nutshell, the family's official choice almost totally explains secondary effects at the end of lower secondary school. In fact, according to the rules and regulations of the French educational system, families first officially express a wish for their child's future track and then teachers and heads of schools make a proposal for a track, *while knowing the family's wishes* (Duru-Bellat 1988). Studying the mechanisms that shape the family's choice in the first place would thus be of key importance but is beyond the scope of this chapter. For the transition at age 18, in the absence of information on students' choice of higher-education track, we showed that the type of *baccalauréat général* passed has a substantial influence on secondary effects in the transition to preparatory classes.

A FINAL OVERVIEW OF GENDER AND ETHNIC
INEQUALITIES

Parental class and education are the most important but not the only
sources of inequalities in educational attainment. We also analyzed gender
and ethnic inequalities at each transition and their decomposition into primary and secondary effects. Our most noteworthy results are now briefly
described.

At each of the five transitions studied, secondary effects are virtually the only mechanism creating gender differentials. At age 15, girls in
both cohorts more frequently enter the academic track of upper secondary school than boys do: the odds ratios are 1.74 and 1.52 for the 1951
and 1984 cohorts, respectively. However, at age 18, taking university and
classes préparatoires together, we identify an interesting historical reversal
in the pattern of gender inequality: the odds ratio comparing girls to boys
amounts to 0.43 in the earlier cohort but 1.20 in the later one. Decomposing these inequalities highlights that no significant gender difference in academic performance can be reported at the end of upper secondary school in
either cohort. However, boys belonging to the 1951 cohort were favored by
secondary effects and, therefore, had higher transition rates than girls into
the academic track of higher education. The opposite occurs in the 1984
cohort. In their review of international studies on gender inequality in education, Buchmann, DiPrete, and McDaniel (2008, 325) also find that the
"proportion of both men and women enrolling in college has increased since
the 1970s, but the increase for women has been much more substantial."
In France this trend is due to the temporal reversal of secondary effects,
which can likely be related to a declining significance of traditional gender-
role attitudes (DiPrete and Buchmann 2006) and particularly to a rise in
women's expectations for future employment (Goldin, Katz, and Kuziemk
2006). Accessing higher education and obtaining a university degree is ob-
jectively an efficient means for women to reduce their relative disadvantage
in the labor market in France (Cacouault and Fournier 1998). That said,
boys remain highly overrepresented in the most prestigious tracks of higher
education. Indeed, women who passed the academic *baccalauréat* are still
only half as likely as men to attend *classes préparatoires*. In this case, secondary effects continue to favor men. In the study of gender differentials,

horizontal inequalities between tracks or subjects within higher education are of key importance (Gerber and Cheung 2008).

As regards ethnic inequality, two approaches are followed: first, focusing on parents' country of birth, which is only possible for the 1984 cohort and, second, considering pupils' citizenship and comparing both cohorts. In the 1984 cohort, primary and secondary effects work in opposite directions to create the observed differentials between second-generation immigrant pupils and the majority group. Notwithstanding that ethnic minority pupils perform noticeably worse than the majority group, they have *higher* transition rates than the children of nonmigrants at a given level of academic achievement. This could be related to ethnic minority families seeming to particularly value education, especially as a means of upward social mobility (Zéroulou 1988; Vallet and Caille 1996; Brinbaum and Cebolla Boado 2007). When comparing the cohorts—using the measure of pupils' citizenship, which is the only measure available for both cohorts—two results are worth noting. In the 1960s and in contemporary France, foreign pupils have lower transition rates than their French schoolmates at age 15 (the odds ratios are 0.65 and 0.59 for the 1951 and 1984 cohorts, respectively), but rates do not significantly differ at age 18. Our results also demonstrate an interesting historical reversal in the role played by secondary effects at age 15. In the 1960s foreign pupils were penalized by primary and, particularly, by secondary effects, whereas now secondary effects favor them. To interpret this change, we put forward three nonexclusive tentative explanations. First, in the period of strong economic growth of the 1960s, foreign migrants were in France to work mainly as manual workers and education was not considered to be a requirement for achieving social mobility. In contemporary France, on the other hand, school success proves to be at the center of upward mobility strategies. In addition, in early waves of labor migration, immigrants were likely to be less positively selected in terms of educational attainment and social status than more recent migrants. This latter-day positive selection of immigrants might be related to higher aspirations (Heath, Rothon, and Kilpi 2008, 223–24). Lastly, the reform that allowed families to have a say in the tracking procedure at the end of lower secondary school was not introduced until the 1970s and could explain the reversal of secondary effects, as foreign families in contemporary France translate their educational aspirations into more ambitious school plans that are taken into account by the teachers' teams (Vallet and Caille 1996).

CONCLUSION

Among the findings presented in this chapter, three main elements are essential. First, upper-class families' demand for the two components of the academic track of higher education, university and *classes préparatoires*, has dramatically changed over time. In the 1960s and 1970s, when few pupils had the opportunity to access higher education, both university and preparatory classes were valued by the upper class. After the two waves of educational expansion in the 1960s to early 1970s and the late 1980s to early 1990s, mass universities, where many working-class pupils study, no longer grant a clear relative advantage to upper-class pupils. Preparatory classes, which are selective and lead to elite schools (*grandes écoles*), have therefore become much more attractive to upper-class families. This type of "horizontal" inequality, which occurs within a given level of schooling, has become increasingly significant (Lucas 2001; Ichou and Vallet 2011). It might thus be argued that in the present-day French school system the selective-versus-non-selective contrast is actually the most relevant for comparison with the older system (Berthelot 1987).

Second, in the course of pupils' educational careers, secondary effects generally increase relative to primary effects. Boudon himself predicted this result. As a matter of fact, only higher achievers from lower-class backgrounds survive the first branching points. Therefore, "after a number of years, differences in school achievement as a function of social background are scarcely observable in a given cohort" (Boudon 1974, 85): primary effects should tend to die out across the school career (similar observations are found in Bourdieu 1966, 334–35). Though true, this upward trend in the relative importance of secondary effects throughout an educational career is not as strong as Boudon supposed. Therefore, the primary-versus-secondary-effects distinction should not be reduced to a temporal opposition between a compulsory school period when all primary effects are created and a postcompulsory-education period during which secondary effects generate all educational inequalities. In the present-day French educational system, primary effects are far from negligible even after compulsory schooling.

Third, we have identified a clear historical rise in the share of the primary effects of social stratification in creating educational differentials. As regards school transitions, academic performance plays a far more important role in contemporary France than it did 40 years ago. Until the 1960s and 1970s, in the context of a tracked school system, lower-class pupils were eliminated very early on the basis of predominantly inherited social characteristics. Now that the school system is more unified, branching points have been postponed and social differentials are increasingly generated through differences in academic achievement. In other words, school achievement has partially replaced social ascription as the basis of educational selection. With the benefit of hindsight, the French historian of education Antoine Prost maintains that the

> reform of the *collèges* has not only consolidated social stratification, it has legitimated it. This stratification is now based on apparently academic criteria rather than overtly social ones. It thus invites the members of the various social groups to internalize their respective social positions and to accept them as a consequence of their unequal merit. . . . It defines as personal merit or incapacity what would have previously been attributed to the accidents of birth. Responsibility for educational inequality is now laid at the door of individuals rather than society.[15] (1999, 62)

The extent to which individuals from different social classes are aware of or have internalized these structural changes in the creation of educational inequalities would require further research. What is certain, however, is that this "meritocratization" of the school system is not devoid of ambiguities. This way of legitimizing educational and thus social inequalities as a fair by-product of individuals' own achievements is not harmless to everyone. Indeed, the painful and long-lasting psychological and social consequences of this selection process for the "losers" should not be underestimated (Goldthorpe 1996b; McNamee and Miller 2004; Duru-Bellat 2009).

NOTES

1. Interestingly, the terms "primary effects" and "secondary effects" were absent from the French version of the text (Boudon 1973), and Boudon first coined the distinction in English. It is only recently, and well after the publication of *Education, Opportunity, and Social Inequality* in 1974, that the terms were translated into French as *effets primaires* and *effets secondaires*.

2. Our translation: "the primary cause of nondemocratization: the influence of family background on the child's development and, in turn, on his or her school success," and "the secondary cause of nondemocratization: even at a given

level of school performance, the likelihood of entering lower secondary school is linked to social background."

3. Put simply, Boudon (1973, 1974) saw secondary effects to be the result of socially differentiated rational choices, while Bourdieu (1966, 1974) insisted on the role of the internalization of objective chances of future success. Each position has been portrayed as being in conflict with the other by commentators and by the authors themselves. The supposed incompatibility of the two positions, however, should not be taken at face value, because the real difference between the authors lies in the level of consciousness and intentionality that is ascribed to the individual. Boudon conceived of social actors as being more conscious and intentional than Bourdieu did (see, e.g., Paradeise 1990).

4. When other measures of prior academic achievement in elementary school and early lower secondary school were added to the logistic models, the share of primary effects rose to 64 percent (Duru-Bellat, Jarousse, and Mingat 1993, 52).

5. In this chapter, the term "cohort" should not be understood in the strict sense of people born in a given year. Here, we use it to designate groups of pupils who left elementary school at the same time (for our two cohorts, the summers of 1962 and 1995), without necessarily having been born in the same year. The two groups will nevertheless be referred to as the 1951 and 1984 cohorts, respectively.

6. For the 1951 cohort we label the transitions as follows: transition 1 from elementary school to lower secondary school, transition 2 from lower to upper secondary school, and transition 3 from upper secondary school to higher education. For the sake of clarity, we add a prime sign to the corresponding transitions for the 1984 cohort, i.e., transition 2′ and transition 3′.

7. This demonstrates that educational expansion has resulted in greater heterogeneity in (often unmeasured) ability variables at each level of schooling, which was precisely Mare's prediction in his 1981 *American Sociological Review* paper (82, especially note 5).

8. The coefficients that we want to compare are the log odds ratios associated with class, conditional and unconditional on academic performance. To do so, we need to neutralize the scaling problems described by Karlson, Holm, and Breen (2012) and Mood (2010). Following the former paper, we compare (1) a logit model including class and academic performance residualized with respect to class (i.e., uncorrelated with class) with (2) a model including both class and the usual academic performance variable. The former model gives the total effect of class, while the latter indicates the secondary effects of class.

9. Given that the performance variable is standardized (mean = 0; standard deviation = 1), we used the following cut points to construct the five categories: –1.5, –0.5, 0.5, and 1.5.

10. As a further robustness check, we used two variables from the 1995 panel study that are not used in the analysis because they do not correspond to any transition: standardized test scores and subjective teacher assessments of pupils, both measured at the beginning of lower secondary school. The former

variable is continuous; the latter is categorical. These two variables thus reproduce the two different ways of assessing pupils' achievement in the 1962 and 1995 surveys. It turns out that the correlation between these two variables is 0.79, which is high and thus means that both variables are quite similar measures of pupils' academic achievement.

11. Using the same two variables described in the previous note, we can confirm that this social bias in teachers' assessment exists, but that it is not strong. We regressed teachers' assessment on social class of origin, *controlling for test scores*, and observed that, for a given test score, teachers tend to give slightly inferior assessments to working-class children and, to a lesser extent, intermediate-class children, compared to pupils belonging to the salariat.

12. No such data are available for the 1951 cohort.

13. For the sake of brevity, detailed tables are not displayed but are available in the web appendix (http://www.primaryandsecondaryeffects.com).

14. The relevant question was asked in a subquestionnaire included in the panel study in 2002: "What qualities would you like your future occupation to have?" followed by the items.

15. Written in French as "La réforme des collèges n'a pas seulement consolidé la stratification sociale : elle l'a légitimée, puisqu'elle l'a fait reposer sur des critères apparemment scolaires et non plus ouvertement sociaux. Elle a invité les membres des différents groupes sociaux à intérioriser leurs positions sociales respectives et à les assumer comme une conséquence de leur inégal mérite. . . . Elle a transformé en mérite ou en incapacité personnelle ce qu'on aurait auparavant imputé aux hasards de la naissance. La charge des inégalités devant l'école n'incombe plus à la société mais aux individus" (Prost 1997, 111).

REFERENCES

Alwin, Duane F., and Robert M. Hauser. 1975. "The Decomposition of Effects in Path Analysis." *American Sociological Review* 40:37–47.

Berthelot, Jean-Michel. 1987. "De la terminale aux études post-bac: itinéraires et logiques d'orientation." *Revue française de pédagogie* 81:5–15.

Blinder, Alan S. 1973. "Wage Discrimination: Reduced Form and Structural Variables." *Journal of Human Resources* 8:436–55.

Boudon, Raymond. 1973. *L'inégalité des chances : la mobilité sociale dans les sociétés industrielles.* Paris: Armand Colin.

———. 1974. *Education, Opportunity, and Social Inequality: Changing Prospects in Western Society.* New York: Wiley.

Bourdieu, Pierre. 1966. "L'école conservatrice: les inégalités devant l'école et devant la culture." *Revue française de sociologie* 7:325–47.

———. 1974. "Avenir de classe et causalité du probable." *Revue française de sociologie* 15:3–42.

Bourdieu, Pierre, and Monique de Saint-Martin. 1975. "Les catégories de l'entendement professoral." *Actes de la recherche en sciences sociales* 1:68–93.

Brauns, Hildegard, and Susanne Steinmann. 1999. "Educational Reform in France, West-Germany and the United Kingdom: Updating the CASMIN Educational Classification." *ZUMA-Nachrichten* 44:7–44.

Breen, Richard, and John H. Goldthorpe. 1997. "Explaining Educational Differentials: Towards a Formal Rational Action Theory." *Rationality and Society* 9:275–305.

Breen, Richard, and Jan O. Jonsson. 2005. "Inequality of Opportunity in Comparative Perspective: Recent Research on Educational Attainment and Social Mobility." *Annual Review of Sociology* 31:223–43.

Brinbaum, Yaël, and Héctor Cebolla Boado. 2007. "The School Careers of Ethnic Minority Youth in France: Success or Disillusion?" *Ethnicities* 7:445–74.

Buchmann, Claudia, Thomas A. DiPrete, and Anne McDaniel. 2008. "Gender Inequalities in Education." *Annual Review of Sociology* 34:319–37.

Buis, Maarten. 2010 "Direct and Indirect Effects in a Logit Model." *Stata Journal* 10:11–29.

Cacouault, Marlaine, and Christine Fournier. 1998. "Le diplôme contribue-t-il à réduire les différences entre hommes et femmes sur le marché du travail?" In *Égalité des sexes en éducation et formation*, edited by Nicole Mosconi, 68–98. Paris: Presses Universitaires de France.

Clerc, Paul. 1964. "La famille et l'orientation scolaire au niveau de la sixième. Enquête de juin 1963 dans l'agglomération parisienne." *Population* 19:637–44.

De Graaf, Nan Dirk, Paul M. de Graaf, and Gerbert Kraaykamp. 2000. "Parental Cultural Capital and Educational Attainment in the Netherlands: A Refinement of the Cultural Capital Perspective." *Sociology of Education* 73:92–111.

DiPrete, Thomas A., and Claudia Buchmann. 2006. "Gender-Specific Trends in the Values of Education and the Emerging Gender Gap in College Completion." *Demography* 43:1–24.

Duru-Bellat, Marie. 1988. *Le fonctionnement de l'orientation. Genèse des inégalités sociales à l'école.* Lausanne, Switzerland: Delachaux et Niestlé.

———. 1996. "Social Inequalities in French Secondary Schools: From Figures to Theories." *British Journal of Sociology of Education* 17:341–50.

———. 2009. *Le mérite contre la justice.* Paris: Presses de Sciences Po.

Duru-Bellat, Marie, Jean-Pierre Jarousse, and Alain Mingat. 1993. "Les scolarités de la maternelle au lycée. Étapes et processus dans la production des inégalités sociales." *Revue française de sociologie* 34:43–60.

Duru-Bellat, Marie, Annick Kieffer, and David Reimer. 2008. "Patterns of Social Inequalities in Access to Higher Education in France and Germany." *International Journal of Comparative Sociology* 49:347–68.

Erikson, Robert, John H. Goldthorpe, Michelle Jackson, Meir Yaish, and David R. Cox. 2005. "On Class Differentials in Educational Attainment." *Proceedings of the National Academy of Sciences* 102:9730–33.

Erikson, Robert, and Jan O. Jonsson, eds. 1996. *Can Education be Equalized? The Swedish Case in Comparative Perspective*. Boulder, CO: Westview.

Fairlie, Robert W. 2005. "An Extension of the Blinder-Oaxaca Decomposition Technique to Logit and Probit Models." *Journal of Economic and Social Measurement* 30:305–16.

Garnier, Maurice A., and Lawrence E. Raffalovich. 1984. "The Evolution of Equality of Educational Opportunities in France." *Sociology of Education* 57:1–11.

Gerber, Theodore P., and Sin Yi Cheung. 2008. "Horizontal Stratification in Postsecondary Education: Forms, Explanations, and Implications." *Annual Review of Sociology* 34:299–318.

Girard, Alain, and Henri Bastide. 1963. "La stratification sociale et la démocratisation de l'enseignement." *Population* 18:435–72.

———. 1973. "De la fin des études élémentaires à l'entrée dans la vie professionnelle ou à l'Université. La marche d'une promotion de 1962 à 1972." *Population* 28:571–94.

Goldin, Claudia, Lawrence F. Katz, and Ilyana Kuziemk. 2006. "The Homecoming of the American College Women: The Reversal of the College Gender Gap." *Journal of Economic Perspectives* 20:133–56.

Goldthorpe, John H. 1996a. "Class Analysis and the Reorientation of Class Theory: The Case of Persisting Differentials in Educational Attainment." *British Journal of Sociology* 47:481–505.

———. 1996b. "Problems of 'Meritocracy.'" In *Can Education Be Equalized? The Swedish Case in Comparative Perspective*, edited by Robert Erikson and Jan O. Jonsson, 255–87. Boulder, CO: Westview.

Heath, Anthony F., Catherine Rothon, and Elina Kilpi. 2008. "The Second Generation in Western Europe: Education, Unemployment, and Occupational Attainment." *Annual Review of Sociology* 34:211–35.

Ichou, Mathieu, and Louis-André Vallet. 2011. "Do All Roads Lead to Inequality? Trends in French Upper Secondary School Analysed with Four Longitudinal Surveys." *Oxford Review of Education* 37:167–94.

INED Survey. 1962–1972. "De la fin des études élémentaires à l'entrée dans la vie professionnelle ou à l'université. La marche d'une promotion de 1962 à 1972." Paris: Institut National d'Études Démographiques.

INSEE (Institut National de la Statistique et des Études Économiques). 2006. "Note by Fabrice Murat: Calcul d'une pondération globale en 2006 pour le panel d'élèves entrés en 6e en 1995." Direction des Statistiques Démographiques et Sociales. Paris: Institut National de la Statistique et des Études Économiques.

Ishida, Hiroshi, Walter Müller, and John M. Ridge. 1995. "Class Origin, Class Destination, and Education: A Cross-National Study of Ten Industrial Nations." *American Journal of Sociology* 101:145–93.

Jackson, Michelle, Robert Erikson, John H. Goldthorpe, and Meir Yaish. 2007. "Primary and Secondary Effects in Class Differentials in Educational Attainment: The Transition to A-Level Courses in England and Wales." *Acta Sociologica* 50:211–29.

Jonsson, Jan O., Colin Mills, and Walter Müller. 1996. "A Half Century of Increasing Educational Openness? Social Class, Gender and Educational Attainment in Sweden, Germany and Britain." In *Can Education be Equalized? The Swedish Case in Comparative Perspective*, edited by Robert Erikson and Jan O. Jonsson, 183–206. Boulder, CO: Westview.

Karlson, Kristian B., Anders Holm, and Richard Breen. 2012. "Comparing Regression Coefficients between Same-Sample Nested Models Using Logit and Probit: A New Method." *Sociological Methodology* 42.

Lareau, Annette, and Elliot B. Weininger. 2003. "Cultural Capital in Educational Research: A Critical Assessment." *Theory and Society* 32:567–606.

Lelièvre, Claude. 1990. *Histoire des institutions scolaires (1789–1989)*. Paris: Nathan.

Lucas, Samuel R. 2001. "Effectively Maintained Inequality: Education Transitions, Track Mobility, and Social Background Effects." *American Journal of Sociology* 106:1642–90.

Mare, Robert D. 1981. "Change and Stability in Educational Stratification." *American Sociological Review* 46:72–87.

Maurice, Marc. 1989. "Méthode comparative et analyse sociétale : les implications théoriques des comparaisons internationales." *Sociologie du Travail* 31:175–90.

McNamee, Stephen J., and Robert K. Miller. 2004. *The Meritocracy Myth*. Lanham, MD: Rowman and Littlefield.

Merle, Pierre. 2007. *Les notes. Secrets de fabrication*. Paris: Presses Universitaires de France.

Ministry of Education Panel Study. 1995–2006. "Panel d'élèves du second degré, recrutement 1995." Direction de l'Évaluation, de la Prospective et de la Performance. Paris: Ministère de l'Éducation nationale.

Mood, Carina. 2010. "Logistic Regression: Why We Cannot Do What We Think We Can Do, and What We Can Do about It." *European Sociological Review* 26:67–82.

Nash, Roy. 2006. "Controlling for 'Ability': A Conceptual and Empirical Study of Primary and Secondary Effects." *British Journal of Sociology of Education* 27:157–72.

Oaxaca, Ronald L. 1973. "Male-Female Wage Differentials in Urban Labor Markets." *International Economic Review* 14:693–709.

Paradeise, Catherine. 1990. "Principes et méthodes. Les théories de l'acteur." *Les Cahiers Français* 247:31–38.

Prost, Antoine. 1992. *L'Enseignement s'est-il démocratisén? Les élèves des lycées et collèges de l'agglomération d'Orléans de 1945 à 1990.* Paris: Presses Universitaires de France.

———. 1997. *Éducation, société et politiques. Une histoire de l'enseignement de 1945 à nos jours.* Paris: Seuil.

———. 1999. "Schooling and Social Stratification: Paradoxes of the Reform of the Middle School in 20th-Century France." In *The Comprehensive School Experiment Revisited: Evidence from Western Europe,* edited by Achim Leschinsky and Karl Ulrich Mayer, 40–63. Frankfurt, Germany: Peter Lang.

Sartori, Giovanni. 1991. "Comparing and Miscomparing." *Journal of Theoretical Politics* 3:243–57.

Selz, Marion, and Louis-André Vallet. 2006. "La démocratisation de l'enseignement et son paradoxe apparent." *Données sociales. La société française (Édition 2006),* 101–7. Paris: INSEE.

Shavit, Yossi, and Hans-Peter Blossfeld, eds. 1993. *Persistent Inequality: Changing Educational Attainment in Thirteen Countries.* Boulder, CO: Westview.

Smith, Herbert L., and Maurice A. Garnier. 1986. "Association between Background and Educational Attainment in France." *Sociological Methods and Research* 14:317–44.

Thélot, Claude, and Louis-André Vallet. 2000. "La réduction des inégalités sociales devant l'école depuis le début du siècle." *Économie et Statistique* 334:3–32.

Vallet, Louis-André. 2004. "The Dynamics of Inequality of Educational Opportunity in France: Change in the Association between Social Background and Education in Thirteen Five-Year Birth Cohorts (1908–1972)." ISA Research Committee 28 on Social Stratification and Mobility Spring Conference, Neuchâtel, Switzerland, May 7–9.

Vallet, Louis-André, and Jean-Paul Caille. 1996. "Les élèves étrangers ou issus de l'immigration dans l'école et le collège français. Une étude d'ensemble." *Les dossiers d'Éducation et Formations* 67:1–153.

Vallet, Louis-André, and Marion Selz. 2007. "Évolution historique de l'inégalité des chances devant l'école : des méthodes et des résultats revisités." *Éducation et Formations* 74:65–74.

Zéroulou, Zaïhia. 1988. "La réussite scolaire des enfants d'immigrés : l'apport d'une approche en termes de mobilisation." *Revue française de sociologie* 29:447–70.

CHAPTER SIX

Social-Origin Inequalities in Educational Careers in Italy

Performance or Decision Effects?

Dalit Contini and Andrea Scagni

A notable feature of Italian society is low average educational attainment in comparison with other late industrial countries (OECD 2009). Over time, the proportion of students obtaining upper secondary education has increased in line with other countries, but the gap between Italy and other nations is still sizable with respect to participation in tertiary education. Italy is also characterized by a low degree of social mobility compared to other European countries (Breen 2004) and the United States (Checchi, Ichino, and Rustichini 1999). Comparative research also points to a high level of inequality of educational opportunity (IEO) in Italy, and although many countries witnessed decreasing IEO over the second half of the 20th century, little change is observed in Italy (Shavit and Blossfeld 1993; Cobalti and Schizzerotto 1994; Shavit and Westerbeek 1998; Breen et al. 2009; Barone 2009). As suggested by Checchi (2003), low intergenerational mobility could be an important limiting factor in educational attainment.

Class differentials in educational attainment can be considered to be a consequence of the operation of primary and secondary effects (Boudon 1974). The former, also known as performance effects, describe the influence of social origin on measured academic ability early in a child's educational career: for example, advantaged parents will be better able to sustain and motivate schoolwork and provide a stimulating environment for their offspring. The latter, also known as decision effects, operate through the choices that students and their families make within the educational system, given the student's level of measured academic ability. A rational action approach that assumes that families wish to avoid intergenerational downward mobility (e.g., Goldthorpe 1996; Breen and Goldthorpe 1997) provides a theoretical explanation for the evidence that, at given levels of ability, schooling decisions vary by social background.[1]

In this chapter we evaluate the relative contributions of primary and secondary effects in creating educational inequalities in Italy at the transitions to upper secondary and tertiary education. After lower secondary education, students can choose between a variety of programs, broadly classified into *lyceums* (constituting the academic track) and technical and vocational schools that are more oriented toward the labor market. In the empirical analysis of the first transition (to upper secondary education), we analyze the divide between the academic track and other educational programs; despite all children with an upper secondary school diploma having access to university, continuation rates are much higher for those from the academic track. For the later transition we consider whether students enroll in university within three years of attaining the diploma.

Given the absence of longitudinal educational surveys in Italy, the empirical analyses are based on a cross-sectional repeated survey of secondary school graduates carried out by the National Statistical Institute for the purpose of investigating transitions to tertiary education and the labor market after upper secondary education. The survey has been conducted every three years since 1998 on approximately 20,000 respondents per graduation cohort, and it collects information on individual educational careers up to three years after attainment of the diploma. Since children who do not enter upper secondary school or who eventually drop out before attaining the degree are not interviewed, the survey is not perfectly suited for studying transitions from lower to upper secondary school. We can view this issue as a problem of nonrandom sample selection; as we show below, if sample selection is ignored, results are biased. Conventional econometric methods for correcting sample selection bias do not apply to our case, and for this reason, we attempt to solve the problem with a simple ad hoc nonparametric approach by employing additional sources of data. First, we use aggregate administrative information supplied by the Ministry of Education and the Population Census. Second, we use a cross-sectional survey of a nationally representative sample of young people aged 15–34.[2] However, sample sizes for each birth cohort are small, and for this reason we use these data in an auxiliary way: (a) to provide information that will allow us to account for sample selection in the graduate survey and (b) to derive a second direct estimate of primary and secondary effects.

In the next section we describe the main features of the Italian educational system. We then review the literature on educational inequality in Italy, before describing the data and variables. Next, we outline the methodological issues faced in the analysis related to specific features of both the available surveys and the Italian educational system. We present results for the transition to upper secondary education and the transition to tertiary education.[3] In our concluding remarks we suggest possible explanations for the high level of IEO in Italy and our findings on the relative importance of secondary effects.

THE ITALIAN EDUCATIONAL SYSTEM

Over the last 50 years the Italian schooling system underwent several major reforms that reduced barriers to accessing education and limited its stratification (Cobalti and Schizzerotto 1994). In today's educational system, children enter the school system at age 6 and follow an eight-year compulsory education period, formally divided into two cycles: primary education, lasting five years, and lower secondary education, lasting three. The current system was established in 1962, when the former lower secondary school system, which included an academic track and a dead-end vocational track, was replaced by a unified three-year comprehensive middle school. Since 1923, education had been compulsory up until age 14, but it was only in 1962 that the law was actively enforced. In recent years the school-leaving age was further increased from 14 to 16 (although for the birth cohorts analyzed here, schooling was compulsory only up until age 14).

Lower secondary school ends with a national examination. After this examination, students choose from a variety of upper secondary educational programs, broadly classified into academic, technical, and vocational tracks. There are no performance-related admission restrictions. The academic track includes various types of lyceums: the *liceo classico*, emphasizing humanities; the *liceo scientifico*, favoring mathematics and science; and the *liceo linguistico*, specializing in foreign languages. The sociopedagogical lyceum (formerly called *istituto magistrale*) was originally designed to prepare for primary school teaching. Although university qualifications are now required, until a few years ago this lyceum provided direct access to a teaching career, and for this reason the sociopedagogical lyceum is not always treated as if it is part of the academic track. Given its specific focus, a similar argument also applies to the artistic lyceum. In contrast, technical schools (*istituti tecnici*) combine general education with vocational training and are considered to be less demanding than lyceums. Lyceums and technical educational programs generally last for five years, while vocational education (provided by *istituti professionali*) lasts for a minimum of three and up to a maximum of five years.[4] After five years of schooling students take a school-type-specific national examination (*esame di maturità*) and eventually attain the upper secondary school diploma.

Upper secondary enrollment has become practically universal. The proportions of students in the different tracks have changed significantly over the last 15 years: the share of children in the academic track has risen from 25 to 31 percent; that in technical, sociopedagogical, and art schools has declined from 53 to 45 percent; and that in vocational education has remained quite stable.

The tertiary-education system in Italy is university based, while higher vocational education is very limited. Access to university, formerly possible only for students with an academic degree, was liberalized in the 1969 reform, which extended eligibility to all those with five-year upper secondary educational qualifications. There are no admission requirements related to previous performance, although transition rates differ markedly between tracks.[5] University degrees have a legal value, in that they certify that the qualification has been attained. The standard required to obtain a degree is officially the same across all higher-education institutions, and as a consequence the prestige of the university awarding the qualification is not particularly important for students' and potential employers' decision processes.

The Bologna process, which aimed to harmonize the structure of university programs across European states, led in 2001 to a major restructuring of the Italian tertiary-education system.[6] This restructuring meant that four- to six-year programs, depending on the discipline, were transformed into three-year undergraduate degree programs and optional two-year master's-level degrees. The shorter undergraduate degree was expected to increase enrollment, reduce dropout rates, decrease inequality of opportunity, and allow faster entrance into the labor market. University attendance indeed witnessed a significant increase immediately after the reform, from 60 to 75 percent, mainly driven by more students coming from the technical track. However, just a few years later enrollment rates fell back to 62 percent, suggesting that the effect of the reform was temporary. Two of the four birth cohorts included in our analysis experienced the postreform system, so despite the very short observation window, we can observe short-term changes in IEO associated with the new arrangement.

The Italian educational system is in the main a public system, and only a modest share of children attend private schools (in 2002 approximately 7 percent at the primary school level, 3.5 percent at lower secondary level, and 6 percent at upper secondary level). With the exception of a few Catholic schools, Italian private schools at the secondary level provide on average lower-quality education than do public schools, and they often play a remedial role for students from rich families who have been held back by repeating school years (Cappellari 2004; Bertola, Checchi, and Oppedisano 2007; Brunello and Rocco 2008).

It is worth mentioning here that a major problem afflicting the Italian educational system is the large attainment gap between the north and south of the country. Bratti, Checchi, and Filippin (2007) report wide differentials in Program for International Student Assessment (PISA) scores and show that the north–south divide is largely attributable to differences in endowments—of individuals, schools, and socioeconomic environment—although there are also differences in school effectiveness between the north and the south.

An overview of transitions occurring throughout the school career for children born in 1985 (the most recent birth cohort of those analyzed here) is shown in Figure 6.1. According to the Population Census of 2001, approximately 3.5 percent of the children in this cohort do not complete compulsory schooling, while 23 percent of the birth cohort leave the educational system before attaining the upper secondary school diploma.[7] About 25 percent of students moving to upper secondary education choose the academic track, with vocational schools capturing a similar share, while about half the children opt for technical programs.[8] Among those attaining the upper secondary degree, nearly 31 percent come from the academic track. The difference between enrollment and completion is due to the significantly higher dropout rates observed for the technical and vocational tracks compared to lyceums and to school transfers (usually induced by poor performance, with transfers occurring in the direction of easier educational programs). Overall, 64 percent of those who are eligible enter tertiary education. However, differences between tracks are marked:

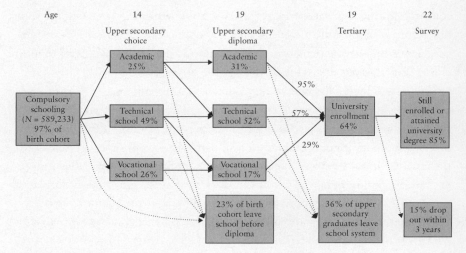

Figure 6.1.   Transitions within the educational system for the 1985 birth cohort

SOURCE: MIUR. *Dieci anni di scuola statale 1998–2007* (upper secondary choices). Our calculations were based on data of the ISTAT survey *Percorsi di studio e di lavoro dei diplomati 2007* (upper secondary diploma and tertiary education); data of ISTAT 2001 Population Census (birth cohort size, percentage leaving before upper secondary diploma).

NOTE: Percentages in boxes refer to the entire cohort at specific ages, with the exception of age 19, where the share of each school track is conditional on enrollment and refers to the 77% who did not leave school before diploma. Percentages in lines between boxes are transition rates of each group.

transition rates vary from over 95 percent for academic track leavers to 29 percent for vocational track leavers. Nearly 15 percent of the children who had enrolled in university report that they have dropped out when interviewed three years after the conclusion of upper secondary education. Although reliable estimates of students leaving the system before they attain a university degree are not available, we believe that this number is considerably larger.[9] Note that Italy lacks a homogeneous body of official statistics on the educational system; for this reason the figures reported in Figure 6.1 are based on a variety of data sources—administrative and survey data—and therefore full consistency is not assured.

RESEARCH ON IEO IN ITALY

The association between social origins and educational attainment seems to be particularly strong in Italy compared to other European countries (Breen et al. 2009) and the United States (Hertz et al. 2008; Checchi, Ichino, and Rustichini 1999). Similarly, in comparative studies, Italy shows a particularly strong association between parents' and child's class position (Breen 2004). Furthermore, Pisati and Schizzerotto show that social fluidity in Italy changed little over the 1980s and 1990s (2004).

Evidence on the evolution of IEO in Italy is inconclusive. Cobalti and Schizzerotto (1993) report no appreciable change in the extent of class inequalities related to the odds of attaining various educational levels for birth cohorts from the 1920s to early 1960s, a conclusion revisited by Shavit and Westerbeek (1998), who find declining effects of father's education on the odds of completing lower levels of the educational hierarchy. These declining effects carried over slightly to the unconditional odds of obtaining an upper secondary school degree, but this did not contribute to an equalization in the chances of attending university. Breen et al. (2009) report a decline in class inequalities in most European countries, but the change is not statistically significant in Italy. Checchi, Fiorio, and Leonardi (2008) show that, despite educational expansion, the differential in the probability of obtaining a university degree related to parental educational levels has not changed substantially over the last 60 years, and Checchi (2003) suggests that this persisting weak intergenerational educational mobility could be the reason for the low level of average educational attainment in Italy.

Several studies focus on upper secondary school transitions. Strong social-origin effects in the type of secondary school attended are reported by Cappellari (2004), Checchi and Flabbi (2007), Mocetti (2008), and Contini and Scagni (2011a). Cappellari employs the first wave of the survey of secondary school graduates that we analyze here and finds that school choices (academic or vocational educational programs, public or private schools) heavily depend on social origin. Checchi and Flabbi (2007) and Contini and Scagni (2011a) exploit PISA data relating to 15-year-olds (Italian children were surveyed one year after tracking had occurred). Checchi and Flabbi (2007) estimate the direct effect of social origin on the probability of entering the academic track, given PISA scores; in comparing Italy and Germany they find higher inequality in the former. Contini and Scagni (2011a) focus instead on total inequality and compare Italy, Germany, and the Netherlands. They observe that Italy falls between Germany (with the highest IEO) and the Netherlands (with the lowest). Using the Italian

Labor Force Survey—conducted by the National Statistical Institute—and aggregate administrative data, Mocetti (2008) investigates the determinants of upper secondary school continuation and track choice and finds that school failure is highly correlated with family background and strongly influences later choices. On the whole, the research on transitions to upper secondary school underlines the existence of high social inequalities at this stage of the school career in Italy.

The transition to higher education is investigated by Cappellari (2004), who reports that graduates from the academic track have a higher probability of continuing to tertiary education and perform better in university; on the other hand, attaining a nonacademic type of diploma improves the quality of the school-to-work transition in terms of employment probabilities (but not in terms of remuneration). These results imply a strong indirect effect of social origins on tertiary education operating via upper secondary school choices. He also finds a sizable direct effect of family background. Bratti, Checchi, and de Blasio (2008) study the effect of the expansion of higher education on IEO during the 1990s. A much wider range of curricula was established at that time, along with establishment of new institutions in small towns. The authors argue that since the expansion was not based on cost-benefit analyses but consisted instead of the widespread allocation of public funds across regions, it acted as an exogenous policy change. They evaluate whether the increased supply of tertiary institutions created a higher demand for tertiary education and indeed find that students had an increased probability of enrolling in tertiary education, although they were not more likely to obtain a degree. Middle-class students benefited most from the reform. The impact of the Bologna process is analyzed in Cappellari and Lucifora (2008): since the reform was not anticipated, it represents an ideal social experiment whose effects can be evaluated. The authors find a 10 percentage point rise in the probability of university enrollment among secondary school graduates, with the growth concentrated among students from backgrounds with low parental occupational and educational levels. Although the overall probability of dropping out increased slightly, on the whole the more able students seem to have benefited from the reform.[10]

Research on primary and secondary effects in educational transitions in Italy is limited. Contini and Scagni (2011b) analyze upper secondary transitions; the work presented in this chapter employs additional data sources and extends the analysis to tertiary education.

DATA AND VARIABLES

Data

No extensive panel survey providing information on schooling careers is available, and for this reason we use two cross-sectional surveys. The main source is the survey "Percorsi di studio e di lavoro dei diplomati," conducted by the National Statistical Institute (ISTAT) every three years since 1998. Each wave includes data on approximately 20,000 upper secondary school graduates, with the aim of investigating the transition from secondary school to tertiary education and the labor market. Individuals are interviewed three years after the attainment of the diploma and longitudinal information is collected retrospectively. We use data from the 1998, 2001, 2004, and 2007 waves, covering (disregarding repetitions) birth cohorts from 1976 to 1985.[11]

The survey is well suited for studying the transition to university. However, when it comes to investigating the transition to upper secondary education, the sample is self-selected: the entire population of children exiting lower secondary school is of interest, but early school leavers are not interviewed. If dropouts mainly belong to lower social strata, when sample selection is ignored both the social-background differentials in the performance distribution and the effect of social background on school choices will be underestimated. To overcome these problems and account for selection bias, we study the transition to upper secondary school by complementing the ISTAT survey data with (a) aggregate administrative data provided by ISTAT (population census and school-system administrative data) and the Ministry of Education and (b) the survey "Condizione Giovanile in Italia," conducted every four years by the Socio-economic and Political Research Institute IARD and including data on young people aged 15–34 (Buzzi, Cavalli, and de Lillo 2007). The survey is designed to investigate young people's attitudes and behavior and includes information on school careers. However, final upper secondary grades are not collected, and samples are small.[12] For these reasons we use IARD data in two different ways: (a) to provide information that will be used to account for sample selection in the ISTAT survey and (b) to derive another direct estimate of primary and secondary effects at the first transition, despite sample size problems, for comparison purposes.

Variables: Transition to Upper Secondary School (Age 14)

Dependent Variable. Upper secondary school track (S_2). Despite the variety of different educational programs at the upper secondary school level and the broad classification into three tracks (academic, technical, and professional), we follow the common practice of focusing on the divide between the academic track and all other choices, including exit from the system, to allow cross-country comparability. In the academic track we include classical, scientific, and linguistic lyceums.

Explanatory Variables

Performance (A_1). Our measure of academic performance is the result from the lower secondary final examination, a national assessment of all disciplines, administered by a school examination board and an external president nominated by the Ministry of Education. The examination is not standardized, but national guidelines for evaluation are provided to ensure some comparability. Grades follow a coarse four-level scale (pass, good, very good, excellent).[13]

Social background (SB). A three-category parental education variable (primary and lower secondary, upper secondary, and tertiary) is defined according to the highest educational level of the parents, whether father or mother.[14] We do not use parental class (as do other chapters of this book and our own analyses of tertiary-education transitions), because we cannot obtain the relevant data needed for sample selection correction from official statistics.

Variables: Transition to Tertiary Education (Age 19)

Dependent Variable. University enrollment (S_3). The dependent variable measures whether the secondary school graduate entered tertiary education within three years of graduation.

Explanatory Variables

Performance (A_2). As a measure of performance we take upper secondary final-examination scores. The examinations are designed and regulated by the Ministry of Education, which also defines broad evaluation criteria. Assessments are designed to correspond to the particular goals of each educational program, so they are school-type specific. Grades range from 60 to 100 for all school types, hence the same score may correspond to quite different levels and kinds of competencies (in Figure 6.2 we show that final score distributions for 2004 graduates are very similar across tracks). As a consequence, grades are not a good measure of proficiency in and of themselves: grades and the educational programs taken together are a much

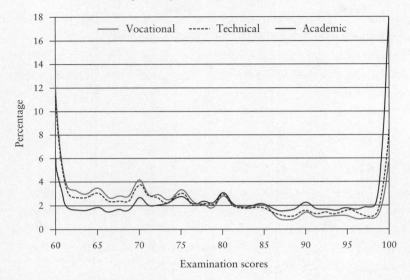

Figure 6.2.   Upper secondary final-examination score distribution in 2004, by track

NOTE: Distributions are analytically interpolated to smooth out irregularities.

better signal of student competency and capacity to successfully complete tertiary education. Upper secondary final-examination scores are affected by another peculiarity compared to the grading systems at work in many other European countries. The grade distributions depicted in Figure 6.2 are clearly not Gaussian and exhibit strong heaping effects on 10s and in particular on the lowest and highest values: this unusual shape is a strong signal of discretion in grade assignment. This suggests that treating grades as if they had a Gaussian distribution would be inappropriate; thus we do not use the standard methodology described in Chapter 2 but instead use a nonparametric version.

Upper secondary school degree (S_2^*). The attained degree in secondary school is treated as a nominal variable with three levels, corresponding to the academic, technical, and vocational tracks; we distinguish here between technical and vocational programs because they differ greatly in curricular content and in tertiary-education participation rates.[15]

Social background (SB). We refer to two alternative indicators: parental education (already described for secondary school transitions) and parental class. Both variables are defined according to the dominance principle: we use either the father's or mother's level, whichever is higher. As regards parental class, we stick as closely as possible to the classification employed by Erikson et al. (2005), which distinguishes the working class, intermediate class, and salariat. We present our results on parental class in the web appendix.

SETUP OF THE ANALYSIS

Transition to Upper Secondary Education (Age 14)

We now turn to the setup of the analysis. In this section we provide a brief overview of the methodology employed to decompose overall inequality into primary and secondary effects (fully described in Chapter 2) and the specific features of the Italian case, and we outline the strategies adopted to overcome sample selection.

Let SB be family social background (typically measured by parental education or class), S_2 the upper secondary school track ($S_2 = 1$ for the academic track, 0 otherwise), and A_1 the lower secondary school final-examination grade. Since final grades follow a coarse four-level scale, the commonly applied normal approximation for A_1 proposed by Erikson et al. (2005) is not appropriate. In this context, we decompose the probability P to enter the academic track given social background as follows:

$$P(S_2 = 1 \mid SB = j) = \sum_{A_1} P(A_1 \mid SB = j) P(S_2 = 1 \mid A_1, SB = j), \qquad (6.1)$$

whose observed counterpart is the percentage of those belonging to social stratum j enrolling in the academic track. On the other hand,

$$p_{jk} = \sum_{A_1} P(A_1 \mid SB = j) P(S_2 = 1 \mid A_1, SB = k) \qquad (6.2)$$

and

$$p_{kj} = \sum_{A_1} P(A_1 \mid SB = k) P(S_2 = 1 \mid A_1, SB = j) \qquad (6.3)$$

are counterfactual, or synthesized, probabilities, the transition probabilities that an individual would experience if he or she had the performance distribution of social class j and the transition probability of social class k (or vice versa). Comparing estimates of p_{jj} and p_{kj} provides information on primary effects, while comparing estimates of p_{jj} and p_{jk} provides information on secondary effects. Differentials between observed and synthesized probabilities are measured by odds ratios and then turned into log odds ratios to allow the definition of an additive decomposition of the total effect of *SB* on S_2 (see Chapter 2).

We are interested in the entire cohort of lower secondary school leavers; however, since ISTAT data refer to secondary school graduates (excluding dropouts), the derived observed distribution of performance and the distribution of the transition probabilities generally differ from the distributions of interest. This is a problem of nonrandom sample selection: as we show below, ignoring it leads to biased results. Note that conventional methods for the correction of sample selection bias (such as Heckman's procedure) do not apply in our case.[16] In what follows we outline our strategies to overcome these problems.

Performance Distribution. Let *G* be a binary variable equal to 1 if the child has attained an upper secondary school degree (in any of the available tracks) and 0 otherwise. The observable distribution $P(A_1 \mid SB, G = 1)$ and the distribution of interest $P(A_1 \mid SB)$ are related by

$$P(A_1 \mid SB, G = 1) = P(A_1 \mid SB) \frac{P(G = 1 \mid A_1, SB)}{P(G = 1 \mid SB)}. \tag{6.4}$$

The two distributions overlap if the probability of graduation is not affected by performance once social background is controlled for, but this would be an unusual situation in practice. Thus, the performance distribution given social background directly derived from the ISTAT survey is likely to be biased: we expect it to overestimate performance, in particular for the lower social strata.

We obtain the distribution of interest by exploiting equation (6.4). The correction factor cannot be estimated directly with official data: the marginal graduation probability at the national level is available but not by performance nor by any measure of social background. However, we can derive a rough indirect estimate of $P(A_1 \mid SB)$ by employing aggregate data on lower secondary final grades and parental education (see the web appendix for details).[17] The correction factor can also be estimated with the IARD survey data; moreover, despite small sample size, this survey can be exploited to derive a direct estimate of the distribution of ability.

Transition Probability. We wish to estimate $P(S_2 = 1 \mid A_1, SB)$, but the ISTAT survey provides an estimate of only $P(S_2 = 1 \mid A_1, SB, G = 1)$. The following relation holds:

$$P(S_2 = 1 \mid A_1, SB, G = 1) = P(S_2 = 1 \mid A_1, SB) \frac{P(G = 1 \mid S_2 = 1, A_1, SB)}{P(G = 1 \mid A_1, SB)}. \quad (6.5)$$

Note that S_2 represents the first choice undertaken after lower secondary schooling (regardless of possible subsequent failures or changes of track). The observed distribution and the distribution of interest coincide if the probability of attaining an upper secondary degree (any degree, regardless of the track) does not depend on which track is first chosen, given performance and social background. Correction factors in (6.5) are estimated with IARD data: the evidence is that track choice does affect the likelihood of attaining the diploma, even after controlling for social background and previous school performance. These estimates are applied to correct the distribution derived from the ISTAT survey. IARD data are also used to obtain direct estimates of the transition probabilities, although the sample size further reduces (see note 12), because lower secondary final grades are collected only in the year 2000 survey.

Summing Up. Since only upper secondary school graduates are interviewed, the ISTAT survey is affected by sample selection and provides biased estimates of overall inequality and of primary and secondary effects in secondary school transitions. Correction factors derived from (6.4) and (6.5) can be estimated with IARD survey data, which, however, suffer from small sample size. Correction factors for the performance distribution are also estimated from official aggregate data and the Population Census. These factors are combined with the corresponding estimates derived from the ISTAT survey: two final performance distributions and one transition function given performance are produced, giving rise to two alternative estimates of overall inequality and of the relative contribution of primary and secondary effects. A third estimate is provided by directly employing IARD data. Summarizing, we conducted the analyses using the following combinations of data sources:

   a. *Main data source*: ISTAT survey
       Correction factor for the ability distribution: Official data source
       Correction factor for the transition function: IARD survey
   b. *Main data source*: ISTAT survey

    Correction factor for the ability distribution: IARD survey
    Correction factor for the transition function: IARD survey
  c. *Data source*: IARD survey (no correction needed)

Combining estimates from different sources is obviously not optimal: it involves different nonsampling errors and makes sampling standard errors difficult to evaluate. Nevertheless, we think that the approach is still valuable. First, other options are simply not available. Second, and more importantly, we produce alternative estimates, derived from independent data sources, that can be compared. As we show, the substantive conclusions are quite robust, giving rise to a clear picture of IEO in secondary school transitions in Italy.

Transition to Tertiary Education

All secondary school leavers are eligible for tertiary education in Italy, provided that they have attained a five-year program degree. However, as we have shown above, markedly different transition rates are observed between educational programs: the great majority of academic track school leavers move to university while only a small fraction of students from vocational schools do. As a consequence, when analyzing transitions to tertiary education we should also take the school track into account. As we discussed above, there is an additional reason for doing so; final secondary school scores are not a good measure of proficiency in and of themselves, and to be meaningful they should be considered together with the educational program.

There are two strategies of analysis: we may adopt a conditional perspective, in which previous choices are taken as given, or an unconditional perspective, in which the focus is on overall IEO. We outline these strategies below.

Conditional Analysis. Let S_3 be a binary variable that equals 1 if the student enrolls in university within three years of attaining the diploma and 0 otherwise. The object of interest is $P(S_3 = 1 \mid SB, S_2^*, G = 1)$, with S_2^* representing the graduation track.[18] We consider past choices (and their outcomes) as given, ignoring IEO in the probability of attaining a secondary school degree in the different tracks and focusing on additional IEO. We accomplish this by separately analyzing school leavers from each track. As we highlighted above, grades in the upper secondary final examination are more comparable within tracks, so they can be used to decompose total inequality into primary and secondary effects in this context.

In general, we expect social background to exert a much weaker influence at this stage. The reason is that the decision to enter tertiary education has largely been anticipated by the choice of secondary school; despite the absence of formal restrictions in university enrollment, families are well aware that the academic track is designed to provide general education and prepare for university, while the other tracks prepare for the labor market. Moreover, by the end of secondary school, children have already been exposed to a selection process, which is stronger for the lower social strata; in fact higher levels of performance and motivation are needed for children of disadvantaged background to successfully complete the more demanding educational programs. Hence social origin should play a more limited role at this point of the educational career.

Unconditional Analysis. There is also an interest in assessing total inequality in tertiary-education enrollment. In this perspective, the aim is to evaluate social-origin differentials:

$$P(S_3 = 1 \mid SB) = P(S_3 = 1 \mid SB, G = 1) P(G = 1 \mid SB). \qquad (6.6)$$

This analysis also requires us to take sample selection into account. We estimate the probability of entering tertiary education given eligibility from the ISTAT graduate survey data, and we use estimates of the graduation probabilities to account for sample selection (see Table 6.1).

Primary and Secondary Effects Decomposition. The decomposition for the conditional analysis is based on

$$P\left(S_3 = 1 \mid SB, S_2^*, G = 1\right) = \sum_{A_2} P\left(S_3 = 1 \mid A_2, SB, S_2^*, G = 1\right)$$
$$\times f\left(A_2 \mid SB, S_2^*, G = 1\right) \quad \forall S_2^*, \qquad (6.7)$$

while that for the unconditional analysis is based on

$$P\left(S_3 = 1 \mid SB\right) = \sum_{A_2} \sum_{S_2^*} P\left(S_3 = 1 \mid A_2, S_2^*, SB, G = 1\right)$$
$$\times f\left(A_2, S_2^* \mid SB, G = 1\right) P\left(G = 1 \mid SB\right), \qquad (6.8)$$

where the sum over G is omitted because the transition probability given $G = 0$ is 0. Changing social background in the tertiary-education transition function given performance provides information on secondary effects;

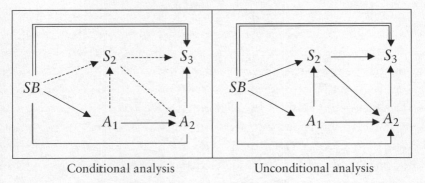

Conditional analysis   Unconditional analysis

Figure 6.3. Primary and secondary effects in tertiary educational transitions

NOTE: Double solid arrows represent secondary effects, single solid arrows represent primary effects, and dotted arrows represent ignored effects.

changing it in all other terms provides information on primary effects. From this perspective, *secondary effects* are defined in both the conditional and the unconditional analyses as the net effect of social origin, given past schooling history (educational program and performance) up to the onset of university studies. *Primary effects* are defined by difference.

Consider the charts in Figure 6.3, depicting all the relevant effects involved in educational choices, at the upper secondary and tertiary levels (to keep the charts simple, let first-choice track S_2 and graduation track S_2^* coincide). Social background affects performance and choices at all levels of schooling; performance is affected by social origins and, at the transition to university, by previous performance; and school choices are influenced, besides by social origins, by performance at the time the choice is undertaken.

When we consider tertiary-educational choices conditional on S_2 (Figure 6.3, left panel) we implicitly ignore the mechanisms that lead to the choice of S_2 (all the paths going to S_2), how that track affects university enrollment, and how it affects performance at the end of upper secondary school A_2 (all the paths going from S_2). If as we have stated above, secondary effects are defined as the net effect of social background given track and performance, primary effects capture the remaining relations: in this case, the influence of social background on university enrollment S_3 occurring via performance but not via the school track.

On the other hand, all the paths connecting SB to S_3 are considered in the unconditional analysis (Figure 6.3, right panel), which refers ideally to an entire birth cohort of children. If primary effects are defined by difference with respect to secondary effects, primary effects here capture the fact that children from advantaged backgrounds perform better during compulsory schooling, have a higher propensity to choose lyceums because they perform better in compulsory school—but also at given levels of performance—and perform better during secondary school and are more likely to obtain an upper secondary school degree. For all these reasons, they are more prone to enter tertiary education. In this sense, naming these effects primary effects might be somewhat improper, because they incorporate decision effects at earlier stages of the educational career.

PROBABILITY OF ATTAINING THE SECONDARY SCHOOL DEGREE GIVEN SOCIAL BACKGROUND

To correct for sample selection in the ISTAT survey—in the upper secondary education transition and for the unconditional analysis of the tertiary-education transition—we evaluate the correction factors in equations (6.4), (6.5), and (6.6). These are ratios of different versions of the probability of attaining a secondary school degree given social background, measured by the highest parental educational level. No official figures are provided by national institutions, so we have derived our own estimates.[19] The estimation procedure is described in the web appendix and results are reported in Table 6.1 (upper panel). The evidence is striking: the chances of attaining

TABLE 6.1

Estimated probability of attaining the upper secondary diploma by parental education (%)

	Birth cohort	PARENTAL EDUCATION			
		High	Medium	Low	All
ISTAT[a]	1976	104	91	49	62
	1979	105	97	56	70
	1982	102	100	53	74
	1985	94	101	56	77
IARD[b]	1975–77	99	85	62	75
	1978–80	96	84	58	73
	1980–82	97	79	57	73

[a]Our own analysis of data from the ISTAT 1998, 2001, 2004, and 2007 surveys and other official data (see web appendix, http://www.primaryandsecondaryeffects.com).

[b]Our own analysis of data from the IARD 1992, 1996, 2000, and 2004 surveys (Buzzi, Cavalli, and De Lillo 2007). We aggregate contiguous cohorts to raise sample size. The last cohort is omitted because there are no observations.

the upper secondary degree (in any of the tracks) are much smaller for those originating from the lowest parental education group, and this result is rather stable over time. Some figures exceed unity: these inconsistencies result from the use of various data sources, each possibly affected by different nonsampling errors[20] (in the analyses that follow, these values are forced to 1). Estimates derived from IARD data (Table 6.1, lower panel) are smaller for those originating from the medium parental education group and somewhat larger for those from the lowest group. Although these differences are not negligible, as we see later the corresponding estimates of the transition probabilities, odds ratios, and relative importance of primary and secondary effects do not change substantially.

RESULTS: TRANSITION TO UPPER SECONDARY SCHOOL (AGE 14)

Estimates of the probabilities of entering the academic track by social background are shown in Table 6.2 (left panel). Given the sample selection problem affecting the graduate survey, direct nonparametric estimates are biased. Hence, we refer to the decomposition used to estimate primary and secondary effects,

$$P(S_2 = 1 \mid SB) = \sum_{A_1} P(A_1 \mid SB) P(S_2 = 1 \mid A_1, SB),$$

and apply the sample corrections according to equations (6.4) and (6.5) to the raw estimates of the performance and transition distributions based on the ISTAT survey, as described above.[21] These estimates are reported in panels a and b of Table 6.2; estimates directly derived from IARD data are shown in panel c, where contiguous cohorts are aggregated to increase sample size.

Results are quite consistent in showing that upper secondary school choices are plagued by strong inequality: transition rates to the academic track vary from between 9 percent and 17 percent for those from low parental education households to over 70 percent for those from high parental education households.[22] The corresponding odds ratios are extremely high (Table 6.2, right panel). For example, take the 1985 birth cohort: the odds of entering the academic track for children from the highest parental education group are 13–21 times higher than those for children from the lowest

TABLE 6.2

*Transition rates (%) to the academic track and overall inequality, age 14
(odds ratios vs. low parental education)*

	TRANSITION RATES BY BIRTH COHORT				ODDS RATIO BY BIRTH COHORT			
			PANEL A					
Parental education	*1976*	*1979*	*1982*	*1985*	*1976*	*1979*	*1982*	*1985*
High	74	79	72	69	29.6	33.5	23.5	21.0
Medium	36	37	36	34	5.9	5.2	5.0	4.8
Low	9	10	10	10	—	—	—	—
			PANEL B					
Parental education	*1976*	*1979*	*1982*	*1985*	*1976*	*1979*	*1982*	*1985*
High	74	79	72	71	20.3	30.5	20.3	21.1
Medium	37	36	34	31	4.4	4.5	3.9	4.0
Low	12	11	11	10	—	—	—	—
			PANEL C					
Parental education	*1975–77*	*1978–80*	*1981–83*	*1984–86*	*1975–77*	*1978–80*	*1981–83*	*1984–86*
High	71	77	70	70	20.9	24.6	11.4	13.2
Medium	35	38	33	41	4.1	4.5	2.4	3.9
Low	11	12	17	15	—	—	—	—

N O T E : Panel a: ISTAT surveys. Performance distribution corrected with official data; transition probability with IARD data. Panel b: ISTAT surveys. Performance distribution and transition probability corrected with IARD data. Panel c: IARD surveys. Observed frequencies.

parental education group; when comparing children from medium and low parental education groups the ratio is 4–5. Odds ratios tend to decrease over the decade under study, in particular between the second and third cohort. These observed differences are statistically significant: the log-linear model that posits constant association between parental education and academic track enrollment over time was tested and rejected. The 1985 birth cohort is the first to experience the after-reform system elicited by the Bologna process, so these results provide evidence that the reform has succeeded (although possibly only temporarily) in reducing social-origin inequalities.

To evaluate the relative importance of primary and secondary effects we derive the synthesized transition probabilities according to equations (6.2) and (6.3). To illustrate the calculations, let us take the 1985 birth cohort and estimates of Table 6.2's panel b as an example. The observed transition probability for a child from the highest parental education group is 71 percent, while that for a child from the lowest group is 10 percent. On the other hand, the probability for an ideal individual exposed to the performance distribution of the highest parental education group and the conditional transition probability of the lowest parental education group is 24 percent, while the corresponding probability for a child with the performance distribution of the lowest parental education group and the transition probability of the highest parental education group is 55 percent (see the web appendix). Comparing these figures we see that primary effects are less important than secondary effects, because changes are more substantial when we replace the transition probability than when we replace the performance distribution.

The observed odds ratio is

$$\frac{0.71/0.29}{0.10/0.90} = 21.1.$$

Two alternative decompositions can be obtained:

$$\ln\frac{0.71/0.29}{0.10/0.90} = 3.09 = \ln\frac{0.71/0.29}{0.55/0.45} + \ln\frac{0.55/0.45}{0.10/0.90} = 0.69 + 2.40,$$

$$\ln\frac{0.71/0.29}{0.10/0.90} = 3.09 = \ln\frac{0.71/0.29}{0.24/0.76} + \ln\frac{0.24/0.76}{0.10/0.90} = 2.05 + 1.04.$$

According to the first, the share due to secondary effects is 2.40 / 3.09 = 0.78, and according to the second, it is 2.05 / 3.09 = 0.66; the average share is 0.72.

The full set of results on the relative importance of primary and secondary effects is reported in Table 6.3. Secondary effects account for over 60–70 percent of the total differential between high and low parental education groups and for 50–70 percent between medium and low education groups, depending on the birth cohort and data sources.[23] We thus conclude that decision-related effects are more important than performance-related effects in shaping social-origin inequalities in upper secondary school choices.

Primary effects are due to the influence of family background on performance and to that of performance on school choices. Assigning values 1–4 to the grades (pass, good, very good, excellent), we computed standardized mean scores for the children of each parental education group.

TABLE 6.3

Performance and decision effects (%) in upper secondary education transitions, age 14
(odds ratios vs. low parental education)

Birth cohort		1976		1979		1982		1985	
	Parental education	High	Medium	High	Medium	High	Medium	High	Medium
Panel a	Log odds ratio	3.39	1.77	3.51	1.65	3.15	1.61	3.04	1.56
	Performance	29.6	42.2	31.2	43.5	36.6	50.7	28.7	46.6
	Decision	70.4	57.8	68.8	56.5	63.4	49.3	71.3	53.4
Panel b	Log odds ratio	2.99	1.41	3.42	1.50	3.01	1.36	3.09	1.39
	Performance	21.1	27.4	27.6	35.5	32.5	40.8	28.0	38.7
	Decision	78.9	72.6	72.4	64.5	67.5	59.2	72.0	61.3
Panel c	Log odds ratio	3.03	1.52	3.91	1.67	2.88	1.22	2.34	1.16
	Performance	23.8	26.1	24.8	33.6	37.2	52.3	44.1	47.5
	Decision	76.2	73.9	75.2	66.4	62.9	47.7	55.9	52.5

NOTE: Panel a: ISTAT surveys. Performance distribution corrected with official data; transition probability with IARD data. Panel b: ISTAT surveys. Performance distribution and transition probability corrected with IARD data. Panel c: IARD surveys. Observed frequencies.

Between-group variance accounts for 5–12 percent of total variability, and mean scores increase by nearly 1 standard deviation when moving from the lowest to the highest parental education group—a rather substantial difference—and this gap appears to be fairly stable over time.[24] Therefore, the relative weakness of primary effects observed at this stage does not seem to be due to the capacity of the system to limit performance differentials across social groups.

RESULTS: TRANSITIONS TO UNIVERSITY (AGE 19)

Conditional Analysis. Tertiary-education participation has increased considerably—in particular for children of low and medium social origin—from the 1982 birth cohort, the first to be affected by the reform enforced in 2001. Transition probabilities to university given eligibility highly depend on social background (Table 6.4, upper panel). We report here only the results pertaining to parental education, leaving those pertaining to parental class to the web appendix. Note that between-group differences are somewhat more marked if we refer to parental education rather than parental class.

The transition probabilities conditional on social origin and upper secondary school track are summarized in Table 6.4 (lower panels). Given

TABLE 6.4

Transition rates (%) to tertiary education and overall inequality, given eligibility and conditional on track, age 19 (odds ratios vs. low parental education)

Track	Parental education	TRANSITION RATES BY BIRTH COHORT				ODDS RATIO BY BIRTH COHORT			
		1976	1979	1982	1985	1976	1979	1982	1985
All	High	89	89	91	90	13.2	14.4	12.9	10.1
	Medium	63	60	68	69	2.8	2.7	2.7	2.5
	Low	38	36	44	47	—	—	—	—
Academic	High	96	98	98	98	2.7	6.7	4.8	6.1
	Medium	94	92	95	96	1.7	1.6	1.9	3.0
	Low	90	88	91	89	—	—	—	—
Technical	High	76	62	75	78	6.4	3.6	4.3	4.2
	Medium	50	47	59	63	2.0	2.0	2.1	2.0
	Low	33	31	41	46	—	—	—	—
Vocational	High	38	40	50	54	2.8	3.8	4.0	3.5
	Medium	26	26	30	33	1.6	2.0	1.7	1.5
	Low	18	15	20	25	—	—	—	—

the goals of the various educational programs, between-track differences are large, although substantial differences are observed even within tracks across social backgrounds.[25] Consistently, the odds ratios are still fairly large (although quite unstable), highlighting that although secondary school decisions are made by taking into account current plans about tertiary education, social background continues to influence educational choices even at later stages of the educational career.

To assess whether the inequalities described above are mainly due to primary or secondary effects, we first analyze the extent to which school performance varies between social groups at the end of secondary school. As we discussed above, final-examination grades reflect performance within tracks but not across tracks, because grades vary in the same range for all educational programs and are awarded in accordance with their specific program goals. Social-background differentials in mean performance within upper secondary school tracks are very small and the percentage of variance between social groups over the total variance is negligible for all cohorts (always <2 percent).[26]

Table 6.5 shows the primary and secondary effects decomposition based on equation (6.7), conditional on the school track. At this point of the educational career, inequality is driven almost entirely by secondary effects. Primary effects explain a very modest proportion of total inequality, and in light of the limited performance differentials across social strata, this is hardly a surprising result. This is true in particular for academic track leavers, who are generally focused on entering university, no matter how they previously performed. Note that an estimate lower than 0 for primary effects indicates that the (synthesized) transition rates that a child of a higher class would experience if he or she were exposed to the performance distribution of a lower class are *higher* than the actual rates. Hence, overall inequality is represented in this case by the difference between secondary and primary effects, and the differential in favor of the children from the more advantaged backgrounds can be entirely attributed to secondary effects.[27]

Unconditional Analysis. The focus of the unconditional analysis is overall inequality in the transition to the tertiary level. Estimates of the probability of entering tertiary education by parental education with respect to the whole birth cohort are summarized in Table 6.6 (left panel). Despite the non-negligible discrepancies between the different estimates, the

TABLE 6.5

Performance and decision effects (%) in tertiary education transitions conditional on track, age 19 (odds ratios vs. low parental education)

Track	Parental education	1976		1979		1982		1985	
		High	Medium	High	Medium	High	Medium	High	Medium
Academic	Log odds ratio	1.03	0.54	2.07	0.46	1.77	0.65	1.76	0.98
	Performance	-0.3	0.1	0.9	-15.7	16.2	10.5	9.6	7.3
	Decision	100.3	99.9	99.1	115.7	83.8	89.5	90.4	92.7
Technical	Log odds ratio	1.91	0.75	1.44	0.67	1.56	0.65	1.43	0.66
	Performance	11.4	12.5	7.8	4.8	14.7	15.5	15.1	15.6
	Decision	88.6	87.5	92.2	95.2	85.3	84.5	84.9	84.4
Vocational	Log odds ratio	0.93	0.57	1.40	0.70	1.38	0.57	1.25	0.38
	Performance	-5.5	4.8	3.2	4.2	8.2	9.9	11.2	12.9
	Decision	105.5	95.2	96.8	95.8	91.8	90.1	88.8	87.1

TABLE 6.6
*Transition rates (%) to tertiary education and overall inequality, age 19
(odds ratios vs. low parental education)*

Parental education	TRANSITION RATES BY BIRTH COHORT				ODDS RATIO BY BIRTH COHORT			
	1976	1979	1982	1985	1976	1979	1982	1985
	PANEL A							
High	89	89	91	85	36.7	32.4	33.8	16.1
Medium	58	58	68	69	6.0	5.5	7.1	6.3
Low	18	20	23	26	—	—	—	—
	PANEL B[a]							
High	88	85	88	—	24.8	22.4	21.2	—
Medium	54	50	54	—	3.8	3.9	3.5	—
Low	24	21	25	—	—	—	—	—
	PANEL C[a]							
High	90	89	86	—	17.5	18.0	17.2	—
Medium	61	59	62	—	4.6	3.2	3.1	—
Low	33	32	26	—	—	—	—	—

NOTE: Panel a: ISTAT surveys. Performance distribution corrected with official data; transition probability with IARD data. Panel b: ISTAT surveys. Performance distribution and transition probability corrected with IARD data. Panel c: IARD surveys. Observed frequencies.

[a]No IARD data available for 1985 cohort.

odds ratios describing overall inequality (Table 6.6, right panel) suggest that social-origin differentials in tertiary-education participation are very large.

Decomposition (6.8) into primary and secondary effects is carried out with respect to Table 6.6's panels a and b only: the IARD survey alone cannot be employed for this purpose because upper secondary grades are not recorded. We find that 70–80 percent of the social origin differential in tertiary-education enrollment is related to primary effects, that is, those performance differences that develop throughout the educational career, earlier decision effects, and differential dropout rates. However, a substantial share—between 20 percent and 25 percent—is accounted for by the secondary (or decision) effects occurring after the attainment of the upper secondary school diploma, given track and grades (Table 6.7).

CONCLUSION

The empirical analyses carried out in this chapter paint a clear picture of IEO in the Italian educational system. We observe very large inequalities related to social background, at both the level of upper secondary and

TABLE 6.7

Performance and decision effects (%) in tertiary education transitions, age 19 (odds ratios vs. low parental education)

Birth cohort		1976		1979		1982		1985	
Parental education		High	Medium	High	Medium	High	Medium	High	Medium
Panel a	Log odds ratio	3.66	1.83	3.58	1.71	3.33	1.84	2.67	1.76
	Performance	74.2	78.7	73.0	76.2	75.0	77.8	74.1	79.1
	Decision	25.8	21.3	27.0	23.8	25.0	22.2	25.9	20.9
Panel b	Log odds ratio	3.24	1.35	3.20	1.36	3.05	1.26	2.95	1.21
	Performance	70.6	71.3	72.7	72.1	74.3	71.3	75.2	74.8
	Decision	29.4	28.7	27.3	27.9	25.7	28.7	24.8	25.2

N o t e : Panel a: ISTAT surveys. Performance distribution corrected with official data; transition probability with IARD data. Panel b: ISTAT surveys. Performance distribution and transition probability corrected with IARD data.

tertiary education. Only a minority of children from the lowest backgrounds enroll in the academic track; although all upper secondary school degrees provide access to university, completion of the academic track is a strong predictor of tertiary-education enrollment, hence inequality at early stages of the school career carries over to university participation. Furthermore, the probability of not attaining any upper secondary school diploma is much higher for the lowest social-origin group, and despite selection effects in operation up to the end of secondary education, additional inequalities that manifest at this point are still sizable: children from advantaged backgrounds are more likely to continue to higher education even within the group of students who have attained the same type of diploma.

Social-origin inequalities can largely be attributed to secondary effects. The estimated share of secondary effects in determining inequality at the first transition is over 60–70 percent when comparing children from high and low parental education groups and 50–70 percent when comparing those from intermediate and low parental education groups (these represent large percentage shares compared to the estimates for the other countries included in this volume). We conclude that although academic performance at this stage strongly depends on social origin, performance is not the major driving force in generating IEO in upper secondary school choices. As regards tertiary-education transitions, almost the entire social-background differential within tracks can be attributed to secondary effects. This is due to performance differentials between social groups being very small at this stage, because only the most able children from the least advantaged groups attain a diploma (in particular in the academic track), in contrast to children from the highest groups, in which the majority attain a diploma. When we consider the entire birth cohort (in the unconditional analysis), we estimate that previous choices and performance differentials account for 70–80 percent of the overall inequality; the remaining 20–30 percent, quite a significant share, is attributable instead to social-background differentials in tertiary-education participation, given upper secondary school track and school performance.

Although performance effects are not negligible, large secondary effects call for policies aimed toward reducing social-origin differentials in educational decisions, in particular at the upper secondary school level. Institutional features are potentially relevant, particularly the strong differentiation of the curricula at age 14. An extensive literature provides evidence that early tracking, favoring the role of families in school choices, enhances social-origin inequalities (Ammermueller 2005; Schuetz, Ursprung, and Woessmann 2005; Hanushek and Woessman 2006; Brunello and Checchi 2007). In light of this literature, some scholars advocate the establishment of a comprehensive educational system up to age 16; this would provide general education for all students for a longer time and postpone the moment of choice, leaving more room for the evaluation of children's attitudes and educational aspirations.

The weakly meritocratic character of the Italian educational system is also potentially related to the creation of inequalities, and secondary effects in particular. First, no performance restrictions are applied: all children have access to the academic track at the upper secondary school level, regardless of previous school performance, and all children with a five-year diploma are eligible for tertiary education.[28] Second, the absence of standardized assessments makes evaluations to some extent school dependent, with the consequence that grades and degrees have limited informative power, reducing the chances of all actors involved (children, families, prospective employers) making objective judgments of a child's ability and, hence, fully informed choices. If children and employers are aware that grades and degrees provide imperfect signals of students' competencies, other features will be given more weight in decision processes, reducing the role of performance and possibly enhancing the direct effect of social origin on educational choices and in the labor market (Cipollone and Visco 2007).

In this context there are no strong incentives to perform well in school, and this could be one of the reasons for the unsatisfactory placement of Italy in PISA results (OECD 2006) and Trends in International Mathematics and Science Study (TIMSS; Mullis, Martin, and Foy 2008). As regards incentives to enter the academic track and tertiary education, returns to education in terms of wages are comparatively low in Italy (Cipollone and Visco 2007), and there is evidence that job-status attainment largely depends on social status (Barbieri, Paugam, and Russell 2000). Hence, despite direct costs of schooling having remained low at all educational levels, opportunity costs are relatively large for those originating in the lowest social groups. On the other hand, children from the most advantaged backgrounds are still encouraged to attain a university qualification, in order not to fall down the social ladder (Breen and Goldthorpe 1997). All these factors contribute to enhancing the role of decision effects rather than performance effects in educational choices and to the creation of large social-origin differentials.

The weakly meritocratic character of the Italian educational system is considered by many scholars to limit both quality and equity, and from this perspective, a reform of the system promoting merit (of students, teachers, and schools) has often been invoked. A key point in this respect is to provide standardized measures of performance, to allow for between-child comparisons. The demand for a move toward accountability is becoming increasingly widespread in the public debate on the Italian educational system. From one perspective it is held that appropriate forms of virtuous competition between schools would foster higher-quality education; from another, the availability of comparable data on child performance would allow the research community to bring the problems of the school system to light and help design adequate policies to overcome them. To this end, an independent evaluation institution was established by the Ministry of Education in 2004.[29] Significant steps toward an accountable educational system have been taken since then. For the first time, in 2010 a set of nationally standardized tests was administered to comprehensive school pupils in different grades, and in the same year a standardized unit was formally included in the lower secondary final examination. Moreover, the full data archive containing test results and contextual information on children, families, and schools is now available. This is a significant improvement, which we hope will have positive consequences for applied educational research in Italy.

NOTES

1. Ability is here understood to be an observed measure of performance (typically grade point average) as opposed to an unobserved measure of cognitive ability, since it is held that it is the former that affects the decision process through the perceived probability of schooling success.

2. The survey "Condizione Giovanile in Italia" (Buzzi, Cavalli, and de Lillo 2007) is carried out by the IARD Institute, a private research center that has been conducting research on Italian youth for 40 years.

3. Additional results are available in the web appendix (http://www.primary andsecondaryeffects.com).

4. Most students attaining a three-year-program qualification continue their studies for another two years.

5. However, in some universities only a predefined number of students are admitted to some study programs (*numero chiuso*). Admission is regulated by

ad hoc tests, while upper secondary examination scores are rarely taken into consideration.

6. The Bologna process formally began in 1999 with the Bologna Declaration, in which 30 countries expressed their willingness to participate in developing an integrated European Higher Education Area, with the aim of ensuring more comparable, compatible, and coherent systems of higher education in Europe (http://www.ehea.info).

7. Those leaving before attaining an upper secondary school diploma include children who follow vocational programs set up at the regional level, which provide no general education, as well as those attaining a three-year vocational qualification from state-level schools.

8. We include teaching and art schools in this category.

9. Official dropout rates overestimate dropout rates in the university system because they do not account for transfers across educational programs provided by different schools.

10. Ballarino and Checchi (2006) address the general issue of inequality in the Italian educational system and discuss results from some of the papers they cite.

11. The sampling procedure is based on a two-stage random selection, with schools as first-stage and children as second-stage units. In the first stage the sample is stratified with respect to administrative regions, school track, and school size.

12. The sample is randomly selected, with proportional stratification with respect to region or city of residence, gender, and age. Approximately 3,000 individuals per wave are interviewed, but since the age range is 15–34, any birth year has only a few cases. By pooling data from different waves (1992, 1996, 2000, and 2004 surveys) and aggregating three contiguous birth cohorts to increase the sample size, we obtain 500–1,500 cases per group. However, data on final grades in lower secondary school—necessary to decompose overall inequality into primary and secondary effects—are available only for the survey carried out in 2000. This means that the relevant samples are further reduced, amounting to approximately 500 cases for the 1975–77 and the 1978–80 birth cohorts and fewer than 250 for the 1981–83 and 1984–86 cohorts.

13. Since 2008 final grades have followed a five-level scale (adding a level to the four-level scale). In the same year a nationally standardized unit was included in final examinations, although its weight in determining the final grade was decided at the school level; since 2010 evaluation criteria have been defined at the national level.

14. In keeping with the definition employed for children, the upper secondary category refers to degrees in any of the tracks.

15. Again, we include the sociopedagogical lyceum and art school in the technical track.

16. Heckman's model assumes that sample selection is determined by the outcome of a probit model not dependent on the y of interest and where the

unobservable component is correlated with the unobservable component of the model for y. In addition, the probability of entering the sample can be estimated from the available data. Our case differs substantially from this situation in that the selection variable (attainment of the upper secondary diploma) comes logically after the y of interest (upper secondary track), so that the former directly depends on the latter. This implies that (a) the underlying model does not fit and (b) the selection probability model cannot be estimated (if we had the data to model it, there would be no sample selection issue).

17. The problem is that the graduates' survey provides no information on lower secondary final grades for upper secondary school dropouts. However, a rough estimate of $P(A_1 \mid G = 0)$ can be obtained by exploiting aggregate data on lower secondary final grades and gross graduation rates, combined with an estimate of the lower secondary final grade distribution for graduates. We find that nearly all the children who did not attain the upper secondary school diploma exited lower secondary school with the lowest grade, and that nearly all the children obtaining higher grades eventually graduated. We show that this result implies that $P(A_1 \mid SB)$ can be obtained from $P(A_1 \mid SB, G = 1)$ and $P(G = 1 \mid SB)$. As we have already noted, graduation rates by social background are not available. But graduation probabilities by parental education can be estimated by exploiting the graduates' survey, gross graduation rates, and the marginal distribution of parental education for selected birth cohorts (derived from Population Census data).

18. S_2^* and S_2 differ in that S_2^* stands for the graduation track and S_2 is the first enrollment track. Students who change track, while a minority, are quite numerous in Italy.

19. To be more precise, for the first transition we estimate the graduation probabilities given social background among those who have successfully completed compulsory schooling. Given the low share of dropouts at this stage, estimates change only slightly and are not reported.

20. All data sources with the exception of the graduate survey cover the whole population of interest; given the survey's large sample size, sampling variability is not a major issue here; standard errors of the estimates are very small and cannot by themselves explain the inconsistencies (standard errors of the estimated proportions due to sampling variability in the graduate survey do not exceed 0.0001).

21. In related work (Contini and Scagni 2011b) we consider the role of gender and geographic area, and although both the performance distribution and the transition probability vary with respect to these variables, the overall picture in terms of IEO does not change much. Given the scope of this book, we report here only national-level estimates, for males and females taken together.

22. These results are consistent with the marginal probability of academic track enrollment having increased over time: although the probabilities conditional on parental education do not change much over the period of interest, the

distribution of parental education varies in that the proportion of students originating from higher education households increases (see web appendix).

23. We do not calculate standard errors for the relative importance of primary and secondary effects because the procedure outlined in Chapter 2 does not fit our case. First, the method applies to simple random samples; standard errors are underestimated in complex sampling designs in which first-stage sampling units are schools. Second, performance scores have to be approximated by a normal distribution, but as shown above, this is not feasible in our case. Third, since we use combinations of different sources of data to correct for sample selection, a proper extension of the method is by no means straightforward. In support of the substantive validity of our results, note that results do not vary greatly across birth cohorts (for which independent samples were drawn) and data sources.

24. These results are detailed in the web appendix.

25. Note that the share of vocational track leavers coming from the uppermost stratum is very small.

26. See the web appendix for evidence on performance differentials at this stage.

27. Consider the comparison between medium and low parental education groups for the 1979 birth cohort. The figure of 115.7 percent indicates that the odds ratio pertaining to secondary effects is larger than the odds ratio measuring total inequality (see Chapter 2 for details).

28. Contini and Scagni (2011a) analyze whether access restrictions reduce IEO. By comparing German states with and without restrictions, they show that there is evidence in favor of the thesis, although no general conclusions can be drawn from a theoretical point of view.

29. INVALSI (Istituto Nazionale Valutazione del Sistema Educativo di Istruzione e di Formazione).

REFERENCES

Ammermueller, Andreas. 2005. "Educational Opportunities and the Role of Institutions." Maastricht: Centre for European Economic Research. http://edocs.ub.unimaas.nl/loader/file.asp?id=1071.

Ballarino, Gabriele, and Daniele Checchi. 2006. *Sistema scolastico e diseguaglianza sociale*. Bologna: Il Mulino.

Barbieri, Paolo, Serge Paugam, and Helen Russell. 2000. "Social Capital and Exits from Unemployment." In *Welfare Regimes and the Experience of Unemployment in Europe*, edited by Duncan Gallie and Serge Paugam, 200–217. Oxford: Oxford University Press.

Barone, Carlo. 2009. "A New Look at Schooling Inequalities in Italy and Their Trends over Time." *Research in Social Stratification and Mobility* 27:92–109.

Bertola, Giuseppe, Daniele Checchi, and Veruska Oppedisano. 2007. "Private School Quality in Italy." *Giornale degli Economisti ed Annali di Economia* 66:375–400.

Boudon, Raymond. 1974. *L'inégalité des Chances*. Paris: Colin.

Bratti, Massimiliano, Daniele Checchi, and Antonio Filippin. 2007. "Territorial Differences in Italian Students' Mathematical Competences: Evidence from PISA 2003." Institute for the Study of Labor (IZA) discussion paper 2603. Bonn, Germany: Forschungsinstitut zur Zukunft der Arbeit. http://ftp.iza .org/dp2603.pdf.

Bratti Massimiliano, Daniele Checchi, and Guido de Blasio. 2008. "Does the Expansion of Higher Education Increase the Equality of Educational Opportunities? Evidence from Italy." *Labour* 22:53–88.

Breen, Richard. 2004. *Social Mobility in Europe*. Oxford: Oxford University Press.

Breen, Richard, and John H. Goldthorpe. 1997. "Explaining Educational Differentials: Towards a Formal Rational Action Theory." *Rationality and Society* 9:275–98.

Breen Richard, Ruud Luijkx, Walter Müller, and Reinhard Pollak. 2009. "Nonpersistent Inequality in Educational Attainments: Evidence from Eight European Countries." *American Journal of Sociology* 114:1475–521.

Brunello, Giorgio, and Daniele Checchi. 2007. "Does School Tracking Affect Equality of Opportunity? New International Evidence." *Economic Policy* 52:781–861.

Brunello, Giorgio, and Lorenzo Rocco. 2008. "Educational Standards in Private and Public Schools." *Economic Journal* 118:1866–87.

Buzzi, Carlo, Alessandro Cavalli, and Antonio de Lillo. 2007. *Rapporto Giovani: Sesta indagine dell'Istituto IARD sulla condizione giovanile in Italia*. Bologna, Italy: Il Mulino.

Cappellari, Lorenzo. 2004. "High School Types, Academic Performance and Early Labour Market Outcomes." Institute for the Study of Labor (IZA) discussion paper 1048. Bonn, Germany: Forschungsinstitut zur Zukunft der Arbeit. http://ftp.iza.org/dp1048.pdf.

Cappellari, Lorenzo, and Claudio Lucifora. 2008. "The 'Bologna Process' and College Enrolment Decisions." Institute for the Study of Labor (IZA) discussion paper 3444. Bonn, Germany: Forschungsinstitut zur Zukunft der Arbeit. http://ftp.iza.org/dp3444.pdf.

Checchi, Daniele. 2003. "The Italian Educational System: Family Background and Social Stratification." Paper presented at the Institute for Studies and Economic Analyses (*Istituto di Studi e Analisi Economica*, or ISAE) conference on *Monitoring Italy*, Rome, October 1. http://checchi.economia.unimi .it/pdf/un15.pdf.

Checchi, Daniele, Carlo V. Fiorio, and Marco Leonardi. 2008. "Intergenerational Persistence in Educational Attainment in Italy." Institute for the Study of

Labor (IZA) discussion paper 3622. Bonn, Germany: Forschungsinstitut zur Zukunft der Arbeit. http://ftp.iza.org/dp3622.pdf.

Checchi, Daniele, and Luca Flabbi. 2007. "Intergenerational Mobility and Schooling Decisions in Germany and Italy: The Impact of Secondary School Tracks." Institute for the Study of Labor (IZA) discussion paper 2876. Bonn, Germany: Forschungsinstitut zur Zukunft der Arbeit. http://ftp.iza.org/dp2876.pdf.

Checchi, Daniele, Andrea Ichino, and Aldo Rustichini. 1999. "More Equal but Less Mobile? Intergenerational Mobility and Inequality in Italy and in the US." *Journal of Public Economics* 74:351–93.

Cipollone, Piero, and Ignazio Visco. 2007. "Il merito nella società della conoscenza." *Il Mulino* 1:21–34.

Cobalti, Antonio, and Antonio Schizzerotto. 1993. "Inequality of Educational Opportunity in Italy." In *Persistent Inequality: A Comparative Study of Educational Attainment in Thirteen Countries*, edited by Hans-Peter Blossfeld and Yossi Shavit, 292–312. Boulder, CO: Westview.

———. 1994. *La Mobilità Sociale in Italia*. Bologna: Il Mulino.

Contini, Dalit, and Andrea Scagni. 2011a. "Inequality of Opportunity in Secondary School Enrolment in Italy, Germany and the Netherlands." Quality and Quantity 45(2): 441–64.

———. 2011b. "Primary and Secondary Effects in Educational Attainment in Italy." In *Statistical Methods for the Evaluation of University Systems*, edited by Massimo Attanasio and Vincenza Capursi, 223–45. Heidelberg, Germany: Springer Physica Verlag.

Erikson, Robert, John H. Goldthorpe, Michelle Jackson, Meir Yaish, and David R. Cox. 2005. "On Class Differentials in Educational Attainment." *Proceedings of the National Academy of Sciences* 102:9730–33.

Goldthorpe, John H. 1996. "Class Analysis and the Reorientation of Class Theory: The Case of Persisting Differentials in Educational Attainment." *British Journal of Sociology* 45:481–506.

Hanushek, Erik A., and Ludger Woessman. 2006. "Does Educational Tracking Affect Performance and Inequality? Differences-in-Differences Evidence across Countries." *Economic Journal* 116: C63–C76.

Hertz, Tom, Tamara Jayasundera, Patrizio Piraino, Sibel Selcuk, Nicole Smith, and Alina Verashchagina. 2008. "The Inheritance of Educational Inequality: International Comparisons and Fifty-Year Trends." *B.E. Journal of Economic Analysis and Policy* 7(2): article 10.

Ministero dell'Istruzione, dell'Università e della Ricerca, Direzione Generale per gli Studi e la Programmazione e per i Sistemi Informativi. 2008. *10 anni di scuola statale: a.s. 1998/99–a.s. 2007/2008: Dati, fenomeni e tendenze del sistema di istruzione*, edited by Mariano Ferrazzano and Sergio Govi. Rome.

Mocetti, Sauro. 2008. "Educational Choices and the Selection Process Before and After Compulsory Schooling." Working paper 691, Banca d'Italia.

Mullis, Ina V. S., Michael O. Martin, and Pierre Foy. 2008. *TIMSS 2007 International Mathematics Report. Findings from IEA's Trends in International Mathematics and Science Study at the Fourth and Eighth Grades.* Boston, MA: IEA TIMSS & PIRLS International Study Center.

OECD. 2006. *PISA 2006: Science Competencies for Tomorrow's World.* Paris: OECD.

———. *Education at a Glance.* Paris: OECD.

Pisati, Maurizio, and Antonio Schizzerotto. 2004. "The Italian Mobility Regime: 1985–97." In *Social Mobility in Europe,* edited by Richard Breen, 149–74. Oxford: Oxford University Press.

Shavit, Yossi, and Hans-Peter Blossfeld, eds. 1993. *Persistent Inequality: Changing Educational Attainment in Thirteen Countries.* Boulder, CO: Westview.

Shavit, Yossi, and Karin Westerbeek. 1998. "Educational Stratification in Italy: Reforms, Expansion, and Equality of Opportunity." *European Sociological Review* 14:15–36.

Schuetz, Gabriela, Heinrich W. Ursprung, and Ludger Woessmann. 2005. "Education Policy and Equality of Opportunity." Institute for the Study of Labor (IZA) discussion paper 1906. Bonn, Germany: Forschungsinstitut zur Zukunft der Arbeit. http://ftp.iza.org/dp1906.pdf.

CHAPTER SEVEN

Ever-Declining Inequalities?

Transitions to Upper Secondary and Tertiary
Education in Sweden, 1972–1990 Birth
Cohorts

Frida Rudolphi

The reduction of educational inequalities is a recurrent item on the Swedish political agenda, with a long-standing political goal that individuals' educational attainment should be independent of their social origin. In line with this ambition, research has consistently shown that Sweden experienced a long-term decline in inequality of educational opportunity (IEO) during the 20th century. The decline in inequality is observed at all educational levels, although it has been more systematic at the transition to upper secondary education than to university education. While this equalization appeared to have leveled off for traditional longer university education by the early 1970s (Erikson and Jonsson 1996a; Gustafsson, Andersson, and Hansen 2000; Jonsson and Erikson 2007), it slowed somewhat later for academic upper secondary education, and inequalities in the chances of making this transition further declined from the late 1980s up until the end of the century (Erikson and Jonsson 1996a; Erikson and Rudolphi 2010; Gustafsson, Andersson, and Hansen 2000).

Remaining educational differentials related to children's class and educational origins arise because privileged children both tend to perform better in school and choose to stay in education and opt for more academically oriented educational routes than children of less advantaged social origin at similar performance levels (Erikson and Jonsson 1996a; Erikson et al. 2005; Jonsson and Erikson 2000). The relative strength of the two processes, commonly labeled primary and secondary effects (Boudon 1974), speaks to the potential mechanisms behind educational inequality and to possible ways of overcoming it. While a social gradient in performance is most likely related to continuous socialization from early ages, choice effects are likely to be the result of active decision making under the constraints of available resources (Boudon 1974; Erikson and Jonsson 1996b; Jonsson and Erikson 2000, 2007). As a consequence, it is quite likely that choice effects and performance effects will differ at different transition points: for example, compared with the transition to upper secondary education, we would expect the transition to university to depend more on economic resources and thus choice effects to be stronger. Accordingly, studying change over time and variation across educational transitions in primary and secondary effects is of utmost importance (see Chapter 1).

This chapter's analysis extends previous research on educational inequality in Sweden in three ways. First, I study inequalities in the transition to upper secondary school for recent cohorts, for which change over time has not yet been studied. Second, I analyze change between transitions within cohorts by comparing social selection over individuals' educational careers. These two extensions are made possible by the availability of high-quality register data comprising all pupils born in 1972–1990 who completed the final year of compulsory school in Sweden. These data enable me to assess the relative importance of primary and secondary effects in producing educational inequalities in the two most consequential educational transitions in the Swedish educational system, the transitions to upper secondary and to tertiary education, for individuals who turned 16 between 1988 and 2006. I follow six full birth cohorts (1972–1977) through their educational careers from compulsory school to upper secondary enrollment up to age 17, to completion by age 20, to enrollment in university education by age 25, and finally to completion of tertiary education (university or university college) by age 30.

The third extension builds on the idea that, alongside educational expansion, stratification may increasingly occur between educational programs or tracks within a given level of education. In accordance with the idea that people of privileged social origins tend to seek out the most prestigious tracks (Lucas 2001; also see Bourdieu 1996, pt. II), recent Swedish research shows that class inequalities in higher education operate along horizontal as well as vertical dimensions (Berggren 2008; Hällsten 2011a; Jonsson and Erikson 2007). Although the ambition here is not to analyze the horizontal dimensions of IEO in detail, I extend the analyses beyond the vertical dimension of education. At upper secondary education, I study the natural science track—the pathway that confers eligibility for the widest range of university programs—as an alternative outcome to all upper secondary academic tracks, and I distinguish enrollment in university education (*universitet*) from enrollment in the recently expanded and less prestigious university college institutions (*högskolor*). Finally, I also pay attention to upper secondary school completion, which in Sweden became a more prominent concern after the upper secondary school reforms of the late 1990s (Swedish National Agency for Education, 2009a). Amid the increasing enrollment rates to academic upper secondary education observed during the 1990s, differential noncompletion rates between social classes are also observed (Erikson and Rudolphi 2010; Svensson 2008). Social-class differences in noncompletion rates have implications for inequality, so that inequality in completion of academic upper secondary schooling may deviate substantially from the picture of equality in enrollment, even if enrollment may be considered to capture educational choice with more precision.

THE SWEDISH EDUCATIONAL SYSTEM

The Swedish educational system is characterized by late formal tracking, free tuition at all educational levels, and no dead ends. After nine years of compulsory schooling, when pupils are normally around 16 years old, the first important transition is made.[1] Pupils can then choose to continue to upper secondary school (which is optional although nearly all students make this choice), and if they continue, they must decide which track to take. Swedish upper secondary education can be described as a parallel system, where pupils can choose between programs that broadly fall into two tracks: vocational or academic. While academic programs mainly prepare for higher levels of study, vocational programs provide more direct training for the labor market. During the 1990s, upper secondary education was reformed and expanded to be more comprehensive (prop. 1990/91:85). Vocational programs increased from two to three years, providing basic eligibility for entry into tertiary education. However, graduation from vocational tracks grants restricted access to tertiary education, as many university programs require additional courses. Moreover, in the reformed system some of the 17 different programs can be regarded as semivocational or semiacademic alternatives. Academic tracks, with much higher enrollment rates to university and university college than other programs (Swedish National Agency for Education 2009a), continued to be the main route for those preparing for higher studies, with the royal road to university education going via the natural science program, which provides eligibility for most tertiary programs.[2]

Universities and university colleges are integrated within the Swedish tertiary educational system, and in the 1990s tertiary education was substantially expanded, mainly through increased enrollment at regional university colleges (Josefsson and Unemo 2003, chap. 5). The most common type of tertiary education is organized in programs of three to five years with a set course structure, but students also have the option of achieving a general degree by taking freestanding courses (students taking the latter alternative more rarely attain a degree than those who enroll in programs [Statistics Sweden 2009]). Professional degrees are organized within a program.

Teacher-assigned grades function as a selection instrument for both upper secondary and tertiary education. At tertiary level the numbers of educational places in specific programs are normally fixed, with a centralized system controlling admissions. Admission to the more popular and prestigious university programs generally requires high grade point averages (GPAs) from upper secondary school, as is the case for other programs with good labor market prospects. Alternative entrance routes to tertiary education have been introduced with the purpose of increasing social diversity in recruitment and widening the pool of applicants. Besides grades, an optional aptitude test, the Swedish Scholastic Assessment Test (SweSAT, *högskoleprovet*), is used as a selection instrument.[3] Equalizing recruitment to tertiary education by establishing alternative entrance possibilities has, however, proved to be difficult, and previous studies suggest that upper-middle-class students and young people with well-educated parents are overrepresented among those who have enrolled through alternative admission rules (Berggren 2007; Cliffordson and Askling 2006).

OVERVIEW AND ANALYTICAL STRATEGY

In Figure 7.1 the flows of individuals across educational transitions are shown for a single birth cohort, providing an overview of the Swedish educational system and a point of departure for describing the analytical strategy. For the sake of parsimony, I concentrate on completion and exclude enrollment in the figure.

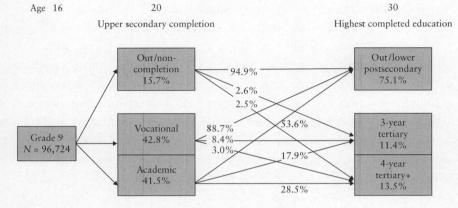

Figure 7.1. Important educational pathways through the stylized Swedish educational system, 1977 birth cohort

NOTE: Includes pupils with conventional grades at age 16, irrespective of immigrant background; 4.2% of the cohort is excluded because of incomplete information on highest educational attainment by age 30. Percentages in boxes are of entire cohort; percentages in lines between boxes are transition rates of each group.

Among ninth graders born in 1977, who normally enrolled in upper secondary education in 1993, almost 42 percent completed an academic up-per secondary education by age 20. A similar proportion completed a vocational track, whereas close to 16 percent did not complete upper secondary education by age 20, a group including both dropouts and delayed students.

With an approximately 42 percent completion rate, academic up-per secondary track is the clear standard educational path to university and university colleges. A significant number of students from vocational tracks—around 11 percent—completed at least three years of tertiary education by age 30. The group with no upper secondary certificate by age 20 had 5 percent completing tertiary education by age 30. That educational decisions are reversible is a key feature of the Swedish educational system and of relevance for how to structure the analysis of university education. In comparison with, for example, Germany and the Netherlands, the Swedish educational system is characterized by more openness, in the sense that the first formal tracking occurs rather late, at around age 16, and subsequent educational decisions are not heavily conditioned by previous ones.

There is no clear-cut analytical approach to the structural openness and complexity of the Swedish educational system as illustrated in Figure 7.1

when analyzing transitions over individuals' careers.[4] While the study of detailed educational careers, taking account of all possible tracks, would be a valuable complement to the vast literature focusing on highest-completed education, the most appropriate strategy for the core question in focus here is to study the standard pathway. The strategy of analyzing the main route to higher education facilitates the separation of primary and secondary effects in the transition to university level, because GPA is not comparable between vocational and academic tracks at the end of upper secondary school (for studies on social inequality in nonstandard pathways, see Breen and Jonsson 2000; Hällsten 2011b). GPA from around age 16 is used as a performance measure for the first transition, from compulsory to academic upper secondary education, while GPA from around age 19 is used for the transition from academic upper secondary education to tertiary education (in both cases, I use the final grade level's GPA, which is also used for admission to the next educational level, though other selection instruments are also applied for the admission to tertiary education). In a complementary analysis of the transition to tertiary education, I study primary and secondary effects by using compulsory-school grades to control for performance. In this case I include all students in compulsory education at around age 16, although the performance measure in this analysis is less suitable for the analysis of primary and secondary effects because GPA at age 16 is not used as a selection instrument for tertiary education, largely because it is superseded by assessments of performance taken later in the educational career.

PREVIOUS RESEARCH

Performance (primary) and choice (secondary) effects of social origin were recognized early in Swedish research. The two processes were acknowledged by Boalt (1947) and Härnqvist (1958) and were later shown to prevail at the transition both from primary to upper secondary school and from upper secondary school to university (Erikson and Jonsson 1993, 1996a). Numerous Swedish studies show that IEO is driven by both processes: children of privileged social origins perform better, measured by grades at around ages 16 and 19 (Berggren 2008; Böhlmark and Holmlund 2011; Gustafsson and Yang-Hansen 2009), and attain higher levels of education at given levels of performance, compared with those of less advantaged social origins

(Erikson and Jonsson 1996a; Gustafsson, Andersson, and Hansen 2000; Hällsten 2011a; Jonsson and Erikson 2007).

Few Swedish studies have aimed to assess the relative importance of primary and secondary effects. Using the same method as employed in this study (see Chapter 2 of this volume; Erikson et al. 2005), in which actual and synthesized transition rates are compared to establish the relative importance of primary and secondary effects, Erikson (2007) examined the transition to upper secondary education for cohorts born in 1953 and 1969. He found a tendency for a somewhat lower proportion of inequality to be attributable to secondary effects (around 30 to 45 percent) when considering enrollment in natural science programs compared with enrollment in all upper secondary programs (around 40 to 65 percent). When analyzing inequality in the transition to academic upper secondary education for four cohorts born between 1967 and 1982, Erikson and Rudolphi (2010) estimated that slightly more than a third (around 35 to 40 percent) of the inequality was determined by secondary effects, using GPA from compulsory school as a performance measure. In a path analysis on the same data for one of the cohorts, Härnqvist (in Erikson and Jonsson 1993, chap. 7) estimated that around 43 percent of the inequality at the transition to upper secondary education was determined by secondary effects. The estimated proportion of secondary effects was larger for the transition to tertiary education (around 54 percent) when grades from upper secondary school were also included in the model. In an analysis of the influence of parents' schooling on the probability of studying at the tertiary level by age 26, Björklund et al. (2010, table 10.1) use data and performance measures similar to Härnqvist's. When several different performance measures from ages 10 to 16 are taken into account, the proportion of secondary effects amounts to around 43 percent, in an estimation based on all pupils in compulsory school.

Changes over Time in Inequality in Transition to Academic Upper Secondary Education

Changes in inequality in educational attainment can be attributed to numerous changes in societal circumstances, of which inequality of condition is probably one of the most important aspects, with the institutional structure of the educational system playing a central role. Previous research suggests social-class inequalities in the transition to academic tracks slightly declined between 1988 and 1998 (Gustafsson, Andersson, and Hansen 2000), with a more or less stable proportion of secondary effects over the period (Erikson and Rudolphi 2010). While it has been suggested that the decline between 1988 and 1993 occurred partly because of demographic factors (Gustafsson, Andersson, and Hansen 2000),[5] a Swedish reform of upper secondary education in the mid-1990s might have contributed to equalization by diminishing the cost differences between vocational and academic routes up until 1998 (Jonsson 2007).[6] What happened to the trend in the years after 1998, during a period when declining proportions of pupils entered academic upper secondary tracks (Statistics Sweden 2007), is less well understood. There is no obvious reason to expect a substantial equalization in choice effects after 1998, given that, among other things, there was no general trend of equalization in living conditions up until 2006 (quite the contrary, in fact: income inequalities increased during this period; see Jonsson, Mood, and Bihagen 2010, fig. 2) and no wide-ranging educational reform was implemented during the latest part of the observed period in this study, 1999–2006. However, a recent analysis based on sibling correlations suggests that inequality in graduating from an academic track did also decline for the cohorts who normally entered upper secondary education between 1999 and 2003 (Böhlmark and Holmlund 2011, fig. 7).

Much attention has been focused on the potential effects of the extensive educational reforms of compulsory and upper secondary education in the 1990s, with decentralization and individualization being two key trends (Björklund et al. 2005, 2010; Böhlmark and Holmlund 2011; Fredriksson and Vlachos 2011; Swedish National Agency for Education 2009b). Some of the reforms have raised equity concerns regarding children's schooling outcomes, but research indicates that grade inequalities at age 16 have remained fairly constant at the individual level. Björklund, Lindahl, and Sund (2003) find stable grade inequalities during the 1990s in three core subjects using sibling analysis, and this development continued up to 2007 according to updated analyses on grades in two of the subjects (Böhlmark and Holmlund 2011, figs. 5, 6a). Recent results suggest a similar pattern for GPAs based on grades in 16 subjects. Contrasting groups on either educational level of the mother or income rank of the father, Fredriksson and Vlachos (2011, fig. 6.6) obtained results indicating stability or a slight decline in the importance of family resources for grades at age 16 between 1990 and 2008. By contrast, an analysis by Gustafsson and Yang-Hansen

(2009, fig. 3.1) suggests GPA inequality between pupils with highly educated parents and other pupils slightly increased between 1996 and 2004, followed by a slight decline up until 2007. If GPA inequality did increase after the mid-1990s, growing performance effects in producing inequality in academic upper secondary attendance might have followed. However, as I demonstrate, GPA inequalities during the 19-year period under study seem to be characterized by a high degree of stability.

Changes over Time in Inequality in Transition to Tertiary Education

The observation window for the tertiary analysis covers birth cohorts who normally graduated from upper secondary school between 1991 and 1996, which was a turbulent economic period in Sweden, occurring alongside an extensive expansion of tertiary education. These features could have promoted a trend toward equalization in the social recruitment to tertiary education. The recession beginning in 1991 might well have increased the propensity of students to continue in education after upper secondary school, because the alternative was to face the risk of unemployment. The reduced costs of staying in education might have been particularly important for youths from low educated families, and we can accordingly expect declining inequalities in secondary (choice) effects.

Diminishing cohort sizes in combination with an expansion of places on programs or courses that applicants can fill most likely reduced the entry requirements for tertiary education, thereby improving the chances of low- and mediocre-performing students enrolling in university education. This development might have led to declining primary effects (Berggren 2006; Gustafsson, Andersson, and Hansen 2000). There are reasons to expect declines in the absolute size of both primary and secondary effects, and it is difficult to predict whether the relative importance of the two effects might change. Predicting change in the total inequality at the transition to tertiary education is also complicated by the prediction hinging on which risk set is selected and on changes in selection at earlier branching points in the educational system.

Changes over Time in Educational Inequality across Transitions

The common finding of declining total IEO across transitions (for Sweden, see Breen and Jonsson 2000; Erikson and Jonsson 1993) could be explained either by increased selection (Mare 1981, 1993)—implying that students become more and more similar in ability and motivation across transitions—or by individuals becoming increasingly independent of their family of origin in their educational decisions as they grow older (Blossfeld and Shavit 1993). From both of these accounts we can expect the total IEO to decrease across transitions, and because economic considerations most likely become more important at the threshold to university studies, I expect the relative weight of secondary effects to increase. While the analyses do not provide any critical test of the alternative explanations, I try to reduce selection effects by controlling for grades from upper secondary level when analyzing the transition to tertiary education.

Findings of decreasing educational inequality across transitions have been questioned for not taking horizontal aspects of educational pathways into account, because the strength of the overall inequality depends on the "exclusiveness" of the studied outcome; social selection to longer, more prestigious tertiary education courses is stronger compared with less prestigious alternatives (Berggren 2008; Hällsten 2011a; Jonsson and Erikson 2007). Building on the idea that children tend to avoid downward social mobility relative to their parents (Breen and Goldthorpe 1997; Erikson and Jonsson 1996b), we would expect the perceived utility (in terms of occupational status and income) of acquiring a prestigious university education to be higher for adolescents with well-educated parents (Jonsson and Erikson 2007). Given that individuals of privileged social origins tend to gain more by choosing high-status educational alternatives, we can expect a higher level of inequality for more prestigious courses—here captured by degrees from longer courses and enrollment in full-time university education—to partly be a consequence of stronger choice effects.[7] The generally higher entrance requirements for longer programs and more prestigious universities are likely to also involve stronger primary effects for these educational routes.

DATA AND METHOD

The data come from the database Sweden over Time: Activities and Relations (STAR), compiled by Statistics Sweden for the Level of Living project at the Swedish Institute for Social Research (SOFI), and comprise a range of population registers where parents and children can be identified through a multigenerational link. Binary educational outcomes are analyzed by applying the decomposition approach described in Chapter 2 of this volume (also see Erikson et al. 2005; Jackson et al. 2007). The estimations are carried out using the STATA command ldecomp (Buis 2010).

Sample Selection

I base my analyses on pupils born between 1972 and 1990 who were found in the Swedish grade nine register during 1988 to 2007, which includes yearly information on all pupils in the ninth, and final, grade of compulsory school from 1988 onward. Some sample restrictions are made. Since I wish to follow individuals' educational careers from the beginning of compulsory schooling onward, children who immigrated to Sweden after the usual age at which pupils start their compulsory schooling (seven years) are excluded, and I restrict the analyses to those who did not emigrate during the normal age for completing upper secondary education (from age 15 to the spring semester in which they turn 19).[8] After also excluding a small proportion of students for whom we lack information on compulsory-school grades, because they attended a school that did not apply the conventional grading system (0.2–0.8 percent in each birth cohort), the total number of observations amounts to 1,900,074 (Table 7.1). When analyzing university and university college education, the observation window is narrower: the enrollment analysis is based on pupils born from 1972 to 1982, and the six oldest birth cohorts are included in the completion analysis. Pupils with nonconventional upper secondary grades are excluded in all tertiary analyses (proportions of missing values on grades are shown in the web appendix, http://www.primaryandsecondaryeffects.com, Table A7.1), and I apply an additional restriction in the enrollment analysis, excluding those who were residing abroad for all or most of the time they would make the transition to tertiary education.

Parental Education

Parent's educational level is obtained from yearly register information on highest educational attainment according to the Swedish standard classification *Svensk utbildningsnomenklatur* (SUN) (Statistics Sweden 2000) when the child is aged around 16. When two parents (biological or step) are present in the household, the higher of the parents' educational levels is assigned. Educational level is coded into three broad categories: (a) compulsory school of nine years or less; (b) upper secondary education of

TABLE 7.1

Distribution of students with different social backgrounds by birth cohort (%)

| | | | EDUCATION | | | | SOCIAL CLASS | | | | |
Birth cohort	Grade 9 cohort (age 16)	N[a]	High	Mid	Low	Missing information	Salariat	Intermediate	Working	No class	Not in census
1972	1988	106,710	14.2	63.3	21.3	1.2	38.7	19.0	36.5	5.8	0.1
1973	1989	105,449	14.9	64.7	20.2	0.2	38.8	18.8	36.5	5.8	0.2
1974	1990	106,477	15.8	65.8	18.1	0.2	39.1	18.3	36.5	5.9	0.2
1975	1991	100,378	16.3	66.0	17.5	0.2	38.8	18.1	36.9	6.1	0.2
1976	1992	95,222	17.1	67.0	15.8	0.1	39.2	17.9	36.6	6.1	0.2
1977	1993	93,373	17.3	67.4	15.2	0.1	38.7	17.5	37.1	6.5	0.3
1978	1994	90,330	17.9	67.4	14.6	0.1	38.3	17.4	37.2	6.7	0.3
1979	1995	93,355	18.5	67.5	13.9	0.1	41.4	18.4	33.4	6.6	0.3
1980	1996	94,486	18.8	67.8	13.3	0.1	41.5	17.9	33.5	6.9	0.2
1981	1997	89,537	19.0	68.2	12.8	0.1	41.1	17.7	34.0	7.0	0.2
1982	1998	90,820	17.7	68.9	13.3	0.1	39.8	17.2	35.0	7.8	0.2
1983	1999	91,018	17.6	69.0	13.3	0.1	39.0	16.7	35.7	8.3	0.2
1984	2000	93,049	19.4	70.2	10.3	0.1	38.1	16.4	36.4	8.6	0.2
1985	2001	97,645	19.5	70.5	10.0	0.1	37.1	15.7	37.2	8.8	0.6
1986	2002	100,765	19.8	70.7	9.5	0.1	35.9	15.5	38.3	8.8	1.2
1987	2003	103,901	19.8	71.3	8.9	0.1	34.9	14.7	38.6	8.8	1.6
1988	2004	111,463	19.8	71.7	8.4	0.2	33.6	14.1	39.5	9.1	3.0
1989	2005	114,710	20.6	71.4	7.9	0.1	33.1	13.9	39.7	9.5	3.7
1990	2006	121,359	21.0	71.6	7.3	0.1	32.6	13.7	39.9	9.9	3.9

NOTE: N = 1,900,074.

[a]In addition to the sample restrictions described in the chapter, 230–330 observations in each cohort were excluded because the students emigrated at the usual age for completing upper secondary education. In the analysis of enrollment in tertiary education, another 90–230 observations per cohort were excluded because the students were residing abroad for all or most of the time they would make the transition.

two–three years, postsecondary education or tertiary education shorter than three years, or three-year "lower" tertiary qualifications (mainly nurses and teachers at lower grades of compulsory school); and (c) higher tertiary education of at least three years.[9] Table 7.1 presents the distributions of educational background for each birth cohort, and we see that the size of the high education group clearly increases over the cohorts.

Social-Class Origin

Social-class origin is coded according to the Swedish standard classification (Statistics Sweden 1982), which is similar to the Erikson-Goldthorpe-Portocarero (EGP) class schema (Erikson and Goldthorpe 1992). I distinguish the salariat (employed and self-employed professionals, managers, and high- and medium-level administrators), the intermediate class (farmers, self-employed, and lower nonmanual employees), and the working class (skilled and unskilled workers, including nonmanual workers in unskilled positions).[10]

Those who are not working or who are working in nonclassified occupations are collapsed into a missing category, which also includes a small group who did not participate in the relevant census. Information on social class stems from two Swedish censuses conducted in 1985 and 1990, which restricts the observation window to children born before 1990 for the analysis of class-origin effects. Pupils born between 1972 and 1981 are coded according to the 1985 census and those born in 1982–1989 according to the 1990 census, thus the age at which social-class origin is measured varies quite substantially over cohorts, from ages 1 to 13. This is reflected in the class distribution over cohorts, as shown in Table 7.1. Pupils in the youngest cohort with information on social class at age 1 have the lowest proportion of salariat-class parents and highest proportion of nonworking parents of all cohorts. Because these systematic discrepancies may affect estimates of change in IEO, I choose to focus the analysis on inequality based on parental education, with results for social class reported in the web appendix. I restrict the analysis to four cohorts for which class origin is measured at a similar age.

Educational Transitions

First, students in academic tracks are contrasted with those who are either in vocational tracks or have left school.[11] Enrollment in an academic upper secondary track is based on program registration at the beginning of the academic year, and completion of an academic upper secondary track is defined as having sufficient grades to earn an upper secondary school certificate from an academic program. In addition, I analyze completion of the natural science track, in which students who completed the natural science program are contrasted with all others.

Enrollment in tertiary education is derived from data on admissions from 1990 to the spring semester of 2007, which allows me to follow students over each semester from age 18 up until the spring semester that they turn 25. I analyze enrollment in tertiary education, irrespective of type of institution and of the length of the course taken. As a complement to this very broadly defined outcome, I study enrollment in full-time university education versus all other routes.[12] Tertiary attainment by age 30 is coded from yearly information on the Swedish standard classification of level of education (SUN) (Statistics Sweden 2000) for 2002–2007. I contrast with all others those who (a) completed a three-year tertiary degree or higher or (b) completed a four- to five-year tertiary degree or higher. Table 7.2 depicts an overview of educational attainment by birth cohort.

Educational Performance

I use teacher-assigned grades awarded just before the educational transitions under consideration, which in the Swedish case are the most appropriate achievement measures when separating performance effects from choice effects (compare Erikson and Rudolphi 2010). Depending on cohort, GPAs or grade sums from the final grade of compulsory and upper secondary school are analyzed.[13] In the most recent compulsory system under study, grades are assigned for up to 20 separate subjects. The grade sum is the sum of the 16 best subject scores, and varies between 0 and 320 points. Pupils who completed compulsory school in 1998 were the first who earned grades in this grading system. Before the 1995–96 academic year, a national relative grading system was used, with grades and GPAs varying between 1 and 5, with the national average fixed at 3 and with grades following a normal distribution. For ease of presentation, grade sums are also labeled GPA. A corresponding change occurred for grades at upper secondary level, and students completing upper secondary education in 1997 were the first large cohort to graduate using a grading system with GPA ranging from 0 to 20.

TABLE 7.2
Educational attainment by birth cohort (%)

Birth cohort	1990	1989	1988	1987	1986	1985	1984	1983	1982	1981	1980	1979	1978	1977	1976	1975	1974	1973	1972
ENROLLMENT UPPER SECONDARY (AGE 17)																			
Academic track	42.5	44.5	45.4	45.6	46.8	48.3	50.3	50.4	52.3	51.6	49.0	47.2	44.9	45.1	46.9	44.7	42.9	41.9	41.3
Vocational track	45.8	46.2	45.6	45.8	44.4	42.5	40.3	40.5	39.4	42.9	45.2	46.5	50.3	49.1	47.3	47.2	46.0	45.7	45.9
Noncoded track	0.0	0.0	0.0	0.0	0.0	0.0	0.0	0.0	0.0	0.0	0.0	0.1	1.5	1.0	0.1	0.0	0.0	0.3	0.4
Not enrolled or prep track (IV)	11.7	9.2	9.0	8.6	8.8	9.2	9.4	9.0	8.3	5.5	5.8	6.2	3.4	4.8	5.7	8.1	11.1	12.1	12.4
COMPLETION UPPER SECONDARY (AGE 20)																			
Academic track (including natural science track)				39.3	40.0	41.3	42.5	42.2	43.4	44.7	41.9	41.5	40.6	42.3	43.4	40.8	39.3	37.6	36.7
Natural science track				8.5	8.7	9.6	13.0	12.9	13.9	14.3	13.3	12.1	10.5	9.3	7.9	7.0	6.4	6.1	5.9
Vocational track				37.5	36.7	34.9	32.6	32.0	30.4	33.2	33.2	36.0	39.2	42.8	43.6	45.1	45.1	44.3	44.2
Noncoded track				0.0	0.0	0.0	0.2	0.0	0.0	0.1	0.0	0.0	0.0	0.0	0.1	0.4	0.3	0.4	0.2
Noncompletion or prep track (IV)				23.2	23.3	23.8	24.7	25.8	26.2	22.0	24.9	22.6	20.1	14.9	12.9	13.7	15.2	17.8	18.8
ENROLLMENT TERTIARY (AROUND AGE 25)																			
Any tertiary									44.6	45.6	44.6	43.5	42.2	41.5	41.0	39.7	38.3	36.3	33.3
University full time									32.0	33.0	32.3	31.1	30.0	30.0	29.0	27.4	25.8	22.8	20.3
University full time, excluding four new universities from 1999 or later									27.1	28.0	27.2	26.3	25.3	25.6	25.3	24.5	23.9	22.2	20.0
Any tertiary, conditional on completion of academic upper secondary track									77.7	77.9	78.7	78.0	77.0	74.7	73.2	73.3	72.9	71.2	67.9
University full time, conditional on completion of academic upper secondary track									58.9	59.6	60.3	59.2	58.4	57.3	55.2	54.2	53.2	49.3	45.5
HIGHEST COMPLETED EDUCATION (AGE 30)																			
3-year tertiary or longer														24.3	23.8	22.6	20.7	19.0	17.1
4-year tertiary or longer														13.1	12.5	11.3	10.3	9.3	8.2
Missing information														3.8	3.7	3.6	3.3	3.2	3.3
3-year tertiary or longer, conditional on completion of academic upper secondary track														44.9	43.1	42.0	40.7	39.1	36.1
4-year tertiary or longer, conditional on completion of academic upper secondary track														27.4	25.6	24.3	23.1	21.5	19.4

NOTE: Cohorts shown in descending order.

RESULTS

For conciseness, I show only the main results in the text. When analyses relate to many cohorts and variables, and thus return many estimates, more comprehensive results are reserved for presentation in the web appendix.

Upper Secondary Education

How have transition rates to academic upper secondary schooling changed over the past two decades? Table 7.2 shows transition rates for the 1972 to 1990 birth cohorts who normally enrolled in upper secondary education when they were around 16 years old, in 1988 to 2006 (note that the cohorts are shown in descending order). A long-term increase in enrollment from the 1972 to 1982 birth cohort was followed by a decline in enrollment that continued up until the youngest cohort, born in 1990.[14] This decline is substantial, amounting to 10 percentage points between the 1982 and 1990 cohorts (see Statistics Sweden 2007; Svensson 2008), with an enrollment rate in 2006 almost on a par with that in 1988. To a large extent, the observed decline is a consequence of declining enrollment in natural science and technical upper secondary education (not shown) (see SOU 2010:28; Svensson 2008).

Furthermore, it is evident from Table 7.2 that increasing enrollment in academic tracks by those born between 1978 and 1982 has been at the cost of declining completion rates. For this period, the growing divergence between enrollment and completion rates is found across all social origins, but thereafter the completion rate among pupils of high educational origin slowly increased while remaining stable for those with parents of low education (Table 7.3).

Upper secondary schooling is largely a gendered market, particularly among vocational tracks (Swedish National Agency for Education 2006a, diagram 23). When programs are categorized into broad groups with regard to their academic content, as in Table 7.2, enrollment levels and trends are on the whole similar for boys and girls, although boys have somewhat lower enrollment rates, and their transition rates take a steeper downward trend from the 1982 cohort compared to girls (not shown).

Figure 7.2 shows GPA differences between pupils of different educational backgrounds. The group differences in mean GPA are standardized for each cohort according to the year-specific standard deviation (Cohen's *d*

TABLE 7.3

Upper secondary attainment by birth cohort and educational background (%)

Birth cohort	1972	1973	1974	1975	1976	1977	1978	1979	1980	1981	1982	1983	1984	1985	1986	1987	1988	1989	1990
Grade 9 cohort (age 16)	1988	1989	1990	1991	1992	1993	1994	1995	1996	1997	1998	1999	2000	2001	2002	2003	2004	2005	2006
ENROLLMENT ACADEMIC TRACK (UP UNTIL AGE 17)																			
High education	76	76	75	76	77	75	75	76	77	79	79	77	75	73	72	69	69	68	65
Mid education	40	40	41	43	44	43	42	44	46	49	50	48	47	44	42	41	41	40	38
Low education	22	22	21	23	25	24	24	24	26	28	30	28	30	28	27	27	28	27	26
COMPLETION ACADEMIC TRACK (UP UNTIL AGE 20)																			
High education	70	71	71	72	73	71	69	69	68	71	69	68	67	66	65	63			
Mid education	36	36	38	39	41	40	38	38	39	42	41	40	39	37	36	35			
Low education	19	19	19	20	22	21	20	20	20	22	21	20	21	21	20	20			
COMPLETION ACADEMIC TRACK (UP UNTIL AGE 20) *among those enrolled* in an academic track (up until age 17)																			
High education	91	92	93	93	93	92	91	90	88	89	86	87	88	89	89	89			
Mid education	88	88	90	90	91	90	87	85	83	84	81	81	81	82	82	82			
Low education	85	86	87	86	88	86	79	78	75	76	70	70	70	71	69	70			
COMPLETION NATURAL SCIENCE TRACK (UP UNTIL AGE 20)																			
High education	18	19	18	19	21	23	25	28	29	30	29	28	28	21	19	18			
Mid education	5	5	5	5	6	7	8	10	11	12	12	11	10	7	7	7			
Low education	2	2	2	2	2	3	3	4	4	5	5	4	5	3	3	3			

NOTE: Values for missing categories on educational origin are not shown.

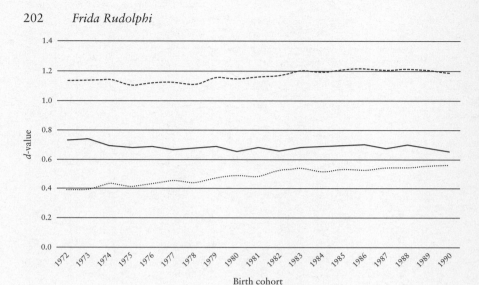

Figure 7.2.   Grade point average differentials at age 16 between children of different educational backgrounds by birth cohort, shown as standardized mean differences (Cohen's *d*). Standardization is carried out for each cohort separately

expresses the difference between two group means divided by the standard deviation for the data; absolute GPA scores for the different background groups are presented in the web appendix, Table A7.1). Concentrating on the gap between pupils of high and low educational origin, the trend is largely characterized by stability, with slightly increasing inequality in grades at age 16 at the beginning of the period; the increase in standardized mean differences is not of substantial size, at around 0.06 of a standard deviation.[15]

There is clearly a growing GPA difference between pupils of mid and low educational origin, amounting to almost 0.20 of a standard deviation. A pressing question is to what extent this development reflects a change in the social composition of the groups. An examination of the relative size of subgroups within the growing category of mid-educated parents reveals that the within-category educational level increases over the studied period (not shown). A change in the social composition of educational categories may be of particular relevance for this large category of mid-educated parents in which very different educational levels are brought together, and I therefore put less focus on group comparisons against this category (see Rudolphi 2011 for more discussion of this issue).

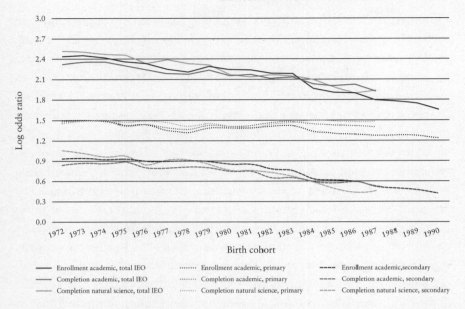

Figure 7.3. Inequality in academic upper secondary education by birth cohort, for high versus low educational background: total IEO, primary effect, and secondary effect

Before turning to the educational transitions to upper secondary education, the results on performance can be summarized as indicating overall stability in the inequality between pupils of high and low educational origins. In contrast, there is a sharp increase in grade differentials between pupils of mid and low educational origin, which is likely to be driven at least in part by a change in the educational composition of the mid category.

Are the fluctuations in transition rates to academic upper secondary schooling associated with changing educational inequality? The association between educational origin and upper secondary outcomes, expressed as log odds ratios, is shown for each birth cohort in Figure 7.3. These log odds ratios are decomposed into primary and secondary effects, using the method explained in Chapter 2 of this volume.

In Figure 7.3 children of high educational background are contrasted with those of low educational background. Declining total inequality is the main story over the period, no matter which academic upper secondary outcome we look at. It is evident that young people with low educated parents improved their upper secondary attainment in relation to their more privileged peers. Over the first 10-year period, when enrollment rates in academic upper secondary education expanded (with the exception of a dip at the beginning of the new program structure, visible in Figure 7.3), total inequality mainly declined, followed by a sharper decline in total IEO in enrollment for the 1984 birth cohort. This decline is related to a structural change in the natural science and technical programs, a pattern that is especially prominent for boys (Rudolphi 2011, appendix 6).

Somewhat surprisingly, Figure 7.3 shows a continuing trend of diminishing inequalities for pupils born in 1982 and later, a period during which transition rates to academic tracks fell. Transition rates to academic programs declined for children of all social origins, particularly for those from highly educated homes, although the rates remained more stable for students with low parental education, who already had low transition rates (see Table 7.3). Equalization of this form is quite unexpected, because declining inequalities have previously been driven by increasing attainment among children of lower social origin in combination with stability or slower improvement among their more privileged peers (Erikson and Jonsson 1993; Erikson and Rudolphi 2010).

Figure 7.3 makes apparent that the main process driving the recent decline in IEO is a decline in secondary effects. From the 1982 birth cohort onward, we observe declining secondary effects and more stable primary effects, meaning that the relative importance of secondary effects in determining IEO diminished over the most recent part of the studied period for cohorts that enrolled in upper secondary education from the late 1990s to 2006. The relative size of primary and secondary effects is shown in Table 7.4, together with decomposition results for other group comparisons.[16]

The long-term reduction in IEO depends on which groups are contrasted (and as will be discussed, how an academic track is defined). When comparing children in families with mid and low levels of education, equalization is observable only for the most recent cohorts. This equalization does not appear to be at all driven by declining primary effects but rather by declining choice effects, which fell to zero by the end of the period. This implies that by the end of the period, all inequality in academic upper secondary education was due to performance differences, although there is no increase in the absolute size of primary effects as secondary effects fall. This is despite the increased grade differentials between those originating in families with mid and low levels of education, largely because the growing

TABLE 7.4

Total inequality and proportion of secondary effects from estimations of primary and secondary effects, respectively, for the transition to academic upper secondary education. Log odds ratios and proportions

Birth cohort	1972	1973	1974	1975	1976	1977	1978	1979	1980	1981	1982	1983	1984	1985	1986	1987	1988	1989	1990
Grade 9 cohort (age 16)	1988	1989	1990	1991	1992	1993	1994	1995	1996	1997	1998	1999	2000	2001	2002	2003	2004	2005	2006
HIGH VS. LOW EDUCATIONAL ORIGIN																			
Proportion secondary effect																			
Enrollment academic	0.38	0.39	0.38	0.40	0.38	0.40	0.40	0.39	0.38	0.38	0.36	0.35	0.32	0.32	0.32	0.29	0.28	0.27	0.25
Completion academic	0.36	0.37	0.36	0.39	0.36	0.36	0.37	0.36	0.34	0.35	0.30	0.31	0.29	0.28	0.30	0.27			
Completion natural science	0.42	0.41	0.39	0.40	0.36	0.39	0.40	0.37	0.35	0.36	0.33	0.32	0.28	0.25	0.22	0.23			
MID VS. LOW EDUCATIONAL ORIGIN																			
Enrollment academic																			
Total inequality	0.88	0.89	0.95	0.91	0.88	0.87	0.81	0.90	0.89	0.88	0.86	0.87	0.73	0.71	0.67	0.62	0.58	0.58	0.54
Proportion secondary effect	0.40	0.41	0.38	0.41	0.37	0.36	0.37	0.36	0.33	0.35	0.28	0.28	0.22	0.21	0.16	0.07	0.04	0.01	−0.07
Completion academic																			
Total inequality	0.89	0.88	0.96	0.92	0.88	0.90	0.87	0.94	0.93	0.94	0.94	0.96	0.85	0.82	0.82	0.77			
Proportion secondary effect	0.40	0.40	0.38	0.41	0.37	0.36	0.38	0.36	0.34	0.36	0.30	0.31	0.26	0.23	0.24	0.18			
Completion natural science																			
Total inequality	0.98	0.91	0.98	0.99	0.93	1.03	1.02	1.01	0.97	0.93	1.04	0.98	0.85	0.79	0.75	0.80			
Proportion secondary effect	0.42	0.39	0.34	0.38	0.32	0.37	0.42	0.37	0.33	0.34	0.34	0.29	0.18	0.14	0.09	0.11			

(continued)

TABLE 7.4 (*Continued*)

Birth cohort	1972	1973	1974	1975	1976	1977	1978	1979	1980	1981	1982	1983	1984	1985	1986	1987	1988	1989	1990
Grade 9 cohort (age 16)	1988	1989	1990	1991	1992	1993	1994	1995	1996	1997	1998	1999	2000	2001	2002	2003	2004	2005	2006
SALARIAT VS. WORKING-CLASS ORIGIN																			
Enrollment academic																			
Total inequality						1.45	1.48				1.34	1.35							
Proportion secondary effect						0.40	0.42				0.38	0.36							
Completion academic																			
Total inequality						1.45	1.46				1.32	1.33							
Proportion secondary effect						0.38	0.39				0.34	0.32							
Completion natural science																			
Total inequality						1.51	1.45				1.29	1.32							
Proportion secondary effect						0.36	0.34				0.32	0.31							

NOTE: Absolute levels are shown in Figure 7.3 for high vs. low educational origin.

grade differentials are offset by a concurrent tendency toward a weakening importance of grades in determining enrollment in academic programs. The last-mentioned development has been shown to occur between the 1972 and 1979 birth cohorts (Gustafsson, Andersson, and Hansen 2000, fig. 15) and continues during the latter part of the studied period between the 1983 and 1990 cohorts (Rudolphi 2011, appendix 6).[17]

How can we understand the declining secondary effects? Shortly after the implementation of prolonged vocational study programs (starting in 1992 and fully implemented in 1995), which coincided with an extraordinarily deep economic recession, enrollment rates in academic programs increased, particularly among those with low educated parents (see Table 7.3). This might have been the result of decreasing differences in costs between vocational and academic study alternatives and perhaps of the poor labor market situation for young people, making the choice of staying on until tertiary level a more viable alternative (Jonsson 2007).

Another possible explanation for the recent decline in secondary effects when comparing pupils of high and low educational origins is the rising popularity of semiacademic tracks (the aesthetic and media programs) among children of highly educated parents and, in particular, among girls. From the mid-1990s, these tracks became increasingly attractive among girls with highly educated parents. In this group, the fastest-growing program was the aesthetic program, whose curriculum is close to the academic social science program.[18] When the definition of academic tracks is extended to the semiacademic aesthetic and media programs (which is the common way of defining academic programs in official educational statistics), the decline in IEO is still present after the 1983 cohort, but the pattern deviates from the results in Figure 7.3 in two respects. First, the IEO level is higher when semiacademic tracks are included in the group of academic programs. Second, the implementation of a new program structure in the mid-1990s was followed by an initial *growth* in IEO between the 1976 and 1978 cohorts (Rudolphi 2011, appendix 6; compare Böhlmark and Holmlund 2011, fig. 7), instead of the decline observable in Figure 7.3. Taken together, these two differences provide a less impressive picture of the long-term decline in total inequality, especially for girls.

Declining interest in academic upper secondary programs among pupils with highly educated parents is a new and unexpected phenomenon, though it remains to be seen whether this change in choice behavior has repercussions for subsequent inequalities in university education. Perhaps young people and their parents after some years of experience with a new upper secondary system have gradually come to value programs with semi-academic profiles as adequate alternatives for those aiming to take higher education later on (which accords with the intentions behind the reform). Alternatively, or additionally, the observed change may be a result of strategic behavior by socially privileged families to improve their children's chances of achieving high grades in the competition for attractive university programs. Strategic behavior in upper secondary education has previously been identified as occurring in relation to course choice within programs (SOU 2004:29, chap. 3).

In Table 7.3 we witness a fall in the strength of primary effects for those born in 1984 when comparing enrollment between the most and least privileged groups. This fall does not appear to follow through to completion of academic upper secondary education. For the cohorts born in 1984 and later, the completion rate among those who enrolled in academic upper secondary programs slightly increased for pupils of high educational origin and remained at more stable (lower) levels for pupils of low educational origin. Completion relies more heavily on previous educational performance than enrollment, and the higher total inequality in completion of an academic upper secondary education compared with enrollment for cohorts 1984 to 1987 is attributable to performance effects.

It turns out that for completion, the proportion of IEO determined by secondary effects was more or less stable up until the 1982 birth cohort, varying between 36 and 40 percent for enrollment in an academic program when comparing the most and least privileged groups (proportions are shown in Table 7.4), which corresponds well with previous results on social-class inequality based on smaller samples and fewer cohorts for the same period (Erikson and Rudolphi 2010). However, from the 1982 cohort onward, the decline in IEO for the transition to academic tracks becomes increasingly attributable to diminishing secondary effects. The relative importance of secondary effects in producing educational inequalities decreased from around 36 percent in 1998 to 25 percent by the end of the period, in 2006. A general pattern for all academic programs is that inequality is somewhat more driven by primary effects when completion is considered rather than enrollment, comparing students of high versus low educational background.

The development and size of total inequality are fairly similar when using alternative measures of academic upper secondary education, though total IEO in natural science education is generally higher compared with other outcomes when children of mid and low educational background are contrasted.[19] Overall, then, my results point to declining secondary effects in the transition to all forms of academic upper secondary education, while primary effects have remained more constant over the period considered.

The focus in the analysis is on academic education, although it should be mentioned that noncompletion of upper secondary education has become of increasing importance when studying education in Sweden. The standards required to achieve a pass grade increased in the mid-1990s, a change that has been most consequential for the completion rates of low-performing students (Björklund et al. 2010). Probably as a consequence, inequality due to family resources increased at the upper secondary level between 1993 and 1999 as measured by completion of any kind of program (Böhlmark and Holmlund 2011, fig. 7; Rudolphi 2011, appendix 6).

Tertiary Education

A substantial share of Swedish young people participates in some kind of higher education. Of the youngest birth cohort within the observation window—those born in 1982—around 45 percent were registered in tertiary education up to age 25. As is the case for several other European countries (OECD 2010), Sweden experienced a significant expansion of higher education (Swedish National Agency for Higher Education 2008, diagram 5). The growth in participation in higher education has been fastest among women, with both entrance and qualification rates increasing at a slower pace for men (e.g., Swedish National Agency for Higher Education 2010, fig. 19). From the 1977 birth cohort onward, the increase in participation rates slowed for university education, which may be related to recovery from the economic recession of the early 1990s (individuals born in 1977 could enter tertiary education from 1996, when the Swedish economy had started to improve). The expansion was sizable at university colleges and universities that earned university status in 1999 or later but less prominent for full-time education at traditional universities (Rudolphi 2011, appendix 8). Not everyone who enrolls in tertiary education takes the examinations necessary to obtain a degree—far from it. Swedish nongraduation rates are high from an international perspective (OECD 2010, chart A4.1), but just as for enrollment, attainment of a degree increases with time over the six cohorts under study.

As illustrated by the flowchart in Figure 7.1, students in higher education are mainly recruited from those who have graduated from an academic upper secondary program. Turning to this positively selected group, around 70 percent or more enroll in tertiary education by around age 25 in most cohorts, but much lower proportions attain a degree by age 30 (see Table 7.2). Interestingly, gender differences in tertiary entrance are small in this restricted sample—once young men complete an academic upper secondary education, they take up tertiary education at almost the same rate as young women (Rudolphi 2011, appendix 9).

Looking at the whole population of 16-year-olds in ninth grade, the social selection in tertiary education is stronger for males, which parallels the pattern for academic upper secondary education (web appendix, Table A7.2). When restricting the analysis to those who graduated from an academic upper secondary program, shown in Table 7.5, the total inequality level is lower (as expected) and the gender difference is reversed for enrollment (with males having lower IEO) while being small for having a degree by age 30.

For men, inequality in enrollment in any kind of tertiary education declined from the 1972 to the 1976 birth cohort among all who attended school up until age 16 (Table 7.6). Berggren (2006) interprets a subsequent rise in IEO as working-class boys' response to an improved labor market situation, increasingly leading them to turn to the labor market instead of higher education. Results shown in Table 7.6 suggest that this is a plausible explanation, since IEO remains at a higher level for six consecutive cohorts after those born in 1976, who all entered higher education while the labor market was recovering. Thus, for young men, decreasing IEO across the older cohorts seems to be of a temporary character for the observed period. For women, declining inequality in enrollment in the full sample of ninth graders is present but much smaller in magnitude, suggesting that young women of low educational background depended less on the labor market situation in their educational decision making than their male peers of similar educational origin during this period.[20]

As expected, the size of inequality is related to the length of education, so that IEO is higher in degrees from longer courses (compare Gustafsson, Andersson, and Hansen 2000). When separating performance from choice

TABLE 7.5

Estimations of total inequality, primary and secondary effects, respectively, for enrollment in tertiary education by around age 25 and attainment of a tertiary degree by age 30. Social-origin comparison: high versus low educational background; salariat versus working-class background. Performance: grade point average from upper secondary education. Population: graduated from academic upper secondary program. Log odds ratios[a]

INCLUDED: GRADUATED FROM ACADEMIC UPPER SECONDARY PROGRAM

HIGH VS. LOW EDUCATIONAL ORIGIN

Birth cohort	WOMEN											MEN										
	1972	1973	1974	1975	1976	1977	1978	1979	1980	1981	1982	1972	1973	1974	1975	1976	1977	1978	1979	1980	1981	1982
Enrollment: any																						
Total	1.60	1.56	1.49	1.55	1.50	1.65	1.51	1.45	1.51	1.61	1.49	1.52	1.28	1.33	1.23	1.25	1.45	1.38	1.36	1.51	1.33	1.49
Primary	0.72	0.73	0.74	0.76	0.83	0.86	0.69	0.72	0.78	0.82	0.83	0.67	0.65	0.74	0.61	0.73	0.76	0.65	0.61	0.68	0.65	0.72
Secondary	0.88	0.83	0.75	0.78	0.68	0.79	0.81	0.73	0.73	0.79	0.66	0.85	0.63	0.60	0.61	0.51	0.69	0.73	0.75	0.85	0.66	0.77
Proportion secondary	0.55	0.53	0.51	0.51	0.45	0.48	0.54	0.50	0.48	0.49	0.44	0.44	0.49	0.45	0.50	0.41	0.47	0.53	0.55	0.55	0.51	0.52
Enrollment: university																						
Total	1.67	1.66	1.55	1.56	1.54	1.57	1.49	1.52	1.48	1.61	1.54	1.62	1.45	1.40	1.29	1.41	1.43	1.33	1.34	1.42	1.26	1.51
Primary	0.66	0.65	0.65	0.70	0.74	0.78	0.61	0.62	0.66	0.70	0.72	0.65	0.61	0.68	0.59	0.71	0.72	0.61	0.58	0.62	0.59	0.66
Secondary	1.00	1.00	0.89	0.86	0.81	0.80	0.88	0.89	0.82	0.91	0.82	0.96	0.84	0.72	0.70	0.70	0.71	0.72	0.76	0.80	0.66	0.85
Proportion secondary	0.60	0.61	0.58	0.55	0.52	0.51	0.59	0.59	0.55	0.57	0.53	0.60	0.58	0.51	0.54	0.50	0.50	0.54	0.57	0.56	0.53	0.56
Degree ≥ 3 years																						
Total	1.08	1.02	0.93	0.99	1.03	1.14						1.02	0.92	0.93	0.90	0.93	1.00					
Primary	0.61	0.59	0.59	0.58	0.64	0.66						0.63	0.56	0.62	0.51	0.61	0.63					
Secondary	0.46	0.43	0.35	0.42	0.40	0.48						0.40	0.36	0.32	0.39	0.32	0.37					
Proportion secondary	0.43	0.42	0.37	0.42	0.38	0.42						0.39	0.39	0.34	0.43	0.34	0.37					

(continued)

TABLE 7.5 (Continued)

Birth cohort	1972	1973	1974	1975	1976	1977	1978	1979	1980	1981	1982
Degree ≥ 4 years											
Total	1.44	1.43	1.29	1.24	1.35	1.39					
Primary	0.78	0.76	0.74	0.73	0.77	0.79					
Secondary	0.66	0.67	0.55	0.51	0.58	0.61					
Proportion secondary	0.46	0.47	0.43	0.41	0.43	0.44					
Enrollment: any											
Total						0.84	0.87				0.85
Proportion secondary						0.37	0.49				0.44
Degree ≥ 3 years											
Total						0.61					
Proportion secondary						0.33					
SALARIAT VS. WORKING-CLASS ORIGIN											
Degree ≥ 4 years											
Total	1.28	1.20	1.30	1.17	1.18	1.17					
Primary	0.76	0.67	0.75	0.63	0.74	0.73					
Secondary	0.52	0.52	0.56	0.54	0.44	0.45					
Proportion secondary	0.41	0.44	0.43	0.46	0.37	0.38					
Enrollment: any											
Total						0.76	0.82				0.89
Proportion secondary						0.41	0.52				0.46
Degree ≥ 3 years											
Total						0.56					
Proportion secondary						0.33					

ᵃOther group comparisons and comparisons between salariat and working-class origin for all tertiary outcomes are shown in the web appendix.

TABLE 7.6

Estimations of total inequality, primary and secondary effects, respectively, for enrollment in tertiary education by around age 25 and attainment of a tertiary degree by age 30. Social-origin comparison: high versus low educational background; salariat versus working-class background. Performance: grade point average in grade 9 (age 16). Population: all in grade 9. Log odds ratios[a]

Birth cohort	WOMEN											MEN										
	1972	1973	1974	1975	1976	1977	1978	1979	1980	1981	1982	1972	1973	1974	1975	1976	1977	1978	1979	1980	1981	1982
Enrollment: any																						
Total	2.34	2.30	2.27	2.24	2.23	2.26	2.15	2.27	2.24	2.29	2.22	2.72	2.60	2.59	2.47	2.41	2.48	2.48	2.53	2.53	2.51	2.52
Primary	1.18	1.20	1.25	1.21	1.26	1.29	1.21	1.31	1.31	1.29	1.35	1.46	1.49	1.44	1.39	1.44	1.46	1.47	1.47	1.46	1.44	1.49
Secondary	1.16	1.10	1.01	1.03	0.97	0.97	0.94	0.96	0.93	0.99	0.87	1.26	1.11	1.15	1.07	0.97	1.03	1.01	1.06	1.07	1.06	1.03
Proportion secondary	0.50	0.48	0.45	0.46	0.44	0.43	0.44	0.42	0.42	0.43	0.39	0.46	0.43	0.45	0.44	0.40	0.41	0.41	0.42	0.42	0.42	0.41
ENROLLMENT: UNIVERSITY																						
Total	2.51	2.49	2.37	2.29	2.32	2.30	2.20	2.33	2.24	2.30	2.29	2.82	2.72	2.65	2.51	2.52	2.55	2.51	2.55	2.55	2.50	2.57
Primary	1.14	1.14	1.17	1.14	1.18	1.23	1.15	1.22	1.20	1.18	1.24	1.41	1.44	1.40	1.35	1.41	1.43	1.42	1.42	1.41	1.40	1.43
Secondary	1.37	1.35	1.20	1.15	1.13	1.07	1.05	1.11	1.04	1.12	1.05	1.41	1.28	1.25	1.16	1.11	1.12	1.08	1.12	1.14	1.10	1.14
Proportion secondary	0.55	0.54	0.51	0.50	0.49	0.46	0.48	0.48	0.46	0.49	0.46	0.50	0.47	0.47	0.46	0.44	0.44	0.43	0.44	0.45	0.44	0.44
Degree ≥ 3 years																						
Total	1.95	1.87	1.84	1.76	1.80	1.85						2.32	2.24	2.30	2.15	2.12	2.15					
Primary	1.07	1.09	1.11	1.05	1.08	1.12						1.35	1.37	1.34	1.28	1.33	1.36					
Secondary	0.88	0.78	0.72	0.71	0.73	0.73						0.98	0.87	0.95	0.87	0.79	0.79					
Proportion secondary	0.45	0.42	0.39	0.41	0.40	0.40						0.42	0.39	0.42	0.41	0.37	0.37					

INCLUDED: ALL IN GRADE 9

HIGH VS. LOW EDUCATIONAL ORIGIN

(continued)

TABLE 7.6 (Continued)

Birth cohort	1972	1973	1974	1975	1976	1977	1978	1979	1980	1981	1982	SALARIAT VS. WORKING-CLASS ORIGIN										
												1972	1973	1974	1975	1976	1977	1978	1979	1980	1981	1982
Degree ≥ 4 years																						
Total	2.49	2.45	2.32	2.17	2.21	2.32						2.59	2.53	2.68	2.45	2.37	2.39					
Primary	1.29	1.29	1.30	1.22	1.23	1.29						1.46	1.51	1.48	1.41	1.43	1.46					
Secondary	1.19	1.15	1.01	0.95	0.98	1.02						1.13	1.02	1.20	1.04	0.94	0.93					
Proportion secondary	0.48	0.47	0.44	0.44	0.44	0.44						0.43	0.40	0.45	0.42	0.40	0.39					
Enrollment: any																						
Total						1.34	1.35				1.30						1.55	1.57				1.52
Proportion secondary						0.39	0.41				0.39						0.39	0.40				0.39
Degree ≥ 3 years																						
Total						1.09											1.39					
Proportion secondary						0.34											0.36					

[a]Other group comparisons and comparisons between salariat and working-class origin for all tertiary outcomes are shown in the web appendix.

effects, I concentrate on students who take the most common route to tertiary education. Decompositions of IEO into primary and secondary effects are summarized in Table 7.5 for those who graduated from academic upper secondary education. The higher level of inequality in degrees from longer programs compared with shorter ones is to a large extent related to choice effects. However, it is also attributable to higher performance effects, presumably because longer programs usually have higher entrance requirements. The relative importance of choice effects in generating educational inequality tends to be slightly higher for degrees from longer educations. The distinction between universities and university colleges appears to be less important than the length of education in determining IEO.[21]

A general conclusion from the decompositions in Table 7.5 is that no overall long-term decline in the strength of primary effects is revealed: men's diminishing inequality in enrollment between the 1972 and 1976 cohorts mainly occurs because of declining secondary effects (a dip in primary effects for the 1975 cohort aside). A tendency toward increased primary effects in IEO in tertiary enrollment is observable for women for the 1979 to 1982 cohorts, although a long-term increase in primary effects does not seem to have occurred over the whole period for women; the absolute level for the 1982 cohort does not exceed the levels for the 1976 and 1977 cohorts, where relatively high primary effects are observed for women and men alike.

In terms of relative importance, secondary effects play a quite decisive role in producing inequalities in tertiary enrollment for people who take the standard pathway, varying between 41 and 56 percent (any tertiary) and 50 and 61 percent (full-time university) of total IEO. As expected, the proportion of secondary effects is higher for tertiary enrollment than for enrollment in academic upper secondary programs. Primary effects play a relatively larger role in generating inequality in attainment of a degree; the proportion of secondary effects in IEO in completing a degree ranges from 34 percent to 47 percent (see Table 7.5).

A complementary analysis based on all who attended compulsory schooling around age 16 is shown in Table 7.6, with primary and secondary effects decomposed on the basis of GPA from compulsory school. The table reveals a higher total level of inequality, and we see that inequality in enrollment is slightly less driven by secondary effects in this nonselective group. Even though grades at age 16 do not function as a selection instrument to tertiary education, performance differences at this age play an important role in producing inequality in higher education later on.

Generally, women tend to have both lower primary and secondary effects than men. For the older cohorts, women's lower total IEO in tertiary education is on the whole due to their weaker primary effects. This means that the relative importance of secondary effects tends to be somewhat larger for women than for men during the first part of the period (a tendency that also holds for younger cohorts for enrollment in full-time university education). The relative importance of secondary effects differs by 4 to 7 percentage points between men and women in the oldest cohorts, while the gender difference is small or nonexistent by the end of the period.

Gender differences in IEO in tertiary education in the full sample of pupils in compulsory school can partly be seen in light of low average graduation rates from academic upper secondary programs for boys with low educational origin (not shown, but see Erikson and Rudolphi 2010; Gustafsson, Andersson, and Hansen 2000 for social class), who in practice were blocked from entering tertiary programs directly after upper secondary schooling (up until the mid-1990s only academic programs provided eligibility for entry into tertiary education without additional schooling). This points to a general and important issue: inequality patterns at lower levels affect social selection at higher levels, even within an educational system without dead ends.

CONCLUSION

In contrast to results for many of the countries portrayed in the influential comparative volume *Persistent Inequality* (Shavit and Blossfeld 1993), the Swedish picture of decreasing educational inequalities during the 20th century has been consistently corroborated by researchers for the period up until the late 1990s for upper secondary education. Through the analysis of register data covering 19 Swedish birth cohorts, my results suggest a continuing trend of declining inequalities in academic upper secondary education from 1999 to 2006, a development that is mainly driven by decreasing secondary effects. Given similar grades, students of low educational origin have come to make upper secondary choices more similar to those of their peers with highly educated parents, while primary effects (performance effects) have remained somewhat stable.

A general conclusion is that primary effects are indeed a prevailing force in producing social inequalities throughout individuals' educational careers. This is particularly the case for the transition to academic upper secondary education, in which 60 to 75 percent of the total inequality is explained by primary effects according to this study. For attainment of a tertiary degree, the proportion of primary effects exceeds 50 percent (53–66 percent) among those who take the most common route to a degree and whose GPA from academic upper secondary education is used as a performance measure. Inequality in enrollment in tertiary education is to a lesser extent driven by performance effects (44–59 percent), in particular enrollment in full-time university education (39–50 percent), compared with inequality in earning a degree. Primary effects account for a substantial part of the inequalities observed across the two most important educational transitions in Sweden, as estimated by contrasting the categories of high and low educational origin.

The analyses of inequality in academic upper secondary education and tertiary education do not suggest any continuous long-term decline in primary effects. The primary effect for inequality in completion of an academic upper secondary education fluctuated somewhat under the studied period, but for the youngest four cohorts (born in 1984 to 1987), most of whom left compulsory school 1999 to 2003, the strength of the primary effect is almost on a par with the estimated level for the 1972 birth cohort.

Efforts to reduce the influence of family background early in the educational career appear to be highly appropriate, because social-origin effects on schooling emerge early and have long-term consequences for subsequent educational attainment. Moreover, slow cognitive development may have negative enduring consequences for individuals' lives beyond their educational achievement. Therefore, a general improvement in the cognitive development of pupils appears to be an important policy aim for reducing educational inequalities and other unwanted effects of ascribed characteristics (compare Erikson and Rudolphi 2011).

"Secondary effects" refer to educational inequalities that are not related to educational performance and ability, and performance is here captured by register information on GPA, which is an important criterion on which students are selected throughout the Swedish educational system. Comparing educational origin effects across educational transitions, the size of secondary effects tends to vary less than does total IEO. This pattern is consistent with the differential selection hypothesis (e.g., Mare 1993), which states that social-origin effects will decline over transitions because students who stay in education become more highly selected on, for example, ability. Compared with the transition to academic upper secondary education, the relative importance of performance in generating IEO at the transition to tertiary education is lower among the positively selected group of academic upper secondary students, which in part may be due to the high average ability in the group. It is indeed a plausible assumption that selection occurs on not only observed factors (in our case, grades) but also unobserved aspects that affect educational success. However, declining educational origin effects across transitions can arise for reasons other than selection processes, for example, if children become gradually less influenced by their parents in their choices (Blossfeld and Shavit 1993). Since the same pattern is consistent with several hypotheses, it is difficult to formulate a critical test of the differential selection hypothesis.

The finding of a recent decline in inequality in academic upper secondary education partly results from a growing interest in semiacademic tracks among students with highly educated parents, especially girls. This may reflect that they, after some years of experience with the current educational system, increasingly regard these programs as an adequate educational pathway to university. The decline perhaps is in part a result of strategic behavior, in that students may choose less academic courses rather than traditional academic programs in the hope of achieving high grades more easily. Whether this is the case is a question that remains to be examined for the youngest cohorts analyzed in this study.

As to the result of declining inequality in upper secondary education, a more general issue concerns the long-term trend of increasing levels of parental education across cohorts. This might have induced a change in the composition of educational groups with regard to academic ability and perhaps also a change in parenting styles and aspirations for children's education. For example, the group of parents with high education might have become less positively selected on these features during the course of educational expansion, which in turn might have increased educational mobility across generations. This could, however, have been counteracted by a corresponding change toward increasing negative selection in the diminishing group of parents at the lowest level of education. On the other hand, rising absolute qualifications in this group, due to improved compulsory schooling, may at the same time lead to diminishing effects of parental education on children's attainment.

Should we expect ever-declining inequalities? From an international perspective, Sweden has been successful in reducing educational inequality in the transition to academic upper secondary schooling during the 20th century, and the results here show a continuing trend of equalization up until 2006. In line with findings and arguments put forward in previous Swedish research (Erikson and Jonsson 1996b), this study points to the potential to reduce IEO by means of attenuating secondary effects. In contrast to primary effects, which are likely to be generated from a very young age and to depend strongly on socialization in the home environment, secondary effects are arguably easier to change, because crucial educational decisions are made when most children can be reached by information and support provided in the school environment. The results showing that declining secondary effects drive equalization in academic upper secondary education to a larger extent than primary effects during recent years are consistent with this assumption.

Nonetheless, I believe that the results raise equality concerns for the future, first, because of the overall stability in primary effects in producing inequality in completion of academic upper secondary education, with no movement toward continuing equalization in performance effects in generating inequality in tertiary education. Second, the focus in this study is on important educational routes that provide good opportunities for entering higher education or advantageous positions in the labor market. When striving for an answer to the question of whether Sweden has experienced declining educational inequalities, it is essential to keep in mind that the key results in this study center on an important, yet incomplete, aspect of the educational system. A shift in the focus toward educational failure and early school dropout leads us to a more pessimistic conclusion. Although my main results suggest a long-term trend in the equalization of academic upper secondary education as a contrast to all other routes, they should be seen in the light of increasing inequality in early school leaving observed during the 1990s.

Remaining social selection to academic upper secondary education now mostly depends on performance inequality, which is a challenge for policy makers to handle. When comparing children of high and low educational background, the estimations indicate that primary effects account for 70 to 75 percent of the inequality in academic upper secondary education for the four most recent cohorts. I expect limited forthcoming equalization without explicit political concern directed toward reducing performance differentials early in the school career. While not directly analyzed here, equalizing performance differences would particularly benefit children of immigrants (Jackson, Jonsson, and Rudolphi 2012; Jonsson and Rudolphi 2011), meaning that such measures would have the potential to reduce educational differences more generally. Improving general societal conditions, ensuring a low level of inequality in children's early living conditions, and including high-quality daycare and preschool for all children may be efficient measures for promoting equality in compulsory and upper secondary performance and hence also in higher education.

NOTES

I am grateful to Jan O. Jonsson and Michelle Jackson for valuable suggestions. I also wish to thank Anders Böhlmark, Robert Erikson, Michael Gähler, Juho Härkönen, and Carina Mood for helpful comments. Financial support from the Swedish Research Council (VR) (721-2004-3454 and 2008-7499); Economic Change, Quality of Life, and Social Cohesion (EQUALSOC); and the Swedish Council for Working Life and Social Research (FAS-centre grant 2006-1515) is gratefully acknowledged.

1. Cohorts born between 1972 and 1977 experienced a tracked course system in two subjects toward the end of compulsory schooling, a system that was abolished in 1994. The choice of track was not decisive for eligibility for upper secondary studies, but the probability of taking the academic routes in upper secondary school was higher among students who took advanced courses (Erikson and Jonsson 1993, chap. 7).

2. A new program structure was implemented in the fall semester of 2011 (prop. 2008/09:199).

3. Two alternative means of acquiring eligibility for entry into tertiary education were available for the cohorts that I study. Municipal adult education (*Komvux*) offered the possibility of pursuing the equivalent to upper secondary education and improving upper secondary school grades. In addition, work experience of four years or more had the potential to increase SweSAT merit up until 2008 (SFS 2007:666; UFB 1992).

4. It is not necessarily appropriate to apply a sequential model (Mare 1980) in the analysis of a sample of students eligible to enter tertiary education directly after upper secondary education, because this excludes a non-negligible fraction of students taking nonstandard routes to higher education. Cameron and Heckman (1998) put emphasis on other potential limitations with sequential modeling, arguing that omitted time-varying variables of importance for all educational transitions (e.g., ability, aspiration, or aspects of family resources) may cause

unobserved heterogeneity across transition models with progressively selective samples, possibly biasing inequality estimates downward. Despite these potential problems, I find it meaningful to analyze how IEO dynamics evolve along educational careers with regard to primary and secondary effects by the use of a sequential transition approach, because it provides empirical results for understanding the role of upper secondary grades in the selection into higher education for the most typical educational route.

5. Declining cohort sizes in combination with a stable or increased number of educational places might have resulted in less competition and lower GPA requirements for entry into academic tracks (Gustafsson, Andersson, and Hansen 2000).

6. Increasing vocational programs from two to three years reduced the alternative costs of choosing an academic program over vocational education.

7. Shorter programs can naturally be assumed to involve lower costs than longer educational alternatives.

8. Birth cohort sizes vary extensively over time, from around 90,000 to 122,000 in the studied population (Table 7.1). The overall pattern of the development of cohort sizes is similar when all foreign-born children are included (Swedish National Agency for Higher Education 2009b, chap. 4).

9. When no register information was available for the year that the child turned 16, I used information for the following year, if available.

10. Categorization of the standard Swedish social-class scheme *socioekonomisk indelning* (SEI) is the following. Salariat: SEI = 60, 56, 46; intermediate class: SEI = 89, 79, 36; working class: SEI = 33, 22, 21, 12, 11 (approximately corresponding to I, II; IIIa, IV, V; and IIIb, VI, VII, respectively, in the EGP classification). Note that medium-level administrators (SEI = 46) are coded into the salariat class, and non-manual workers in unskilled positions (SEI = 33) are coded into the working class, which is not conventional within Swedish stratification research but makes for better international comparisons because the categorization lies closer to the ones applied in other chapters of this volume.

11. Up until 1992 the five academic tracks were three to four years long, providing eligibility for tertiary education. In the most recent system under study, fully implemented in 1995, the most equivalent tracks are either programs for natural science or technology or programs for humanities or social sciences, including international baccalaureate. Special programs can be either academic or vocational. When appropriate register information for special programs was not available (for 0.2–3.8 percent in the 1979–1990 birth cohorts in the analyzed sample), I used GPAs of pupils in the program at school level as a guide for assigning type of track. The terms "program" and "track" are used interchangeably.

12. Full-time education is defined as accumulating 15 credits during one semester (20 ECTS scores in 2007), which is lower than a regular full-time student, who scores 20 credits (30 ECTS scores in 2007). For students who are registered in more than one course, I use information on university status from the most extensive course.

13. I consider upper secondary transitions and grades from three register years—the normal age for completing grade nine plus or minus one year for slightly underage and overage pupils. This means that GPA data relate to pupils ages 15 to 17 for compulsory school and upper secondary enrollment and to pupils ages 18 to 20 for upper secondary completion. Two exceptions are made. Only two years are considered for the 1981 (age 15–16) and 1982 (age 16–17) birth cohorts for grades from compulsory school, because of a change in the grading system. The same applies for upper secondary grades for the 1977 (age 18–19) and 1978 (age 19–20) birth cohorts. The proportions of missing cases are therefore larger for these cohorts (see web appendix Table A7.1).

14. It has been proposed that the dip in enrollment rates to academic programs after the 1976 birth cohort partly originated from the initial optimism shown by pupils toward the new three-year vocational programs being replaced by skepticism after a few years (Broady et al. 2000, 72; see Gustafsson, Andersson, and Hansen 2000, figs. 12 and 13 for the development of transition rates to academic programs for the 1972–1979 birth cohorts comparable to those shown in Table 7.2).

15. Restricting the analysis to grades in mathematics and English and by use of more broadly defined categories of high and low educational background, Böhlmark and Holmlund (2011, fig. 6a) find no increase in standardized mean differences. This somewhat different result from the one shown in Figure 7.2 appears to arise mainly from different categorizations of educational background rather than from dissimilarities in the outcomes (for a more detailed discussion of different results based on diverse measures and methods, see Rudolphi 2011). Furthermore, a trend of stability or no clear trend of explained variance in grades by family resources, measured in various ways, has previously been documented (Böhlmark and Holmlund 2011, fig. 5; Rudolphi 2011; Swedish National Agency of Education 2006b, 28).

16. The main trends visible in Figure 7.3 and Table 7.4 are statistically significant. In Figure 7.3, the total inequality in enrollment in an academic upper secondary track between children of high and low educational origin is significantly higher for pupils born in 1982 compared with students born in 1972, though the relative importance of primary and secondary effects is not significantly different. For the second part of the period, covering pupils born in 1982 and 1990, both the total inequality level and the relative importance of secondary effects differ significantly between the youngest and oldest birth cohorts.

17. This tendency, in turn, is related to changes in the supply and demand for academic upper secondary education. Shrinking birth cohorts may be the main explanation for the first period, a demographic development that in combination with the accessible number of educational places probably resulted in increased availability of educational places for pupils who aspired to take academic tracks (Gustafsson, Andersson, and Hansen 2000, 172). From 1998 onward, the weakening association between grades and enrollment in academic tracks may be related to a general downturn in the demand for academic upper secondary

education. The decline in transition rates from the 1982 birth cohort onward is plausibly related to decreasing demand rather than supply of academic upper secondary education. Although cohort sizes increased between 1998 and 2006, so did the number of upper secondary schools (Swedish National Agency for Education 2011a, diagram 3, 2011b).

18. The aesthetic program is a much less common route than the main academic tracks. Although transition rates to tertiary education are lower from aesthetic and media programs compared with academic tracks, they are still fairly high. Around 76 percent of the pupils who completed the natural science program in 2005 enrolled in higher education within three years. The corresponding rate for the social science track was 54 percent, followed by the aesthetic and media programs with 40 percent and 31 percent, respectively (Swedish National Agency for Education 2009a).

19. Contrary to my expectation, the results for completion of the natural science track do not stand out as showing relatively stronger primary effects than those for completion of academic programs as a whole.

20. The IEO development for women from the 1976 cohort onward is perhaps related to a slower improvement of the employment possibilities in female-dominated segments of the labor market. A decline in class inequalities in enrollment during the first part of the studied period is more notable for girls when transitions only up to age 21 are taken into consideration (Berggren 2006; Gustafsson, Andersson, and Hansen 2000).

21. Interpreting the change in IEO in university enrollment is complicated by a compositional change in university institutions, since three university colleges earned university status in 1999.

REFERENCES

Berggren, Caroline. 2006. "Labour Market Influence on Recruitment to Higher Education: Gender and Class Perspectives." *Higher Education* 52:121–48.
———. 2007. "Broadening Recruitment of Higher Education through the Admission System: Gender and Class Perspectives." *Studies in Higher Education* 32:97–116.
———. 2008. "Horizontal and Vertical Differentiation within Higher Education: Gender and Class Perspectives." *Higher Education Quarterly* 62:20–39.
Björklund, Anders. Melissa A. Clark, Per-Anders Edin, Peter Fredriksson, and Alan B. Kreuger. 2005. *The Market Comes to Education: An Evaluation of Sweden's Surprising School Reforms.* New York: Russell Sage Foundation.
Björklund, Anders, Peter Fredriksson, Jan-Eric Gustafsson, and Björn Öckert. 2010. *Den svenska utbildningspolitikens arbetsmarknadseffekter: vad säger forskningen?* Report 2010:13. Uppsala, Sweden: Institute for Evaluation of Labour Market and Education Policy (IFAU).

Björklund, Anders, Mikael Lindahl, and Krister Sund. 2003. "Family Background and School Performance during a Turbulent Era of School Reforms." *Swedish Economic Policy Review* 10:111–36.

Blossfeld, Hans-Peter, and Yossi Shavit. 1993. "Persisting Barriers: Changes in Educational Opportunities in Thirteen Countries." In *Persistent Inequality: Changing Educational Attainment in Thirteen Countries*, edited by Yossi Shavit and Hans-Peter Blossfeld. Boulder, CO: Westview.

Boalt, Gunnar. 1947. *Skolutbildning och skolresultat för barn ur olika samhällsgrupper i Stockholm*. Stockholm: P. A. Norstedt and Söner.

Böhlmark, Anders, and Helena Holmlund. 2011. *20 år med förändringar i skolan: Vad har hänt med likvärdigheten?* Stockholm: Centre for Business and Policy Studies (SNS).

Boudon, Raymond. 1974. *Education, Opportunity, and Social Inequality. Changing Prospects in Western Society*. New York: Wiley.

Bourdieu, Pierre. 1996. *The State Nobility*. Cambridge: Polity Press.

Breen, Richard, and John H. Goldthorpe. 1997. "Explaining Educational Differentials: Towards a Formal Rational Action Theory." *Rationality and Society* 9:275–305.

Breen, Richard, and Jan O. Jonsson. 2000. "Analyzing Educational Careers: A Multinomial Transition Model." *American Sociological Review* 65:754–72.

Broady, Donald, Mats B. Andersson, Mikael Börjesson, Jonas Gustafsson, Elisabeth Hultqvist, and Mikael Palme. 2000. "Skolan under 1990-talet: sociala förutsättningar och utbildningsstrategier." In *Välfärd och skola. Antologi från Kommittén välfärdsbokslut*. Swedish Government Official Report (SOU) 2000:39. Stockholm: Fritzes.

Buis, Maarten L. 2010. "Direct and Indirect Effects in a Logit Model." *Stata Journal* 10:11–29.

Cameron, Stephen V., and James. J. Heckman. 1998. "Life Cycle Schooling and Dynamic Selection Bias: Models and Evidence for Five Cohorts of American Males." *Journal of Political Economy* 106:262–333.

Cliffordson, Christina, and Berit Askling. 2006. "Different Grounds for Admission: Its Effects on Recruitment and Achievement in Medical Education." *Scandinavian Journal of Educational Research* 50:45–62.

Erikson, Robert. 1984. "Social Class of Men, Women and Families." *Sociology* 18:500–514.

———. 2007. "Social Selection in Stockholm Schools: Primary and Secondary Effects on the Transition to Upper Secondary Education." In *From Origin to Destination. Trends and Mechanisms in Social Stratification Research*, edited by Stefani Scherer, Reinhard Pollak, Gunnar Otte, and Markus Gangl. Frankfurt, Germany: Campus Verlag.

Erikson, Robert, and John H. Goldthorpe. 1992. *The Constant Flux: A Study of Class Mobility in Industrial Societies*. Oxford: Clarendon Press.

Erikson, Robert, John H. Goldthorpe, Michelle Jackson, Meir Yaish, and

David R. Cox. 2005. "On Class Differentials in Educational Attainment." *Proceedings of the National Academy of Sciences* 102:9730–33.

Erikson, Robert, and Jan O. Jonsson. 1993. *Ursprung och utbildning. Social snedrekrytering till högre studier.* Stockholm: Fritzes.

———. 1996a. "The Swedish Context." In *Can Education Be Equalized?* edited by Robert Erikson and Jan O. Jonsson. Boulder, CO: Westview.

———. 1996b. "Introduction. Explaining Class Inequality in Education: The Swedish Test Case." In *Can Education Be Equalized?* edited by Robert Erikson and Jan O. Jonsson. Boulder CO: Westview.

Erikson, Robert, and Frida Rudolphi. 2010. "Change in Social Selection to Upper Secondary School: Primary and Secondary Effects in Sweden." *European Sociological Review* 26:291–305.

———. 2011. "Social snedrekrytering till teoretisk gymnasieutbildning." In *Utvärdering genom uppföljning. Longitudinell individforskning under ett halvt sekel*, edited by Allan Svensson, 305. Gothenburg, Sweden: Acta Universitatis Gothoburgensis.

Fredriksson, Peter, and Jonas Vlachos. 2011. *Reformer och resultat: kommer regeringens utbildningsreformer att ha någon betydelse?* Studier i Finanspolitik 2011/3. Stockholm: Finanspolitiska rådet.

Gustafsson, Jan-Eric, Anette Andersson, and Mikael Hansen. 2000. "Prestationer och prestationsskillnader i 1990-talets skola." In *Välfärd och skola.* Swedish Government Official Report (SOU) 2000:39. Stockholm: Fritzes.

Gustafsson, Jan-Eric, and Kajsa Yang-Hansen. 2009. "Resultatförändringar i svensk grundskola." In *Vad påverkar resultaten i svensk grundskola? Kunskapsöversikt om betydelsen av olika faktorer.* Swedish National Agency for Education. Stockholm: Fritzes.

Hällsten, Martin. 2011a. "The Structure of Educational Decision-Making and Consequences for Inequality: A Swedish Test Case." *American Journal of Sociology* 116:806–54.

———. 2011b. "Late Entry in Swedish Tertiary Education: Can the Opportunity of Lifelong Learning Promote Equality over the Lifecourse?" *British Journal of Industrial Relations* 49:537–59.

Härnqvist, Kjell. 1958. *Reserverna för högre utbildning. Beräkningar och metoddiskussion. 1955 års universitetsutredning III.* Swedish Government Official Report (SOU) 1958:11. Stockholm: Idun.

Jackson, Michelle, Robert Erikson, John H. Goldthorpe, and Meir Yaish. 2007. "Primary and Secondary Effects in Class Differentials in Educational Attainment: The Transition to A-Level Courses in England and Wales." *Acta Sociologica* 50:211–29.

Jackson, Michelle, Jan O. Jonsson, and Frida Rudolphi. 2012. "Ethnic Inequality in Choice-Driven Education Systems: A Longitudinal Study of Performance and Choice in England and Sweden." *Sociology of Education* 85:158–78.

Jonsson, Jan O. 2004. "Equality at a Halt? Social Mobility in Sweden, 1976–

1999." In *Social Mobility in Europe*, edited by Richard Breen. Oxford: Oxford University Press.

———. 2007. "Gymnasiets yrkesutbildningar efter reformen: mer valvärda alternativ?" In *Utbildningsvägen: vart leder den? Om ungdomar, yrkesutbildning och försörjning*, edited by Jonas Olofsson. Stockholm: Centre for Business and Policy Studies (SNS).

Jonsson, Jan O., and Robert Erikson. 2000. "Understanding Educational Inequality: The Swedish Experience." *L'Année Sociologique* 50:345–82.

———. 2007. "Sweden: Why Educational Expansion Is Not Such a Great Strategy for Equality: Theory and Evidence." In *Stratification in Higher Education: A Comparative Study*, edited by Yossi Shavit, Richard Arum, and Adam Gamoran. Stanford, CA: Stanford University Press.

Jonsson, Jan O., Carina Mood, and Erik Bihagen. 2010. "Poverty in Sweden, 1991–2007: Change, Dynamics, and Intergenerational Transmission of Poverty during Economic Recession and Growth." Working paper 10/2011, Swedish Institute for Social Research. English version of *Social Rapport*. Stockholm: National Board of Health and Welfare.

Jonsson, Jan O., and Frida Rudolphi. 2011. "Weak Performance—Strong Determination: School Achievement and Educational Choice among Ethnic Minority Students in Sweden." *European Sociological Review* 27:487–508.

Josefsson, Anneli, and Lena Unemo. 2003. *Bilaga 10, Långtidsutredningen 2003*. Swedish Government Official Report (SOU) 2003:96. Stockholm: Fritzes.

Lucas, Samuel. R. 2001. "Effectively Maintained Inequality: Education Transitions, Track Mobility, and Social Background Effects." *American Journal of Sociology* 106:1642–90.

Mare, Robert D. 1980. "Social Background and School Continuation Decisions." *Journal of the Statistical Association* 75:295–305.

———. 1981. "Change and Stability in Educational Stratification." *American Sociological Review* 46:72–87.

———. 1993. "Educational Stratification on Observed and Unobserved Components of Family Background." In *Persistent Inequality: A Comparative Study of Educational Attainment in Thirteen Countries*, edited by Yossi Shavit and Hans-Peter Blossfeld. Boulder, CO: Westview.

OECD. 2010. *Education at a Glance 2010—OECD Indicators 2010*. Paris: OECD Publishing.

Proposition 1990/91:85. *Att växa med kunskaper: om gymnasieskolan och vuxenutbildningen*. Regeringens proposition.

Proposition 2008/09:199. *Högre krav och kvalitet i den nya gymnasieskolan*. Regeringens proposition.

Rudolphi, Frida. 2011. "Ever Declining Inequalities? Primary and Secondary Effects in Sweden in the Transition to Upper Secondary and Higher Education for Students Born in 1972–1990." In *Inequality in Educational Outcomes. How Aspirations, Performance, and Choice Shape School Careers in Swe-*

den. PhD diss. 86. Stockholm: Stockholm University, Swedish Institute for
Social Research.

SFS. 2007. *Ändring 2007:666 i Högskoleförordningen 1993:100.*

Shavit, Yossi, and Hans-Peter Blossfeld, eds. 1993. *Persistent Inequality: A Comparative Study of Educational Attainment in Thirteen Countries.* Boulder,
CO: Westview.

SOU. 2004. *Tre vägar till den öppna högskolan.* Betänkande av Tillträdesutredningen. Swedish Government Official Report (SOU) 2004:29. Stockholm:
Fritzes.

———. 2010. *Vändpunkt Sverige: ett ökat intresse för matematik, naturvetenskap, teknik och IKT.* Swedish Government Official Report (SOU) 2010:28.
Stockholm: Fritzes.

Statistics Sweden. 1982. *Socioekonomisk indelning (SEI).* MIS 1982:4. Stockholm: Statistiska centralbyrån.

———. 2000. *Svensk utbildningsnomenklatur, SUN 2000.* MIS 2000:1. Stockholm: Statistiska centralbyrån.

———. 2007. *Utbildningsstatistisk årsbok 2008. Utbildning och forskning.*
Örebro, Sweden: Statistiska centralbyrån.

———. 2009. *Education in Sweden 2009.* Örebro: Statistiska centralbyrån.

Svensson, Allan. 2008. *Genomströmningen i gymnasieskolan. En studie av
elever som antogs till gymnasieskolan hösten 2003.* IPD-rapport nr 2008:02.
Gothenburg, Sweden: Göteborgs universitet, Institutionen för pedagogik och
didaktik.

Swedish National Agency for Education. 2006a. *Könsskillnader i måluppfyllelse
och utbildningsval.* Report 287. Stockholm: Fritzes.

———. 2006b. *Vad händer med likvärdigheten i skolan? En kvantitativ analys av
variation och likvärdighet över tid.* Report 275. Stockholm: Fritzes.

———. 2009a. *Beskrivande data 2009. Förskoleverksamhet, skolbarnomsorg,
skola och vuxenutbildning.* Report 335. Stockholm: Fritzes.

———. 2009b. *Vad påverkar resultaten i svensk grundskola? Kunskapsöversikt
om betydelsen av olika faktorer.* Stockholm: Fritzes.

———. 2011a. *Skolor och elever i gymnasieskolan, läsåret 2010/2011.* PM 2011-
02-24. Dnr 71-2011-00014. Stockholm: Skolverket.

———. 2011b. Tables available at http://www.skolverket.se/forskola_och_
skola/2.300/fristaende-skolors-utveckling-1.100553 (in Swedish).

Swedish National Agency for Higher Education. 2008. *Women and Men in
Higher Education.* Report 2008:48 R. Stockholm: Högskoleverket.

———. 2010. *Universitet & högskolor. Högskoleverkets årsrapport 2010.* Report
2010:10 R. Stockholm: Högskoleverket.

UFB. 1992. *Utbildningsväsendets författningsböcker* (UFB) *1992/93. Del 3.
Högskolans utbildning och forskning.* Stockholm: Fritzes.

CHAPTER EIGHT

Dentist, Driver, or Dropout?

Family Background and Secondary Education
Choices in Denmark

Anders Holm and Mads Meier Jæger

Although Denmark belongs to the Scandinavian comprehensive welfare state family, rich evidence suggests that social-class background still has a substantial impact on educational success in this national context. In terms of the *quantity* of inequality, social-class differences in educational attainment decreased over most of the 20th century in Denmark (e.g., Benjaminsen 2006; Thomsen 2008; for evidence on other countries, see Breen and Jonsson 2005; Breen et al. 2009). Nevertheless, class inequalities in educational attainment remain fairly strong. In terms of the *quality* of inequality, recent research shows that social-class differences in educational attainment in Denmark are mainly driven by social-class differences in cultural resources (Jæger and Holm 2004; Jæger 2009), but also to some extent by differences in economic and social resources (e.g., McIntosh and Munk 2007; Jæger 2007a; Jæger and Holm 2007).

In this chapter we synthesize previous research on Denmark by decomposing the total effect of family background on educational attainment into primary and secondary effects. As explained in more detail in Chapter 1 of this volume, the distinction between primary and secondary effects was popularized by Boudon (1974). Existing research suggests that both primary and secondary effects matter in Denmark. First, there is compelling evidence that family background, typically measured by social-class background and parents' educational attainment, is strongly linked to academic ability; that is, primary effects exist (e.g., Andersen et al. 2001; Jæger 2009). Second, research also documents substantial effects of family background on educational outcomes even after controlling for demonstrated academic ability; that is, secondary effects exist (e.g., Hansen 1995; McIntosh and Munk

2007; Jæger 2009). Secondary effects have been linked to factors such as students' desire to preserve the relative social position of the family of origin (Holm and Jæger 2008) and to their beliefs about the future economic and social returns to educational decisions (Jæger 2007b).

Although previous research shows that primary and secondary effects exist, this chapter is the first to systematically identify the relative importance of primary and secondary effects of family background on educational success in Denmark. In doing so, we seek to assess the position of Denmark in comparison to other countries in terms of the relative importance of primary and secondary effects (see Erikson et al. 2005; Erikson 2007; Jackson et al. 2007). Furthermore, in addition to cross-sectional analysis we carry out cross-time analysis by comparing primary and secondary effects for two birth cohorts, born around 1954 and 1984, respectively, who made the first educational transition around 1970 and 2000, respectively. This analysis allows us to assess whether the relative importance of primary and secondary effects has changed over time.

The chapter focuses on the primary and secondary effects of family background on the transition that students make at around age 16, from elementary school to different types of secondary education. This transition is very important in the Danish educational system because at this stage students choose whether to pursue an academic or a vocational track. Furthermore, because there is very little migration between the two tracks, the decision not to enter the academic track at age 16 is in practice irreversible and has long-term consequences for students' later educational careers and socioeconomic outcomes (Jæger and Holm 2007).

The Danish educational system has some idiosyncrasies that we also address in the chapter. Unlike England or the United States, in which students decide whether to continue in an academically oriented secondary education track (A-levels in England and high school degree in the United States), the choice set in Denmark includes two *qualitatively different* options: academic upper secondary education and vocational secondary education. Existing research finds that students who choose the academic upper secondary education track are very different from students who choose the vocational secondary education track in terms of average academic ability, family background, and educational aspirations (e.g., Jæger and Holm 2007; Jæger 2007a, 2009). In our empirical analysis we take the more complex set of educational options in Denmark into account by estimating primary and secondary effects in a multinomial (rather than binary) analytic framework.

THE DANISH EDUCATIONAL SYSTEM

The Danish educational system combines features of a German-oriented path-dependent system and a Scandinavian equality-oriented system. There is no tracking in the elementary school system (tracking similar to that found in Germany existed previously but was abolished in two reforms, in 1958 and 1975). Students normally finish elementary school after the 9th grade at age 16. An optional 10th grade also exists. Respondents in our 1954 cohort were exposed to tracking from the 7th grade of elementary school (into an academic or a nonacademic type of lower secondary education), whereas respondents in our 1984 cohort were not exposed to any tracking. However, respondents in the 1954 cohort who were placed in the nonacademic track in lower secondary education were not formally limited with respect to their educational options after elementary school. Consequently, even when tracking existed it was much less stringent than in, for example, the German system and did not preclude any educational choices at later stages.

Educational Choices after Elementary School

The first and arguably most important educational transition that students make in the Danish educational system is the choice after elementary school. Here, students have three options: (1) leave the educational system, (2) enter upper secondary education, or (3) enter vocational secondary education.

Upper secondary education is a three-year, academically oriented track that prepares students for higher education. The most common type of upper secondary education is the *Gymnasium*, which focuses on general-education academic subjects (Danish, foreign languages, sciences, history, etc.). Today, around 50 percent of students enter the *Gymnasium*. A second type of upper secondary education, the *HF* (*Højere Forberedelseseksamen*, or higher preparatory examinations), was introduced in 1968. The *HF*, which grants eligibility for higher education, was designed for late-starting students who did not enter the *Gymnasium* immediately after elementary school but who wished to obtain upper secondary level credentials (the *HF* is similar to the General Educational Development certificate in the United States). Both types of upper secondary education, the traditional *Gymnasium* and the *HF*, were available to our respondents in the two cohorts. In the 1980s two new types of upper secondary education specializing in, respectively, technical (HTX) and mercantile (HHX) subjects were introduced; in our analysis, only the 1984 cohort could enroll in these programs. The HTX and the HHX offer an academic track with a practical flavor and may therefore attract some students from lower-class backgrounds who might have the academic ability to pursue academic credentials but who may feel uncomfortable with traditional academic teaching styles in the old *Gymnasium*. Therefore one might expect that the academic track has become more attractive to lower-class students in the 1984 cohort compared to the 1954 cohort.

Vocational secondary education normally takes three to four years and consists of a combination of school-based training (mechanics, bricklaying, hairdressing, etc.) and on-the-job training as an apprentice with an employer. Upon completion of their training, students receive a certificate that attests to their educational qualifications, and they enter the labor market (often with the employer with whom they apprenticed).

Figure 8.1 shows transition probabilities for the 1954 and the 1984 cohorts. The figure shows that 52 percent of the respondents in the 1954 cohort left the educational system after elementary school, 26 percent completed vocational secondary education, and 22 percent completed upper secondary education. In the 1984 cohort 35 percent left the educational system after elementary school, 20 percent completed vocational secondary education, and 45 percent completed upper secondary education.[1]

Educational Choices after Upper Secondary Education

A second educational transition exists for students who complete upper secondary education. These students may enter one of two types of higher education: university college and university.

University college (three–four years) comprises a range of courses typically targeted at jobs in the public sector. These include, for example, schoolteacher, nurse, social worker, child care worker, and some types of engineering. Today, almost all types of courses at university colleges require applicants to have completed upper secondary education. When the 1954 cohort went through the educational system it was possible to be admitted to some courses at university colleges without first having completed upper secondary education. However, very few people used this option.

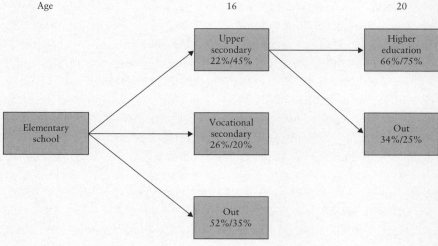

Figure 8.1.   Flowchart for educational pathways
N O T E : First percentage represents the 1954 cohort, second the 1984.

University (five–six years) includes all types of education at the university level. Courses include, for example, medicine, law, economics, architecture, civil engineering, and natural sciences. Today, almost all university-level courses are built around a three-year bachelor's (BA, BSc) degree and a two-year master's (MA, MSc) degree. A doctorate normally takes three years after completing a master's degree. When the 1954 cohort went through the educational system most university degrees took five or six years to complete, and there was no formal distinction between BA and MA levels.

In Figure 8.1 we have merged university college and university into a single group labeled higher education. The figure shows that in the 1954 cohort two-thirds of those who completed upper secondary education also later completed some type of higher education. Unfortunately, data on tertiary-level education are not available for the 1984 cohort. Instead, in Figure 8.1 we plot national figures for tertiary-level completion rates for similarly aged cohorts (figures are from Undervisningsministeriet 2010, 72–77), which show that around three-quarters of those who complete upper secondary education later complete some type of higher education.

DATA AND VARIABLES

Data

We use two data sources. Our first data source is the Danish Longitudinal Survey of Youth (DLSY). The DLSY is a cohort study with a nationally representative sample of 3,151 participants who were born around 1954 (see Jæger and Holm 2007; Jæger 2007b). The DLSY respondents were first interviewed in 1968 at age 14 (when they attended the seventh grade of elementary school), and they have since been interviewed in 1970, 1971, 1973, 1976, 1992, 2001, and 2004. The response rate in the DLSY has remained high throughout its history. In the 2001 wave, 2,507, or 79.6 percent, of the original sample members were successfully interviewed. In this chapter we analyze data from the early DLSY waves (1968–1976), in which there was practically no attrition among the primary respondents.[2]

Our second data source is the Program for International Student Assessment Longitudinal (PISA-L) survey. The PISA-L is a follow-up survey of the original participants in the Danish PISA survey, which was carried out in 2000. The Danish PISA 2000 sample of eighth-grade elementary school students (i.e., 15- or 16-year-olds born around 1984) was reinterviewed in 2004 when the students had reached their late teens or early 20s. The PISA-L focused on postelementary schooling decisions, occupational aspirations, and a range of other topics. Of the nationally representative sample of 3,954 participants in the 2000 PISA sample, interviews were successfully carried out with 3,084 respondents in the 2004 PISA-L survey. This yielded a response rate of 78 percent (Andersen 2005).

The DLSY and the PISA-L allow us to analyze the primary and secondary effects of social-class background on educational choices after elementary school because both surveys include information on (1) educational choice after elementary school, (2) academic ability at around age 14, and (3) family background characteristics (parental social class and parental education).

Variables

Table 8.1 shows descriptive statistics for all variables used in the analysis. The dependent variable measures type of secondary education, with the three possible outcomes being no education beyond elementary school, vocational secondary education, and upper secondary education. Our measure

TABLE 8.1

Descriptive statistics: Percentages (categorical variables), means,
and standard deviations

Variable	1954 COHORT (DLSY)		1984 COHORT (PISA-L)	
	%	SD	%	SD
Secondary education choice				
No education beyond elementary school	51.4		35.1	
Vocational secondary education	26.2		19.5	
Upper secondary education	22.4		45.4	
Academic ability	0	1.0	0	1.0
Social class background				
Salariat	13.1		22.6	
Intermediate	32.9		50.5	
Working class	50.5		14.0	
Missing	3.5		12.9	
Parental education				
High	9.0		49.2	
Medium	36.9		33.2	
Low	37.9		10.6	
Missing	16.2		7.0	
Gender (= female)	43.4		51.1	
Number of observations	3,038		3,073	

NOTE: DLSY = Danish Longitudinal Survey of Youth; PISA-L = Program for International Student Assessment Longitudinal.

of secondary education pertains to completion of the different types of secondary education rather than to enrollment, because in the 1954 cohort we have reliable information on completion but not reliable information on enrollment (but noncompletion).

The principal explanatory variables are academic ability, social-class background, and parental education. In the DLSY our measure of academic ability is the first component from a principal component analysis of three cognitive tests measuring respondents' mathematical, verbal, and spatial ability, carried out when respondents were 14 years old. This measure of academic ability accounts for 67 percent of the total variance in the three cognitive tests. In the PISA-L our measure of academic ability is the respondent's score on the PISA reading ability test carried out at age 15 (see OECD 2000). Both academic ability variables are standardized. Unfortunately, the DLSY and PISA-L do not include any information on respondents' academic performance, for example, their grade point average (GPA) from the final examinations after ninth grade. As a consequence, we are not able to include any measure of academic performance that is observable to the respondent. However, not being able to control for academic performance such as GPA may be less of a problem in the Danish case than elsewhere for two reasons. First, unlike in other countries, student GPA from elementary school has no formal bearing on the range of available educational options after elementary school. Danish students typically apply for upper second-ary or vocational secondary education in the spring of their ninth-grade year and several months before their final examinations at the end of the ninth grade. Consequently, students do not know what their GPA will be when they decide to apply for secondary education. Second, GPA is not important when secondary education schools (academic and vocational) admit students because schools are not allowed to select students based on GPA and because schools do not know applicants' GPA when they admit students (in most cases admission is based on the proximity of a student's home to the school). Consequently, because of the lack of formal require-ments students have a de facto free choice in the secondary education they select (but not necessarily the particular school).[3]

Our measure of social class is based on the Erikson-Goldthorpe-Porto-carero (EGP) class schema (see Erikson and Goldthorpe 1992). We use the dominance principle and assign the social-class position of the respondent's father or mother, whichever is higher, as our indicator of social-class back-ground. We use three class categories: (1) salariat (EGP classes I and II), (2) intermediate (EGP classes IIIa, IVabc, and V), and (3) working class (EGP classes IIIb, VI, and VII). We also include an indicator for missing data on social-class background (for example, if neither parent was active in the labor market or if information on social class was missing). Table 8.1 shows that the distributions of social-class background differ across the two co-horts. In the 1954 cohort around half the respondents have working-class backgrounds, whereas this was the case for less than a quarter of the 1984 cohort. In the 1984 cohort only 14 percent of respondents have a working-class background, while relatively more respondents have an intermediate-class background. Consequently, our data suggest a comparatively high level of social mobility between the two generations.

Our measure of parental education is based on the highest level of edu-cation of the respondent's father or mother. We distinguish three levels of education: (1) low (elementary school only), (2) medium (vocational or upper secondary education but no higher education), and (3) high (university college or university education). From Table 8.1 we also see marked differences across cohorts in parental education. In the 1954 cohort, less than 10 percent of the parents had high education; in the 1984 cohort, almost half the parents had high education. Our data indicate increasing levels of parental educational attainment.

RESULTS

In this section we present results from the empirical analysis of primary and secondary effects on educational choices in Denmark. First, we provide summary evidence of primary effects in both cohorts. Then, for secondary effects we present two sets of results. Our first set of results concerns primary and secondary effects with regard to the probability of completing upper secondary education, that is, the academic track in Danish secondary education. We carry out this analysis to ensure that our results are comparable with previous studies analyzing the educational systems in the United States and Great Britain, in which students decide whether to continue in the academic track. Next, we present results that take into account the particular trichotomous choice set that Danish students face after elementary school (i.e., the choice between no education, upper secondary education, and vocational secondary education). In the binary case we decompose the total effect of social-class background and parental education on secondary education choice into primary and secondary effects using the method described in Chapter 2 of this volume. In the trichotomous case we use our own methodological approach, which is similar conceptually to the one used in the binary case but somewhat different technically.

Primary Effects

Table 8.2 shows results from linear regressions of academic ability on social-class background and parental education. These effects can be interpreted as benchmark estimates of primary effects, and because the academic ability variables are standardized, the effects of the family background variables are scaled as changes in the distribution of academic ability in fractions of a standard deviation. For both cohorts we find that both social-class background and parental education are statistically significant predictors of

TABLE 8.2

Results from linear regressions of academic ability on
social-class background

Variable	1954 cohort	1984 cohort
Social-class background		
Salariat	0.519***	0.633***
Intermediate	0.234***	0.443***
Working	—	—
R^2	0.05	0.05
Parental education		
High	0.599***	0.856***
Medium	0.233***	0.590***
Low	—	—
R^2	0.05	0.08
N	2,452	2,579

N O T E : Models do not include observations with missing values on
social-class background or parental education.
***$p < 0.001$.

academic ability at around age 14. In the 1954 cohort, respondents whose
parents were in the salariat or intermediate class or who had high or medium education display 0.5–0.6 and 0.2–0.3 of a standard deviation, respectively, higher academic ability compared to respondents whose parents
were in the working class or who had low (i.e., elementary school) education. In the 1984 cohort results are very similar for social-class background,
while differences in academic ability by parental education appear to be
somewhat larger. Consequently, it seems that over time parental education became a stronger predictor of academic performance. Our findings
resemble previous results on Denmark (e.g., Hansen 1995; Jæger 2007a,
2009; Jæger and Holm 2007).

Secondary Effects for Upper Secondary Education

Table 8.3 shows results from binary logistic regressions of the probability
of completing upper secondary education. This type of education is the
academic track in secondary education in Denmark, and it is the gateway
to higher education. We model the probability of completing upper secondary education as a function of either social-class background or parental
education and of academic ability at around age 14. The effects of social
class and parental education on the probability of completing upper secondary education conditional on academic ability can be interpreted as

TABLE 8.3

Results from logistic regressions of upper secondary education. Log-odds coefficients and average partial effects (APEs)

Variable	1954 COHORT		1984 COHORT	
	Coefficient	APE	Coefficient	APE
Academic ability	1.505***	0.215	0.489***	0.112
Social-class background				
Salariat	1.425***	0.239	0.562***	0.132
Intermediate	0.815***	0.120	0.319**	0.073
Working	—	—	—	—
Pseudo R^2	0.214		0.044	
Academic ability	1.490***	0.203	0.458***	0.106
Parental education				
High	2.271***	0.392	0.786***	0.181
Medium	0.935***	0.126	0.620***	0.140
Low	—	—	—	—
Pseudo R^2	0.243		0.047	
N	2,452		2,579	

NOTE: Models do not include observations with missing values on social-class background or parental education.

**$p < 0.01$; ***$p < 0.001$.

benchmark estimates of secondary effects of family background on educational success.

Table 8.3 reports log-odds coefficients and average partial effects (APEs). The APEs express the expected change in the probability of completing upper secondary education (averaged over the whole sample) for respondents with different values on the social-class and parental education variables. In the 1954 cohort we find that, after taking into account academic ability, there are highly significant differences in the likelihood of completing upper secondary education for respondents with different social-class backgrounds and parental educational levels. The estimated log odds ratio between the salariat and the working class is 1.425, which is equivalent to an APE of 0.239. Consequently, after holding constant academic ability, respondents with salariat backgrounds are on average 24 percent more likely to complete upper secondary education compared to respondents with working-class backgrounds. This result is similar to those reported in previous research. Educational gradients are also strong in the 1954 cohort. Together, these results suggest very large secondary effects in the 1954 cohort. We also find highly significant social-class and parental education effects in the 1984 cohort, but their substantive magnitude is much smaller. In the 1984 cohort the APE for the contrast between salariat and working-class background is 0.132 (about half that in the 1954 cohort). The gradient by parental education is also much smaller in the 1984 cohort. The difference in the strength of secondary effects might be a result of the large expansion of upper secondary education and the introduction of the practically flavored academic tracks (HTX and HHX) that occurred between the two cohorts. We discuss this possibility in more detail below.

Primary and Secondary Effects in Choosing Upper Secondary Education

In this section we decompose the total effect of social-class background and parental education on secondary education choice to calculate the relative importance of primary and secondary effects. We use the methods described in Chapter 2 of this volume (see also Erikson et al. 2005 and Jackson et al. 2007).

We begin by assessing the impact of primary effects on educational transitions. Tables 8.4a and 8.4b show synthesized transition rates into upper secondary education for respondents with different social class and parental education backgrounds. We analyze the impact of primary effects by assuming that respondents with a certain family background characteristic (e.g., working class) happen to have the academic ability distributions of respondents with a different family background characteristic (e.g., salariat). We analyze the impact of secondary effects by assuming that respondents with a certain family background characteristic happen to have the decision probabilities of respondents with a different family background characteristic. In Tables 8.4a and 8.4b the Decision columns refer to respondents' social-class or parental education group, respectively, and the Performance rows refer to academic ability distributions for those groups.

Table 8.4a shows that in the 1954 cohort the transition rate into upper secondary education was 49.9 percent for respondents of salariat background and the academic ability of the salariat. If respondents with salariat background had instead had the academic ability of those of working-class background, their transition rate would have been 35.0 percent on average, i.e., their synthesized transition rate is 14.9 percentage points lower. By contrast, respondents of working-class background have an actual transition rate of 14.3 percent and would have had a transition rate of 25.9 percent

TABLE 8.4A
Estimated factual and synthesized transition rates by social-class background

| | 1954 COHORT | | |
| | Decision | | |
Performance	Salariat	Intermediate	Working
Salariat	49.9	39.0	25.9
Intermediate	41.6	30.4	18.3
Working	35.0	24.8	14.3
	1984 COHORT		
	Decision		
Performance	Salariat	Intermediate	Working
Salariat	52.7	46.9	39.4
Intermediate	50.5	44.7	37.4
Working	45.4	39.8	32.7

NOTE: Calculated using ldecomp in Stata (see Buis 2010).

TABLE 8.4B
Estimated factual and synthesized transition rates by parental education

| | 1954 COHORT | | |
| | Decision | | |
Performance	High	Medium	Low
High	64.0	38.0	22.1
Medium	54.3	29.0	15.7
Low	47.5	23.4	12.0
	1984 COHORT		
	Decision		
Performance	High	Medium	Low
High	50.4	46.4	32.3
Medium	46.4	42.5	28.8
Low	41.2	37.4	24.7

NOTE: Calculated using ldecomp in Stata (see Buis 2010).

had they had the ability distribution of the salariat, i.e., a positive difference of 11.6 percentage points. In general, for both cohorts the synthesized transition rates show that respondents of all class backgrounds increase their transition rate if they have the academic ability of a higher social class and decrease their transition rate if they have the academic ability of a lower class. As shown in Table 8.4b, the picture is similar when we use parental education rather than social class as our indicator of family background.

When comparing the two cohorts we find that the gaps in transition rates for respondents with different social-class and parental education backgrounds decrease from the 1954 cohort to the 1984 cohort. In other words, it seems that primary effects are moderately more important in the 1954 cohort than in the 1984 cohort because substituting academic ability distributions between social classes has a larger effect on the synthesized transition rates in the 1954 cohort than in the 1984 cohort. This result might be attributable to the existence of a moderate level of tracking in the 1954 cohort (from the seventh grade) that did not exist in the 1984 cohort and that might have led to more substantial inequalities in academic ability before the transition into upper secondary education. However, as we show in our multinomial decomposition below, the picture is somewhat more complex because, in addition to upper secondary education, students have the option of choosing to enroll in vocational secondary education.

Tables 8.5a and 8.5b show the relative importance of secondary effects for educational success calculated using both social-class background and parental education as indicators of family background. The tables express the relative importance of secondary effects as the percentage of the total effect of, respectively, social-class background and parental education on transition rates into upper secondary education that is *not* attributable to academic ability. From Table 8.5a we see that in the 1954 cohort secondary effects account for between 60 and 70 percent of the total effect of social class on the likelihood of completing upper secondary education. Figures for parental education (Table 8.5b) are remarkably consistent at around 70 percent. Our results suggest that secondary effects account for most of the observed social-background inequalities in the likelihood of completing upper secondary education.

In the 1984 cohort we find that the secondary effects of social-class background are very similar to those found in the 1954 cohort. In the 1984 cohort secondary effects account for about 60 percent of the total class differences in transition rates when comparing the salariat and intermediate class and 65 percent when comparing the salariat and the working class. The secondary effects of social class are slightly lower when comparing the intermediate and working classes (60.2 percent in the 1984 cohort compared to 70.6 percent in the 1954 cohort). When using parental education

TABLE 8.5A
Relative importance of secondary effects, social-class background (%)

Class	1954 COHORT		
	Salariat	Intermediate	Working
Salariat	—	59.1 (0.128)	65.4 (0.065)
Intermediate	59.1 (0.128)	—	70.6 (0.091)
Working	65.4 (0.065)	70.6 (0.091)	—
Class	1984 COHORT		
	Salariat	Intermediate	Working
Salariat	—	60.0 (0.143)	65.1 (0.134)
Intermediate	60.0 (0.143)	—	60.2 (0.318)
Working	65.1 (0.134)	60.2 (0.318)	—

NOTE: Estimates show the relative importance of secondary effects, expressed as the percentage of the total social-class effect on transition rates into upper secondary education that is not attributable to academic ability. Standard errors in parentheses (calculated using the R package DECIDE).

TABLE 8.5B
Relative importance of secondary effects, parental education (%)

Education	1954 COHORT		
	High	Medium	Low
High	—	72.6 (0.097)	73.7 (0.063)
Medium	72.6 (0.097)	—	73.5 (0.076)
Low	73.7 (0.063)	73.5 (0.076)	—
Class	1984 COHORT		
	High	Medium	Low
High	—	49.6 (0.140)	67.0 (0.085)
Medium	49.6 (0.140)	—	73.8 (0.096)
Low	67.0 (0.085)	73.8 (0.096)	—

NOTE: Estimates show the relative importance of secondary effects, expressed as the percentage of the total parental education effect on transition rates into upper secondary education that is not attributable to academic ability. Standard errors in parentheses (calculated using the R package DECIDE).

as the measure of family background we find that in the 1984 cohort secondary effects account for between 50 percent (difference between high and medium educated parents) and 74 percent (difference between medium and low educated parents) of the total educational gradient in the likelihood of completing upper secondary education. Consequently, it seems that across the two generations born 30 years apart secondary effects have become relatively less important in explaining differences in educational outcomes.

A Multinomial Decomposition of Primary and Secondary Effects

Unlike in England or the United States, secondary education in Denmark includes two very different tracks: the academic upper secondary track and the hands-on vocational track. Thus, upon completion of elementary school at around age 16, Danish students must decide not only whether to continue in the educational system but also which of the two tracks they wish to pursue. In this section we take this particular institutional feature of Danish secondary education into account by presenting results from a multinomial decomposition of primary and secondary effects of social-class background and parental education on the choice of secondary education. Existing research shows that students' choices of track differ significantly in terms of their family background characteristics and academic ability (e.g., Jæger and Holm 2007; Jæger 2009). Consequently, it is likely that the relative importance of primary and secondary effects will differ across the two educational choices.

Because the choice set is now trichotomous (no education, vocational secondary education, or upper secondary education) rather than binary (no education or upper secondary education), the decomposition method used in the previous sections no longer applies. Instead, we employ a technically different but substantively similar method introduced by Karlson, Holm, and Breen (forthcoming), which is adapted for multinomial outcome variables. The method yields results very similar to those of the methods employed in the previous sections when applied to binary models (Karlson and Holm 2010). The idea behind the method in Karlson, Holm, and Breen is simple. First, we run a linear regression of academic ability on the social-class and the parental education variables (one regression for each family background variable). Second, we use the residuals from these regression models (which by definition are uncorrelated with the social-class and parental education variables) instead of the original academic ability variable in a multinomial logistic regression of secondary education choice. We use the new residualized academic ability variable instead of the original ability variable to correct for differences in the scale of the residual variances in the multinomial logistic regression model. This procedure allows us to directly compare log-odds coefficients across nested models. We then proceed by estimating two multinomial logistic models: one model that includes the residualized academic ability variable and one model that includes the original academic ability variable. The first model measures the *total* effect of social class and parental education on educational choice, because in this model social class and parental education is uncorrelated with academic ability (because all shared variance between the social class and parental education and academic ability variables has already been purged in the linear regression). The second model, which uses the original academic ability variable, measures the *conditional* effect of social class and parental education on educational choice (i.e., the effect of social class and parental education conditional on its indirect effect running through academic ability). The two models are statistically equivalent in the sense that they have the same fit to the data. We interpret the percentage-wise change in the log-odds coefficients of the social class and parental education variables from the first model (total social class and parental education effect) to the second model (conditional social-class and parental education effect) as a measure of the relative importance of secondary effects. Unlike in the previous analysis, we include gender as an explanatory variable (a dummy variable for women) because there are significant gender differences in the choice of (especially vocational) secondary education in Denmark.

Tables 8.6a and 8.6b summarize results from the multinomial decompositions in the 1954 and the 1984 cohorts. Columns M1 and M2 show results from the two multinomial logistic regression models using, respectively, the residualized and the original academic ability variable. The RSE (relative secondary effect) column shows our measure of secondary effects, that is, the percentage reduction of the log-odds coefficient for the social-class and parental education variable when comparing M1 and M2.

We begin by analyzing primary and secondary effects in the likelihood of completing upper secondary education versus no education. In the 1954 cohort we find highly significant effects of both academic ability and social-class background and parental education when comparing the likelihood of choosing upper secondary education over no education. Our RSE for social-class background is 63.2 when comparing salariat versus working class and 72.6 when comparing intermediate versus working class. These results indicate that secondary effects account for between 63 and 73 percent of social-class differences in the likelihood of choosing the academic upper secondary track over no education. Results are very similar for different levels of parental education. Consequently, we obtain essentially the same results for the decomposition analysis of primary and secondary

T A B L E 8 . 6 A

Results from multinomial logistic regression models of secondary education choice on parental social class. Reference category is low education (no education beyond elementary school)

	1954 COHORT			1984 COHORT		
	M1	*M2*	*RSE*	*M1*	*M2*	*RSE*
VOCATIONAL SECONDARY EDUCATION VS. LOW EDUCATION						
Academic ability	−0.042	−0.042	—	−0.650***	−0.650***	—
Social-class background						
Salariat	−0.361**	−0.334**	92.5	−0.750***	−0.338	45.1
Intermediate	0.302**	0.314***	104.0	−0.226	0.062	27.4
Working	—	—	—	—	—	—
Gender (= female)	−0.326***	−0.326***		−1.008***	−1.008***	
UPPER SECONDARY EDUCATION VS. LOW EDUCATION						
Academic ability	1.226***	1.226***	—	0.239***	0.239***	—
Social-class background						
Salariat	2.099***	1.326***	63.2	0.607***	0.455***	74.9
Intermediate	1.275***	0.926***	72.6	0.461***	0.355***	77.0
Working	—	—	—	—	—	—
Gender (= female)	−0.054	−0.054		−0.107	−0.107	
Pseudo R^2	0.119	0.119		0.067	0.067	

N O T E : M1 = model with residualized academic ability; M2 = model with observed academic ability; RSE = relative secondary effect (social-class coefficient in M2 as percentage of coefficient in M1).

**p < 0.01; ***p < 0.001.

effects as those reported in Tables 8.5a and 8.5b using a different technique. Together, these results again show that in the 1954 cohort secondary effects account for most of the inequalities in the likelihood of completing upper secondary education.

Results for the 1984 cohort are remarkably similar to those for the 1954 cohort. Tables 8.6a and 8.6b show that academic ability and social class and parental education all matter, with those of high academic ability and more privileged class backgrounds or better-educated parents being more likely to choose upper secondary education compared to those of low ability and less privileged backgrounds. Furthermore, the relative sizes of secondary effects, as expressed by the RSEs, resemble those found in the 1954 cohort. We find that in the 1984 cohort secondary effects account for over 70 percent of social-class differences in the likelihood of choosing upper secondary education over no education (the RSEs are 74.9 and 77.0 for parents' social class and 78.9 and 86.5 for parents' education). In sum, our

TABLE 8.6B

Results from multinomial logistic regression models of secondary education choice on parental education. Reference category is low education (no education beyond elementary school)

	1954 COHORT			1984 COHORT		
	M1	M2	RSE	M1	M2	RSE
VOCATIONAL SECONDARY EDUCATION VS. LOW EDUCATION						
Academic ability	−0.031	−0.031	—	−0.627***	−0.627***	—
Parental education						
High	−0.726**	−0.703**	96.8	−0.779***	−0.242	31.1
Medium	−0.047	−0.038	80.9	−0.046	0.261	−567.4
Low	—	—	—	—	—	—
Gender (= female)	−0.310**	−0.310**		−1.037***	−1.037***	
UPPER SECONDARY EDUCATION VS. LOW EDUCATION						
Academic ability	1.221***	1.221***	—	0.224***	0.224***	—
Parental education						
High	2.962***	2.071***	69.9	0.910***	0.718***	78.9
Medium	1.268***	0.923***	73.5	0.813***	0.703***	86.5
Low	—	—	—	—	—	—
Gender (= female)	−0.014	−0.014		−0.091	−0.091	
Pseudo R^2	0.134	0.134		0.070	0.070	

NOTE: M1 = model with residualized academic ability; M2 = model with observed academic ability; RSE = relative secondary effect (social-class coefficient in M2 as percentage of coefficient in M1).

**$p < 0.01$; ***$p < 0.001$.

results suggest that despite an overall decline in the socioeconomic gradient in educational attainment over time in Denmark (Benjaminsen 2006) the relative balance between primary and secondary effects has changed very little. This is a noteworthy result.

Cross-temporal results are somewhat different when we compare the relative importance of primary and secondary effects on the likelihood of completing vocational secondary education compared with no education. In the 1954 cohort we find no significant effect of academic ability on the likelihood of choosing vocational secondary education over no education. This result suggests that in this cohort those who choose vocational secondary education do not have better academic skills than those who choose not to pursue any type of secondary education (previous research finds similar results, see, e.g., Jæger and Holm 2007; Jæger 2009). However, as regards secondary effects, we do find highly significant social-class effects after accounting for academic ability and less strong parental education effects. Our results thus suggest that respondents whose families belong to the salariat or whose parents are highly educated are less likely to choose vocational secondary education over no education compared to respondents with working-class backgrounds or respondents whose parents are poorly educated. When comparing the social-class and parental education effects across M1 and M2 in the 1954 cohort, we find that their effects on the likelihood of choosing vocational education over no education change very little when we adjust for primary effects. This result suggests that for the 1954 cohort the difference in the likelihood of choosing vocational secondary education over no education is almost entirely driven by secondary effects. This finding might be attributable to vocational occupations generally having low social status in the 1954 cohort (being associated with working-class jobs), especially among socioeconomically advantaged families. Consequently, it may be preferable for children from advantaged backgrounds who know that they are not going to enter upper secondary education (maybe because of poor academic ability or lack of motivation) not to pursue any type of secondary education rather than to obtain a vocational education because the latter alternative may be socially stigmatizing. Other mechanisms, for example, advantaged families exploiting social or informational resources rather than (or as a supplement to) investing in academic skills to promote their children's long-term socioeconomic success (e.g., Jæger and Holm 2004, 2007) might also explain why secondary effects dominate.

In the 1984 cohort the results are somewhat different. In this cohort we find a significant negative effect of academic ability on the probability of choosing vocational secondary education over no education. Although counterintuitive, this finding has been reported in previous research (e.g., Jæger 2009). One explanation may be that students are increasingly being selected into vocational secondary education (being distinctly hands-on rather than academic) on the basis of poor academic skills. This trend would concentrate academic low achievers in vocational secondary education. Regarding secondary effects, we find only marginally significant effects of social-class background and parental education after controlling for academic ability. RSEs are also rather low and should be interpreted with caution, because in most cases the class and parental education effects are not statistically significant. Our analysis suggests that primary effects (negative selection on ability) are much more important in explaining family background differences in the choice of vocational secondary education versus no education in the 1984 cohort than in the 1954 cohort. A possible explanation for this might be that when the 1954 cohort completed elementary school the vocational education system was much less institutionalized and recognized (in the sense of providing students with formally recognized and marketable skills) than it is today. As a consequence, gaining an apprenticeship position and subsequent success in the labor market (and eventually acquiring high social status) depended to a larger extent on family social connections and access to information, that is, factors that were unrelated to a child's actual academic ability but which are arguably captured by the social-class and parental education variables. By contrast, when the 1984 cohort left elementary school the vocational secondary education system had become much more institutionalized and educational institutions themselves helped students find apprenticeship positions. Possibly, this change in the organization of vocational secondary education has reduced the usefulness of parents' informal resources (secondary effects), and in combination with increasing negative selection on academic ability, these trends may have increased the relative importance of primary effects.

Our results for the multinomial decomposition can be summarized as follows. The first conclusion is that in both the 1954 and the 1984 cohorts we find that family background differences in the likelihood of completing upper secondary education are mainly driven by secondary effects. Our results show that in both cohorts secondary effects account for approximately 70 percent of the association between social-class background and educational outcome and the association between parental education and educational outcome. Given the considerable expansion of upper secondary education between the 1954 cohort and the 1984 cohort, it is remarkable that the relative balance of primary and secondary effects has remained so stable over time (around one quarter of the 1954 and similarly aged cohorts completed upper secondary education, while this was the case for around half of the 1984 and similarly aged cohorts). Indeed, in the context of the expansion of upper secondary education one would expect primary effects to have become less important over time, since academic ability is arguably less discriminating in terms of securing access to upper secondary education today than it used to be. However, upper secondary education remains the only gateway to higher education in Denmark, which means that family factors other than those that go into the production of children's academic ability (intergenerational status preservation, other noneconomic returns to education, etc., see Jæger 2007a; Jæger and Holm 2007) arguably continue to be important for educational decision making. This situation would explain the persisting importance of secondary effects.

Our second main conclusion is that primary effects have become relatively more important vis-à-vis secondary effects over time with respect to explaining family background differences in the likelihood of choosing vocational secondary education relative to no education. A possible explanation of this finding might be that the vocational education system has become much more institutionalized over the period that we study and parents' noneconomic resources (social connections, information) are of lesser importance today compared to the past.

CONCLUSION

We decompose the total effect of family background on choice of secondary education in Denmark into primary and secondary effects. We compare the relative magnitude of primary and secondary effects across two cohorts: an older cohort that made the transition from elementary to secondary education around 1970 and a younger cohort that made this transition around 2000. We also extend the traditional approach to modeling primary and secondary effects to accommodate the institutional structure of the Danish secondary education system, which offers two (rather than one) tracks: the academic upper secondary track and the hands-on vocational track.

Our empirical analysis suggests that in Denmark secondary effects make up the lion's share of observable family background inequalities in the likelihood of succeeding in the academic track in secondary education. Secondary effects arguably arise from social-class differences in educational decision-making strategies, cultural capital, and other noncognitive resources, all factors that have previously been shown to be important in Denmark. Interestingly, we find that the relative importance of secondary effects on the likelihood of completing upper secondary education has changed very little over the period that we study (1970–2000) despite the rapid expansion of upper secondary education and lower overall inequality in educational opportunity. We argue that the role of upper secondary education as the exclusive gateway to higher education, alongside its consistently academic profile (a profile that remained largely unchanged over the period that we study), is likely to be the principal explanation of this finding. The contrast between those who do not complete any type of secondary education and those who complete vocational secondary education shows radically different results. We find that in the 1954 cohort academic ability does not matter and that almost all observable differences in the likelihood of completing vocational secondary education by social-class background and parental education are driven by secondary effects. We speculate that parents' social resources (and in particular their ability to help their child find an apprenticeship position or a job) and a fragmented vocational educational system at the time were key ingredients in generating strong secondary effects. By contrast, in the 1984 cohort we find that primary effects now dominate and secondary effects are of little importance. We argue that this change over time may be due to a rapid institutionalization and professionalization of vocational secondary education in Denmark, which has reduced the usefulness of parents' social resources and has led to an increasingly negative selection of students into vocational secondary education based on poor academic skills.

Our analysis shows that inequality in educational outcomes exists in Denmark and furthermore that secondary effects, at least with respect to the likelihood of completing upper secondary education, are particularly strong compared to most other countries (with the exception of Italy). Consequently, in Denmark, social-class background and parental education have large direct effects on educational outcomes after accounting for their impact on academic ability. The reason for the dominance of secondary effects might be attributable to, first, no tracking in elementary school; second, enrollment in upper secondary education at the end of elementary school not formally being linked to academic ability (unlike, for example, in Germany); and third, upper secondary education being very academically oriented. These conditions allow academically weak students to gain easy access to upper secondary education (thereby reducing the impact of primary effects on enrollment), but once students get in, they do not have an easy time because of the strong academic orientation of upper secondary education (thereby increasing the importance of secondary effects on completion, such as those resulting from differences in parental cultural and social resources). In this sense the Danish hybrid between a German-oriented path-dependent and a Scandinavian equality-oriented educational system gives rise to strong secondary effects.

NOTES

1. Educational noncompletion is somewhat overestimated in the 1984 cohort because respondents were interviewed in their late teens or early 20s. Consequently, some respondents who reported at age 19 not having completed any education beyond elementary school would eventually complete some type of secondary education (see Jæger 2009).

2. For more information on the DLSY, see http://www.sfi.dk/dlsy. The missing data that we observe on the family background variables arise from information on parental social class and parental education being collected from parents themselves in a separate postal survey in 1968 (the primary DLSY respondents also made retrospective reports of their parents' education and occupation in later surveys, and we have used this information whenever information from parents themselves was not available).

3. Jæger (2009) reports that in 1996, of all students who applied for upper secondary education, 97.2 percent were admitted.

REFERENCES

Andersen, Annemarie Møller, Niels Egelund, Torben Pilegaard Jensen, Michael Krone, Lena Lindenskov, and Jan Mejding. 2001. *Forventninger og færdigheder: danske unge i en international sammenhæng.* Copenhagen: AKF, DPU og SFI-Survey.

Andersen, Dines. 2005. *4 år efter grundskolen. 19-årige om valg og veje i ungdomsuddannelserne.* Copenhagen: Institute of Local Government Studies.

Benjaminsen, Lars. 2006. *Chanceulighed i det 20. århundrede.* Copenhagen: PhD diss., Sociologisk Institut, Københavns Universitet.

Boudon, Raymond. 1974. *Education, Opportunity, and Social Inequality: Changing Prospects in Western Society.* New York: Wiley.

Breen, Richard, and Jan O. Jonsson. 2005. "Inequality of Opportunity in Comparative Perspective: Recent Research on Educational Attainment and Social Mobility." *Annual Review of Sociology* 31:223–43.

Breen, Richard, Ruud Luijkx, Walter Müller, and Reinhard Pollak. 2009. "Nonpersistent Inequality in Educational Attainment: Evidence from Eight European Countries." *American Journal of Sociology* 114:1475–521.

Buis, Maarten. 2010 "Direct and Indirect Effects in a Logit Model." *Stata Journal* 10:11–29.

Erikson, Robert. 2007. "Social Selection in Stockholm Schools: Primary and Secondary Effects on the Transition to Upper Secondary Education." In *From Origin to Destination: Trends and Mechanisms in Social Stratification Research,* edited by Stefani Scherer, Reinhard Pollak, Gunnar Otte, and Markus Gangl, 35–76. Frankfurt, Germany: Campus Verlag.

Erikson, Robert, and John H. Goldthorpe. 1992. *The Constant Flux: A Study of Class Mobility in Industrial Societies.* London: Clarendon Press.

Erikson, Robert, John H. Goldthorpe, Michelle Jackson, Meir Yaish, and David R. Cox. 2005. "On Class Differentials in Educational Attainment." *Proceedings of the National Academy of Sciences* 102:30–33.

Hansen, Erik Jørgen. 1995. *En generation blev voksen.* Copenhagen: Socialforskningsinstituttet.

Holm, Anders, and Mads Meier Jæger. 2008. "Does Relative Risk Aversion Explain Educational Inequality? A Dynamic Choice Approach." *Research in Social Stratification and Mobility* 26:199–220.

Jæger, Mads Meier. 2007a. "Educational Mobility across Three Generations: The Changing Impact of Social Class, Economic, Cultural, and Social Capital." *European Societies* 9:527–50.

———. 2007b. "Economic and Social Returns to Educational Choices: Extending the Utility Function." *Rationality and Society* 19:451–83.

———. 2009. "Equal Access but Unequal Outcomes: Cultural Capital and Educational Choice in a Meritocratic Society." *Social Forces* 87:1943–71.

Jæger, Mads Meier, and Anders Holm. 2004. "Penge, (ud)dannelse, forbindelser eller *brains*? En test af fire forældreressourcers betydning for unges uddannelsesvalg i Danmark." *Dansk Sociologi* 15:67–83.

———. 2007. "Does Parents' Economic, Cultural, and Social Capital Explain the Social Class Effect on Educational Attainment in the Scandinavian Mobility Regime?" *Social Science Research* 36:719–44.

Karlson, Kristian B., and Anders Holm. 2010. "Decomposing Primary and Secondary Effects: A New Decomposition Method." *Research in Social Stratification and Mobility* 29:221–37.

Karlson, Kristian B., Anders Holm, and Richard Breen. Forthcoming. "Comparing Regression Coefficients between Same-Sample Nested Models Using Logit and Probit: A New Method." *Sociological Methodology.*

McIntosh, James, and Martin D. Munk. 2007. "Scholastic Ability vs. Family Background in Educational Success: Evidence From Danish Sample Survey Data." *Journal of Population Economics* 20:101–20.

OECD. 2000. *PISA Technical Report.* Paris: OECD.

Thomsen, Jens Peter. 2008. *Social differentiering og kulturel praksis på danske universiteter.* Roskilde, Denmark: Roskilde Universitetsforlag.

Undervisningsministeriet [Ministry of Education]. 2010. *Tal, der taler 2009. Uddannelsesnøgletal 2009.* Copenhagen: Ministry of Education.

CHAPTER NINE

Social Background and Educational Transitions in England

Michelle Jackson

When in 1996 Tony Blair gave his final speech to the Labour Party conference before becoming prime minister the following year, he famously said, "Ask me my three main priorities for government, and I tell you: education, education, education." This statement struck a chord with politicians and the public alike, for who could argue that education should not be a main priority for any government? Even John Major, the prime minister at the time, could only respond, "My priorities are the same, but in a different order" (quoted in Smithers 2001, 405). One feature of modern British social and political rhetoric is an almost unquestioning acceptance that education offers social and economic benefits and that it is essential for the effective functioning of a modern, postindustrial society. This rhetoric appears to have driven the significant educational expansion and reform observed over the past century.

Over the 20th century, England witnessed a movement from (almost) universal primary education at the beginning of the century; through universal secondary education, formalized in the 1944 Education Act; to a system of mass higher education by the end of the century. The 1944 Education Act revolutionized secondary education and was supposed to mark a move away from an institutional structure that strongly favored the social elite. The act made state secondary education free of charge for all pupils in England and compulsory up to age 15, thereby ensuring that previously marginalized groups could work their way through the education system.[1] A tripartite system was set up, so that talented students of all social backgrounds could be channeled into the academic-focused grammar schools, while the less talented could be directed toward secondary modern (and to a much lesser extent, secondary technical) schools. As Ranson writes, "The Act realized for the first time [the] ideal of universal free secondary education for all directed to the needs and capacities of youngsters rather than dependent upon the material well-being, status and power of their parents" (1988, 4).

Over time, dissatisfaction grew with the tripartite system. The 11-plus examination, used to identify the talented students who would attend grammar schools, drew criticism from scholars who highlighted class bias in test questions and a far from impressive level of precision in identifying the top students who would benefit from a grammar school education (see Halsey and Floud 1957). Concerns were also raised about the quality of many of the secondary modern schools. By the 1960s comprehensive schools were beginning to spread across England, until in 1965 Anthony Crosland (the secretary of state for education) instructed local education authorities to move from the tripartite to the comprehensive system. Today, the majority of secondary schools in England are comprehensives, although a small number of local education authorities continue to preserve the tripartite system.

At the university level, although the number of students studying for degree courses steadily increased in the second half of the 20th century, it was not until 1992 that there was rapid expansion in this sector, as a consequence of the Further and Higher Education Act. All institutions previously classified as polytechnics, and thus not eligible to award university degrees, were reclassified as universities and given equivalent degree-awarding power. This laid the foundation for the system of mass higher education that is in place today (see Cheung and Egerton 2007 for a more detailed discussion of the expansion of tertiary education in Great Britain).

Figure 9.1 shows an overview of the English educational system as it currently stands, with estimates of the proportion of students who pass through the different transition points.[2] It is now compulsory for all children to be enrolled in formal education up until age 16, after which they can continue in education to take formal academic courses (typically leading to Advanced-Supplementary or Advanced qualifications, known as AS- and A-level, respectively) or vocational courses (such as the Vocational Certificate of Education, or VCE), or alternatively they may leave the educational system and enter the labor market.[3] In general, the academic courses leading to A-level qualifications are more prestigious than other courses, and they offer the best chances for students intending to continue to university.

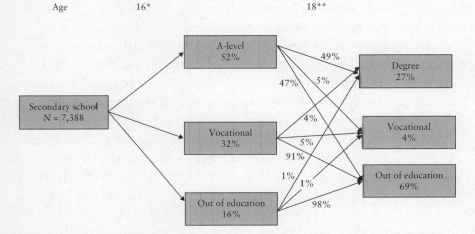

Figure 9.1.   Important educational pathways through the stylized English educational system

NOTE: Estimated using weighted data drawn from Youth Cohort Study 11 (students born in 1986); students were selected if they were present in the first and third sweeps of Youth Cohort Study 11. The sample of students included in this analysis differs from the sample in the later analyses (e.g., Figure 9.2); in the later analyses, students are included in the sample only if there is additional information on their social origins and performance. Percentages in boxes are of entire cohort; percentages in lines between boxes are transition rates of each group.

*Transition at age 16 from compulsory to noncompulsory education.

**Transition at age 18 to university degree.

As the figure shows, the majority of English schoolchildren make the transition to A-level education (52 percent), while 32 percent enter vocational education. The second main transition in the English system is that at age 18, when students decide whether to apply to university. Of the 52 percent of students who continued to A-level courses, 49 percent go on to study for a degree.

Research on educational inequality in England shows that class inequalities are both considerable and significant (e.g., Halsey, Heath, and Ridge 1980; Heath and Clifford 1990; Kerckhoff and Trott 1993; Jonsson, Mills, and Müller 1996; Cheung and Egerton 2007; Jackson et al. 2007). In *Origins and Destinations*, Halsey, Heath, and Ridge show that students of advantaged social-class background are much more likely to progress through the education system to enter university education than those from working-class homes. They conclude, "If the 'hereditary curse upon English education is its organisation upon lines of social class,' [Tawney 1931, 142] that would seem to be as true in the 1960s as it was . . . when Tawney wrote" (1980, 205). Recent studies on the changing extent of class inequalities suggest that over the first half of the 20th century the association between class background and educational attainment in Great Britain declined somewhat, but in the latter half of the century inequalities were relatively stable (see Breen et al. 2009).

In this chapter, I examine social-background inequalities in educational attainment in England, focusing on the two main educational transitions in the academic track: the transition at age 16, from compulsory to A-level education, and the transition at age 18, from A-level to university degree. I consider both parental class and parental education as measures of social background. I ask whether the associations between social background and educational transitions have changed over a 30-year period.

DATA

The data in this chapter are drawn from three major British cohort studies: the National Child Development Study (NCDS), the British Cohort Study (BCS), and the Youth Cohort Study (YCS).

The NCDS is a nationally representative cohort study of all children born in Britain in one week in March 1958. Measures were taken from birth, and cohort members have been followed throughout their childhood and adult life. In this chapter, I use measures from the sweeps taken at ages 11, 16, and 23.

Similarly, the BCS is a nationally representative cohort study of all children born in Britain in one week in September 1970. I use measures from the sweeps taken at ages 10, 16, 26, and 29.

The YCS is a series of cohort studies focusing on students from England and Wales.[4] The first YCS was carried out in 1985, and to date, a total of 13 cohorts have been surveyed. The structure of each YCS is similar, with an initial survey of a sample of 16-year-olds and follow-up surveys of the same individuals in subsequent years. The primary mode of completion is a postal questionnaire, with computer-assisted telephone interviewing being used in more recent YCS surveys to encourage nonresponders to participate[5] (DCSF 2008). In this chapter, to present as comprehensive a picture as possible of trends in educational inequality in England, I analyze all the datasets from the YCS surveys for which comparable measures are available: YCS3 (students born in 1971), YCS5–YCS11 (students born in 1975 through 1986), and YCS13 (students born in 1991). Unfortunately, the most recent two studies in the series, YCS12 and YCS13, have known problems, and thus I exclude YCS12 entirely and use data from YCS13 only for analyses of the first transition.[6] Weights are supplied in the YCS datasets to correct for problems arising from the sampling design, and the weights are applied in all analyses.

In the following analyses, to ensure that comparable populations are studied across the three different datasets, I consider only those students who reside (and study) in England. Sample sizes for the cohorts range from approximately 3,000 to 12,000 cases. I refer to the cohorts by the birth year of the respondents.

MEASURES

I obtain consistent measures of the social class and educational qualifications of the respondent's parents, the respondent's academic performance at ages 16 and 18, information on whether the respondent made the transition from General Certificate of Secondary Education to A-level education, and whether the respondent made the transition from A-level to degree-level education.

Parental Social Class

The social class measure takes account of information on both father's and mother's occupation to build a measure of household class.[7] In the earlier cohorts, father's and mother's occupations are coded to Socio-Economic Groups (SEGs), which are subsequently recoded into the Erikson-Gold-thorpe-Portocarero (EGP) class schema (Erikson, Goldthorpe, and Porto-carero 1979) according to an algorithm developed by Heath and McDonald (1987). In the later cohorts (from YCS5 onward) father's and mother's occupations are coded to the National Statistics Socio-Economic Classification (NS-SEC), which is a version of the EGP schema adopted by Britain's Office for National Statistics (Rose, Pevalin, and O'Reilly 2005).

I use a three-class version of the schema, which I consider to be hierarchical: salariat (higher and lower managerial and professional occupations), intermediate (intermediate and petty bourgeoisie occupations), and working class (semiroutine and routine occupations). To obtain the household measure, I use a dominance approach to determine whether the father's or mother's class should be taken as better representing the class of the household (Erikson 1984). I therefore compare the individual class positions of the respondent's father and mother and take the higher class position as the household class (where information on one parent is missing, the household class is determined by the remaining parent's class).

Parental Education

The parental education measure represents the dominant educational level of the household. The educational qualifications of the respondent's father and mother are separately classified into three categories: degree, A-level, and no qualifications (this category includes qualifications below A-level). The household educational level is taken to be that of the parent with the higher level of educational qualifications, and once again, where information on one parent is missing, household education is determined by the remaining parent's educational level.

Descriptive statistics show that, over time, a general upgrading of social background occurs, whether considered in terms of social class or education. The size of the working class decreases from the beginning to the end of the period, with a concurrent increase in the size of the salariat. Similarly, over the period considered in this chapter the proportion of students from a household in which at least one parent holds a degree increased substantially while the proportion of students with poorly qualified parents decreased (the distribution of students across the social background groups for the 1958 and 1991 cohorts is shown in the web appendix, http://www .primaryandsecondaryeffects.com, Figure A9.1).

Academic Performance

Academic performance at age 16 is measured as performance in public examinations in mathematics and English language (Ordinary-level qualification, or Certificate of Secondary Education [CSE] in the case of NCDS, BCS, and YCS3 and performance in the General Certificate of Secondary Education [GCSE] in the case of later YCS surveys). These examinations are usually taken at the end of compulsory schooling, that is, the year in which the student turns 16. Of the range of subjects studied, both mathematics and English language are effectively compulsory, meaning that virtually all students will have grades (Jackson et al. 2007). The grades range from a high of A* to a low of G (below this, grades are "unclassified").

To create the age-16 performance measure, scores were attached to the mathematics and English language grades following Jackson et al. (2007). The final performance measure was standardized to have a mean of 0 and standard deviation of 1, with higher scores indicating higher levels of performance.

Academic performance at age 18 is measured as performance in the A-level public examinations, usually taken two years after the end of compulsory schooling, in the year in which the student turns 18. Students normally take three A-level examinations but can choose to take more. A-level grades range from a high of A to a low of E (below which grades are again described as "unclassified").

The age-18 performance measure was created by assigning points to each grade, adding those points over all subjects studied, and then standardizing the points score to have a mean of 0 and standard deviation of 1. In some datasets an average points score was the only measure of performance available, and here again the score was standardized to have a mean of 0 and standard deviation of 1. The distributions of performance and the relationships between performance and the other variables in the analyses do not appear to be influenced by whether a total points score or an average points score is used.

Transitions

The first transition variable—the transition to A-level—distinguishes between students who continued in education after age 16 to take A-level courses and those who dropped out of education or took vocational courses. The NCDS and BCS have no direct measures of whether students continued to A-level education, so instead the age that the respondent left full-time education is used as a proxy. Those respondents who left education at age 16 or younger are assumed to have dropped out of academic education, while those who left after age 16 are assumed to have made the transition to A-level (see Jackson et al. 2007). In the YCS surveys, a question in the first sweep identifies respondents who are currently studying for A- or AS-levels.

The second transition variable distinguishes between students who after their A-levels continued to take degree courses and those who dropped out of academic education. In contrast to the previous transition, the at-risk population for the degree transition is the subsample of students who took A-level examinations. In the NCDS and BCS, there are again no direct measures of whether the respondent made the transition to degree-level education, only separate measures of the age that the respondent left full-time education and of whether the respondent achieved a degree. Respondents who left full-time education after age 18 and achieved a degree-level qualification are assumed to have made the transition to degree level, in contrast to those who left education earlier or did not achieve a degree-level qualification. While this measure is clearly not an ideal measure of the transition, in that it excludes those respondents who made the transition but dropped out of degree-level education before achieving the qualification, it is reasonable to assume that these dropouts are not so numerous as to substantially bias the results. In the YCS surveys, a question in the third sweep of the survey (conducted when the respondents were aged 18–19) identifies respondents who are currently studying for a degree.

RESULTS

I consider social-background inequalities in the two main transitions in the English education system, presenting results pertaining to students who were born between 1958 and 1991.

The Transition at 16: A-level

The total percentage of all students who made the transition to A-level education increased from 30 percent for the 1958 birth cohort to 52 percent for the 1991 birth cohort, a considerable upgrading over a 30-year period. However, despite this general increase, there are significant inequalities in the propensity to make the transition related to social-background characteristics. Figure 9.2 shows transition rates to A-level education for students originating in the three social classes for all birth cohorts between 1958 and 1991. Figure 9.3 shows equivalent transition rates for those originating in the three parental educational groups.[8]

It is clear that social background, whether operationalized through social class or education, plays an important differentiating role in the transition to A-level. Across the whole period, students from advantaged social-background groups are more likely to make the transition to A-level rather than to leave academic education than students from the least

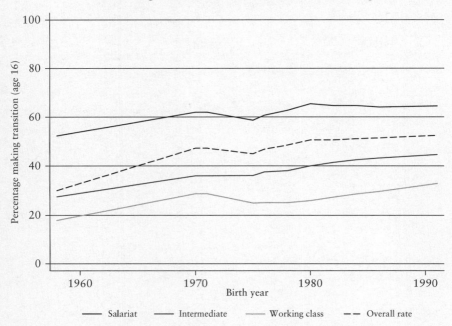

Figure 9.2. Transition rates to A-level education for students originating in the salariat, intermediate, and working classes (overall transition rate shown as a dotted line)

NOTE: Transition rates have been smoothed using a five-year moving average.

advantaged social-background groups. If we calculate odds ratios on the basis of these transition rates, we see that students of salariat background in the most recent cohort are almost four times more likely to make the transition to A-level rather than not than students from the working class. As regards changes over time, in the context of an overall increase in the proportion of all students making the transition to A-level education, the odds ratios decline from the beginning to the end of the period; the odds ratio for the salariat–working-class comparison declines from 5.0 to 3.7 between 1958 and 1991, while the odds ratio for the high–low-parental-education comparison declines from 7.7 to 3.8 in the same period. Log-linear models show that for both class and educational background the constant association model must be rejected. As regards social class, a model positing a constant association between class and transition over the cohorts must be rejected according to conventional criteria ($G^2 = 90.9$, 20 degrees of

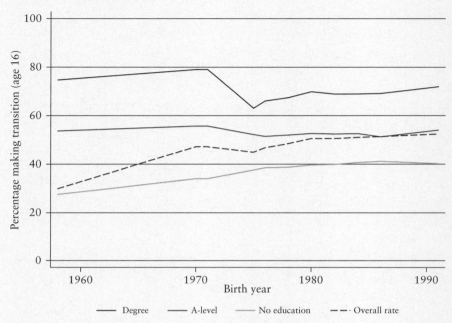

Figure 9.3. Transition rates to A-level education for students originating in the degree, A-level, and no-education groups (overall transition rate shown as a dotted line)

NOTE: Transition rates have been smoothed using a five-year moving average.

freedom [d.f.], $p = 0.000$), although the UNIDIFF model, which posits a uniform change over time in the association between class and transition, must also be rejected ($G^2 = 21.9$, 10 d.f., $p = 0.000$) (Erikson and Goldthorpe 1992; Xie 1992). Furthermore, the UNIDIFF parameters suggest that while changes over time may be detected, these constitute little more than trendless fluctuation. As regards educational background, the constant association model is again rejected ($G^2 = 204.8$, 18 d.f., $p = 0.000$), as is the UNIDIFF model ($G^2 = 55.2$, 9 d.f., $p = 0.000$). Here, however, the UNIDIFF parameters suggest that there was a sharp reduction in the size of the odds ratios between the 1958 and the 1971 cohorts but that from that point forward there was no systematic movement in the odds ratios characterizing the relationship between educational background and transition.

Finally, we may consider the cross classification of social class against educational background (see web appendix, Figure A9.2). There are rather sizable inequalities between the most advantaged and least advantaged groups, with students born in 1991 and originating in the salariat-by-degree-qualifications group being over seven times more likely to make the transition to A-level rather than to leave education than students from working-class-by-no-education households. Log-linear models show that the model of constant association between class-by-educational background and the transition to A-level must be rejected ($G^2 = 325.5$, 72 d.f., $p = 0.000$), although again the UNIDIFF model does not fit the data well ($G^2 = 253.5$, 63 d.f., $p = 0.000$). In common with the findings for the educational-background-by-transition association, the UNIDIFF parameters suggest that there was a declining association between class-by-educational background and transition between the 1958 and 1971 cohorts but that the association remained rather constant after that point.

Having established that there is a significant and substantial association between social background and transition, whether social background is operationalized through class, education, or a cross classification of the two, I now move on to ask how this association is generated. In particular, I ask whether the inequalities can be attributed to the primary effects of differences in performance between the different social-background groups or whether they should be attributed to the secondary effects of differences between the groups in the educational choices that are made, conditional on performance.

Figure 9.4 shows the mean of the performance score for each class across the cohorts. Two features of the figure should be highlighted, which are common to the patterns exhibited when we consider the means by education and the class-by-education groups (not presented). First, the performance scores differ systematically across the social-background groups. Students of more advantaged background have higher average performance scores than students of less advantaged background. In addition to higher average performance scores, in the higher-social-background groups there is less deviation around the mean scores (the standard deviations for performance are smaller in the more advantaged groups than in the less advantaged groups). The range of average performance scores appears to be similar across the different operationalizations of social background: in the 1991 cohort, the average performance scores of the salariat and working class are separated by 0.87 of a standard deviation, while the average performance scores of degree and no-education households (not shown) are

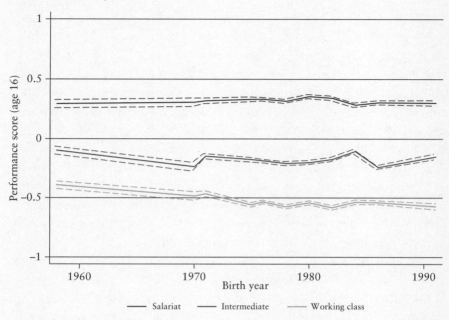

Figure 9.4. Mean performance scores at age 16 for the salariat, intermediate, and working classes, with upper and lower confidence bounds in dashed lines

separated by 0.77 of a standard deviation. It is only in the cross classification of class by educational background that larger differences between the most and least advantaged groups emerge. Second, there is no evidence that the differences in performance scores between social-background groups are reduced over the period considered. Indeed, Figure 9.4 suggests that average performance scores are slightly more differentiated by class in the later cohorts than in the earlier cohorts.

The foregoing analyses have demonstrated significant and substantial inequalities in the propensity to make the transition to A-level related to social background and significant and substantial inequalities in average performance scores between different social-background groups. I now move on to ask how far the differences in performance scores can explain inequalities in the propensity to make the transition to A-level, or in other words, whether these inequalities can be attributed to primary or to secondary effects.

I use the method described in Chapter 2 to estimate the relative importance of primary and secondary effects (see also Erikson et al. 2005; Jackson

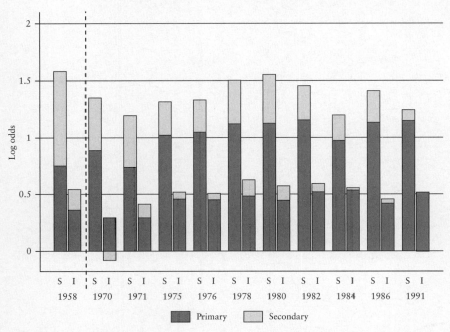

Figure 9.5.   Log odds ratios representing the expected size of class inequalities at age 16 if only primary or secondary effects are operating (relative to working class)

NOTE: S = salariat; I = intermediate class.

et al. 2007). I calculate synthesized log odds ratios for the class and educational background groups, comparing higher groups to the lowest background group. So, for example, I calculate the log odds ratio that would be expected when comparing salariat and working-class students if secondary effects were eliminated, thus representing the inequality that would be expected if only *primary* effects were operating to create differences between the salariat and working class. Similarly, I calculate the size of the inequality that would be expected if only *secondary* effects were operating. Figures 9.5 and 9.6, respectively, show the total inequalities between the higher classes (relative to the working class) and the higher-education groups (relative to the no-education group), broken down to show the contribution of primary and secondary effects in creating those inequalities, between 1958 and 1991.

The figures show the general decline in social-background inequalities over time that was identified earlier, a decline that appears to be driven

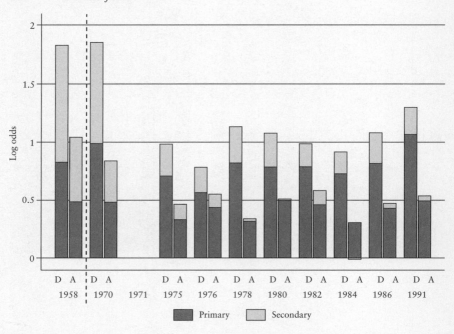

Figure 9.6.   Log odds ratios representing the expected size of educational background inequalities at age 16 if only primary or secondary effects are operating (relative to no education)

NOTE: D = degree; A = A-level. Data on parental education are not available for the 1971 birth cohort (see note 6).

by both a small increase in the absolute size of primary effects and a large reduction in the absolute size of secondary effects.[9] To take as an example the comparison between the salariat and working class in Figure 9.5, the log odds ratio that would be expected if only primary effects were in operation progressively increases from 0.8 in 1958 to 1.2 in 1991. But at the same time, the log odds ratio that would be expected if only secondary effects were in operation decreases, from 0.8 in 1958 to 0.1 in 1991. And as the overall inequality between classes declines over time, the *relative* size of primary effects in creating this inequality increases. For the salariat–working-class comparison just described, the relative importance of secondary effects declines from 51 percent for the 1958 cohort to only 8 percent for the 1991 cohort, a difference that is significant at the 5 percent level.[10]

The relative importance of primary and secondary effects seems to be similar across the different operationalizations of social background, so that although the total size of the inequalities differs depending on whether class or educational background is used, the relative importance of performance and choice is somewhat constant. Indeed, significance tests show that estimates of the relative importance of secondary effects do not differ significantly across the different operationalizations of social background. The patterns shown in relation to class and educational background are maintained when we consider the class-by-education cross classification (see web appendix, Figure A9.3). In the context of what appears to be a declining association between the class-by-education groups and the transition, the magnitude of primary effects shows a small increase across the cohorts. The reduction in the log odds ratios comparing the class-by-education groups to the lowest group, working-class-by-no-education, largely comes about through a substantial reduction in the size of secondary effects between the earlier and later cohorts. In the 1991 cohort, primary effects account for around 84 percent of the total inequality between the highest and lowest groups, with only 16 percent contributed by secondary effects.

The results for the transition at age 16 show that social background exerts an influence on the transition over the whole time period considered, whether social background is operationalized through social class, educational background, or the cross classification of the two measures. The results show that a model of constant association between the transition and social background, however operationalized, must be rejected, although there is no clear evidence for a *systematic* weakening of this association over time. Where there is reduction in the size of the odds ratios expressing inequalities, this reduction seems to be largely due to a reduction in the size of secondary effects.

The Transition at 18: University Degree

I now consider inequalities in the chances of making the transition from A-level education to university degree. As discussed above, the population of interest in this analysis is of course much more highly selected in comparison to the population in the previous analysis of the transition to A-level education. The focus is now on a group of students for whom we have grades in A-level examinations, information on social background, and the choice made in the transition to degree-level education. Given data constraints, the most recent cohort to be included in the analysis was born

Figure 9.7. Transition rates to degree-level education for students (with A-level grades) originating in the salariat, intermediate, and working classes (overall transition rate shown as a dotted line)

NOTE: Transition rates have been smoothed using a five-year moving average.

in 1986, and in this cohort just under 60 percent of students with A-level qualifications went on to make the transition to university degree. In Figures 9.7 and 9.8 I present the transition rates to university degree for the classes and educational groups for all cohorts in the analysis. For this transition it is not possible to conduct analyses for the cross classification of class and educational groups, because the number of cases included in the analysis is substantially reduced and some of the cross classified groups contain very few individuals.

The most immediate difference between this transition and the previous one is that the associations between social background and the transition to university degree are clearly weaker than the equivalent associations at the transition to A-level. For example, for the 1986 cohort, the odds ratio describing the inequality between the degree and the no-education groups is 3.2 for the transition to A-level education but only 1.5 for the transition

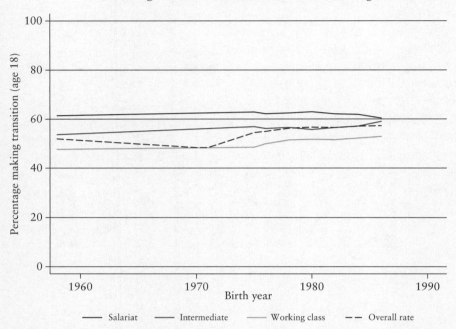

Figure 9.8. Transition rates to degree-level education for students (with A-level grades) originating in the degree, A-level, and no-education groups (overall transition rate shown as a dotted line)

NOTE: Transition rates have been smoothed using a five-year moving average.

from A-level to university degree. Additionally, the comparison between the lower two social-background groups (intermediate against working class, and A-level against no education), shows that there are often only very small differences in the rates of transition to university degree. The strength of the associations between class and transition and between educational background and transition do not change over time, and constant-association log-linear models positing no change fit the data well (for class, the constant association model fit statistics are $G^2 = 21.5$, 16 d.f., $p = 0.159$; for education, $G^2 = 22.8$, 14 d.f., $p = 0.064$). In general, then, while inequalities in the transition to university degree are smaller than those at the first transition, class and educational background inequalities are still present and they persist over time. But should these inequalities be attributed to primary or to secondary effects? As before, I use the method described in Chapter 2 to determine the relative importance of primary and secondary effects in

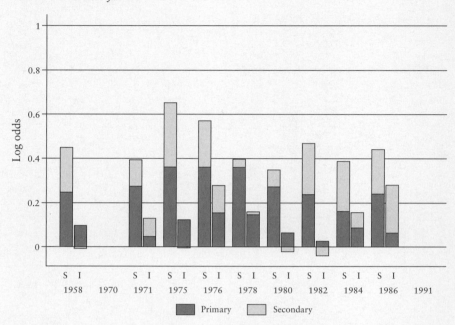

Figure 9.9.   Log odds ratios representing the expected size of class inequalities at age 18 if only primary or secondary effects are operating (relative to working class)

N O T E : Data on the transition are not available for the 1970 or 1991 birth cohorts (see note 6).

creating the inequalities in the transition to university degree, and the results are presented in Figures 9.9 and 9.10.

Figure 9.9 shows the contribution of primary and secondary effects to the overall log odds ratios describing class inequalities. We see that, just as total inequalities between classes remain fairly constant across the period, so does the relative importance of primary and secondary effects. Secondary effects account for around 45 percent of the salariat-to-working-class inequality in both the 1958 cohort and the 1986 cohort. When social background is operationalized through parental qualifications, secondary effects account for just under 48 percent of the inequality between those from degree households and those from no-education households in the 1958 cohort, and for almost 30 percent of the inequality in the 1986 cohort.[11] Although there is no evidence for a systematic or significant change in the relative importance of primary or secondary effects over time, there is some variation over the cohorts. While it would be unwise to draw far-reaching

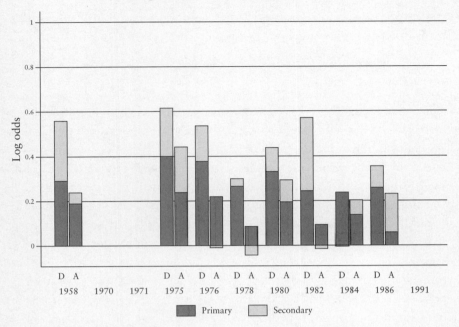

Figure 9.10. Log odds ratios representing the expected size of educational background inequalities at age 18 if only primary or secondary effects are operating (relative to no education)

NOTE: D = degree; A = A-level. Data on parental education and transition are not available for the 1970, 1971, or 1991 birth cohorts (see note 6).

conclusions on the basis of this variation, we should note that secondary effects appear to be weaker when the overall log odds ratios expressing inequalities are smaller and stronger when the log odds ratios are larger. In other words, secondary effects appear to be stronger when the association between social background and the transition is stronger.

The results for the transition to university degree have many commonalities with the results for the transition to A-level, although there are also some differences. Both class and educational background are associated with making the transition to university degree, although these associations are weaker than for the transition to A-level education at age 16. In contrast to the transition at 16, the constant association model is a good fit to the data, indicating that there is no significant change over time in the relationship between social background and the transition to university degree. Finally, the relative importance of primary and secondary effects is rather stable over time, and secondary effects maintain a larger influence at this transition than at the previous transition to A-level education.

CONCLUSION

The foregoing analyses have shown that social background, whether operationalized through class or parental education, significantly influences the chances of making the major transitions in the English educational system. Social-background inequalities are most marked at the first transition, the transition to A-level at age 16, but they are also evident at the second transition, at age 18, from A-level to university degree. The reduction in social-background inequalities at age 18 is not particularly surprising given that the population at risk of making this transition is much more highly selected than the population considered in the previous transition, in that these students have already taken A-level examinations and have made a positive choice in an earlier transition. The first transition is therefore the more important transition in determining *overall* inequalities in educational attainment. The association between social background and the transition at age 16, to A-level education, is not constant over time but instead exhibits trendless fluctuation, with no evidence of a systematic movement toward greater equality, although where changes in the association do occur, these changes appear to be in the direction of greater equality. In contrast, the association between social background and the transition at 18, to degree-level education, remains rather stable over time.

The persisting associations between social background and the transitions are notable in the context of changes in social structure over the past 30 years. The class structure has gradually upgraded over this period, so that increasing numbers of students originate from households in which at least one parent has an occupation in the salariat and decreasing numbers of students originate from working-class homes. Similarly, the educational structure has changed over the past 30 years, so that increasing numbers of students originate in households in which at least one parent holds a degree. Indeed, there has been a fourfold increase in the number of students coming from a degree household, and the number of students originating in households where neither parent holds educational qualifications has halved. The results here show that, on the whole, privileged families are able to maintain their children's advantage over the children of less privileged families, even while increasing numbers of students originate from privileged homes.

Although the results clearly indicate that both parental class and educational background continue to exert an influence over children's educational chances, it is reasonable to ask why the associations between social background and the transition at age 16 are not stable over time (and may be weakening), while the associations between social background and the transition at age 18 remain stable. This finding is of course largely in keeping with the maximally maintained inequality thesis: as educational systems expand, and the participation rates of students from advantaged backgrounds reach their maximal level, continuing expansion must be driven by increasing participation rates of students from less advantaged backgrounds, and the association between social background and the transition will subsequently weaken (Raftery and Hout 1993). On this basis, we might argue that social-background inequalities in the transition at age 16 are susceptible to change because almost all the capable students of advantaged background now make the transition to A-level education and that inequalities in the transition to university degree remain constant because the advantaged social groups have not yet reached their maximal transition rates to university degree.

Decomposing the social-background inequalities so as to reveal the influence of primary and secondary effects shows that at the first transition, to A-level education, primary effects increase in importance over the cohorts, with secondary effects declining in importance, both in absolute and relative terms. At the second transition, to university degree, there is little evidence of change over time in the importance of secondary effects. Perhaps the most striking result of the analyses is that when there are changes toward a weaker association between social background and the transitions there are also changes toward weakening secondary effects, and when the association is stable over time secondary effects tend to be stable too.

The declining importance of secondary effects at the transition to A-level education is perhaps due in part to educational expansion removing the perceived barriers to continuing at this level: as soon as a large proportion of the population makes the transition to A-level education, the perceived chances of succeeding at this level presumably also rise. Furthermore, as the opportunities for employment for those with only compulsory education have decreased over time, the opportunity costs of continuing in education have also decreased. It may also be that government policy has had some effect in reducing secondary effects at the transition to A-level, by emphasizing an ideology of aspiration and more importantly, for recent cohorts, by offering financial incentives for students from low-income households who continue in education after the compulsory period (the Education Maintenance Allowance, which paid students from poor households up to £30 per week to continue in education, with bonuses of £100 for high achievers). As Jackson et al. (2007) argue, secondary effects would seem to be amenable to policy intervention, and the evidence so far suggests that offering financial incentives to disadvantaged students may well increase the transition rates of students from these groups (see Payne 2003 for a review of pilot studies of the allowance).

The stability of secondary effects at the transition to university degree may, again, reflect the fact that a university education is still far from universal. At this transition point, less advantaged students face a decision of whether to continue with a costly and risky educational path or to leave academic education for the labor market. It seems that the perceived barriers to success, alongside the costs of continuing in education, faced by those from disadvantaged families lead to persisting secondary effects at the transition to university.

The continuing importance of primary effects implies that social background continues to be successfully transmitted through performance. Clearly, parents with higher-class jobs and higher education have many resources available to them to support their children's educational performance. They may offer direct support and informal teaching to their children, use their superior economic resources to buy extra tuition, and more generally, offer a secure and prosperous home environment that is conducive to learning. All these factors are likely to lead to their children's improved performance relative to children from less advantaged homes. But arguably one of the most important changes in the educational system over the past 30 years is the move toward basing GCSE and A-level grades increasingly on coursework rather than examinations. This means that around 20–40 percent of a GCSE mathematics or English grade might be based on coursework undertaken at home rather than on an examination taken at school (in some subjects, coursework may contribute a large percentage of the final grade). It would seem reasonable to hypothesize that coursework undertaken at home is more vulnerable to parental influence than examinations taken at school. Subsequently, at the same time that government policy has focused on reducing inequalities related to social background, the educational system has changed in a way that may continue to offer advantages to children from privileged households.

In the final chapter of *Origins and Destinations*, Halsey, Heath, and Ridge (1980) argued that there was room for both optimism and pessimism when considering social-background inequalities in educational attainment. Now, 30 years later, it seems that both optimists and pessimists might again find support for their position. Optimists might point to the nonconstant association between social background and the transition at 16 and the constant association between social background and the transition at 18 and suggest that we should appreciate that there has been no strengthening of these associations, even during a period of dramatic takeoff in income inequality that might have been expected to tighten the link between social background and educational outcomes (see, e.g., Blanden et al. 2004). They might also argue that the reduction over time in the size of secondary effects in the transition to A-level points toward the possibility that policy can be effective in reducing inequality and that, in time, primary effects might be effectively tackled through policy too. However, pessimists would be obliged to respond that, even after decades of government and public emphasis on equality of opportunity through education, social class and educational background remain important determinants of the two main transitions in the English education system. They may also note with some sadness that the Conservative–Liberal Democrat coalition government recently abolished the Education Maintenance Allowance, while introducing economic cuts that are likely to negatively affect those from disadvantaged homes (Toynbee 2010a, 2010b). Perhaps the optimist and pessimist would both agree that, for inequalities in educational attainment to lessen in the future, more effective measures must be introduced to improve the performance of children from disadvantaged households and to encourage and support those children in making ambitious educational choices.

NOTES

I thank John Goldthorpe, Martin Neugebauer, and participants in the Center for Research on Inequalities and the Life Course (CIQLE) Workshop (Yale University), Institute for the Study of Societal Issues (ISSI) Colloquium (University of California at Berkeley), and Stanford Sociology Colloquium Series for helpful comments on this chapter.

1. In this chapter I examine inequalities in educational attainment only in England (not in the other countries of the United Kingdom); the 1944 Education Act, along with other educational policies that I discuss in the chapter, applied to Wales as well as to England.

2. Figure 9.1 is based on data drawn from Youth Cohort Study 11 (Jarvis, Exley, and Tipping 2003), which follows a cohort of young people who were born in 1986 and thus reached the first transition point in 2002. More details on the Youth Cohort Study data are provided in the "Data" section.

3. As of 2013 all children will be required to continue in education or formal training until age 17, and from 2015, until age 18. These reforms, introduced in the Education and Skills Act 2008, are designed to increase skill levels, thereby meeting the perceived demands of technological change and the global economy.

4. YCS13, the most recent cohort in the series, sampled students only in England.

5. Because of declining response rates to YCS questionnaires, YCS13 broke with the design of previous studies and introduced face-to-face interviews. The response rate for the first sweep of YCS13 was 69 percent (DCSF 2008), in line with the response rates for the early YCSs, in contrast to 47 percent for the first sweep of YCS12 (TNS Social, Prior, and Hall 2005).

6. I exclude YCS1 and YCS2 because of data quality issues and YCS4 because some important measures are missing. Further details on why some datasets from the YCS series were excluded are available from the author.

The following cohorts are included in the analysis of the transition to A-level: 1958, 1970 (for class only), 1971, 1975, 1976, 1978, 1980, 1982, 1984, 1986, and 1991.

The following cohorts are included in the analysis of the transition to university degree: 1958, 1971, 1975, 1976, 1978, 1980, 1982, 1984, and 1986.

7. Information on father's and mother's occupation and education is collected when the students are 11 years old in NCDS, 10 years old in BCS, and 16 years old in YCS.

8. The transition rates presented in Figures 9.2, 9.3, 9.7, and 9.8 have been smoothed using a five-year moving average. Figures based on the raw transition rates are available on request.

9. In some cases (e.g., the intermediate-working-class comparison in 1970) the bar for primary effects is positive while the bar for secondary effects is negative; the overall log odds ratio is the sum of the two bars. The opposing directions of the bars should be interpreted as follows: if primary effects were eliminated and only secondary effects were operating in 1970, working-class children would actually be advantaged over intermediate-class children in the transition to A-level, while if only primary effects were operating, working-class children would be more disadvantaged relative to intermediate-class children.

10. Significance tests were carried out to establish whether the estimates of the relative importance of secondary effects were different from 0 within each

cohort, whether these estimates differed significantly depending on which operationalization of social background was used, and whether differences in estimates of the relative importance of secondary effects differed significantly between cohorts (see Chapter 2 of this volume). Full results of the significance tests are available in the web appendix.

11. Once again, estimates of the relative importance of secondary effects do not differ significantly across the different operationalizations of social background.

REFERENCES

Blair, Tony. 1996. Speech to the Labour Party Conference. October 1.

Blanden, Jo, Alissa Goodman, Paul Gregg, and Stephen Machin. 2004. "Changes in Intergenerational Mobility in Britain." In *Generational Income Mobility in North America and Europe*, edited by Miles Corak, 122–46. Cambridge: Cambridge University Press.

Breen, Richard, Ruud Luijkx, Walter Müller, and Reinhard Pollak. 2009. "Non-persistent Inequality in Educational Attainment: Evidence from Eight European Countries." *American Journal of Sociology* 114:1475–521.

Cheung, Sin Yi, and Muriel Egerton. 2007. "Great Britain: Higher Education Expansion and Reform: Changing Educational Inequalities." In *Stratification in Higher Education: A Comparative Study*, edited by Yossi Shavit, Richard Arum, and Adam Gamoran, 195–219. Stanford, CA: Stanford University Press.

DCSF (Department for Children, Schools and Families). 2008. *Youth Cohort Study: Cohort 13*. BMRB Social Research.

Erikson, Robert. 1984. "Social Class of Men, Women and Families." *Sociology* 18:500–514.

Erikson, Robert, and John H. Goldthorpe. 1992. *The Constant Flux: A Study of Class Mobility in Industrial Societies*. Oxford: Clarendon Press.

Erikson, Robert, John H. Goldthorpe, Michelle Jackson, Meir Yaish, and David R. Cox. 2005. "On Class Differentials in Educational Attainment." *Proceedings of the National Academy of Sciences* 102:9730–33.

Erikson, Robert, John H. Goldthorpe, and Lucienne Portocarero. 1979. "Intergenerational Class Mobility in Three Western European Societies: England, France and Sweden." *British Journal of Sociology* 33:1–34.

Halsey, A. H., and Jean Floud. 1957. "Intelligence Tests, Social Class and Selection for Secondary Schools." *British Journal of Sociology* 8:33–39.

Halsey, A. H, Anthony F. Heath, and John Ridge. 1980. *Origins and Destinations: Family, Class and Education in Modern Britain*. Oxford: Clarendon Press.

Heath, Anthony F., and Peter Clifford. 1990. "Class Inequalities in Education in the Twentieth Century." *Journal of the Royal Statistical Society*, Series A, 153:1–16.

Heath, Anthony F., and McDonald, Sarah K. 1987. "Social Change and the Future of the Left." *Political Quarterly* 58:364–77.

Jackson, Michelle, Robert Erikson, John H. Goldthorpe, and Meir Yaish. 2007. "Primary and Secondary Effects in Class Differentials in Educational Attainment: The Transition to A-Level Courses in England and Wales." *Acta Sociologica* 50:211–29.

Jarvis, Lindsey, Sonia Exley, and Sarah Tipping. 2003. *Youth Cohort Study: Survey of 16 Year Olds (Cohort 11, Sweep 1), Technical Report*. London: Department for Education and Skills.

Jonsson, Jan O., Colin Mills, and Walter Müller. 1996. "A Half Century of Increasing Educational Openness? Social Class, Gender and Educational Attainment in Sweden, Germany and Britain." In *Can Education Be Equalized? The Swedish Case in Comparative Perspective*, edited by Robert Erikson and Jan O. Jonsson, 183–206. Boulder, CO: Westview.

Kerckhoff, Alan C., and Jerry M. Trott. 1993. "Educational Attainment in a Changing Educational System: The Case of England and Wales." In *Persistent Inequality: A Comparative Study of Educational Attainment in Thirteen Countries*, edited by Yossi Shavit and Hans-Peter Blossfeld, 133–54. Boulder, CO: Westview.

Payne, Joan. 2003. *Choice at the End of Compulsory Schooling: A Research Review*. Research Report RR414. London: UK Department for Education and Skills.

Raftery, Adrian E., and Michael Hout. 1993. "Maximally Maintained Inequality: Expansion, Reform and Opportunity in Irish Education." *Sociology of Education* 66:41–62.

Ranson, Stewart. 1988. "From 1944 to 1988: Education, Citizenship and Democracy." *Local Government Studies* 14:1–19.

Rose, David, David J. Pevalin, and Karen O'Reilly. 2005. *The National Statistics Socio-Economic Classification: Origins, Development and Use*. Basingstoke, UK: Palgrave Macmillan.

Smithers, Alan. 2001. "Education Policy." In *The Blair Effect*, edited by Anthony Seldon, 405–26. London: Little Brown.

Tawney, R. H. 1931. *Equality*. London: Unwin Books.

TNS Social, Gillian Prior, and Louise Hall. 2005. *Youth Cohort Study: Survey of 16 Year Olds (Cohort 12, Sweep 1), Technical Report*. London: Department for Education and Skills.

Toynbee, Polly. 2010a. "Sorry, Students, But You're Low in the Pain Pecking Order." *Guardian* (UK), November 6.

———. 2010b. "How to Turn 60,000 Students into Unqualified Drop-Outs." *Guardian* (UK), November 20.

Xie, Yu. 1992. "The Log-Multiplicative Layer Effect Model for Comparing Mobility Tables." *American Sociological Review* 57:380–95.

CHAPTER TEN

Class Origins, High School Graduation, and College Entry in the United States

Stephen L. Morgan, Michael W. Spiller, and Jennifer J. Todd

In sociological studies of intergenerational mobility in the United States, models of educational attainment have received more attention than the analysis of early child development, the transition to work, career advancement processes, or the direct inheritance of capital. This focus was encouraged by the attention of early scholars of inequality in the United States, such as Pitirim Sorokin, who wrote that

> the school is primarily a testing, selecting, and distributing agency. . . . [O]ut of the many pupils who enter the door of the elementary school only an insignificant minority reach the stage of university graduation. The great majority . . . are eliminated, not only from school, but automatically thereby from climbing up this ladder to high social positions. (1927, 188–89)

The subsequent concurrence of Talcott Parsons (1953, 1959) that schooling is central to stratification processes was then decisive in establishing models of schooling as a core concern of research on mobility processes.

The models of primary and secondary effects of social-class origins on educational attainment that are developed and deployed in this volume do not currently have a prominent place in empirical scholarship in the United States. In this chapter, we hope to demonstrate why this is the case, after first reviewing the educational system in the United States and the sociological literature that has examined pathways through it in recent decades. We then provide results on primary and secondary effects in the United States, offering analysis of high school graduation and college entry, with data from the 2002 through 2006 Education Longitudinal Study. We conclude with a discussion of the future utility of models of primary and secondary effects, considering some of the unresolved challenges that these models must confront in establishing warranted causal assertions about the relative sizes of primary and secondary effects.

EDUCATION IN THE UNITED STATES IN HISTORICAL CONTEXT

In this section, we present the modal pattern of age-grade progression through the educational system in the United States. Then we discuss the evolution of this educational system, focusing on the most important transitions for students.

Basic Contours of the Current Education System

In the United States, children begin compulsory schooling at age 6 when they enter the first grade, although kindergarten is now nearly universal for 5-year-olds. Compulsory schooling continues until students reach age 16, at which time they may discontinue schooling in most states. During the period of compulsory attendance, most students enroll in three schools: an elementary school (typically grades 1 through 6), a junior high or middle school (typically grades 7 and 8), and a high school (typically grades 9 through 12). Because schooling is compulsory through to age 16, most adolescents continue their formal education through the 10th grade, unless they have repeated a grade, in which case they may reach age 16 in an earlier grade.[1]

The first crucial educational transition in the United States is high school graduation, which is achieved for most students at age 18 after completing grade 12.[2] High school graduates may then continue their education by attending one of many postsecondary possibilities, including trade schools, community colleges, liberal arts colleges, and comprehensive universities. Most of these institutions accept all applicants who pay tuition and fees, but there is a stratum of elite institutions to which access is restricted.

Historical Development

Educational institutions in the United States are diverse in size and structure because of a legacy of local control that has allowed the emergence of a differentiated and loosely coordinated system of institutions (see Tyack 1974). This system has comparatively weak constraints on enrollment levels, and it has expanded rapidly over the past 150 years in response to the increasing demands of the economy and the citizenry (see Goldin and Katz 2008). Formal barriers to entry for each level of education are also comparatively weak, but the quality of education experienced can differ dramatically depending on the particular school a student attends. The following brief historical narrative captures the essence of the conventional wisdom on the institutional development of education in the United States.

From its earliest days as an independent nation, and in particular through the Land Ordinance Act of 1785, the federal government vested responsibility for education in local communities. Townships were granted land, which they could use or sell, to support the schooling of their children. Most local governments then established taxes to fund the operating expenses of local schools, which allowed communities to provide elementary schooling without charging fees.

Over the course of the 19th century, compulsory schooling laws proliferated, and by the 1870s free elementary education was provided for all youth. Tuition-funded high schools continued to prepare elite youth to attend college, but free public high schools began to emerge. Between 1889 and 1939, the number of students in public high schools then increased from 6.7 percent to 73.3 percent, propelled by increases in the demand for education from parents seeking to educate their children for the prized positions in the rapidly expanding industrial sector (Trow 1961). During this period, the character of the American high school changed substantially. The majority of preexisting high schools had been preparing the children of the elite to attend universities. The main objective of many new public high schools in the early 20th century was to provide a general education for students who were not destined to attend college but who instead needed skills necessary for employment in the expanding industrial sector.

The expansion of higher-education institutions was similarly rapid, following the massive growth of high school education. Provincial colleges that had been established to train youth from elite families were gradually transformed into modern universities with national constituencies (see Karabel 2005). These institutions were joined by rapidly growing state universities. Following World War II, enrollments diversified and grew in response to the Servicemen's Readjustment Act of 1944 (commonly known as the GI Bill), which provided financial support for World War II veterans to attend institutions of higher education (Bound and Turner 2002). Then, as part of the space race with the Soviet Union, the federal government invested heavily in its higher-education system, introducing an array of programs between 1958 and 1973 that provided financial support to institutions and directly to individual students. College attendance rates then continued to increase through the end of the 20th century, spurred by increasing labor market returns to college degrees. In total, the number of students enrolled in colleges and universities increased from 2.7 million in 1950 to 14.8 million in 2000 (Snyder, Dillow, and Hoffman 2009).

During this expansion, the stratification of higher-education institutions changed in character. At the top, elite private institutions formerly attended by only the wealthy became more firmly established as national universities for students from all backgrounds (at least nominally, since these institutions were opened only to those who performed well on standardized tests, a capacity that is substantially shaped by the quality of earlier schooling that parents are able to purchase for their children; see Lemann 1999). State-sponsored institutions came to serve the vast majority of college students, providing educations that many argue vary too widely in quality. At the bottom, a patchwork of community colleges emerged to offer two-year associate's degrees and many forms of vocational training. These open-access community colleges proved particularly attractive to less academically prepared, lower-socioeconomic-status, and first-generation college students, in part because of their low costs. Credits from community colleges can be transferred to most bachelor's degree institutions, but the rate of bachelor's degree completion among those who initially enter community colleges remains low (see Rosenbaum, Deil-Amen, and Person 2006; Bowen, Chingos, and McPherson 2009). Community colleges have not been able to shake the characterization of Burton Clark (1960), that they are institutions that serve a cooling-out function in society, wherein the aspirations of ambitious but disadvantaged students with weak preparation for college are convinced to abandon higher education and pursue nonprofessional careers.

In summary, education has expanded dramatically over the past 150 years in the United States. Because of the rapidity and demand-from-below nature of this expansion, the overall relationship between students' origins and high school completion has weakened over time (Hout and Dohan 1996). Now that high school attendance rates have reached near saturation and college entry rates may be shaped more by student interest and preparation than by rigid structural barriers, scholars are beginning to argue that the goal of providing basic access to educational opportunity through high schools and colleges is nearing completion. All agree that, holding these possible advances aside, a current and future challenge is to ensure that students who begin high school and college are able to stay on course to attain the degrees that they initially desire.

MODELS OF PRIMARY AND SECONDARY EFFECTS IN THE UNITED STATES

Against this background of educational expansion, social stratification researchers in the United States have devoted considerable effort to modeling the effects of social background on educational attainment. The types of models considered in this volume—which are typically attributed to Boudon's (1974) conception of primary and secondary effects but which have been developed in the empirical work of Erikson and Jonsson (1996), Erikson et al. (2005), and Jackson et al. (2007)—have not received much attention. This is somewhat surprising, since Boudon (1974), when developing his distinction between primary and secondary effects, drew inspiration from the structural theory of Keller and Zavalloni (1964), which was based on observations of educational inequality in the United States.

Several factors account for this dearth of attention. Perhaps most important, the sociology of education in the United States has had its own variants of primary and secondary effects modeling, dating from the 1950s. Parsons (1953) wrote that many working-class students, regardless of inherent ability, are likely to eliminate themselves from further schooling because of their adherence to a "security" rather than a "success" goal. His student Kahl (1953) then emphasized the extent to which working-class families have reason to consider the costs and benefits of education differently. These ideas were progressively incorporated into the status attainment tradition, best represented by Sewell, Haller, and Portes (1969) and Sewell, Haller, and Ohlendorf (1970). Here, the consideration of goals and the differential weighting of costs and benefits were mostly lost, as status attainment researchers subordinated such processes to aspiration and motivation-based social-psychological mechanisms.[3]

Nearly as important an explanation for the lack of attention to Boudon's work in the United States is the scathing critique offered by Robert Hauser in an 18-page review essay published in 1976 in the *American Journal of Sociology*. His overall summary of Boudon's book was issued early:

> The premises of Boudon's thesis prove to be sociologically naïve, and the argument lacks cogency. The relationship between evidence and conclusions is often weak, is sometimes artifactual, and in a few instances is contradictory. The analytical and observational evidence is frequently flawed by errors of fact, of method, and of logic. (Hauser 1976, 912–13)

Hauser argued that Boudon's assumptions about class differences in the relative costs and benefits of educational attainment were incoherent because they were premised on the denial of direct class effects on adult social standing. Hauser then argued that Boudon had no evidence to deny the validity of value theories of educational inequality, and he demonstrated that Boudon's reanalysis of Kahl's 1953 article was incorrect. It stands to reason that few *AJS* subscribers then carried on to read the remaining 13 pages of Hauser's review or, more relevant here, Boudon's book itself.[4]

For reasons that are less clear, Boudon's distinction has not been used in the United States in response to its revival in European sociology in the 1990s. We have found no references to the distinction in pieces where one would most expect it, such as in the choice-sympathetic theoretical work of Morgan (2005), Hout (2006), and Lucas (2009).[5] Moreover, methodological and empirical work has similarly proceeded without its consideration, as in Breen and Jonsson (2000, 2005), Lucas (2001), and Roksa et al. (2007).

This state of affairs is regrettable, not just because of a lost opportunity for cross Atlantic cooperation. Primary and secondary effects should be considered in the United States because, as Jackson et al. (2007) demonstrate, their measurement is relevant to concerns in the United States about lost talent in response to college affordability.

In the United States, the federal government's role in promoting access to higher education has been vigorously debated in the past two decades. To some extent, this renewed attention is a direct result of the concern over escalating tuition costs at both public and private universities. Scholars do not agree on the extent that short-term credit constraints prevent students who would otherwise attend college from attending (Kane 1999; Cameron and Taber 2004). Some argue that college entry rates increased at the same time that college costs increased and that many of the prospective students who are eligible for Pell grants—the federal government's main tuition grant for low-income college students—do not even apply for them. Others have countered that these surprisingly low take-up rates are evidence, not that low-income students have sufficient access to credit on their own, but that the application forms for federal grants are too complex, intimidating, and burdensome for families with little past experience with higher education (King 2006; Dynarski and Scott-Clayton 2006). Thus, although various scholars estimate that a $1,000 increase in financial aid is associated with an increase in the rate of attending college of between 3.5 and 6 percent, it is not clear how to effectively deliver this aid to students in the United States (Leslie and Brinkman 1988; Dynarski 2003).

More generally, in recent years two opposite positions have crystallized in the debate over how to decrease the effect of social origins on educational attainment and social standing (see Heckman and Krueger 2003). One position calls for the expansion of government programs for adolescents and young adults, including strengthening vocational high school training programs and displaced-worker training programs, and providing subsidies to relieve short-term credit constraints that prevent able students from attending college. The other position, in contrast, maintains that policies targeted at adolescents and young adults have low social returns because academic and career successes are determined earlier in the life course. If the goal is to increase the skills and attainments of the workforce in the long run and to break down rates of intergenerational transmission of poverty, policies should provide more support for programs for young children.

How is the literature on primary and secondary effects relevant to this debate? Jackson et al. (2007) argue that the existence of meaningful secondary effects has direct policy implications. These effects provide support for the argument against the increasingly dominant position in the United States' policy dialogue that investments in early childhood education have a high social rate of return but policies that promote access to higher education have a comparatively low social rate of return. Jackson et al. (2007, 225) argue further that "the possibility must be recognized that any gains that may be made in reducing primary effects via interventions in early years—at a probably high cost—will be at least in some degree offset in so far as the further problem of secondary effects is not addressed." The literature on primary and secondary effects is therefore at the frontier of policy debate, helping determine, in the best traditions of European welfare states research, how to develop the optimal mix of development subsidies from cradle to grave.[6]

In the remainder of this chapter, we estimate primary and secondary effects for a three-class model of social stratification, following the basic framework worked out by Erikson et al. (2005) and Jackson et al. (2007).[7] We consider the two most important transitions discussed in the literature on educational attainment in the United States: high school graduation and college entry. In conclusion, we offer plausible interpretations of the results and we raise some methodological concerns that this strand of literature should confront to gain the attention of a wider range of scholars of inequality and education.

METHODS

Data and Analysis Sample

Data were drawn from the 2002 base year through 2006 second-follow-up waves of the Education Longitudinal Study (ELS), which is a nationally representative sample of students in public and private high schools collected by the National Center for Education Statistics of the U.S. Department of Education. We restricted the analysis to respondents who participated in all three waves of the survey, using a weight to account for sample attrition between the sophomore year (in 2002) and the two follow-up surveys in 2004 and 2006. The resulting analysis sample includes 12,546 students for the high school graduation models. For the college entry models we dropped students who did not complete high school, resulting in an analysis sample of 11,400 students for the college entry models. Substantial detail on the definition of the analysis sample, procedures for developing weights, and decisions for handling missing data are available in the web appendix (http://www.primaryandsecondaryeffects.com).

Measures

High School Graduation and College Entry. Our respondents were sampled in 2002 as enrolled high school sophomores (i.e., second-year high school students, typically age 15 or 16). We coded high school graduates as those who obtained high school diplomas before the second follow-up in 2006. We did not include General Educational Development (GED) diploma recipients among our high school graduates.[8] Of the 12,546 students who had complete data for high school graduation and social class, 89.8 percent graduated from high school. Approximately 2 percent of these high school graduates experienced a delay in their graduation, defined as receiving a diploma between the summer of 2004 but before data collection in 2006.

College entry is defined strictly as having made the transition to a four-year college within six months of high school graduation, regardless of whether high school graduation was delayed. Of the 11,400 students who were high school graduates and who had complete data for college entry and social class, 44.3 percent entered a four-year college within six months of high school graduation.

Social Class. Following established procedures for estimating primary and secondary effects in the sociology of education, we adopt the three-tiered Erikson-Goldthorpe-Portocarero (EGP) class schema of salariat, intermediate, and working classes. First, we coded the broad occupational categories of fathers and mothers (or male and female guardians) into the nine-category EGP schema. Then we collapsed these nine-category classes to the three tiers of salariat, intermediate class, and working class, after which we then further collapsed father's and mother's class position into an overall family measure. In this family class coding, we very slightly privileged father's class, as explained in the web appendix.

Academic Performance. Respondents were administered achievement tests in both the 2002 base year and the 2004 first-follow-up waves. Base-year respondents were administered mathematics and reading achievement tests, but only mathematics tests were administered in 2004. Our sophomore year academic performance measure is a standardized composite of 2002 mathematics and reading scores estimated by item response theory (IRT). Our 2004 academic performance measure is a standardized composite of 2004 mathematics and 2002 reading IRT-estimated scores. A 2004 measure of academic performance that included 2004 results from a reading test would have been preferable, but this was not available. That such a measure is absent, however, should not be very consequential. Prior work shows considerable stability in relative rankings throughout high school for reading achievement, and this is one of the reasons that the U.S. Department of Education employs an updated mathematics test for the 2004

ELS but not an updated reading test. In contrast, mathematics achievement continues to evolve as a function of social class, mostly because of greater differentiation of courses taken through the final two years of high school.

Modeling Strategy

We first estimate logit models for the two educational transitions of high school graduation and then college entry. We do not employ the smoothing techniques developed by Erikson et al. (2005) but instead estimate models directly on the observed data. For each transition, we estimate pooled logit models for all three classes. To calculate primary and secondary effects, we then estimate models that include academic performance interacted with the indicator variables for class. In so doing, we create parameter estimates that are equivalent to what could be obtained by class-specific logit models. We then calculate marginal observed and what-if transition rates across classes, which Erikson et al. (2005) and Jackson et al. (2007) label counterfactual but which are generally labeled synthesized in this volume (see Chapter 2). These rates are equal to the sort of class-by-class analysis used in this research tradition, with the added benefits that no smoothing assumptions are introduced and the calculation of standard errors is straightforward. (In the web appendix, we also estimate the same models for three education groups and for nine class-education groups.)

Each of these logit models is weighted by the estimated inverse probability of being in the analysis sample, multiplied by the panel weight developed by the data distributors (F2BYWT). To sharpen counterfactual projections, we estimated two sets of inclusion probabilities for the college entry models, as fully explained in the web appendix. The first set of probabilities is estimated with a logit model that includes only those who had graduated from high school. The resulting weight generates college entry rates that can be generalized only to high school graduates. Since this group is not selected at random from the full population of high school students who could *ex ante* enter college, we also estimated a second set of probabilities derived from a broader baseline logit model that includes even those who do not graduate from high school. These probabilities are then used to generate weights that deliver college entry rates that can be generalized to all high school sophomores, as if they had all graduated from high school by 2006 and were available in theory to enter college immediately. We show later that this broader set of estimated college entry rates is generally lower, as expected, but the overall pattern is the same as when the weights permit generalizations only to the selected group of students who are observed to have graduated from high school.

MODELS OF PRIMARY AND SECONDARY EFFECTS

Table 10.1 presents observed transition rates for both high school graduation and college entry, separately by class and for the full sample. Within each panel, means and standard deviations of the performance measure are presented, separately by class and for the full sample. The results show clearly that class in the United States is a strong baseline predictor of both transition rates and performance in high school, as measured by standardized achievement tests.

Table 10.2 presents six logit models in three separate pairs. In the first column of each pair, the educational transition under consideration is modeled solely as a function of social-class origins. In the second column of each pair, primary and secondary effects are modeled by estimating coefficients for social class, performance, and the interaction between performance and class. Because of the parameterization chosen, wherein class is represented by two dummy variables, each of which is interacted with performance, these models produce the same predicted probabilities of making the educational transitions that could be obtained by three class-specific logit models with performance as the sole predictor variable in each.

For the high school graduation model, class and performance both predict whether sophomores complete high school. The association between performance and the probability of graduating high school appears to be slightly weaker for lower classes, although this difference is modest at best and well within sampling error. The predicted probabilities from this model are then presented in panel a of Table 10.3, and they are reported as estimated true and estimated what-if rates (labeled synthesized rates elsewhere in this volume). The nine cells of the panel give the estimated probability for each of the three classes that would prevail if they (1) kept their own performance distribution but (2) went through the estimated transition regime for each of the three classes. The diagonal of the panel includes simple estimated probabilities of graduating high school for each class, which are 0.933 for the salariat class, 0.886 for the intermediate class, and 0.848 for the working class.[9] The values off the diagonal are estimated what-if

TABLE 10.1

Means and standard deviations (SDs) of variables used in the analysis, separately for all high school sophomores and for all high school graduates

	SALARIAT CLASS		INTERMEDIATE CLASS		WORKING CLASS		FULL SAMPLE	
	Mean	*SD*	*Mean*	*SD*	*Mean*	*SD*	*Mean*	*SD*
(A) ALL SOPHOMORES (I.E., SECOND-YEAR HIGH SCHOOL STUDENTS)								
High school graduation	0.933		0.886		0.848		0.898	
Performance in 10th grade (standardized test)	0.275	0.967	−0.141	0.993	−0.368	0.917	0.001	1.000
Number of respondents	6,704		2,434		3,408		12,546	
(B) HIGH SCHOOL GRADUATES								
College entry	0.541		0.406		0.285		0.443	
Performance in 12th grade (standardized test)	0.331	0.943	−0.072	0.986	−0.296	0.923	0.076	0.986
Number of respondents	6,293		2,185		2,922		11,400	

SOURCE: Education Longitudinal Study of 2002–2006.

NOTE: Means and SDs are weighted, but the numbers of respondents are the observed numbers in the data. For the proper weighted distribution of class, see the final column of Table S10.1 in the web appendix. The mean and SD of performance in the 12th grade are not 0 and 1 in the second panel because the variable was standardized across all 12,546 high school sophomores but then presented for this panel only for the 11,400 students from the high school graduate subsample.

TABLE 10.2
Logit models for high school graduation and college entry

	High school graduation		College entry (among high school graduates)		College entry (weighted to the distribution of all high school sophomores)	
Constant	2.64	2.75	0.16	−0.25	0.07	−0.31
	(0.07)	(0.08)	(0.04)	(0.05)	(0.04)	(0.05)
Class						
Intermediate	−0.59	−0.28	−0.54	−0.19	−0.58	−0.19
	(0.10)	(0.14)	(0.06)	(0.07)	(0.06)	(0.07)
Working	−0.92	−0.50	−1.08	−0.54	−1.12	−0.56
	(0.09)	(0.11)	(0.06)	(0.07)	(0.06)	(0.07)
Performance		0.97		1.27		1.28
		(0.07)		(0.05)		(0.05)
× Intermediate		−0.06		0.03		0.04
		(0.12)		(0.09)		(0.09)
× Working		−0.09		−0.14		−0.13
		(0.10)		(0.08)		(0.08)
Wald chi-square	105.9	469.8	336.7	1,206.0	354.0	1,213.1
N	12,546	12,546	11,400	11,400	11,400	11,400

SOURCE: See Table 10.1.

NOTE: Standard errors in parentheses.

transition rates. For example, the value 0.901 in the upper-right-hand cell of the panel is the estimated probability that the salariat class would graduate from high school, assuming the salariat class retains its distribution of performance but moves through the transition regime of the working class. Rather than moving through a logit model with an index function of 2.75 + (0.97)*Performance* as its argument, they move through a logit model with an index function of (2.75 − 0.5) + (.97 − 0.09)*Performance* as its argument. For every value of performance, the predicted probability is then lower. Similar comparisons across columns reveal a strict ordering of transition rates, as determined by the distribution of performance and the estimated logit parameters. Higher classes have lower transition rates when they pass through the transition regimes of lower classes and vice versa.

What about comparisons across rows within columns? For example, consider the difference between 0.933 in the upper-left-hand cell of the panel and 0.892 in the lower-left-hand cell. This difference is produced by the alternative distributions of performance in the salariat and the working classes, as would be observed if they both passed through the transition

TABLE 10.3

High school graduation and college entry rates by class origin, estimated from the models in Table 10.2 that adjust for prior performance

(A) HIGH SCHOOL GRADUATION RATES
What-if class

Observed class	Salariat	Intermediate	Working
Salariat	0.933 (0.004)	0.917 (0.007)	0.901 (0.006)
Intermediate	0.906 (0.006)	0.886 (0.009)	0.866 (0.007)
Working	0.892 (0.007)	0.870 (0.010)	0.848 (0.007)

(B) COLLEGE ENTRY RATES (FOR HIGH SCHOOL GRADUATES ONLY)
What-if class

Observed class	Salariat	Intermediate	Working
Salariat	0.541 (0.009)	0.507 (0.013)	0.423 (0.013)
Intermediate	0.439 (0.011)	0.406 (0.012)	0.336 (0.011)
Working	0.380 (0.009)	0.346 (0.012)	0.285 (0.010)

(C) COLLEGE ENTRY RATES (WEIGHTED TO THE DISTRIBUTION OF
ALL HIGH SCHOOL SOPHOMORES)
What-if class

Observed class	Salariat	Intermediate	Working
Salariat	0.518 (0.009)	0.484 (0.013)	0.399 (0.013)
Intermediate	0.409 (0.009)	0.375 (0.012)	0.307 (0.010)
Working	0.352 (0.009)	0.318 (0.012)	0.259 (0.009)

SOURCE: See Table 10.1.

NOTE: Observed transition rates on the diagonal and what-if transition rates on the off diagonal. Standard errors in parentheses.

regime of the salariat class. Likewise, the difference between 0.901 in the upper-right-hand cell and 0.848 in the lower-right-hand cell is produced by the same difference in distributions of performance between the salariat and the working classes, but in this case the comparison holds under the alternative scenario in which both classes move through the transition regime of the working class.

Figure 10.1 plots all of these predicted probabilities by observed levels of performance, separately by class. Because the logit functional form is constrained to have its largest marginal effect where its S curve crosses the value of 0.5, and because probabilities of graduating high school in the United States are quite high (for samples of sophomores), the predicted values over the observed data range reveal only the upper tail of the underlying S curve. Each of the point values in panel a of Table 10.3 corresponds to one of nine separate points that lie along the dashed lines of predicted

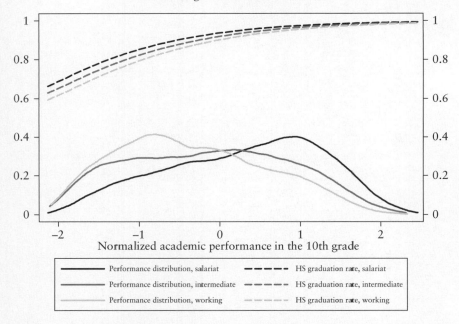

Figure 10.1. Smoothed performance distributions and estimated high school (HS) graduation rates by social class

probabilities in Figure 10.1. The values in the first column of panel a are the corresponding points on the three dashed lines that intersect a vertical line that could be drawn through the mean of the performance distribution of the salariat class. The values in the second and third columns are then three points on the dashed lines that intersect vertical lines that could be drawn through the mean of the performance distributions for the intermediate and working classes, respectively.

Returning to Table 10.2, the models for college entry are presented in the last four columns, in pairs separately for the two weighting schemes discussed earlier. For the first pair, college entry rates are estimated by logit models that are weighted toward the distribution of high school graduates. For the second pair, the same logit models are weighted toward the distribution of all high school sophomores. The logit coefficients suggest that the college entry rate is lower for all three classes when weighted toward all high school sophomores, as indicated for the first model in each pair by the decline in the intercept from 0.16 to 0.07 as well as declines in the class

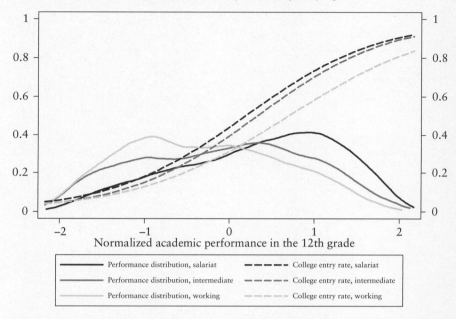

Figure 10.2. Smoothed performance distributions and estimated college entry rates among high school graduates by social class

dummies from −0.54 to −0.58 and −1.08 to −1.12. When performance is added to the predictor variables, these differences persist, although the coefficients for performance do not vary substantially across models.

As shown in panels b and c of Table 10.3, college entry rates are considerably lower than high school graduation rates in the United States. The probability that a high school graduate will enter college within six months of high school graduation is only 0.541, 0.406, and 0.285 for the salariat, intermediate, and working classes, respectively. These rates are slightly lower, at 0.518, 0.375, and 0.259, respectively, when weighted toward the characteristics of high school sophomores. Similarly to Figure 10.1, the full set of predicted probabilities from the college entry models akin to those in panels b and c are presented in Figures 10.2 and 10.3. The predicted probabilities are lower on average than is the case for high school graduation, and thus most of the corresponding logistic S curves are observed over the data range of performance. Moreover, performance more strongly predicts college entry than was the case for high school graduation. When these two factors are combined, the predicted probabilities of college entry increase from less than 0.1 for all classes to greater than 0.8 for all classes.

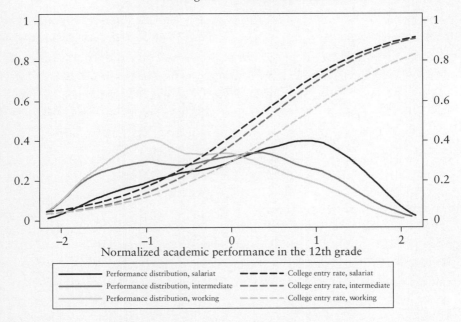

Figure 10.3. Smoothed performance distributions and estimated college entry rates among high school graduates by social class, weighted toward the full distribution of high school sophomores

With reference to the established literature on primary and secondary effects and the new contributions in this volume, four basic patterns are clear from the analysis:

1. Class and performance predict educational transitions in an orderly fashion in the United States, similar to what is observed in other industrial and postindustrial societies when a similar modeling framework is deployed.

2. The absolute rate of high school graduation is quite high in the United States (for a sample of sophomores) compared with analogous rates in other countries that have more finely differentiated forms of secondary education.

3. The absolute rate of entry into four-year colleges in the United States is substantially lower than the high school graduation rate in the United States.

We offer results, available in the web appendix, that support a fourth conclusion:

4. Family class and family education have separable associations with both high school graduation and college entry. The associations cumulate in complementary fashion, but family education is a slightly stronger predictor of both high school graduation and college entry than is social class.

Beyond the summary of our findings just offered, we are less comfortable making additional comparative statements about the relative sizes of primary and secondary effects, both across transitions in the United States and across countries. We leave these comparisons to this volume's editor for the concluding chapter, which uses comparisons of log odds ratios drawn from our results. In the next section, we conclude our chapter with a discussion of our hesitancy, as a set of general concerns that may be particularly pronounced in the stratification system of the United States.

DISCUSSION

We are comfortable stating that primary and secondary effects are surely both present in the United States, as in other countries. We support the basic position that students make choices that determine educational attainment, at least in some fashion and to some extent. Thus, a secondary effect exists, under our implicitly assumed theoretical model. Moreover, since we also see no reason to suspect that such a choice process can explain anything more than a portion of the association between class origins and educational attainment, we must also assume that a primary effect exists. Nonetheless, we have some general concerns that suggest a reorientation of these methods of analysis, especially when applied to educational attainment in the United States. We conclude with this cautionary perspective, which we hope reads as an appeal for further work within this mode of analysis rather than as a reason to abandon it (see also Morgan 2012).

To fix ideas for this concluding discussion, we will define primary and secondary effects for the college entry decision, using graphs as in Erikson et al. (2005). We consider the primary effect of stratification to be the effect of class origins (*Class*) on college entry (*G*) that operates indirectly via academic performance (*P*) in prior schooling. The secondary effect is then the remaining direct effect of class origins on college entry. The causal graph in Figure 10.4a is consistent with these definitions, and it is equivalent in structure to Figure 2(a) of Erikson et al. (2005).[10] The primary and secondary effects of stratification are the causal pathways *Class* → *P* → *G* and *Class* → *G*, respectively.

As shown in the causal graph, the secondary effect is a traditional net direct effect. A causal graph with the same basic content is presented in Figure 10.4b. For this augmented graph, the primary and secondary effects

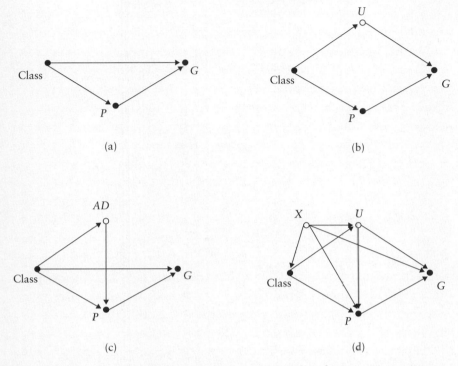

Figure 10.4. Alternative causal graphs of primary and secondary effects (see text for description)

of stratification are defined as two separable causal pathways. As before, the primary effect is *Class* → *P* → *G*. Now, the secondary effect is *Class* → *U* → *G*, where *U* is the choice mechanism that leads students of different class origins to choose differently. The graph in Figure 10.4a is best regarded as a simplification of the graph in Figure 10.4b, which is permissible because *U* is unobserved.[11]

The recent literature on primary and secondary effects suggests that the causal model in Figure 10.4b is too simple. Erikson et al. (2005) extend their simple "potentially causal model," which is represented by the graph in Figure 10.4a, to an elaborated one that is closer to the graph presented in Figure 10.4c. They call this graph a "more realistic model," and it includes a path that is equivalent to the path *Class* → *AD* → *P* → *G* in Figure 10.4c. For Erikson et al. (2005), *AD* is an unobserved anticipatory decision made some years before the actual educational transition (and which they call an "unobserved early choice component"). The anticipatory decision structures P in the run-up to the educational transition. The secondary effect of stratification then operates through two causal pathways, $Class \rightarrow G$ and $Class \rightarrow AD \rightarrow P \rightarrow G$, the second of which is mixed in with what remains the primary effect conceptually, $Class \rightarrow P \rightarrow G$, if AD is unobserved. As a result, standard methods attribute the effect of $Class$ on AD to the association between $Class$ and P, which shifts some of the true secondary effect to the estimated primary effect. The result is that the estimate of the secondary effect is downwardly biased and the estimate of the primary effect is upwardly biased. Or stated in terms of our results, the differences across columns in the what-if transition rates in Table 10.3 are too small because the differences across rows are too large.

Although the reasoning of Erikson et al. (2005) on anticipatory decisions is correct, the full set of causal identification challenges is more extensive. Indeed, Erikson et al. (2005) also allow for the direct effect of AD on G in their "more realistic model," and that creates complications for the conclusion that the anticipatory decision necessarily biases downward estimates of the secondary effect.

We would argue for a baseline model that is more complex than those in Figure 10.4a through 10.4c. We see it as essential to include exogenous variables summarized by X and to also allow the intermediate unobserved variable U to encompass more than just an anticipatory decision. This baseline model is presented in Figure 10.4d, and we argue that the burden of effort, in justifying present methods and direct legacies of them, should be to make the case to delete some of the arrows in the model in Figure 10.4d.

Consider some of the variables that the literature on educational attainment in the United States suggests belong in the background cause X in relation to some of the variables presumed to belong in U. It is often argued that, for many educational transitions in many contexts, race serves as a variable in X while perceptions about the opportunity structure serve as a variable in U (and thereby broadening its default definition from simply an omnibus choice-theoretic mediator). Accordingly, race is a common cause of both class position and beliefs about the opportunity structure. The backdoor paths $Class \leftarrow X \rightarrow U \rightarrow G$ and $Class \leftarrow X \rightarrow U \rightarrow P \rightarrow G$ then follow from the positions in the literature that perceptions of the opportunity structure, U, determine G directly and also determine G indirectly via prior preparation P. Furthermore, the backdoor path $Class \leftarrow X \rightarrow P \rightarrow G$

is supported by the literature that argues for racial bias in performance evaluations, whether generated by tests of dubious quality or by teachers with biased expectations.

Although race is perhaps the most obvious variable to include in X, at least for educational transitions in the United States, other variables that signify categorical distinctions may also belong in X, such as place of residence in contexts where neighborhood disadvantage leads to forms of social isolation. In addition, institutional features of schooling, such as between-school differences in instructional quality and within-school curriculum differentiation, create similar problems.

Accordingly, the causal graph in Figure 10.4b does not appear to give a solid foundation to current modeling practices when applied to the educational system in the United States (nor, possibly, in other countries). Using standard methods is tantamount to replacing the many pathways through X with a simple stand-in path $Class \rightarrow U \rightarrow G$. In this case, U is regarded as an unobserved intervening variable that serves no purpose other than transmitting the net direct effect of $Class$ to G. Treating U in this way will probably lead to overestimation of the secondary effects of stratification because structural effects will then be let in through the backdoor and attributed (by nothing more than an assumption of simple choice-driven behavior) to choice-interpreted secondary effects. At the same time, the estimate of the primary effect, usually represented by $Class \rightarrow P \rightarrow G$, is then confounded by similar additional pathways, although in less clear ways than for the simple case of a sole anticipatory decision considered by Erikson et al. (2005). Overall, the bias in estimates of primary and secondary effects from standard estimation practices will contain many countervailing sources, making a priori claims about the direction of biases impossible. Thus, for example, stating that the differences across columns in the what-if transition rates in Table 10.3 are too small because of omitted variables is true only if an anticipatory decision is the only omitted variable that generates additional dependence in the true causal graph.

Overall, we regard the causal identification challenges just discussed to be sufficient grounds for caution in interpreting differences between what-if transition rates from these models as causal quantities that reflect choice-based secondary effects. Yet these are identification challenges, not barriers, and we look forward to further empirical and theoretical work designed to overcome them. The first step is to model additional causal pathways that emanate from social class, in order to isolate backdoor associations that commingle with narrower forms of primary and secondary effects. The second step is to directly model the choice mechanism that constitutes the conjectured secondary effect, considering how information about costs and benefits is differentially available and differentially used by students and parents from alternative locations in the structure of social advantage.

NOTES

We thank Theo Leenman and Kelly Andronicos for excellent research assistance and Michelle Jackson, Louis-André Vallet, seminar participants at Yale's Center for Research on Inequalities and the Life Course, and seminar participants at Nuffield College, Oxford, for their stimulating comments.

1. However, see Oropesa and Landale (2009) for evidence that a non-negligible proportion of immigrant youth never enrolls in a school after entering the United States.

2. Following Mare (1981), high school graduation is considered a school continuation decision in the United States (see also Mare 1995). Models of primary and secondary effects have focused more frequently on transitions between levels of education, as in our college entry models. We will therefore focus most of our explanatory attention on the college entry decision because it is considered by all traditions of analysis to be an important school continuation decision and an important educational transition.

3. Still, in the broader status attainment research tradition, the effects of family background on educational attainment are routinely decomposed into indirect effects that operate through mediating variables such as academic performance as well as net direct effects that cannot be attributed to the same mediators.

4. Both Boudon's book and Hauser's review covered more ground than primary and secondary effects, and the contention here is simply that Hauser's review prompted many readers to ignore the primary and secondary effects distinction.

5. It is notable that other recent contributions to theories of educational inequality have drawn inspiration from it, particularly Goldthorpe (1996, 2000), Breen and Goldthorpe (1997), and the work that has developed to consider their models of relative risk aversion (see Goldthorpe 2007 for a review). This theoretical work has also had more influence in European sociology than in the United States.

6. And here there are complementarities that need to be assessed. For example, existing evidence suggests that the benefits of early childhood programs for children living in poverty may evaporate as these children enter relatively poor-performing public schools (McKey et al. 1985; Puma et al. 2010). This erosion of

a promising early treatment effect suggests that broad swaths of the public school system may need to be fixed for the benefits of early childhood programs to be sustained until students approach the college entry decision.

7. For comparison with other chapters in this volume, we also estimate primary and secondary effects for education groups and for nine class-education groups. These additional results are presented in the web appendix (http://www.primaryandsecondaryeffects.com).

8. The GED is a test that, if passed, certifies that an individual has academic skills at the level of a high school graduate. A GED is also known as a general equivalency diploma (or degree).

9. These rates of high school graduation among high school sophomores are higher than many standard estimates of overall high school completion, and this is partly attributable to having estimated the high school graduation rate of high school sophomores only. Thus, students who drop out before the sophomore year, because they have reached age 16 early (possibly because they were retained in grades earlier in their school careers) are not in our models. Even so, there is no clear baseline number against which to compare our rates. In part because of the constraints of administrative records, as well as debates about definitional issues, little consensus exists on the absolute levels and trends in high school completion since 1970. For example, estimates produced by the U.S. National Center for Education Statistics, using data and methods similar to ours, suggest that high school graduation rates have slowly increased since 1970 to a current rate of 85 percent (Laird et al. 2008). By contrast, Swanson (2004) reports a decline in the rate to 68 percent, and Heckman and LaFontaine (2007) report a relatively stagnant rate of 75 percent.

10. Erikson et al. (2005, 9732–33) present graphs, or path diagrams, that they also describe as a "potentially causal model" for their Figure 2(a) and a "more realistic model" for their Figure 2(b). Because their article uses counter-factual language throughout and, moreover, cites the work of Rubin (1974), Rosenbaum (2002), and Holland (1986) in the section where these figures are introduced, we regard their path diagrams as putative causal models meant to open up a discussion of causal identification issues.

11. For causal graphs, such simplifications are permissible because we often think of causal arrows as black boxes that indicate the existence of an unobserved mechanism that, in theory, could be observed. In this tradition of analysis, the causal arrow in *Class* $\rightarrow$ *G* is given a choice-theoretic characterization, which justifies granting the pathway an omnibus mediating variable U in Figure 10.4b. See Morgan (2012) for a more specific model for U.

REFERENCES

Boudon, Raymond. 1974. *Education, Opportunity, and Social Inequality: Changing Prospects in Western Society.* New York: Wiley.

Bound, John, and Sarah Turner. 2002. "Going to War and Going to College: Did the G.I. Bill Increase Educational Attainment for Returning Veterans?" *Journal of Labor Economics* 20:784–815.

Bowen, William G., Matthew M. Chingos, and Michael S. McPherson. 2009. *Crossing the Finish Line: Completing College at America's Public Universities.* Princeton, NJ: Princeton University Press.

Breen, Richard, and John H. Goldthorpe. 1997. "Explaining Educational Differentials: Towards a Formal Rational Action Theory." *Rationality and Society* 9:275–305.

Breen, Richard, and Jan O. Jonsson. 2000. "Analyzing Educational Careers: A Multinomial Transition Model." *American Sociological Review* 65:754–72.

———. 2005. "Inequality of Opportunity in Comparative Perspective: Recent Research on Educational Attainment and Social Mobility." *Annual Review of Sociology* 31:223–43.

Cameron, Stephen V., and Christopher Taber. 2004. "Estimation of Educational Borrowing Constraints Using Returns to Schooling." *Journal of Political Economy* 112:132–82.

Clark, Burton R. 1960. "The 'Cooling-out' Function in Higher Education." *American Journal of Sociology* 65:569–76.

Dynarski, Susan M. 2003. "Does Aid Matter? Measuring the Effect of Student Aid on College Attendance and Completion." *American Economic Review* 93:279–88.

Dynarski, Susan M., and Judith Scott-Clayton. 2006. "The Cost of Complexity in Federal Student Aid: Lessons from Optimal Tax Theory and Behavioral Economics." *National Tax Journal* 59:319–56.

Erikson, Robert, John H. Goldthorpe, Michelle Jackson, Meir Yaish, and D. R. Cox. 2005. "On Class Differentials in Educational Attainment." *Proceedings of the National Academy of Sciences* 102:9730–33.

Erikson, R., J. H. Goldthorpe, and L. Portocarero. 1979. "Intergenerational Class Mobility in Three Western European Societies: England, France and Sweden." *British Journal of Sociology* 30:415–41.

Erikson, Robert, and Jan O. Jonsson. 1996. "The Swedish Context: Educational Reform and Long-Term Change in Educational Inequality." In *Can Education Be Equalized? The Swedish Case in Comparative Perspective*, edited by R. Erikson and J. O. Jonsson, 65–93. Boulder, CO: Westview.

Goldin, Claudia Dale, and Lawrence F. Katz. 2008. *The Race between Education and Technology.* Cambridge, MA: Belknap Press of Harvard University Press.

Goldthorpe, John H. 1996. "Class Analysis and the Reorientation of Class Theory: The Case of Persisting Differentials in Educational Attainment." *British Journal of Sociology* 47:481–505.

———. 2000. *On Sociology: Numbers, Narratives, and the Integration of Research and Theory.* Oxford: Oxford University Press.

————. 2007. "The Theory Evaluated: Commentaries and Research." In *On Sociology*, vol. 2, 73–100. Stanford, CA: Stanford University Press.

Hauser, Robert M. 1976. "On Boudon's Model of Social Mobility." *American Journal of Sociology* 81:911–28.

Heckman, James J., and Alan B. Krueger. 2003. *Inequality in America: What Role for Human Capital Policies?* Cambridge, MA: MIT Press.

Heckman, James J., and Paul A. LaFontaine. 2007. "The American High School Graduation Rate: Trends and Levels." National Bureau of Economic Research, Working paper 13670, Cambridge, MA.

Holland, Paul W. 1986. "Statistics and Causal Inference." *Journal of the American Statistical Association* 81:945–70.

Hout, Michael. 2006. "Maximally Maintained Inequality and Essentially Maintained Inequality: Crossnational Comparisons." *Sociological Theory and Methods* 21:237–52.

Hout, Michael, and Daniel P. Dohan. 1996. "Two Paths to Educational Opportunity: Class and Educational Selection in Sweden and the United States." In *Can Education Be Equalized? The Swedish Case in Comparative Perspective*, edited by R. Erikson and J. O. Jonsson, 207–31. Boulder, CO: Westview.

Jackson, Michelle, Robert Erikson, John H. Goldthorpe, and Meir Yaish. 2007. "Primary and Secondary Effects in Class Differentials in Educational Attainment." *Acta Sociologica* 50:211–29.

Kahl, Joseph. 1953. "Educational and Occupational Aspirations of Common Man Boys." *Harvard Educational Review* 23:186–203.

Kane, Thomas J. 1999. *The Price of Admission: Rethinking How Americans Pay for College*. Washington, DC: Brookings Institution Press.

Karabel, Jerome. 2005. *The Chosen: The Hidden History of Admission and Exclusion at Harvard, Yale, and Princeton*. Boston, MA: Houghton Mifflin.

Keller, Suzanne, and Marisa Zavalloni. 1964. "Ambition and Social Class: A Respecification." *Social Forces* 43:58–70.

King, Jacqueline E. 2006. "Missed Opportunities Revisited: New Information on Students Who Do Not Apply for Financial Aid." Washington, DC: American Council on Education.

Laird, Jennifer, Emily F. Cataldi, Angelina Kewal Ramani, and Chris Chapman. 2008. "Dropout and Completion Rates in the United States: 2006." Washington, DC: U.S. Department of Education, National Center for Education Statistics, Institute of Education Sciences.

Lemann, Nicholas. 1999. *The Big Test: The Secret History of the American Meritocracy*. New York: Farrar, Straus, and Giroux.

Leslie, Larry L., and Paul Brinkman. 1988. *The Economic Value of Higher Education*. New York: Macmillan.

Lucas, Samuel R. 2001. "Effectively Maintained Inequality: Education Transitions, Track Mobility, and Social Background Effects." *American Journal of Sociology* 106:1642–90.

———. 2009. "Stratification Theory, Socioeconomic Background, and Educational Attainment: A Formal Analysis." *Rationality and Society* 21:459–511.

Mare, Robert D. 1981. "Change and Stability in Educational Stratification." *American Sociological Review* 46:72–87.

———. 1995. "Changes in Educational Attainment and School Enrollment." In *State of the Union: America in the 1990s*, vol. 1, edited by R. Farley, 155–213. New York: Russell Sage Foundation.

McKey, Ruth H., Larry Condelli, Harriet Ganson, Barbara J. Barrett, Catherine McConkey, and Margaret C. Plantz. 1985. "The Impact of Head Start on Children, Families, and Communities: Final Report of the Head Start Evaluation, Synthesis, and Utilization Project." Washington, DC: CSR Inc. and U.S. Department of Health and Human Services.

Morgan, Stephen L. 2005. *On the Edge of Commitment: Educational Attainment and Race in the United States*. Stanford, CA: Stanford University Press.

———. 2012. "Models of College Entry in the United States and the Challenges of Estimating Primary and Secondary Effects." *Sociological Methods and Research* 41:17–56.

Oropesa, R. S., and Nancy S. Landale. 2009. "Why Do Immigrant Youths Who Never Enroll in U.S. Schools Matter? School Enrollment among Mexicans and Non-Hispanic Whites." *Sociology of Education* 82:240–66.

Parsons, Talcott. 1953. "A Revised Analytical Approach to the Theory of Social Stratification." In *Class, Status, and Power: A Reader in Social Stratification*, edited by R. Bendix and S. M. Lipset, 92–128. Glencoe: Free Press.

———. 1959. "The School Class as a Social System." In *Social Structure and Personality*, edited by T. Parsons, 129–54. New York: Free Press.

Puma, Michael, Stephen Bell, Ronna Cook, and Camilla Heid. 2010. "Head Start Impact Study: Final Report." Administration for Children and Families, U.S. Department of Health and Human Services, Washington, DC.

Roksa, Josipa, Eric Grodsky, Richard Arum, and Adam Gamoran. 2007. "United States: Changes in Higher Education and Social Stratification." In *Stratification in Higher Education: A Comparative Perspective*, edited by Y. Shavit, R. Arum, A. Gamoran, and G. Menahem, 165–91. Stanford, CA: Stanford University Press.

Rosenbaum, James E., Regina Deil-Amen, and Ann E. Person. 2006. *After Admission: From College Access to College Success*. New York: Russell Sage.

Rosenbaum, Paul R. 2002. *Observational Studies*. New York: Springer.

Rubin, Donald B. 1974. "Estimating Causal Effects of Treatments in Randomized and Nonrandomized Studies." *Journal of Educational Psychology* 66:688–701.

Sewell, William H., Archibald O. Haller, and George W. Ohlendorf. 1970. "The Educational and Early Occupational Status Attainment Process: Replication and Revision." *American Sociological Review* 35:1014–24.

Sewell, William H., Archibald O. Haller, and Alejandro Portes. 1969. "The Educational and Early Occupational Attainment Process." *American Sociological Review* 34:82–92.

Snyder, Thomas D., Sally A. Dillow, and Charlene M. Hoffman. 2009. *Digest of Education Statistics 2008*. Washington, DC: National Center for Education Statistics, Institute for Education Sciences, U.S. Department of Education.

Sorokin, Pitirim. 1927. *Social Mobility*. New York: Harper.

Swanson, Christopher B. 2004. "Who Graduates? Who Doesn't? A Statistical Portrait of Public High School Graduation, Class of 2001." Washington, DC: The Urban Institute.

Trow, Martin. 1961. "The Second Transformation of American Secondary Education." *International Journal of Comparative Sociology* 2:144–66.

Tyack, David B. 1974. *The One Best System: A History of American Urban Education*. Cambridge, MA: Harvard University Press.

CHAPTER ELEVEN

Why Does Inequality of Educational Opportunity Vary across Countries?

Primary and Secondary Effects in Comparative Context

Michelle Jackson and Jan O. Jonsson

This volume has asked to what extent social-background inequalities in educational attainment can be attributed to the primary effects of differences in academic performance between members of different social groups or to the secondary effects of differences in the choices made by members of different social groups, conditional on their previous performance. Using the methods described in Chapter 2, inequalities in educational attainment at important educational transitions have been fully decomposed into a part determined by primary effects and a part determined by secondary effects. In each chapter, the authors have used the best available national data to analyze the contribution of the two effects to overall inequality in educational opportunity (IEO) at given transitions. Throughout the volume, we have seen that the magnitude of the effects and of IEO differs across countries, across transitions within countries, and over time. But can these differences be understood as a consequence of differences in the setup of national educational systems? Or is there a systematic logic underlying how primary and secondary effects combine to produce IEO that obtains across all countries? In this chapter we aim to place the findings from the country chapters in a comparative context. We present macrolevel analyses that draw on the results from all the foregoing country chapters and ask whether general and overarching patterns can be found.

As discussed in Chapter 1, distinguishing between primary and secondary effects allows for greater theoretical precision in understanding IEO, because the mechanisms that produce the part of IEO attributable to primary effects are likely to differ from the mechanisms that produce the part of IEO attributable to secondary effects. Social-background inequalities in performance are likely to result from those genetic, cultural, and social features of the family that generate basic academic abilities and that transform academic abilities into school performance. Secondary effects, on the other hand, are likely to result from differences between students of more and less advantaged social backgrounds in the costs, benefits, and risks of pursuing given educational transitions. While primary effects thus find their origin in the early years of childhood and in family life, secondary effects are more likely to depend on the situation at the time of crucial educational choices. Consequently, disentangling primary and secondary effects is important for educational and social policy, because the policy interventions required to reduce IEO depend on whether primary or secondary effects are more important.

Through our comparative approach, we ask whether it is possible to identify features of educational systems or inequality regimes that generate particularly large (or small) primary and secondary effects and IEO. These features could provide us with important clues about the conditions that generate primary and secondary effects and how to reduce overall IEO. Of course, sensu stricto, the eight different countries in this volume represent eight different institutional settings and inequality regimes, but our aim here is to assess whether countries with relatively similar characteristics exhibit similar patterns with regard to primary and secondary effects and IEO.

Our main concern in this chapter, therefore, is to examine the relationships between primary effects, secondary effects, and IEO. We ask how the magnitude of primary and secondary effects varies across countries and whether the magnitude of these effects differs according to institutional features of the countries and educational systems under study. We also ask whether there is a relationship between primary and secondary effects: if primary effects are strong, should we expect strong secondary effects too, or are the two effects unrelated? Although we do not focus on changes over time in this chapter, for some of the countries in this volume we do have data relating to several different cohorts, and we will therefore comment on over-time changes where appropriate. Our results are intriguing, and lead us to conclude with an optimistic discussion of the value of distinguishing between primary and secondary effects when studying IEO and of the possibility of reducing IEO through educational policy.

VARIATION ACROSS COUNTRIES

Inequality of educational opportunity is a consequence of the interaction
between the resources and aspirations of students and their families and
the institutional features of an educational system. Inequalities between
students (and their families) in the economic, social, and cultural resources
available, that is, inequality of condition, may be exacerbated or counteracted by the structure of educational institutions.

Numerous features of the educational system are potentially implicated
in the generation of IEO, and previous research provides an abundance of
classifications and categorizations.[1] For our purposes, however, we single
out two dimensions that are particularly important when understanding
IEO as produced by primary and secondary effects: stratification (or vertical differentiation) and selectivity (choice).

The *stratification* of an educational system describes its vertical differentiation at a given school grade. A highly stratified system consists of
clearly demarcated tracks or schools of very different quality or status.
Placement in, or choice of, tracks and schools is likely to lead to very different outcomes in terms of access to higher education and in terms of
the chances of getting a good job. All educational systems are more or
less differentiated at their higher levels, but some systems embrace early
stratification too; highly stratified systems are those in which students are
already filtered into different tracks during compulsory schooling. Thus,
highly stratified systems also entail early tracking, such that at around age
10 or 11, students are assigned to different tracks and schools.

The *selectivity* of an educational system is the degree to which track
placement is a function of previous school performance rather than the free
choices of students and their parents. In highly selective systems, students'
progress through the educational system is determined by their performance, as measured by teacher-assigned grades or by results in standardized tests and examinations.[2] In choice-driven (or demand-driven) systems,
student choice holds a far more prominent role, so that, in the extreme, any
student may choose to pursue any educational track, regardless of level of
ability or performance.[3] Note, however, that even in highly selective systems
students and their parents still maintain an influence over the tracking decision. It is always possible for students and their parents to reject placement
in an advanced track (an option exercised predominantly by children from

disadvantaged socioeconomic origins), just as there is often some leeway for ambitious students and parents to influence and improve recommendations when the original track recommendation is inferior to that desired.[4]

Distinguishing between stratification and selectivity is uncommon, but because we expect these features to have independent implications for the generation of primary and secondary effects, we believe that the distinction is an important one. This distinction is not normally recognized in part because the stratification of an educational system often goes hand in hand with its selectivity: by and large, highly stratified systems are also highly selective systems and weakly stratified systems are nonselective. The coincidence of stratification and selectivity in educational systems is far from accidental. It would be difficult to preserve a highly stratified system, in which track placement was consequential for labor market success, in the absence of merit-based track selection criteria offering legitimacy. In contrast, mass educational systems with a low level of stratification would hardly be possible without low selectivity. It seems likely that variation in the degree of selectivity might occur only in countries with an intermediate level of stratification—where some tracking occurs but students are also able to move between tracks or where tracking takes place at a relatively late age.

Table 11.1 characterizes the relationship between the level of stratification and the level of selectivity at the secondary or upper secondary level of education for the countries in our analysis. The positioning of the countries in Table 11.1 underlines the point made above that the stratification and selectivity of educational systems are empirically related. We consider the systems of Germany and the Netherlands to be highly stratified (because early selection occurs around age 10–11) and highly selective. England and the United States are classified as weakly stratified with low levels of selectivity.[5] Countries with intermediate levels of stratification are France, Denmark, Italy, and Sweden. France combines an intermediate level of stratification with high levels of selectivity; this is a system in which grades are intended to be consequential for track placement. The Danish, Swedish,[6] and Italian systems exhibit moderate levels of stratification at the secondary level, alongside moderate levels of selectivity: choices about educational transitions are constrained by the level of performance achieved but are otherwise freely made.

In this chapter, we largely focus on stratification and selectivity at the secondary school level, because subsequent educational transitions depend

TABLE II.I

The relationship between stratification and selectivity at the secondary or upper secondary level for the educational systems in place toward the end of the 20th century in the countries in the analysis

	SELECTIVITY		
Stratification	High	Intermediate	Low
High	Germany Netherlands		
Intermediate	France	Denmark Italy Sweden	
Low			England United States

on the transitions negotiated in secondary education. In the country chapters, authors have studied the transition to university education made by those pupils following the (conventionally understood) standard routes that lead to academic success (A-levels in England, the *Abitur* in Germany, for example). The groups of pupils at risk of making the transition to university education therefore differ across countries, with selection into these risk sets differing across countries in an unknown way. As a consequence, it is difficult to make predictions about country differences in IEO at the university level. We emphasize that the placement of countries in Table 11.1 on the stratification and selectivity dimensions is the situation that obtains for secondary or upper secondary education, and it is likely that the placements would be slightly different if the university level were included. Most notably, England and the United States exhibit greater stratification and more selectivity at the university level. In the United States, the major educational hurdle is the transition to college level, where the stratifying choice has (as in many countries) come to be increasingly related to the internal stratification of tertiary education (Shavit, Arum, and Gamoran 2007).

VARIABILITY IN PRIMARY AND SECONDARY EFFECTS

We have identified inequality of condition and the stratification and selectivity of educational systems as country features that are likely to influence the magnitude of primary and secondary effects and of IEO.

As regards educational systems, we expect stratification and selectivity to be most consequential for the generation of *secondary* effects, because selectivity structures the opportunities to make choices and stratification speaks to the importance of making the "right" choices. Primary effects, in contrast, are likely to be influenced to a much lesser degree by stratification and selectivity. In part this is due to a high degree of cross-national similarity in both the practice of assessment and the acquisition of educational abilities, so that it would be hard to identify *any* institutional feature in our sample of countries that could overcome the tendency toward similarity in primary effects. Across countries, there is a high degree of similarity in the types of cognitive and noncognitive skills and aptitudes rewarded by schools.[7] And the mechanisms by which children acquire these skills and aptitudes are also likely to be similar across countries; whether parents pass cognitive and noncognitive traits to their children via genetics or via socialization, we expect very little cross-national variability in how these mechanisms operate (e.g., Erikson and Jonsson 1996). But quite aside from any universal relationship between social background and performance, for additional reasons stratification and selectivity would be expected to influence the magnitude of secondary effects but not the magnitude of primary effects.

Stratification describes the structure of the educational system faced by students and parents, but insofar as IEO is influenced by stratification, we expect the mechanism for this influence to operate through secondary rather than primary effects. Highly stratified systems, in which educational tracks are clearly demarcated from an early age, would no more encourage a closer link between social background and performance than would weakly stratified systems, with little or no tracking. It is the choices that students make, and thus the secondary effects, that are altered by the structure of the educational system. In highly stratified systems, the choice of track is particularly consequential, and recognizing this, students from advantaged backgrounds are given every encouragement and parental support to choose the advantageous track. We therefore expect secondary effects to be larger in size in a highly stratified system than in a weakly stratified system.

Selection describes the extent to which performance drives track placement rather than the free choices of students and parents. Once again, we would expect selection to influence the magnitude of secondary effects but not the magnitude of primary effects. In a weakly selective system with a great deal of free choice, advantaged parents can have substantial influence over whether their child continues to higher levels of education. In a highly selective system in which educational transitions are strongly determined by student performance, there is much less room for choice. Therefore, we would expect secondary effects to be smaller in size in a highly selective system than in a weakly selective system. Selection is not, however, predicted to greatly influence the magnitude of primary effects. As performance is consequential for horizontal differentiation in even nonselective systems, parents in every country aim to translate their resources into performance as effectively as possible, thus leading to rather stable primary effects cross-nationally.

In sum, while increasing stratification is expected to lead to larger secondary effects, increasing selectivity is expected to lead to smaller secondary effects: in a system with much room for free choice, advantaged parents are able to push their children through the school system regardless of potential constraints such as lack of ability. The more stratified the system, the more effort those same parents will put in to ensure that the correct educational choices are made. Primary effects are expected to be similar across countries with different levels of stratification and selectivity. As stratification and selectivity are empirically related, but work at cross-purposes as described above, it is difficult to make predictions about the precise magnitude of secondary effects in our sample of countries. For example, the high stratification of the German system would be expected to generate strong secondary effects, but the system is also characterized by high selectivity, which would be expected to lead to weaker secondary effects. Secondary effects would be predicted to be weaker in England and the United States, where stratification is rather weak, but these are countries in which selectivity is also weak, which would be expected to lead to stronger secondary effects.

On top of the empirical association between stratification and selectivity, which complicates predictions about primary and secondary effects, the effects of these features of educational systems are likely to differ depending on the level of inequality of condition in a country. Differences (and changes) in inequality regimes have the potential to influence primary and secondary effects and thus IEO. In countries where, for example, the income differentials between social classes are large, we would expect higher levels of IEO, because income inequality emphasizes the primary effects of differences in performance between those of different class background (e.g., Reardon, 2011) and the secondary effects of differences in choices made conditional on that performance. Greater economic inequality between classes both increases the capacity of advantaged classes to provide high-quality child care and extra tuition, increasing the size of primary effects, and changes the decision calculus surrounding educational transitions, increasing the size of secondary effects. Thus, inequality of condition has the potential to influence both primary and secondary effects, although because all the countries in this volume are similarly advanced affluent societies (albeit ones with differing levels of income inequality), we might expect this potential to be somewhat muted and thus the degree of variation between countries to be suppressed.

DATA AND VARIABLES: STANDARDIZATION
ACROSS COUNTRIES

As far as possible, the country chapters in this volume followed a standardized approach to data selection, variable construction, and analysis. A summary of the data analyzed and the variable construction for each country is in Table 11.2. For most countries, estimates of the magnitude of primary and secondary effects, and of IEO, are based on the analysis of high quality, nationally representative data with measures of students throughout their educational careers. In some countries, cohort studies that followed children from birth onward could be marshaled to piece together educational trajectories. In others, educational panel surveys of samples of school-age children provided appropriate data. Where access to such data was not possible (for example, in Italy), authors tried to mitigate the effects of sample selection and to therefore provide estimates of the effects of interest that could be compared with those of other countries in the volume.

Sample sizes are generally large and are in almost all cases sufficient to give rather precise estimates of IEO. However, sample sizes do differ substantially among countries and even among datasets within countries: some datasets contain a few thousand individuals and others capture the entire population of students (as is the case in Sweden, where population register data are used). In all countries, we are able to identify a cohort of students born in the mid- to late-1980s or early 1990s, who reached the transition to university toward the end of the first decade of the 21st century. This recent cohort provides the basis for our analyses of the contemporary state of IEO and of the relative importance of primary and secondary effects in creating

TABLE 11.2
Summary of data sources and variable construction

Country	Data source	Cohort represented (decade)	Social-background measure	Performance measure
Denmark	Cohort	1950s, 1980s	Class and education	Standardized test
England	Cohort	1950s, 1970s, 1980s, 1990s	Class and education	Grades
France	Cohort	1950s, 1990s	Class	Grades
Germany	Cross-sectional	1990s	Class and education	Grades
Italy	Cross-sectional	1970s, 1980s	Class and education	Grades
Netherlands	Cohort	1960s, 1970s, 1980s	Education	Standardized test
Sweden	Register	1970s, 1980s, 1990s	Class and education	Grades
United States	Cohort	1990s	Class and education	Standardized test

IEO. In some countries we are further able to examine changes over time in the magnitude of these effects, with the analysis of data relating to cohorts born as long ago as the 1950s.

The measures were as far as possible standardized across the countries. As discussed in Chapter 1, both parental class and parental education were used, where available, as separate measures of social origin. The estimates of the relative importance of primary and secondary effects and of the size of IEO appear to be similar across the different operationalizations of social background. Therefore, for countries for which we have estimates based on both parental class and parental education we report the average of those estimates. Where only one of the measures was available, we report the estimates on the basis of that measure.

Measures of performance offer more challenges when attempting to standardize across countries, because grades are inextricably linked to the institutional structure of a country's educational system. On the whole, the educational systems represented in this volume are ones in which measures of performance are of high quality, in that grades are finely differentiated and students are often aware of both their absolute score and their relative position in the distribution of performance across their cohort. We do not aim to establish an equivalence in grades across countries and instead consider grades to provide information to students about their performance and ranking relative to others *within* a given educational system. The estimates of the relative importance of primary and secondary effects are subsequently comparable across countries, because they show us, within any individual country, what proportion of IEO is determined by differences in the distributions of performance between social groups and what proportion is determined by differences in the choices made, conditional on that performance.

There are, however, two issues related to performance that should be highlighted. In one country, Italy, performance is measured relatively weakly within the educational system and grades at age 14 offer little information to students; grades are reported in just four categories, ranging from "pass" to "excellent," and a large proportion of students achieves excellent grades. The second issue relates not to the measure of performance in the educational system but to the measurement of performance in the datasets available for analysis. As discussed in Chapter 1, it is preferable to employ grades as measures of performance rather than test scores or measures that are unknown to the student. The microlevel model underlying the concepts of primary and secondary effects implies that students make choices on the basis of information about their educational performance, and it is therefore more appropriate to incorporate known grades into our models of primary and secondary effects rather than test scores or other measures known only to academic researchers. In Denmark, the Netherlands, and the United States, the performance measures in the analyses are derived from general-ability tests rather than institutionalized measures of academic performance. As a consequence, we might expect the estimated magnitude of primary and secondary effects in these countries to differ from what would be found if grades were used instead. For example, Jackson et al. (2007) and Erikson and Rudolphi (2010) show that secondary effects account for a larger proportion of IEO when cognitive tests are used as a measure of performance rather than grades.

The estimates that we report in this chapter are taken from the core analyses of each country chapter, in which the magnitude and relative importance of primary and secondary effects were derived following the method described in Chapter 2 (see Erikson et al. 2005; Jackson et al. 2007). The estimates reported here can be found in (or can be derived from) the results reported in each chapter or the web appendix. Inevitably, in an analysis of this type we must focus on the broad picture, and we therefore discuss only the main findings from the individual countries; readers are encouraged to refer to the individual country chapters for the fine details of the analyses summarized here.

DEFINING TRANSITIONS

The most significant challenge in comparing primary and secondary effects and IEO across countries is determining which transitions should be treated as equivalent. Educational transitions represent different sets of opportunities within different countries; in some countries, a transition represents the choice between academic and vocational education, with no possibility of dropout, while in other countries students have the option of deciding between academic education, vocational education, and dropping out. Furthermore, transitions occur at different ages in different countries.

In our analysis, we distinguish three educational transitions: an early transition, which offers a choice between different educational tracks within the period of compulsory schooling (T1); a later transition that occurs at the end of the period of compulsory education and offers a choice between educational tracks and dropping out (T2); and a third transition that marks the transition from secondary education to university education (T3). Table 11.3 describes these transitions and shows which countries are represented in each transition.

While we distinguish between T1 and T2 in Table 11.3, in the analyses below we often combine these transitions. No country in our analysis has both transition T1 and T2, and we therefore consider both transitions

TABLE 11.3

Definition of transitions in each country

Transition	Country	Nature of transition
T1: Ages 10–12	Germany	Primary to Gymnasium
	Netherlands	Primary to VWO
T2: Ages 14–16	Denmark	Compulsory to academic upper secondary
	England	Compulsory to A-level
	France	Compulsory to academic upper secondary
	Italy	Compulsory to lyceum
	Sweden	Compulsory to academic upper secondary
	United States	High school graduation
T3: Ages 18–19	Denmark[a]	—
(conditional)	England	A-level to university degree
	France	Baccalaureate to university degree
	Germany	Gymnasium to university degree
	Italy	Academic upper secondary to university degree
	Netherlands	VWO to WO
	Sweden	Academic upper secondary to university degree
	United States	High school graduation to university degree

[a]Not included in the T3 analysis.

to represent the first major transition in our sample of countries at which primary and secondary effects might come into play. This first major transition, at which students choose whether to pursue academic education, is likely to be extremely consequential for IEO (e.g., Breen and Jonsson 2000; Breen et al. 2009). At the first major transition a substantial proportion of the student population is filtered out of academic education and into vocational education or the labor market.

At around age 18, students face the T3 transition, from upper secondary education to university education. In some countries, only completion of upper secondary education confers eligibility for university entrance, while in other countries all forms of secondary education (academic and vocational) allow students to continue to university. On the whole, we focus on the conditional transition to university and take into account only those students who are eligible to enter university education (compared to the unconditional rate, which refers to the proportion of a cohort who made the transition, regardless of eligibility). As discussed above, the risk set of students who are eligible to enter university education differs across countries and is in several countries difficult to identify with any precision, but we try to achieve some degree of comparability by focusing on those students who have completed academic upper secondary education in our analyses of the conditional rates (see Table 11.3).[8]

TRANSITION RATES ACROSS COUNTRIES

Figure 11.1 shows the percentage of students from the most recent cohort in each country making each of the transitions. The figure demonstrates a high degree of variability in the percentage of students making the transitions across countries. In the first major transition for each country (T1 or T2), the percentages highlight a division between countries in which this transition to academic education represents an elite track (Germany, the Netherlands, and Italy) and countries that have embraced undifferentiated mass education (most notably, the United States), with other countries in an intermediate position.

There is much less variability across countries in the unconditional transition to academic tertiary education (T3), although the countries with the lowest and highest transition rates to university education are still separated by around 30 percentage points (the Netherlands[9] and Italy,

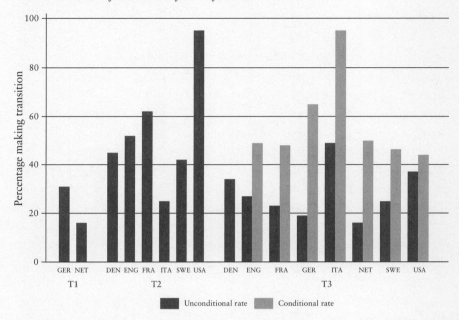

Figure 11.1. The percentage of students in each country making the transitions

NOTE: Denmark is not included in the analyses of conditional T3 because of lack of data.

respectively).[10] Inevitably, the conditional transition rates are in all countries higher than the unconditional rates, and in all countries over 40 percent of those students who were in the risk set for making the transition to university did make the transition.[11] In the following analyses we focus on these conditional transition rates, as it is possible to assess the magnitude of primary and secondary effects only for those students who were eligible to make the transition.

PATTERNS OF INEQUALITY

The percentage of students who make each transition differs between social-background groups, and we now move on to consider inequalities in the chances of making the transitions, as expressed in the log odds ratios comparing the most advantaged and least advantaged groups. In some countries this comparison is between the salariat and working class, in others it is a comparison between the high and low parental education

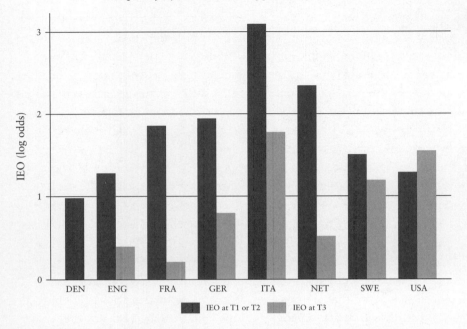

Figure 11.2. Log odds ratios describing inequalities between advantaged and disadvantaged social groups in the first major transition (T1 or T2) and in the transition to university education (T3) for each country

NOTE: Denmark is not included in the analyses of conditional T3 because of lack of data.

categories, and in the countries with both measures of social origin, we take the mean of the aforementioned inequalities related to parental class and education. Figure 11.2 presents log odds ratios describing these inequalities for the most recent birth cohort in each of our countries at the first major transition (T1 or T2) and the transition to university (T3).

Figure 11.2 shows that there is substantial variation across the countries in our sample in the level of IEO between the highest and lowest social-background groups at our defined transitions. At the first major transition, Italy stands out as having a particularly high level of IEO, with a log odds ratio of around 3 for the most recent birth cohort, implying that those of advantaged background are around 20 times more likely to make the transition than not compared to those of disadvantaged background. But IEO is also moderately high in France, Germany, and the Netherlands. Levels of IEO are much weaker in Denmark, England, and the United States.

It is immediately clear that the selected risk set that we define for transition T3 generates a lower level of IEO, probably because of increased homogeneity in the sample in terms of ability and other school-related characteristics and also perhaps because educational decisions made at older ages are less dependent on social origin. A different pattern across the countries emerges, and for those students at risk of making the transition, IEO is relatively low in England, France, and the Netherlands but higher in Italy, Sweden, and the United States.[12]

It is appropriate to ask whether there is any relationship between the level of IEO at the transitions and the stratification or selectivity of a country's educational system. A weak pattern does emerge from the results in Figure 11.2. The highly stratified and highly selective systems of Germany and the Netherlands generate relatively high levels of IEO at the first transition, while the weakly stratified and weakly selective systems of England and the United States are associated with lower-than-average levels of IEO. But the countries that are classified as in an intermediate position on stratification and selectivity—Denmark, Italy, and Sweden—are not clustered in an intermediate position with respect to IEO. Denmark exhibits the lowest level of IEO in our sample, while Italy has the highest level of inequality between the most and least advantaged social-background groups. It is possible that the substantial differences in inequality of condition that prevail between countries in this intermediate group can account for the observed differences in IEO, but without additional country cases this must remain a hypothesis for future research.

At T3 the picture regarding stratification and selectivity is even less clear, because the lowest levels of IEO are found in England, France, and the Netherlands, while Germany, Sweden, and the United States have moderate and similar levels of IEO. The pattern in the observed levels of IEO therefore cuts across differences in educational systems and also across differences in inequality of condition between the countries.

We turn now to consider the contribution of primary and secondary effects to IEO at two transitions: the first major transition in each of our countries and the transition to university. In Figure 11.3 we see the relative importance of secondary effects in determining the IEO between the highest and lowest social-background groups, as expressed as a percentage of the log odds ratio describing the inequality. Once again, the estimates relate to the most recent birth cohort in each of the countries.

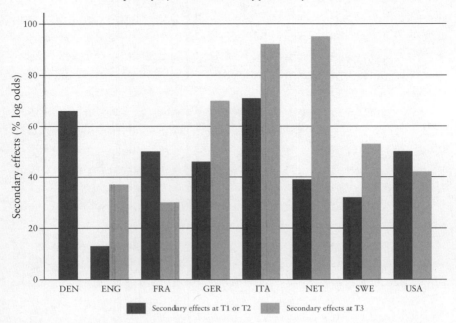

Figure 11.3. The influence of secondary effects at the first major transition (T1 or T2) and the transition to university education (T3) for each country

NOTE: Denmark is not included in the analyses of conditional T3 because of lack of data.

The most important feature of this figure is that secondary effects contribute to IEO in all of the countries in the sample at both transitions. In Italy and the Netherlands over 90 percent of the IEO at T3 between the highest and lowest groups is determined by secondary effects, and for 8 of the 15 country-by-transition estimates around half or more of the total IEO is due to secondary effects. In all countries and at both transitions, with the exception of England at T2, the relative importance of secondary effects is around one-third or higher. Thus, the choices made by students of different social origins, conditional on their performance, contribute substantially to overall inequalities in educational attainment.

THE RELATIONSHIP BETWEEN SECONDARY EFFECTS AND IEO

We now consider the role of primary and secondary effects in the generation of IEO. We have seen that the level of IEO differs across countries and that the relative importance of secondary effects in creating IEO also differs. But arguably of more interest than the relative importance of secondary effects is the absolute size of primary and secondary effects across countries and how primary and secondary effects combine to produce overall inequalities.

In attempting to understand variation across countries in the overall level of IEO, it is important to consider the different pathways through which IEO is created. We propose three main types of educational inequality regimes in which primary and secondary effects operate to produce IEO. We label these regimes Uniform Reproduction, Compensatory Reproduction, and Incremental Reproduction. Figure 11.4 shows how primary and secondary effects are associated in these ideal type regimes.

We plot log odds ratios describing the magnitude of secondary effects (*x* axis) against the log odds ratios describing the magnitude of primary effects (*y* axis) for our three regime ideal types. The letters represent

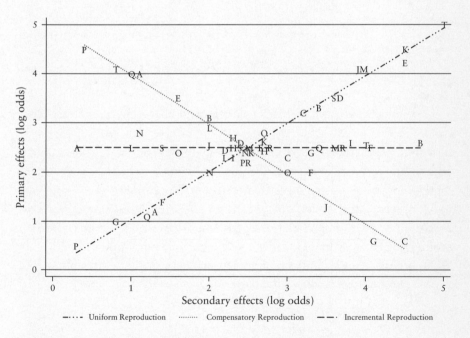

Figure 11.4. The relationship between primary and secondary effects in the hypothetical Uniform Reproduction, Compensatory Reproduction, and Incremental Reproduction regimes

N O T E : Letters represent hypothetical countries.

hypothetical countries, and the lines for each regime represent the ordinary least squares (OLS) regression describing the relationship between secondary and primary effects for that regime.

The relationship between the absolute magnitude of secondary and primary effects is inevitably consequential for the overall level of IEO, which is the sum of the two effects. In Figure 11.5, we plot the log odds ratios describing the magnitude of secondary effects (x axis) against the overall level of IEO for the three regime types (y axis). The lines describe the (linear) relationship between secondary effects and IEO.

Under the Uniform Reproduction regime, secondary effects and primary effects are equal and therefore perfectly positively associated (the correlation, r, equals 1): as secondary effects increase so do primary effects and at the same rate. The overall level of IEO increases rapidly in this regime; because secondary effects are matched in magnitude by primary effects, the IEO is simply twice the magnitude of the secondary effects (i.e., the β coefficient for the regression of IEO on secondary effects is 2, while $r = 1$). In

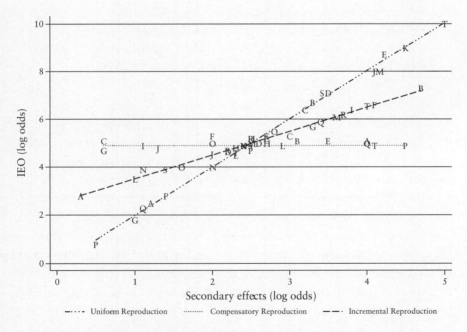

Figure 11.5. The relationship between secondary effects and IEO in the hypothetical Uniform Reproduction, Compensatory Reproduction, and Incremental Reproduction regimes

a Uniform Reproduction regime, therefore, social-background inequalities are expressed equally through performance and through the choices made by members of different groups conditional on performance. Under this regime, students from advantaged social backgrounds are just as successful in securing advantages through their educational performance as they are in securing advantages conditional on that performance.

In contrast, under the Compensatory Reproduction regime, secondary and primary effects are perfectly negatively correlated ($r = -1$), so that as the magnitude of secondary effects increases, the magnitude of primary effects decreases. As a consequence, as Figure 11.5 shows, this is a regime in which the overall level of IEO is effectively constant as secondary effects change (i.e., the β coefficient for the regression of IEO on secondary effects is 0). From the standpoint of individual action, parents have a given bundle of resources that they might employ to further their child's educational career, and they can choose whether to direct those resources toward improving the performance of their child or toward encouraging the educational choices of their child. In such a regime, class will always find a way. Policy interventions and institutional changes might have success in reducing, say, primary effects, but any reduction in primary effects will be offset by an increase in secondary effects. In this regime, therefore, the advantaged classes are always able to maintain their offspring's favorable opportunities, and institutional factors can have an effect only on *how* this IEO is produced.

Finally, in the Incremental Reproduction regime, the magnitude of secondary effects increases while the magnitude of primary effects remains constant ($r = 0$). In other words, the extent to which social-background inequalities operate through performance is limited (to around 2.5 in this case), while the extent to which social background influences the choices that students make conditional on performance is unconstrained.[13] Under this regime, as the magnitude of secondary effects increases, the level of IEO also increases, but at a slower rate than under the Uniform Reproduction regime (the β coefficient under the Incremental Reproduction regime is 1, and r is also 1). In such a regime, stable primary effects are produced because school-relevant abilities are genetically transmitted or inculcated during early class-socialization processes across all countries to a similar extent, and differences between countries are found because country-specific institutional factors determine whether secondary effects are large or small (Erikson and Jonsson 1996, 50, 56–57; see also Goldthorpe 2007).

The ideal types laid out above represent different ways that primary and secondary effects might combine to produce IEO at a given educational transition, and we now ask which regime type best characterizes the results from our sample of countries. In Figure 11.6 we first plot the magnitude of secondary effects against primary effects (measured as log odds ratios between the advantaged and disadvantaged social groups) for each of our countries, for both the first major transition (T1 or T2) and the transition to tertiary education (T3). The most recent birth cohort in each country is represented, and we also add data, if available, for previous birth cohorts. The data points represent birth cohorts within countries (*n* = 19 for T1 or T2, *n* = 17 for T3), and the solid black and gray lines are the OLS regression slopes describing the relationship between secondary and primary effects for T1 or T2 and T3, respectively.

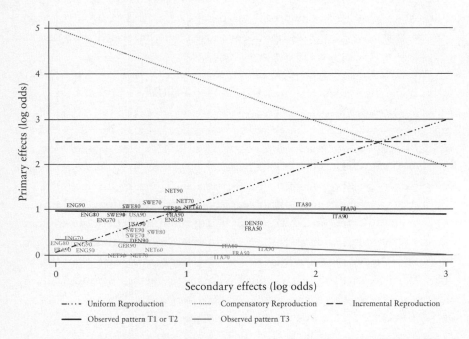

Figure 11.6. The relationship between primary and secondary effects at the first major transition (T1 or T2) and the transition to university education (T3) (log odds ratios for advantaged vs. disadvantaged social-background groups)

The regression line for the observed relationship between secondary and primary effects at the first major transition (T1 or T2) is almost parallel to the regression line for the transition to university (T3). A mean shift separates the two lines, in that primary effects are generally higher at T1 or T2 than at T3, but the regression lines have a strikingly similar slope. At T1 or T2 the β coefficient for the regression of primary effects on secondary effects is -0.02, $p = 0.817$, while at T3 the β coefficient is -0.11, $p = 0.391$. In other words, the slopes are extremely shallow, neither β coefficient differs significantly from 0, and on the basis of this evidence we must conclude that there is no correlation between primary and secondary effects in our data.[14]

The results of this analysis provide us with a strong indication that the relationship between secondary and primary effects in our sample of countries is best described as an Incremental Reproduction regime, in which there is much less variation in the magnitude of primary effects than in the magnitude of secondary effects. The lines for the observed patterns at both transitions are similar to the line for the Incremental Reproduction regime, and statistically the slopes for all three lines are 0. Figure 11.6 confirms, therefore, that at each transition, countries are distinguished from one another by the size of their secondary effects.[15]

We now see how secondary effects are related to overall inequalities in educational attainment. Figure 11.7 shows, for the same data as previously, the relationship between secondary effects and IEO. Figure 11.7 confirms that the observed relationship between secondary effects and IEO is effectively the same as what would be observed in an Incremental Reproduction regime. At both transitions, the regression lines describing the relationship are virtually parallel to that of the Incremental Reproduction regime. At T1 or T2, the β coefficient for the regression of IEO on secondary effects is 0.98, $p = 0.000$, while at T3, the β coefficient is 0.89, $p = 0.000$ (in an Incremental Reproduction regime, the β coefficient is 1; the standard errors for both β coefficients indicate that neither coefficient is statistically different from 1). Therefore, the variation in IEO across countries is almost entirely driven by variation in the size of secondary effects.

DISCUSSION

We have shown that cross-national differences in inequalities in educational opportunity between members of advantaged and disadvantaged social

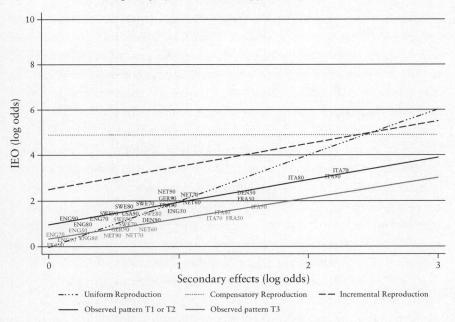

Figure 11.7. The relationship between secondary effects and IEO at the first major transition (T1 or T2) and the transition to university education (T3) (log odds ratios for advantaged vs. disadvantaged social-background groups)

groups are fundamentally driven by cross-national differences in the size of secondary effects, that is, by social differences in educational choice at given levels of school performance. Where secondary effects are large, IEO tends to be large, and where they are small, overall educational inequalities between social groups are smaller. In contrast, there is much less variation in the size of primary effects across countries. This sample of countries can therefore be characterized as displaying an IEO regime that we have labeled Incremental Reproduction. This suggests that in all countries alike there is a floor level of IEO established by social-origin differences in the abilities and aptitudes reflected in performance, but above that floor level there is considerable variation in the way that educational choices play out to establish the overall level of IEO.

Why should secondary effects have such an important role in explaining cross-national variability in IEO? Secondary effects are an area in which advantaged families can bring all of their considerable resources to bear. Students of advantaged background will be encouraged to continue in education even with relatively modest levels of performance, and they will face few risks or costs in comparison with those from less advantaged backgrounds. In fact, the main constraint on the size of secondary effects may not be the extent to which advantaged students can be persuaded to continue in education regardless of their performance but the extent to which *disadvantaged* students do not do the same. Educational choices are forward-looking decisions, reflecting students' preferences about what to study and their labor market ambitions. These choices are guided by estimations of the costs and benefits of different educational alternatives, alongside estimations of the probability of succeeding in these alternatives (e.g., Erikson and Jonsson 1996; Breen and Goldthorpe 1997). Economic security and access to reliable and relevant information are important components of the decision-making process, and students originating in disadvantaged homes are likely to lack these assets. The way in which this lack of assets feeds into the decision-making process depends on institutional and particularistic factors that vary across countries and over time.

Although primary effects have been shown to be much less important than secondary effects in explaining cross-national *variability* in IEO, it is clear that these effects are nevertheless consequential for generating IEO in all countries. As described in the above analyses, in an Incremental Reproduction regime primary effects are much less variable across countries than secondary effects (primary effects average across countries to a log odds ratio of around 1 at T1 or T2 and around 0.4 at T3). One might ask why primary effects show such stability across countries. It seems likely that there is a natural limit in the extent to which social-background differences can feed through into differences in performance. In modern educational systems, an ideology of meritocracy implies that schools must aim to identify and reward talented students, so that inherent academic ability should be reflected in performance. But in conflict with this is the influence that social background exerts on performance, because advantaged families work hard to translate whatever abilities their children have into the highest possible levels of performance. The primary effects are thereby the result of advantaged groups using their resources to maximize their advantage over disadvantaged groups, within the constraints placed by educational systems.

A seemingly puzzling feature of our results has been the lack of association between the stratification and selectivity of educational systems and the contribution of primary and secondary effects to IEO. We believe that the failure to find systematic differences between countries that are highly and weakly stratified and between countries that are highly and weakly selective is due in part to the empirical association between stratification and selectivity: the highly stratified systems that would be expected to encourage the development of secondary effects are also highly selective systems, where secondary effects are likely to be attenuated. Furthermore, even if it were possible to find an educational system that was weakly stratified but highly selective, in which both institutional features acted in the same direction to encourage weak secondary effects, in practice, every educational system leaves plenty of room for maneuver. For example, even in the most selective systems represented in this volume, students are sometimes given a free choice of tracks, they may be given opportunities to prove themselves on higher tracks than their performance qualifies them for, and their parents are able to lobby teachers for more advantageous track placements. And at the same time, in every selective system those students who have qualified for higher tracks are given the opportunity to drop out, an option that is likely to be taken up disproportionally by those from disadvantaged backgrounds because they lack economic resources or have lower educational aspirations. Any compromise of this sort makes even selective systems vulnerable to secondary effects. Ultimately, only a weakly stratified system that strictly allocated educational places on the basis of performance, with no negotiation, would eliminate secondary effects.[16]

As we discuss above, it seems likely that structural features of educational systems will interact with inequality of condition to generate primary effects, secondary effects, and IEO. We unfortunately have too few cases and insufficient variation between countries in inequality of condition to formally assess the role that inequality of condition plays. But our results do suggest that inequality of condition influences the level of IEO in this sample of countries. For example, we observe a higher level of IEO in the more unequal Germany than in the Netherlands, despite similarly selective and stratified school systems. The relatively high level of IEO in Italy may also be attributable to the relatively high level of income inequality in that country (OECD 2008, fig. 11.1). Further tests of the interaction between inequality of condition and the two structural features of educational systems identified here would seem to be a promising area for future research on primary and secondary effects.

POLICY POTENTIAL

The decomposition of IEO into primary and secondary effects draws attention to the ways policy might intervene to equalize educational inequalities.

We have seen that there is much less variation in primary effects across countries than in secondary effects, and we have argued that primary effects may constitute a floor level of IEO that secondary effects build on. We would not, however, wish to argue that primary effects could never in principle, nor in practice, be reduced from the levels that we observe here. In recent years there has been a good deal of interest in policies that intervene in the early years of children's lives, with particular emphasis on the provision of high-quality preschool. These policies have shown potential for equalizing school performance between children of different social backgrounds (e.g., Heckman 2006; Barnett 2008). Similarly, allocating more resources to primary schools and reducing class sizes may have equalizing effects (Krueger 2003). But policy interventions to reduce primary effects must be radical in their scope and are consequently extremely expensive (Jackson et al. 2007). In addition, because primary effects are likely to depend to a very large extent on socialization processes ongoing throughout children's formative years, some might argue that the differences in performance between children of different social groups are normatively defensible and often in fact desirable, arising as they do from legitimate parental partiality, which should be protected from state intervention (Swift 2005).

Although we should certainly not rule out the possibility of reducing primary effects through policy interventions, the fact that secondary effects exhibit such variation across countries and over time suggests that overall IEO could be manipulated more successfully by reducing these secondary effects. Given that any policy designed to reduce secondary effects would be required to ensure that students from different social origins made similar educational choices, encouraging qualified students from disadvantaged backgrounds to make educational transitions must be a priority.[17]

A common theme in political and popular discussions of educational choice is that children from disadvantaged homes lack appropriate ambitions and educational aspirations and that some form of reeducation would ensure that these children made sensible choices when faced with educational transitions. But the appeal to aspirations when explaining why such children are less likely to make educational transitions ignores the material

circumstances that prevail in disadvantaged households that shape ambitions and aspirations. Eliminating secondary effects would require the
costs, risks, and chances of success associated with different educational
options to be no different for students of disadvantaged background than
for those of advantaged background.

We see great potential for manipulating the costs associated with different educational tracks that are faced by disadvantaged children. The economic security that enables children from advantaged homes to take up even
risky educational options is often not in place for those from disadvantaged
homes, and policies that offer a financial safety net can go a long way toward
improving the transition rates of disadvantaged children. For example, in
England, pilot studies showed that the Education Maintenance Allowance,
which offered financial incentives to students from low-income households
who made the transition to postcompulsory education, increased the transition rates of students from these households (Payne 2003; see also Chapter
9 of this volume). But policy changes also have the potential for negative
effects on transition rates. At the transition to university, one recent development in many European countries is the introduction of substantial tuition
fees, to be covered by student loans and grants. Although the increased costs
of university education will in principle be the same for those from advantaged and disadvantaged backgrounds, the risk associated with taking on
increased costs will be much more consequential for those from disadvantaged backgrounds, and increasing secondary effects are likely to result.
Therefore, unless the up-front costs of university education are mitigated,
increasing tuition fees would be expected to have a strongly negative effect
on the rates of transition of students from disadvantaged households.

Aside from the direct manipulation of financial costs, a general strategy for reducing secondary effects would be to aim to replicate the strong
push factors that advantaged parents excel in through policy mechanisms
designed to push and pull well-qualified but socioeconomically disadvantaged students through the educational system. Push mechanisms might
include persuasive and forceful professional guidance for able students,
which would perhaps emphasize both the benefits of more prestigious educational tracks and the student's chances of success (a policy that assumes
that students from disadvantaged households are to some extent myopic in
their assessment of the benefits and chances of success attached to different
educational tracks). Pull mechanisms, on the other hand, would involve

active recruitment by the higher-education institutions, whereby talented students from lower educational tracks are identified and pulled up to the higher tracks (Erikson and Jonsson 1993). It is probable that policies concerned with the behavior of educational institutions, alongside fiscal policies, would have some success in reducing secondary effects. In addition, they come at a low cost.

A final feature of institutional policy that might have an impact on secondary effects is the age at which important transitions are made. Previous research has indicated that decisions made at young ages are more dependent on family background than those made at older ages and thus that IEO is weaker at later transitions (Mare 1980, 1981; Shavit and Blossfeld 1993). In this volume we have also seen that the level of IEO and secondary effects is in most countries substantially weaker at T3 than at T1 or T2 (see Figure 11.2).[18] In general, ceteris paribus, we would expect transitions taken at older ages to be less susceptible to secondary effects because the amount of information available to students about their own abilities and their chances of success at higher levels of education must only increase as their exposure to formal education increases, and we expect talented students with more information to be more likely to make transitions than those with less information. Evidence from analyses of Sweden's comprehensive school reform in the 1960s, which delayed the first transition from age 11–13 to age 16, supports this assertion (Erikson 1996; Meghir and Palme 2005).

CONCLUSION

The results presented in this chapter have only reinforced the argument that, in trying to understand IEO, we must consider the role of primary and secondary effects. Too much of the research on inequalities in educational attainment treats these inequalities as arising only from differences in academic performance between different social groups. We have shown that, in fact, performance inequalities between social groups are but one part of the story. In every country in this volume, secondary effects have been found to be implicated in IEO, and from a cross-national perspective it is clear that secondary effects generate differences in IEO. We argue that this is in fact a parsimonious model of how cross-national differences in IEO are generated, in that we are able to point to differences in the choices made by members of different social groups, conditional on performance, as the crucial *explanandum*. This in turn directs our focus to the economic resources and aspirations available to students at the time that they make decisive educational choices. Bringing in secondary effects has shown us, perhaps, a dark side of choice, in which choices are associated with greater inequality. But knowing this will, in the longer term, show us the way to reducing inequalities between students from different social-background groups.

NOTES

We thank the authors of the country chapters for their generosity and patience in sharing with us the results reported here. We also thank participants in the EQUALSOC final conference (Amsterdam), the Center for Research On Inequalities and the Life Course (CIQLE) Workshop (Yale University), the Institute for the Study of Societal Issues (ISSI) Colloquium (University of California at Berkeley), and the Stanford Sociology Colloquium Series and Robert Erikson, John Goldthorpe, and David Grusky for helpful comments on this chapter.

1. Subsequent to early work by Husén (1967) and Hopper (1968), there have been many variations on a handful of themes when it comes to the classification of educational systems, themes that include stratification, standardization, universalism, and degree of vocational specificity. For a recent review discussing classifications of educational systems in relation to performance (primary) effects, see Van de Werfhorst and Mijs (2010).

2. One might assume, in the same vein as Van de Werfhorst and Mijs (2010), that standardization of selection criteria in the form of centralized tests would provide as objective a view as possible of students' abilities and that IEO would be reduced as a consequence. However, very few countries use standardized tests as a basis of track allocation (in this volume the Netherlands alone uses such a system).

3. In identifying choice as an important dimension along which educational systems might be classified, we are in line with Kerckhoff (2001), and indeed his findings on differences in IEO between countries are similar to our own. Where we differ is in our focus on the impact of social origin on educational choice as expressed in secondary effects; these effects were not the focus of Kerckhoff's analysis.

4. For example, in most *Bundesländer* (states) in Germany, children's performance is assessed by teachers at age 10–12 and the teacher makes a track recommendation on the basis of that performance. *Bundesländer* differ with respect to whether the teacher's recommendation is binding on the student's track placement, but even where the recommendation is binding, students and parents can

influence which track is pursued. See Chapter 3 of this volume for a full description of the German school system.

5. Although the United States has the most undifferentiated educational system of all of the countries up to high school diploma level, the quality of schooling varies more than in other countries (and, as in England, a small private sector offers elite education). While this differentiation by school quality leads to great variation in the level of preparedness for college education among students, any high school diploma confers eligibility for college education (see Kerckhoff 2001).

6. In Denmark and Sweden, although schooling is comprehensive, there is also a substantial degree of tracking at the upper secondary level and a significant proportion of students is engaged in vocational education (just as in Germany and the Netherlands).

7. This is not to say that there is no room for variation in principle. For example, the free schools movement encourages nonstate individuals or groups to set up schools with different curricula and values from the mainstream school system. If such a school were to reject a cultural model in which the virtues traditionally associated with advantaged groups are rewarded, the evaluation of performance may be altered and thus the association between social background and performance. (In practice, the free school concept has been embraced most readily by the advantaged classes, with as yet no wholesale rejection of prevailing norms about performance assessment.)

8. Due to data and space limitations, we will concentrate on the main stratifying transition at T3. However, in several of our countries there are at least two 'levels' of tertiary education, one short-cycle (often more vocationally oriented), and one traditionally 'academic' degree level. For a thorough analysis of social origin differences within the tertiary level from a comparative perspective, see Shavit, Arum, and Gamoran (2007).

9. The Netherlands may at first glance appear to have a lower transition rate for T1 than might be expected by scholars of education, but note that the transition under consideration is that from primary to VWO, the most exclusive academic track.

10. While our results suggest that transition rates to university degree differ across countries, we should note that Organization for Economic Cooperation and Development (OECD) figures show that when it comes to attainment there is very little variation across the countries included in this volume. In all but two of our countries, OECD figures show that slightly more than 30 percent of 25–34-year-olds attain academic tertiary education (type A) (OECD 2009, table A1.3a). A smaller proportion of 25–34-year-olds attains academic tertiary education in Germany and Italy (in both countries, the proportion is under 20 percent). In comparing these attainment figures with our own figures for rates of transition, we see that Italy shows a great discrepancy between transition and attainment rates. This well-known feature of the Italian tertiary sector, in which very high proportions of students drop out after making the transition, suggests

that the decision about whether to pursue tertiary education may be qualitatively different in Italy compared to our other countries.

11. Denmark is not included in the analyses of conditional T3 because of lack of data.

12. We should emphasize that our measures of IEO cannot be straightforwardly translated into a country ranking of all IEO generated by a given educational system. As discussed in Chapter 1, we focus on IEO at particular educational transitions rather than attempting to obtain a summary measure of all inequalities generated within an educational system. However, if IEO at the first major transition is taken to be indicative of this summary measure of IEO, our findings in Figure 11.2 are reasonably consistent with the country rankings that obtain in other studies of IEO and in studies of social fluidity.

13. We may also imagine a regime in which secondary effects are constant while primary effects can vary, but as these circumstances are unlikely to exist in societies with well-developed educational systems, we do not consider this regime here.

14. The number of cases in our analysis is relatively small, and we have therefore checked the results reported in Figure 11.6 for robustness. A plot of the normalized squared residuals against the leverage for each observation established that the OLS regression results were not driven by any individual case.

15. We also note that, with the exception of Italy, variation *within* countries suggests that secondary effects are the most prone to change over time. Although there are few cases in our analysis, insofar as we are able to detect a trend it is toward generally decreasing secondary effects over time combined with stability of primary effects.

16. Clearly, there may be disadvantages associated with a system set up in this way. It is generally believed, for example, that allowing children to make educational choices will encourage engagement with their educational career and increase the level of both effort that students put into their studies and parental involvement. In addition, such a system would be extremely vulnerable if students could not be reassured that grades and test results were fair and did not reflect features unrelated to merit.

17. An alternative would be to *discourage* weak students from advantaged backgrounds from making educational transitions. This may, however, be undesirable, as the average level of educational attainment would fall as a consequence. And as a policy of this sort would most likely be highly unpalatable to the advantaged classes, political effort is probably best directed elsewhere.

18. Some caution must be taken in interpreting these findings, because diminishing IEO across transitions may simply be a consequence of the student body becoming more and more selected on unobserved characteristics (e.g., Mare 1981; Cameron and Heckman 1998; but see Lucas 2001). However, research that controls for this unobserved heterogeneity shows that the finding of diminishing IEO across transitions is maintained (Breen and Jonsson 2000).

REFERENCES

Barnett, W. Steven. 2008. "Preschool Education and Its Lasting Effects: Research and Policy Implications." Boulder, CO: Education and the Public Interest Center and Education Policy Research Unit. http://epicpolicy.org/publication/preschooleducation.

Breen, Richard, and John H. Goldthorpe. 1997. "Explaining Educational Differentials: Towards a Formal Rational Action Theory." *Rationality and Society* 9:275–305.

Breen, Richard, and Jan O. Jonsson. 2000. "Analyzing Educational Careers: A Multinomial Transition Model." *American Sociological Review* 65:754–72.

Breen, Richard, Ruud Luijkx, Walter Müller, and Reinhard Pollak. 2009. "Non-Persistent Inequality in Educational Attainment: Evidence from Eight European Countries." *American Journal of Sociology* 114:1475–521.

Cameron, Stephen V., and James J. Heckman. 1998. "Life Cycle Schooling and Dynamic Selection Bias: Models and Evidence for Five Cohorts of American Males." *Journal of Political Economy* 106:262–311.

Erikson, Robert. 1996. "Explaining Change in Educational Inequality: Economic Security and School Reforms." In *Can Education Be Equalized? The Swedish Case in Comparative Perspective*, edited by Robert Erikson and Jan O. Jonsson, 95–112. Boulder, CO: Westview.

Erikson, Robert, and Jan O. Jonsson. 1993. *Ursprung och Utbildning.* Stockholm: Statens Offentliga Utredningar, Fritzes.

———. 1996. "Introduction: Explaining Class Inequality in Education: The Swedish Test Case." In *Can Education Be Equalized? The Swedish Case in Comparative Perspective*, edited by Robert Erikson and Jan O. Jonsson, 1–64. Boulder, CO: Westview.

Erikson, Robert, and Frida Rudolphi. 2010. "Change in Social Selection to Upper Secondary School: Primary and Secondary Effects in Sweden." *European Sociological Review* 26:291–305.

Erikson, Robert, John H. Goldthorpe, Michelle Jackson, Meir Yaish, and David R. Cox. 2005. "On Class Differentials in Educational Attainment." *Proceedings of the National Academy of Sciences* 102:9730–33.

Goldthorpe, John H. 2007. "Class Analysis and the Reorientation of Class Theory. The Case of Persisting Differentials in Educational Attainment." In *On Sociology.* 2nd ed. Stanford, CA: Stanford University Press.

Heckman, James J. 2006. "Skill Formation and the Economics of Investing in Disadvantaged Children." *Science* 312:1900–1902.

Hopper, Earl I. 1968. "A Typology for the Classification of Educational Systems." *Sociology* 1:29–46.

Husén, Torsten, ed. 1967. *International Study of the Achievements in Mathematics: A Comparison of Twelve Countries.* Vol. 2. Stockholm: Almqvist and Wicksell.

Jackson, Michelle, Robert Erikson, John H. Goldthorpe, and Meir Yaish. 2007. "Primary and Secondary Effects in Class Differentials in Educational Attainment: The Transition to A-Level Courses in England and Wales." *Acta Sociologica* 50:211–29.

Kerckhoff, Alan C. 2001. "Education and Social Stratification Processes in Comparative Perspective." *Sociology of Education* supplement 74:3–18.

Kruger, Alan B. 2003. "Economic Considerations and Class Size." *Economic Journal* 113:F34–F63.

Lucas, Samuel R. 2001. "Effectively Maintained Inequality: Education Transitions, Track Mobility, and Social Background Effects." *American Journal of Sociology* 106:1642–90.

Mare, Robert. 1980. "Social Background and School Continuation Decisions." *Journal of the American Statistical Association* 75:295–305.

———. 1981. "Change and Stability in Educational Stratification." *American Sociological Review* 46:72–87.

Meghir, Costas, and Mårten Palme. 2005. "Educational Reform, Ability, and Family Background." *American Economic Review* 95:414–24.

OECD. 2008. *Growing Unequal? Income Distribution and Poverty in OECD Countries*. Paris: OECD.

———. 2009. *Education at a Glance*. Paris: OECD.

Payne, Joan. 2003. *Choice at the End of Compulsory Schooling: A Research Review*. Research Report RR414. London: UK Department for Education and Skills.

Reardon, Sean F. 2011. "The Widening Academic Achievement Gap between the Rich and the Poor: New Evidence and Possible Explanations." In *Whither Opportunity? Rising Inequality, Schools, and Children's Life Chances*, edited by Greg J. Duncan and Richard J. Murnane, 91–115. New York: Russell Sage.

Shavit, Yossi, Richard Arum, and Adam Gamoran, eds. 2007. *Stratification in Higher Education. A Comparative Study*. Stanford, CA: Stanford University Press.

Shavit, Yossi, and Hans-Peter Blossfeld, eds. 1993. *Persistent Inequality: A Comparative Study of Educational Attainment in Thirteen Countries*. Boulder, CO: Westview.

Swift, Adam. 2005. "Justice, Luck and the Family: The Intergenerational Transmission of Economic Advantage from a Normative Perspective." In *Unequal Chances: Family Background and Economic Success*, edited by Samuel Bowles, Herbert Gintis, and Melissa Osborne-Groves, 256–76. Princeton, NJ: Princeton University Press.

Van de Werfhorst, Herman G., and Mijs, Jonathan J. B. 2010. "Achievement Inequality and the Institutional Structure of Educational Systems: A Comparative Perspective." *Annual Review of Sociology* 36:407–28.

INDEX

Italic page numbers indicate material in tables or figures.